National Security Intelligence

Second Edition

To Loch Lomond Bentley,

RAF pilot,

1913–1941,

who paid the ultimate price in defense of the democracies

NATIONAL SECURITY INTELLIGENCE

Secret Operations in Defense of the Democracies

Second Edition

Loch K. Johnson

polity

First published in 2012 by Polity Press;
This second edition published in 2017

Polity Press
65 Bridge Street
Cambridge CB2 1UR, UK

Polity Press
350 Main Street
Malden, MA 02148, USA

ISBN-13: 978-1-5095-1304-8
ISBN-13: 978-1-5095-1305-5(pb)

A catalogue record for this book is available from the British Library.

Library of Congress Cataloging-in-Publication Data

Name: Johnson, Loch K., 1942– author.
Title: National security intelligence / Loch Johnson.
Description: Second edition. | Cambridge, UK ; Malden, MA : Polity, 2017. | Includes bibliographical references and index.
Identifiers: LCCN 2016039810 (print) | LCCN 2016059847 (ebook) | ISBN 9781509513048 (hardback) | ISBN 9781509513055 (paperback) | ISBN 9781509513079 (Mobi) | ISBN 9781509513086 (Epub)
Subjects: LCSH: Intelligence service–United States. | National security–United States. | BISAC: POLITICAL SCIENCE / Globalization.
Classification: LCC JK486.I6 J64 2017 (print) | LCC JK486.I6 (ebook) | DDC 327.1273–dc23
LC record available at https://lccn.loc.gov/2016039810

Typeset in 10.5 on 12 pt PalatinoLTStd-Roman
by Toppan Best-set Premedia Limited
Printed and bound in Great Britain by Clays Ltd, St. Ives PLC

For further information on Polity, visit our website: www.politybooks.com

Contents

About the Author   vi
Figures and Tables   viii
Abbreviations   x
Preface to the Second Edition: Roadmap to a Hidden World   xv
Acknowledgments   xxii

1 National Security Intelligence: The First Line
   of Defense   1

2 Intelligence Collection and Analysis: Knowing
   about the World   36

3 Covert Action: Secret Attempts to Shape History   82

4 Counterintelligence: The Hunt for Moles   116

5 Safeguards against the Abuse of Secret Power   155

6 National Security Intelligence: Shield and Hidden
   Sword of the Democracies   202

Notes   215
Suggested Readings   249
Index   258

About the Author

Loch Kingsford Johnson is the Regents Professor of Public and International Affairs at the University of Georgia, as well as a Meigs Distinguished Teaching Professor. He is the author of more than 200 articles and essays, and the author or editor of more than 30 books, on U.S. national security. The books include, most recently, *American Foreign Policy and the Challenges of World Leadership* (Oxford, 2015); *Essentials of Strategic Intelligence* (ABC-Clio/Praeger, 2015, editor); *A Season of Inquiry Revisited: The Church Committee Confronts America's Spy Agencies* (Kansas, 2015); *The Threat on the Horizon: An Inside Account of America's Search for Security After the Cold War* (Oxford, 2011); and *The Oxford Handbook of National Security Intelligence* (Oxford, 2010, editor). He has published editorials in the *New York Times*, the *Washington Post*, the *Chicago Tribune*, the *Philadelphia Inquirer*, the *Atlanta Journal-Constitution*, the *Baltimore Sun*, and elsewhere.

Professor Johnson served as special assistant to the chairman of the Senate Select Committee on Intelligence (1975–76); as a staff aide on the U.S. Senate Foreign Relations Committee (1976–77); as the first staff director of the Subcommittee on Intelligence Oversight, U.S. House Permanent Select Committee on Intelligence (1977–79); as a senior staff member on the Subcommittee on Trade and International Economic Policy, Committee on Foreign Affairs, U.S. House of Representatives (1980); and as special assistant to Chairman Les Aspin of the Aspin–Brown Commission on the Roles and Missions of Intelligence (1995–96). He was the Issues Director in a presidential campaign (1976); served as a foreign policy adviser to President Jimmy Carter in his 1980 re-election campaign (coauthoring the *Presidential Briefing Book on Foreign Policy* used during the presidential debates); and is currently a consultant to several government and civic organizations.

Professor Johnson has won the "Certificate of Distinction" from the National Intelligence Study Center in Washington, DC; the "Studies in Intelligence Award" from the Center for the Study of Intelligence in Washington, DC; the "Best Article Award" from the Century Foundation's Understanding Government Project; and the V.O. Key "Best Book" Prize (with Charles S. Bullock III) from the Southern Political Science Association. He has served as secretary of the American Political Science Association, and has led its Intelligence Studies Organized Group. He has also been president of the International Studies Association, South.

Professor Johnson is senior editor of the international journal *Intelligence and National Security*, and he serves on the editorial advisory board for several other journals, including the *Journal of Intelligence History* and the *Journal for Intelligence, Propaganda, and Security Studies.* In 2008–09, he was named a Phi Beta Kappa Visiting Scholar, and is now on the Phi Beta Kappa National Board for the Visiting Scholar Program. He has been a Distinguished Visiting Scholar at Yale University and at Oxford University. In 2012, he was selected as the inaugural "Professor of the Year" by the consortium of fourteen universities in the Southeast Conference (SEC). At the 2014 Annual Meeting of the International Studies Association, he was awarded the "Distinguished Professor" prize, a recognition bestowed occasionally by the Intelligence Studies Section; and, in 2015, he was presented with a Lifetime Achievement Award from the International Association for Intelligence Education.

Born in Auckland, New Zealand, Professor Johnson received his PhD in political science from the University of California, Riverside. In postdoctoral activities, he was awarded an American Political Science Association Congressional Fellowship. He has also studied nuclear weapons policy at Harvard University and MIT. Professor Johnson has lectured at more than 140 universities and think-tanks worldwide. At the University of Georgia, he led the founding of the School of Public and International Affairs in 2001, the first new college at the university since the 1940s.

Figures and Tables

Figures

1.1 Basic human motivations and the quest for national
security intelligence: a stimulus–response model   8
1.2 The U.S. Intelligence Community (IC) in 2016   17
1.3 The CIA during the Cold War   21
1.4 The CIA's Operations Directorate during the Cold War   22
2.1 The intelligence cycle   38
2.2 The relationship between a nation's sense of acceptable
risk and its resources committed to intelligence
collection and analysis   43
2.3 Frequency of NIEs by year, 1950–2005   66
3.1 Herblock on blow back   89
3.2 The ebb and flow of covert actions by the United States,
1947–2010   95
3.3 A partial ladder of escalation for covert actions   107
4.1 Key recommendations in the Huston Plan, 1970   119
5.1 An example of a statement accompanying a
presidentially approved covert action: the *contra*
portion of the Iran–*contra* finding, 1981   159
5.2 Auth on the relationship between Congress and the
CIA prior to 1974   161
5.3 The cycle of intelligence shock and reaction by
congressional overseers, 1975–2006   181
5.4 A typology of roles assumed by intelligence overseers
in the U.S. Congress   193
5.5 Illustrations of role migration and stability among
intelligence overseers in Congress, 1977–2004   196

Tables

5.1 Type of stimuli and oversight responses by lawmakers,
     1974–2016   183
6.1 National security intelligence: a reform agenda for
     the United States   211

Abbreviations

ATC	air traffic control
BENS	Business Executives for National Security
CA	covert action
CAS	Covert Action Staff
CASIS	Canadian Association of Security and Intelligence Studies
CE	counterespionage
CHAOS	cryptonym (codename) for CIA domestic spying operation
CI	counterintelligence
CIA	Central Intelligence Agency (the "Agency")
CIAB	Citizens' Intelligence Advisory Board (proposed)
CIG	Central Intelligence Group
COCOM	combatant commander (Pentagon)
COINTELPRO	FBI Counterintelligence Program
comint	communications intelligence
COS	Chief of Station (the top CIA officer in the field)
CTC	Counterterrorism Center (CIA)
D	Democrat
DA	Directorate of Administration
DBA	dominant battle field awareness
DC	District of Columbia (Washington)
DCI	Director of Central Intelligence
DCIA or D/CIA	Director of the Central Intelligence Agency

DDI	Deputy Director for Intelligence
DDNI	Deputy Director of National Intelligence
DDO	Deputy Director for Operations
DEA	Drug Enforcement Administration
DHS	Department of Homeland Security; also, Defense Humint Service (DoD)
DI	Directorate of Intelligence (CIA)
DIA	Defense Intelligence Agency
DIAC	Defense Intelligence Agency Center
DNC	Democratic National Committee
DNI	Director of National Intelligence
DO	Directorate of Operations (CIA), also known at times earlier in the CIA's history as the Clandestine Services and the National Clandestine Services
DoD	Department of Defense
DS	Directorate of Support
DS&T	Directorate for Science and Technology (CIA)
elint	electronic intelligence
FBI	Federal Bureau of Investigation
FISA	Foreign Intelligence Surveillance Act
FISA Court	Foreign Intelligence Surveillance Court
fisint	foreign instrumentation intelligence
GAO	Government Accountability Office (U.S. Congress)
geoint	geospatial intelligence
GID	General Intelligence Directorate (the Jordanian intelligence service, also known as the Mukhabarat)
GPS	Global Position Service
GRU	Soviet Military Intelligence
HPSCI	House Permanent Select Committee on Intelligence
humint	human intelligence (espionage assets)
IC	Intelligence Community
ICBM	intercontinental ballistic missile
IG	Inspector General
imint	imagery intelligence (photography)
INR	Bureau of Intelligence and Research (Department of State)
ints	intelligence collection methods (as in "sigint")
IOB	Intelligence Oversight Board

IRBM	intermediate-range ballistic missile
IRTPA	Intelligence Reform and Terrorism Prevention Act (2004)
ISA	Inter-Services Intelligence (the Pakistani intelligence service); also, International Studies Association
ITT	International Telephone and Telegraph (an American corporation)
I & W	indicators and warning
JENNIFER	Codename for CIA Soviet submarine retrieval operation in the 1970s (also known as Project AZORIAN)
KGB	Soviet Secret Police and Foreign Intelligence: Committee for State Security
KJ	Key Judgment (NIE executive summary)
KSM	Khalid Sheikh Mohammed, the Al Qaeda terrorist said to have mastermined the 9/11 attacks
MAGIC	Allied codebreaking operations against the Japanese in World War II
masint	measurement and signatures intelligence
MI5	British Security Service
MINARET	cryptonym for NSA warrantless telephone taps against Americans (pre-1975)
MIP	Military Intelligence Program
MI6	Secret Intelligence Service (SIS – United Kingdom)
MRBM	medium-range ballistic missile
NCA	National Command Authority
NCS	National Clandestine Service
NCTC	National Counterterrorism Center
NGA	National Geospatial-Intelligence Agency
NIC	National Intelligence Council
NIE	National Intelligence Estimate
NIM	National Intelligence Manager (ODNI)
NIO	National Intelligence Officer
NIPF	National Intelligence Priorities Framework
NIP	National Intelligence Program
NOC	non-official cover
NPIC	National Photographic Interpretation Center
NRO	National Reconnaissance Office
NSA	National Security Agency

NSC	National Security Council
NSI	National Security Intelligence
NSL	national security letter
OBE	overtaken by events
OC	official cover
ODNI	Office of the Director of National Intelligence
OLC	Office of Legal Counsel (Justice Department)
OPEC	Organization of Petroleum Exporting Countries
osint	open-source intelligence
OSS	Office of Strategic Services
PDB	*President's Daily Brief*
PDD	Presidential Decision Directive
PFIAB	President's Foreign Intelligence Advisory Board (as of 2008, PIAB)
phoint	photographic intelligence
PIAB	President's Intelligence Advisory Board
PM ops	paramilitary operations
PRC	People's Republic of China
PRISM	Codename for controversial NSA sigint program targeting, without a court warrant, suspected terrorists – including some Americans (post-9/11)
RFE	Radio Free Europe
R	Republican
RL	Radio Liberty
SA	special activities
SAM	surface-to-air missile
SCIF	sensitive compartmented information facility
SDO	support to diplomatic operations
SecDef	Secretary of Defense
SHAMROCK	cryptonym for NSA program to read international cables from and to American citizens (pre-1975)
sigint	signals intelligence
SLBM	submarine-launched ballistic missile
SMO	support to military operations
SNIE	Special National Intelligence Estimate
SOG	Special Operations Group (CIA)
SOVA	Office of Soviet Analysis (CIA)
SR-21	U.S. spy plane (see U-2)

SSCI	Senate Select Committee on Intelligence
STELLARWIND	generic cryptonym for controversial NSA warrantless wiretaps and metadata collection programs (post-9/11)
SVR	Foreign Intelligence Service of the Russian Federation (KGB successor)
techint	technical intelligence
telint	telemetry intelligence
TIARA	tactical intelligence and related activities
TIMBER SYCAMORE	CIA PM operation against Syria
TOR	Terms of Reference (for NIE drafting)
215	Code number for NSA communications metadata program targeting U.S. citizens (post-9/11)
UAE	United Arab Emirates
UAV	unmanned aerial vehicle (drone)
USIA	United States Information Agency (Department of State)
U-2	CIA spy plane (with later Air Force Variations known as the A-12 and the SR-71)
VC	Viet Cong
WMD	weapons of mass destruction
YAF	Young Americans for Freedom (student group)

Preface to the Second Edition

Roadmap to a Hidden World

National security intelligence is a vast, complicated, and important topic, with both technical and humanistic dimensions – all made doubly hard to study and understand because of the thick veils of secrecy that surround every nation's spy apparatus. Fortunately, from the point of view of democratic openness as well as the canons of scholarly inquiry, several of these veils have lifted in the past four decades. The disclosures have been a result of public government inquiries into intelligence failures and wrongdoing (especially those in 1975 that looked into charges of illegal domestic spying in the United States), accompanied by a more determined effort by academic researchers to probe the dark side of government. The endnotes in the chapters of this volume are a testament to the burgeoning and valuable research on national security intelligence that has accrued from steady scholarly inquiry into intelligence organizations and their activities.

Much remains to be accomplished, and – quite properly – national security imperatives will never permit full transparency in this sensitive domain. In a democracy, though, the people must have at least a basic comprehension of all their government agencies, even the shadowy world of intelligence. Within the boundaries of maintaining the sanctity of properly classified information, it is incumbent on scholars, journalists, and public officials to help citizens understand the hidden dimensions of their governing institutions.

The Cold War was, in large part, a struggle between espionage organizations in the democracies and in the communist bloc, illustrating the centrality of a nation's secret agencies.[1] Sometimes spy services have been the source of great embarrassment to the democracies, as with America's Bay of Pigs disaster (1961), along with the questionable assassination attempts against foreign leaders carried out by the Central Intelligence Agency (CIA, known as "the Agency" by insiders), acting under ambiguous authority from the Eisenhower and Kennedy administrations. Harmful to the reputation of America's democracy, too, were the domestic espionage scandals of the mid-1970s, the Iran–*contra* scandal a decade later, and, most recently, revelations about torture and other forms of prisoner abuse, as well as dragnet "metadata" collection of information about American citizens by the National Security Agency (NSA), employed by the CIA and military intelligence agencies in the struggle against global terrorism. Intelligence mistakes of analysis can have enormous consequences as well, as when the United Kingdom and the United States invaded Iraq in 2003, based in part on a faulty assessment that Saddam Hussein, the Iraqi dictator, was developing weapons of mass destruction (WMD) that could soon strike London and Washington. Further, intelligence organizations and operations are a costly burden on taxpayers – some $80 billion a year in the United States, according to statements by America's Director of National Intelligence (DNI) in 2010. For all of these reasons, national security intelligence deserves the attention of the public, closer study by the scholarly community, and improved accountability inside democratic regimes.

The challenge is daunting. To some extent, a society's intelligence agencies and its community of scholars are at loggerheads: the government prefers secrecy, while scholars hope for access to information – openness. Still, recent experience underscores that a nation can encourage intelligence scholarship and still have an effective secret service. Indeed, the more a public knows about intelligence, the more likely it is that citizens will support the legitimate – indeed, vital – protective services of these agencies, as long as they operate within the boundaries of the law and accepted ethical probity.

In 2009, a survey of scholarship on intelligence in the United States concluded:

> The interdisciplinary field of intelligence studies is mushrooming, as scholars trained in history, international studies, and political science examine such subjects as the influence of U.S. and foreign intelligence on national decisions during the cold war, the Vietnam War, and Watergate; how spycraft shaped reform efforts in the Communist bloc; the relationship of intelligence gathering to the events of September 11, 2001; and abuses and bungles in the

"campaign against terrorism." As the field grows, it is attracting students in droves.[2]

More recently, a study of the intelligence studies literature finds "path-breaking" new research that has brought in scholars from multiple disciplines and has attracted the attention of more women researchers.[3]

Hundreds of British, Canadian, and American universities and colleges now offer formal courses on national security intelligence, and these classes are always in high demand. The interest stems in large part from the widely reported intelligence failures related to the 9/11 attacks and the flawed predictions about WMD in Iraq that preceded the Second Persian Gulf war in 2003. Students want to know why these failures occurred and what can be done to prevent intelligence errors in the future. Many of them hope to join their governments in some capacity, whether as diplomats, lawmakers, staff aides, intelligence officers, or soldiers, to engage in activities that will help protect the democracies against attacks and assist the cause of international peace. Others realize that governmental decision-making is based on information and, whether in the groves of academe or within a think-tank, they want to pursue a life of learning about the relationship between information and decisions. Some, raised on James Bond movies, are drawn to the study of national security intelligence because it is a fascinating topic – although they soon discover that the writings of the sociologist Max Weber, an expert on bureaucracy, provide greater insight into the real world of spy organizations than the dramatic license exercised by novelist Ian Fleming.

In recent years, the most important development in the study of national security intelligence has been the effort by scholars to move beyond spy memoirs toward a rigorous application of research standards that address such questions as how nations gather and analyze information on threats and opportunities at home and abroad, and how and why they engage in covert action and counter-intelligence operations. Important, as well, as least for democratic nations, has been the question of how to erect safeguards against the abuse of power by secret agencies, at home and abroad. Moreover, studies on intelligence are increasingly offering empirical data, testable hypotheses, and theoretical frameworks – the underpinnings of rigorous scholarly inquiry.[4]

Further, scholars in the field have been conducting in-depth interviews with intelligence practitioners, and have benefited in addition from the extensive number of intelligence documents released by governments in recent decades. Among these documents are, for example, in the United States: the Church Committee Report in 1975–6 (on domestic spying, covert action, and secret assassination plots); the Aspin–Brown Commission Report in 1996 (on counter-intelligence and, more broadly, the state of U.S. intelligence after the Cold War); the Kean Commission Report in 2004 (on the 9/11 intelligence failures); and the Silberman–Robb Commission in 2005 (on WMD in Iraq). In the United Kingdom, the list of valuable new government reports includes the House of Commons Select Committee on Foreign Affairs Report and the Intelligence and Security Committee Report (both in 2003), as well as the Butler Report and the Hutton Report (both in 2004) and the Chilcot Committee (2010), with its report published in 2016 – all of which examined the flawed aspects of British intelligence reporting on WMD in Iraq prior to the outbreak of war in 2003. In Canada, the McDonald Commission Report on domestic intelligence abuse is another valuable source for intelligence researchers (1981).

When the leaders of a nation make a decision, the quality of information before them can be a significant determinant of success or failure. Researchers engaged in intelligence studies seek to know more about this information: where it comes from, its accuracy, how it is used (or misused), and what might be done to improve its reliability and timeliness. The discipline of intelligence studies attempts, as well, to learn more about covert action, which has led to much controversy in world affairs, as with the Bay of Pigs fiasco in 1961. More recently, America's use of Predator and Reaper unmanned aerial vehicles (UAVs or drones), armed with Hellfire and other types of missiles, is a new and highly lethal form of covert action, unleashed against Taliban and Al Qaeda *jihadists* in mountainous regions of northwest Pakistan and Afghanistan, and sometimes inflicting deaths accidentally among noncombatants. As well, drone attacks have been carried out by the Pentagon and the CIA against terrorist targets on the Horn of Africa and across the Maghreb in Northwest Africa, as well as in Syria and Iraq – wherever radical terrorist factions opposed to the democracies are encamped or engaged in their dark arts. Intelligence researchers also study the question of treason: why it occurs and what counterintelligence methods can be employed to reduce its incidence. Further, they explore the question of how democracies can best maintain a balance between the secret operations of intelligence agencies, on the one hand, and the privileges of a free and open society, on the other hand – the ongoing search by the democracies for a workable equilibrium between security and liberty.

National security intelligence is a rich and exciting field of study, for researchers, policymakers, government reformers, intelligence professionals, students, and attentive citizens in every democratic regime. This volume offers an introductory look at this subject, with hopes of encouraging further study by scholars of all ages, along with a renewed dedication to intelligence reform by government officials and citizen activists.

The second edition of this book, like the first, begins in Chapter 1 with an overview of the three major intelligence missions: collection-and-analysis, covert action, and counterintelligence – each of which is replete with its own challenges and controversies. This opening chapter also looks at the multiple dimensions of intelligence, including as a cluster of organizations, as a product, and as a set of activities. Further, Chapter 1 introduces the seventeen agencies that make up America's "Intelligence Community" (IC); suggests why accountability is vital to ensure that these secret organizations adhere to the basic principles of democracy (which has not always been the case); and explores why the American intelligence services have been plagued by a lack of both structural integration and a culture of working together seamlessly toward providing the President and other policy officials with accurate and timely information.

The next three chapters examine more closely each of the core missions, beginning in Chapter 2 with collection-and-analysis. The concept of an "intelligence cycle" is introduced as a useful way to envision how the United States gathers information from around the world and moves it toward helpful analytic reports for the White House and other high councils of government. The steps that intelligence takes while moving from the field to the Oval Office ("the Oval" in Washington lingo) are susceptible to many potential mistakes and distortions, as this chapter reveals.

Chapter 3 takes up the most controversial of the mission triad in the world of intelligence: the use of covert action, such as secret drone attacks in Pakistan. Can, and should, the United States seek to channel the flow of history in a favorable direction by way of hidden interventions abroad – which is the essence of the covert action mission?

Then Chapter 4 peers into the heavily veiled topics of counterintelligence and counterterrorism. These intelligence disciplines are designed to protect the United States from hostile spies and terrorists. The failure of America to thwart the terrorist attacks aimed at New York City and Washington, DC in September 2001, as well as the many other terrorist assaults this nation and its allies have suffered since 9/11, are painful reminders of how significant – and difficult – this responsibility for shielding the democracies can be.

Finally, Chapter 6 reviews why national security intelligence will continue to be a subject of central concern in international affairs, for as long as this world remains a fragmented, uncertain, and dangerous place. The chapter concludes with a discussion of how intelligence activities in the United States and in other open societies might be reformed, both to enhance their effectiveness in providing security for the democratic nations and to ensure the allegiance of the secret services to the core principles of liberty and privacy in these nations.

Much has happened in the world since Polity published the first edition of this book in 2012. This second edition addresses in greater depth the subject of cybersecurity, a growing threat driven home to Americans and their allies by the ceaseless activities of computer hackers against the democracies by autocratic foreign governments, terrorist organizations, and old-fashioned criminals using this new "safe-cracking" tool. Russia has even been accused by U.S. authorities of trying to tamper with the American presidential election of 2016 by hacking into the computers of the Democratic National Committee (DNC), as well as the election boards of various U.S. states (such as Arizona).

Of interest, too, in this new edition are the controversies that have arisen over warrantless wiretaps conducted by the NSA, as well as its massive collection of "metadata" consisting of telephone and social media communication logs of citizens in the democracies – however innocent these individuals might be. The secret agencies in the United States, the United Kingdom, and other democracies adopted this dragnet approach to intelligence collection after the 9/11 attacks – a fact revealed in a leak of classified internal documents in 2013 by a U.S. government contractor, Edward J. Snowden.

Coming to light as well since the first edition has been the extent to which the CIA adopted torture as a counterterrorism interrogation technique in the aftermath of 9/11, along with the rendition of suspected terrorists who have been swept off the streets of their hometowns overseas and kidnapped to foreign prisons for harsh questioning. Critics of these operations wonder if, in combating terrorism, the United States has lost its way, becoming more like the very terrorist factions opposed by democracies and staining the good reputation for ethical behavior that the open societies have enjoyed in many parts of the world. Deep questions of morality have accompanied these startling disclosures, including concerns about the emergence of "surveillance states" even within the free nations. As this book emphasizes, intelligence is not only about security; it is also about safeguarding the traditional democratic values of fair play and the honoring of ethical considerations.

The role of intelligence in support of America's two longest wars – in Iraq and in Afghanistan in the aftermath of the 9/11 attacks – is given added attention in this second edition. So is the unsettling rise of so-called ISIS, a terrorist organization concentrated in Syria, Iraq, and Libya, but with aspirations to create a new "caliphate" or Islamic nation in the Middle East – an empire based on a narrow form of Islamic radicalism with little tolerance for anything modern, such as the rights of women to an education, to a professional career, or even to drive an automobile. The ISIS leaders have inspired "lone wolf" terrorist attacks in the West, including in recent years mass killings in Paris; Brussels; San Bernardino, California; Nice; and Orlando, Florida. Other topics given closer scrutiny in this edition are the complex relationship between intelligence officers and the policymakers they serve; and the important legal and ethical debates surrounding the use of drones to kill suspected terrorists, some of whom have been citizens of the democratic nations.

The second edition, moreover, has expanded sections on the organizational tensions that exist within the U.S. Intelligence Community, especially between the Department of Defense and the CIA; on the expansion of CIA paramilitary covert actions; on the technical means of gathering intelligence; and on how intelligence can become a political football, "politicized" by some individuals to advance their policy initiatives – even if it means "cooking" (slanting) the information to suit their own political ends. Here is the cardinal sin of intelligence.

While this second edition is a little longer than the first, I have been determined not to turn these pages into an encyclopedic treatise. My goal from the beginning has been to provide a manageable primer on the subject of national security intelligence, without drowning the reader in too many details. Once the fundamentals of intelligence presented in this book are understood, the reader can then turn to the more detailed works offered in the "Suggested Readings" section at the end of this volume.

The study of intelligence is an exciting and meaningful pursuit. The subject ranges across many topics and academic disciplines. It has a certain flare that only secret operations, hidden rendezvouses with foreign agents, long-distance spying by glittering satellites in space, mole-hunting, and drone-warfare can impart. Welcome to the second edition, and to the mysterious and fascinating world of modern-day espionage.

Athens, Georgia

Acknowledgments

With pleasure, I acknowledge the well-springs of my understanding about national security intelligence, namely: the authors of the works that are cited in this book; the many intelligence officers who have responded to my endless questions and requests for interviews over the years since 1975; and lawmakers Les Aspin, Frank Church, Wyche Fowler, and Walter F. Mondale (who also served as Vice President during the Carter Administration) who provided wise counsel on the view from Capitol Hill. This work has benefited, too, from my own opportunities to work as a staff aide in the Senate, the House of Representatives, and the White House during the 1970s and 1990s. I would like to express my appreciation as well to Dr. Louise Knight, who originally approached me about writing this book for Polity. She is a wonderful editor and I am grateful for her guidance and friendship. Helpful, too, at Polity was Nekane Tanaka Galdos, who provided valuable guidance throughout the preparation of this second edition, and to Sarah Dancy for her sure-handed copyediting. As well, I want to thank Marie Milward and Lieutenant Colonel James Borders – both PhD recipients in International Affairs at the University of Georgia – for their research assistance and insights; and Markus M. L. Crepaz, head of the Department of International Affairs at the University of Georgia, for his support and encouragement. My greatest debt, as always, is to Leena S. Johnson, my discerning "in-house editor" and wife of many blissful years; and to Kristin E. Swati, our daughter, and her husband Jamil Swati – both a constant source of infectious enthusiasm and good judgment. Their encouragement and unbending support made life much easier for me as an author.

1 National Security Intelligence

The First Line of Defense

Only a few puffs of white cloud marred a perfect blue sky as American Airlines Flight 11 prepared to depart from Boston's Logan International Airport at 7:59 on Tuesday morning, September 11, 2001. Destination: Los Angeles. Passenger Mohamed Atta, short in stature and dour in countenance, had seated himself in 8D, business class. Four other men from the Middle East, equal to Atta in their unfriendly demeanor, sat near him in business and first class.

In the cockpit of the Boeing 767, Captain John Ogonowski and First Officer Thomas McGuinness went through the usual pre-flight checklist at the control panel. Everything was in order. The Captain backed the plane out of its berth and taxied down the runway. He pulled back on a lever and headed for an altitude of 26,000 feet. Eighty-one passengers settled in for the scheduled five-hour flight and the crew's nine flight attendants bustled about in the kitchens, preparing for cabin service. At 8:14, fifteen minutes into the journey, a routine radio message from the Federal Aviation Administration's center for air traffic control (ATC) in Boston requested that Captain Ogonowski take his aircraft to a higher elevation, 35,000 feet. Contrary to standard procedure, the Captain failed to acknowledge these instructions. A commotion on the other side of the cockpit door had distracted him.

Just as the ATC message arrived in the cockpit of Flight 11, two of the men who had boarded the aircraft with Atta sprang from their seats in first class. With knives, they stabbed two flight attendants who were wheeling a beverage cart down the aisle. One of the attendants collapsed, mortally wounded; the other shrieked and clasped a hand over a cut on her arm. The assailants moved quickly to the cockpit door and forced their way inside.

In their wake, Atta raced from his seat and commandeered the controls of the airplane. Back in the passenger cabin, another of his companions knifed a male passenger in the throat and began to spray Mace throughout the business and first-class sections. The poisoned air drove some passengers down the aisle, away from the front of the airplane; others huddled low in their seats. Wielding his knife in plain sight, the killer – muscular, intense, ready to strike again – warned in a heavy Middle Eastern accent that he had a bomb. One of his allies added in flawless English: "Nobody move. Everything will be okay. If you try to make any moves, you'll endanger yourself and the airplane. Just stay quiet." In the coach section, passengers remained unaware of the danger, believing that a medical emergency had arisen in first class.

Filled with Mace, the air in the front cabin was proving impossible to breathe. A flight attendant hid by the curtain that separated the coach and business sections and tried to reach the Captain in the cockpit with an on-board telephone. When this failed, she called the American Airlines operations center in Fort Worth, Texas, and, with remarkable composure, explained in a low voice that a violent hijacking of Flight 11 was under way. Officials in Fort Worth also had no success with their repeated calls to the cockpit.

Twenty-five minutes had elapsed since take-off. The airplane was now flying erratically. It made a lurch southward, circled in a wide arc, and went into a sharp descent. Perhaps it was bound for the John F. Kennedy Airport in New York and a round of bargaining on the tarmac: a demand for a ransom, in exchange for the release of the aircraft and its hostages.

But the plane was flying so low. Far too low.

At 8:46, Flight 11 slammed into the ninety-sixth floor of the North Tower at the World Trade Center in lower Manhattan.

Instant inferno. Temperatures above the melting point for steel. Metal wrenching against metal. Immediate death for all those on board the airplane and an unknown number of office workers – the lucky ones who at least escaped the fiery end that would soon consume others in the building. Some people above the impassable impact site chose to leap from windows toward the streets, an eternity below, rather than perish in the searing flames.

Another aircraft – United Airlines Flight 175 – had also set off for Los Angeles from Logan Airport. Hijacked in coordination with Flight 11, it soon turned to the south as well, arced back toward the east, and plunged toward the skyscrapers of New York City, their windows glittering in the morning sunlight. The plane struck the South Tower at 9:03, about seventeen minutes after the North Tower impact.

Two other teams were part of the hijacking plot, later traced to Al Qaeda, a terrorist group sheltered by the Taliban regime in Afghanistan. Instead of New York City, however, they directed their confiscated airplanes toward the nation's capital city. At 9:27, American Airlines Flight 77, originally on its way to L.A. from Washington Dulles, smashed into the Pentagon like a huge missile, traveling at a speed of 530 miles per hour.

When terrorists took over the fourth plane, United 93, on its way to San Francisco, its passengers had heard – in heart-wrenching cell phone calls with loved ones – about the fate of American 11 and United 175. At 9:57, several of the passengers decided as a group to rush the hijackers in a desperate attempt to prevent the plane from reaching its target – perhaps the Capitol or the White House. Their brave struggle lasted for several minutes, as the terrorist pilot at the controls attempted to throw them off balance by jerking the steering column from side to side and up and down. Undeterred by these maneuvers, the passengers fought their way to the door of the cockpit. About to be overwhelmed, the terrorists chose to destroy the plane rather than surrender. The counterfeit pilot turned a lever hard to the right and rolled the aircraft over on its back. Within seconds, it fell from the sky and exploded in a fiery ball across a barren Pennsylvania field. In another twenty minutes of flying time it would have reached Washington.

In New York, the tragedy was not over. Under the extreme heat caused by the impact of large and fast-flying airplanes filled with volatile aviation fuel, the structural girders of the Twin Towers buckled and soon collapsed, sending office workers, tourists on the observation deck, and rescuing firefighters and police officers into a downward free fall to their deaths. Steel, glass, furniture, and bodies plummeted from the heavens. Massive grey and black plumes of dust and pulverized metal billowed throughout lower Manhattan as thousands of people in the streets below fled from the crumbling 125-story buildings. Blackness blotted out the sky, as if the sun had died that morning along with all the innocents in the Twin Towers.

When the dust settled, nearly 3,000 Americans had perished in New York City, in Washington, and in smoldering farmland near Shanksville, Pennsylvania. The United States had suffered its worst attack since the British burning of Washington, DC in the War of 1812, surpassing the horrific Japanese bombing of Pearl Harbor in 1941.[1]

The importance of national security intelligence

The terrorist attacks on the United States carried out by Al Qaeda on September 11, 2001, were a brutal reminder of the importance of national security intelligence (NSI) – in this instance, information provided to a nation's leaders by secretive government agencies to protect citizens against threats posed by domestic or foreign sources. If only the CIA, America's most well-known espionage service, had been able to place an agent high in the Al Qaeda organization, a "mole" who could have tipped off U.S. authorities about the planned hijackings. If only the Federal Bureau of Investigation (FBI), America's premier domestic intelligence agency, had been more successful in tracking down the hijackers in California earlier in 2001. If only the National Security Agency (NSA), the largest of the U.S. spy organizations, had translated more quickly from Farsi into English intercepted telephone messages between Al Qaeda lieutenants that hinted at an approaching attack on the United States from the skies. If only airport security officers and American pilots had been warned about the immediacy of possible hijackings and been provided with profiles and photographs of at least some of the 9/11 terrorists, which the CIA and the FBI had on file. Mistakes were made by intelligence officers and political leaders alike that might have halted the aerial terrorism that claimed so many innocent lives that awful day.

In the hours and days after the attacks, no one in the United States knew if the tragic events of 9/11 were just the first of many assaults that would follow, perhaps using chemical, biological, or even nuclear devices rather than airplanes as weapons. Fortunately, no more immediate attacks occurred in the United States, but anxiety remained over possible fresh outbreaks of violence against American citizens at home and abroad. After 9/11, Al Qaeda and its loosely affiliated factions targeted other locations around the globe – London, Madrid, and Bali, for example. In more recent years, this terrorist organization, whose leaders (Osama bin Laden chief among them) were thought to be hiding in the rugged mountain terrain of North Waziristan in Pakistan, has lurked behind assaults on American, British, and other international armed forces in Iraq and Afghanistan. Al Qaeda has openly proclaimed its presence in Somalia, Yemen, and in parts of Pakistan as well, along with sleeper agents in all the major democracies. Al Qaeda terrorist factions have been aided and abetted by *jihadists* associated with the Taliban, the insurgent organization that provided Bin Laden and his associates with a safe haven in Afghanistan prior to and during the terrorist operations directed against the United States from 1998 to 2001.

In defense against Al Qaeda and the Taliban, nations in the West have escalated their intelligence activities in the Middle East and Southwest Asia, in hopes of both acquiring prior knowledge of future attacks and crippling the terrorists by way of aggressive paramilitary operations. This approach bore fruit in May 2011 when a U.S. Navy SEAL team, supported by intelligence gathered by America's spy agencies, raided a private compound in Abbottabad (a city near the Pakistani capital, Islamabad) and killed Osama bin Laden.

Soon after Bin Laden's death, another global terrorist faction came to the forefront in the Middle East and North Africa, known as ISIS, a brutal army of insurgents in Syria, Iraq, and Libya, which has demonstrated a sophisticated use of social media to recruit young men and women to its cause. The abbreviation ISIS stands for Islamic State in Iraq and Syria, also known as the Islamic State, ISIL (Islamic State of Iraq and the Levant), or, in Arabic, *Daesh*. This organization claimed credit for attacks not only in the Middle East and Libya, but also in Paris, Brussels, and Nice. Further, adherents to ISIS's anti-Western agenda have engaged in mass shootings on its behalf in California (San Bernardino) and Florida (Orlando). Al Qaeda remains high on the U.S. and allied lists of major threats, but has been edged out of the top tier by the growing virulence and ability of ISIS to spawn "lone wolf" attacks against the democracies.

Mysteries and secrets

Intelligence practitioners speak of "mysteries" and "secrets." Mysteries are subjects that a nation (or some other entity, such an international peacekeeping organization) would like to know about in the world, but which are difficult to fathom in light of the limited capacity of human beings to forecast the course of history – say, the question of who might be the next leader of Russia or China, or whether Pakistan will be able to survive the presence of Taliban warriors and Al Qaeda terrorists based inside its borders. In contrast, secrets are more susceptible to human discovery and comprehension, although even they may be difficult to unveil – say, the number of nuclear submarines in the Chinese Navy, the identity of Russian agents who have infiltrated the North Atlantic Treaty Organization (NATO), or the efficiencies of North Korean rocket fuel and the range of its long-distance missiles.

With the right spy in the right place, with surveillance satellites in the proper orbit, or with reconnaissance aircraft that can penetrate enemy airspace, a nation might be able to uncover secrets. With mysteries, though, leaders must rely largely on the thoughtful assessments of intelligence analysts about the contours of an answer, based on hunches and as much empirical evidence as can be found in open sources or through espionage. Prudent nations establish an intelligence capability to ferret out secrets and, as best they can, to ponder mysteries.

Central themes

This is a book about a nation's efforts to unravel secrets and mysteries, as its leaders attempt to understand world affairs and make sound decisions in a hostile global environment. It has two unifying themes that focus on intelligence failures and scandals. The first theme argues that intelligence agencies in the West have helped protect the democracies against a variety of dangers, from bellicose totalitarian regimes to terrorist organizations at home and abroad, but that these agencies have often fallen short in meeting their responsibility to provide a "first line of defense" against threats. The events of 9/11, along with subsequent erroneous predictions about weapons of mass destruction (WMD) in Iraq, have vividly and tragically underscored the possibility of error by American and other Western intelligence organizations.

Nations and other organizations have periodically experienced significant intelligence mistakes, some of which have led to disaster. Hitler's espionage services predicted that Britain would be weak-kneed and unwilling to react with force against a Nazi invasion of Poland. Joseph Stalin assumed that he could depend on the Third Reich to honor a non-aggression pact signed with the Soviet Union early in the Second World War. President Franklin D. Roosevelt and his intelligence aides assumed that Japan would not be so bold as to strike Pearl Harbor in 1941. As a result of human error and bureaucratic blunder, intelligence misjudgments have haunted leaders and organizations in regimes of every stripe. Intelligence failure is far more the norm than it is a rare exception. Self-delusion; mirror-imaging (that is, assuming other nations will behave in the same manner as one's own nation, despite cultural differences); bureaucratic rivalries that hinder intelligence-sharing; the lack of human agents or surveillance satellites in the right place – the list of reasons for failure goes on. How prescient was the philosopher of war Karl von Clausewitz (1730–1831) when he concluded that "many intelligence reports in war are contradictory, even more are false, and most are uncertain."[2] The same is true in times of peace. This reality about the limits of intelligence is the uncomfortable truth woven like a dark thread through the pages of this volume.

Another truth, and the second theme presented here, is that – regrettably – intelligence agencies (in the manner of other organizations, whether governmental or private sector) often fall prey to Lord Acton's well-known prophecy that "power tends to corrupt and absolute power corrupts absolutely."[3] He might have added: "especially secret power, hidden as it is from the guardians of liberty."[4] History reveals that time and again a nation's secret services have turned their disquieting capabilities for surveillance and manipulation against the very citizens they were meant to shield. Efforts within democratic regimes to maintain accountability over intelligence agencies ("oversight," in the awkward expression of American political scientists) has proven difficult and has often failed.

Neither of these themes – the inability to predict future events with precision, and the acknowledgment that secret government organizations can be a danger to open societies – should astound the reader. After all, intelligence agencies are comprised of human beings – flawed by nature and devoid of a crystal ball; consequently, one can anticipate failures and abuses. (The famous "Grand Strategy" course at Yale University begins with the reading of *Paradise Lost*, a drama by John Milton on the seeds of human corruption.) No mere mortal is omniscient, nor can any mere mortal lay claim to Kantian purity in government affairs. Yet societies seem regularly taken aback by the occurrence of intelligence failures and scandals. Citizens and policymakers alike express amazement and dismay that their espionage services have been unable to provide a clairvoyant warning of impending danger; or that these agencies have spied even at home, not just against enemies abroad. In contrast to this naivety, the American founder James Madison and his colleagues understood that nations were led not by angels but by human beings of flesh and blood; failure and scandal were inevitable.

With the admirable common sense of a Midwesterner, President Harry S. Truman echoed Madison's cautionary words found in *Federalist Paper 51* about the importance of constitutional safeguards against government abuse. "You see," Truman said, "the way a government works, there's got to be a housecleaning every now and then."[5] Citizens in the democracies can throw up their hands in despair over the fact that intelligence errors and misdeeds are

1 The search for information (The intelligence cycle)
2 Protection of information (Counterintelligence)
3 The search for an added advantage (Covert action)
4 Protection against the abuse of secret power (Accountability)

Figure 1.1   Basic human motivations and the quest for national security
intelligence: a stimulus–response model

inescapable, or they can acknowledge the limits and the foibles
of humans and adopt measures to lessen their effects. That is the
challenge laid down in this book.

Given the reality of persistent forecasting miscues and periodic
corruption in government (which is especially hard to discern within
the dark crevasses of the polity), why do nations dedicate substantial resources to the establishment and support of secret agencies?
Are not the mistakes, as well as the risks to civil liberties, too
great for democratic societies to tolerate the presence of clandestine
organizations and their shadowy activities within the interstices of
their free and open government institutions? The answer is that
all living species have a primordial desire to shield themselves
from threats to their well-being; thus, they establish – as well as
they can – prudent defenses, whether radar installations erected
by human societies to detect the presence of enemy bombers, or
by motion-sensitive webs spun by spiders to warn of an intruder.
As fundamental as the atom is to physics, so is the human instinct
for survival to the creation of government institutions, including
secret intelligence agencies. Moreover, reformers in the open societies continue to hope that corruption within intelligence agencies
might be discovered early enough and rooted out before improper
espionage activities manage to corrode the bedrock principles and
procedures of democracy.

Beyond survival, humans are motivated by a sense of ambition
(see Figure 1.1). Intelligence agencies can assist leaders in their
efforts to know in advance not only about threats they may face, but
about opportunities that may arise to advance the national interest.
This book focuses on intelligence agencies within nation-states; but
they are not the only organizations drawn to espionage. The basic

drives of survival and ambition apply as well to non-state organizations and factions around the world; they, too, often have their own intelligence apparatus.

Given the peril of modern WMD – or even the simpler but still catastrophic use of such low-tech methods as aerial terrorism (as occurred in the 9/11 attacks) or a large truck aimed at pedestrians (used in Nice in 2016) – nations hope that their intelligence agencies, however imperfect, might provide at least some degree of warning or leverage in dealings with foreign adversaries or domestic subversives. Nations are prepared to spend vast sums from their treasury on the gathering of information about threats near and far, in an attempt to avoid devastating surprises likes the 9/11 attacks, or to gain an advantage over foreign competitors in a world of military, commercial, cultural, and political rivalries.

The intelligence missions

Collection and analysis

In myriad ways, the activities of intelligence agencies are vital for understanding international affairs.[6] The most important intelligence mission is to gather reliable, timely information about the world, as well as to assess its meaning accurately. At the heart of decision-making in every nation is a scene where policy officials are seated around a table in a well-guarded government conference room, as they decide which direction to take their society in its relations with other nations and international organizations. These deliberations are based on information from many sources – a vast flow of ideas and recommendations from personal aides, cabinet members, lobbyists, the media, academics, think-tank experts, friends, and family. Vital in this "river of information," to use a metaphor favored by several American intelligence directors, are data collected by a nation's secret services. Often this source of information sets the government's agenda and shapes final decisions, especially in a time of crisis. One cannot fully comprehend the choices that a nation makes without an understanding of how these secret agencies operate, and without knowing something about the scope and quality of the information they provide. Despite the many sources of data and guidance available to leaders, national security intelligence resides at the center of a nation's decision-making, largely because secret agents and spy machines can pry out information from foreign governments that is available only through clandestine methods.

As a nation's intelligence services have erred, so have its global strategies and its defenses against internal subversion; and as a nation's intelligence agencies have abused their secret powers, so have its citizens suffered domestic scandals and foreign policy embarrassments. Conversely, as examples throughout this book will attest, reliable information has led to better decisions; and democratic safeguards have curbed intelligence abuses.

Covert action

While primarily interested in the collection and analysis of information, intelligence agencies may also engage in a second mission: covert action – an attempt to change the course of history secretly, through the use of propaganda, political and economic operations, and paramilitary activities (that is, warlike endeavors, which can include assassination plots against the leaders of other nations and terrorist groups). These "dirty tricks," as they are characterized by critics, can be attractive to leaders who seek quick and (they hope) quiet measures to gain an advantage over global competitors. Yet sometimes covert action has brought grief and disrepute to a nation for violating the canons of propriety and international law.

Counterintelligence

Every nation's intelligence service has a third important mission known as counterintelligence, of which counterterrorism is a part. Here the purpose is to guard a nation's secrets and institutions against secret penetration and deception by hostile foreign governments or factions – or, in the case of terrorists, their outright attack against the nation. Foreign adversaries will attempt to burrow into a rival (and sometimes even a friendly) government, mole-like, in search of secrets or to sow disinformation. The Soviets succeeded in penetrating the CIA and the FBI at high levels during the Cold War, as well as the British, German, and French intelligence services, with harmful effects for the West.

Reports from the FBI and British intelligence indicate that Russian and Chinese intelligence officers have been spying against Western nations even more aggressively in recent years, mainly in a quest for technical, military, and commercial secrets. Russia is thought to have the capacity to disrupt the electricity grid in the United States, raising the prospect of cyber-warfare against this crucial national infrastructure. Every nation seeks to thwart the presence of foreign spies or terrorist "sleeper cells" in its midst. The end result is a game of cat and mouse played between malevolent intruders and spy-catchers within the inner sanctums of national capitals around the world.

The challenge of intelligence accountability

Further, for democratic regimes, the matter of intelligence account-ability is critical to those who fear the possible rise of a Gestapo within their own society. In the United States, media investigators discovered in 1974 that the CIA had resorted to spying against American citizens whose only transgression had been to protest the war in Vietnam or to participate in the nation's civil rights movement – activities protected by the First Amendment of the U.S. Constitution. In response to the disclosure of these intelligence abuses, Congress moved to reform America's spy agencies and promulgate safeguards against a repeated misuse of their secret trust. This intelligence reform movement in the United States spread around the world, and continues to be a subject of scholarly discus-sion and practical experimentation inside the world's existing and would-be democracies.

This book's purpose

The objective of this book is to place the topic of national security intelligence under a microscope, particularly with an eye toward examining its flaws and how they might be addressed in order to strengthen a nation's shield against terrorists and other enemies of democracy. This subject is often overlooked, because it is especially difficult to conduct research into the hidden domain of government. This opening chapter offers an introduction to national security intelligence in the United States by presenting some basic defini-tions and organizational diagrams necessary to understand how secret agencies operate.

Ideally a book on national security intelligence would examine the approaches taken in various democratic and non-democratic societies. Some work of this nature has been undertaken.[7] This volume, though, will explore the American experience for the most part. One day, when more data become available about intelligence activities in South America, Europe, Asia, Africa, and elsewhere, a reliable comparative analysis of espionage services will likely yield significant insights into the evolution and function of intelligence agencies around the globe. Until that time, as the French intelligence studies scholar Sébastien Laurent has put it, "the Anglo-Saxon school of intelligence is the only show in town and currently enjoys an unrivaled global hegemony."[8]

In sum, this volume attempts to provide readers with a sense of the failures and scandals that ineluctably accompany the existence of secret agencies. Drawing upon the American example, it demonstrates how each of the intelligence missions is plagued by periodic error and misdeed. It investigates what might be done to mitigate failure and abuse – how a democracy can improve its odds for accurate indications and warnings (I & W) of danger, while promoting the rule of law even inside the government's darkened recesses. Despite the inevitability of failure and scandal, steps can be taken to reduce their incidence. America's intelligence agencies have also recorded many notable successes in defense of democracy and they are examined as well in these pages.

National security intelligence is frustrating because of the inherent weaknesses that attend the imperfections of humankind; nonetheless, on a trouble-ridden world stage characterized by uncertainty, ambiguity, fear, and danger, no nation can afford to be without the shield – the eyes, the ears, and the mind of collection and analysis, and sometimes the sword (covert action and counterespionage) – that intelligence agencies can provide. A good starting place to develop an appreciation for the complexity of this topic is an exploration of the various meanings evoked by the phrase "national security intelligence."

The multiple dimensions of national security intelligence

Intelligence as secret information

Observers, and even intelligence specialists and practitioners, do not always agree on the precise meaning of national security intelligence. The major point of disagreement usually pivots around whether a definition of intelligence ought to be narrow or broad. Defined narrowly (as is most commonly the case), national security intelligence focuses on the primary mission of a nation's secret agencies: the gathering and analysis of information that might help to illuminate policy decisions made by its leaders. Refined still further, the definition may focus strictly on the actual product of the collection and analysis process: a written report or an oral briefing that conveys a blend of secretly and openly derived information to a government official. The CIA has defined intelligence simply as the "knowledge and foreknowledge of the world around us – the prelude to Presidential decision and action."[9] In this instance, national security intelligence means information. Some choose to limit the meaning even further to just *secret* information: that is, the findings gathered clandestinely by spies, satellites, reconnaissance aircraft, and electronic interceptions, and then interpreted by analysts.

Intelligence as a set of missions

More broadly, national security intelligence can refer as well to the three primary intelligence missions: collection and analysis, covert action, and counterintelligence. One might imagine a policy official in Israel asking an intelligence director: "What mixture of secret operations might be most effective in finding out more about, and then stopping, Iran's development of a nuclear bomb?" Here the emphasis is on national security intelligence as a mélange of activities, or secret options, that a leader might adopt to achieve a foreign policy goal. In this case, then, national security intelligence means a catalogue of basic missions carried out by secret government agencies.

Intelligence as a process

A third usage of the term may refer solely to the most preeminent among the trio of missions: collection and analysis. In this instance, the concept of national security intelligence points to the means or the process by which information is gathered from the field – say, a document stolen by a British agent from a safe in Beijing, or a photograph snapped by a camera on a U.S. surveillance satellite passing over a North Korean vessel steaming through the South China Sea – and then transmitted to a government's decision-makers.

Intelligence as organization

Finally, national security intelligence may refer to a building, or perhaps a tent staffed by intelligence officers in an encampment of soldiers bivouacked on a remote battlefield. The people responsible for the information gathered and interpreted by intelligence agencies belong to bureaucratic organizations. "Get intelligence on the line," a general might order, referring to a specific structural entity – perhaps a reconnaissance unit on the front edge of a battlefield – that the commander wants to contact.

A holistic view of national security intelligence

In light of these various dimensions of national security intelligence, thinking of the term purely as a final paper product or an oral briefing that combines secretly acquired and open-source information is too limiting – although certainly national security intelligence is precisely that at its core. Still, intelligence is what intelligence does, and the secret agencies spend much of their time engaged in covert action and counterintelligence, too, not just collection and analysis. Indeed, during times of overt warfare, and sometimes in between, aggressive overseas intelligence operations in the form of covert action can become preeminent – the tail that wags the intelligence dog.

During the 1980s, for instance, the Reagan Doctrine was the most important approach to American foreign policy adopted by President Ronald Reagan and his National Security Advisers. This "doctrine" (a description coined by the media, not the Administration) relied on the CIA to combat Soviet intervention in the developing world – a bold escalation in the funding, magnitude, and frequency of covert actions directed against the Soviet Union and its operations in poor countries around the globe (but especially in Nicaragua and Afghanistan). If one assumed during the 1980s that U.S. national security intelligence was all about the writing of top secret reports on world affairs (or the reports themselves), one would have missed the profound significance of intelligence as a covert action mission considered vital by the Reagan Administration.

Similarly with counterintelligence. Every intelligence officer has an obligation to protect government secrets, augmenting those offices within the spy agencies that are officially responsible for this mole-catching mission. Relegating counterintelligence to orphan status increases the odds of dangerous foreign penetrations, which in turn can lead to the riddling of an intelligence agency with traitors who have succumbed to blandishments (typically, secret cash payments) to spy against their own country. The end result of counterintelligence failures: a nation's own agents abroad are identified, captured, and often killed; its clandestine overseas operations are rolled up; and its reporting is contaminated by the machinations of double agents and disinformation. To focus on secret reports as the be-all and end-all of national security intelligence is to lose sight of the indispensable counterintelligence responsibility to protect a nation's secrets and otherwise shield the public against hostile agent penetrations and terrorist attacks.

Accountability is also often dismissed by some as something that is at best tangential to the subject of national security intelligence. In a democracy, however, intelligence officers and their managers – not to mention the squadrons of lawyers who counsel them (135 in the CIA today, up from six in 1975 and two in 1947) – spend a fair amount of time dealing with overseers: inspectors general (IGs), executive oversight boards, legislative review committees, special panels of inquiry, and select commissions. Again, assuming that intelligence is what intelligence officers do, one would have to include that – at least in democratic regimes – national security intelligence involves time spent with intelligence supervisors, in all three branches of government in the United States, who understand the warnings of Madison and Lord Acton.

National security intelligence is decidedly not covert action alone or counterintelligence; neither is it just responding to oversight panels of inquiry. But it is certainly more than gathering information about threats and opportunities, sitting with a cup of coffee and a computer (or a pencil), writing up what it all means (analysis), and delivering reports to policy officials. Intelligence officials carry out a combination of all these activities. Collection and analysis is usually of premier importance, but occasionally covert action will rush to the forefront of the intelligence agenda. When an Aldrich Ames (CIA) or a Kim Philby (MI6 in Britain) is discovered to be an agent of treason within one's own government – in both of these cases, pawns of the Russian spy services – suddenly intelligence managers rue their lack of sufficient attention to the counterintelligence mission. Or when the acronyms of a nation's secret services – say, CIA, FBI, MI6, or MI5 – are splashed across the newspaper headlines with allegations of failed analysis or scandalous conduct, intelligence managers will wish they had devoted more time to keeping those who fund them in Congress properly informed as they seek to carry out their oversight responsibilities.

Some, quite possibly most, practitioners and scholars alike, will continue to prefer a narrow definition of national security intelligence: the idea of intelligence as information – indeed, just secret information. Others, though, including the author of this book, will adopt a more encompassing view, along the lines suggested by British intelligence scholars Peter Gill and Mark Phythian:

> Intelligence is the umbrella term referring to the range of activities – from planning and information collection to analysis and dissemination – conducted in secret, and aimed at maintaining or enhancing relative security by providing forewarning of threats or potential threats in a manner that allows for the timely

implementation of a preventive policy or strategy, including, where deemed desirable, covert activities.

The ultimate purpose of intelligence is to provide policymakers with a decision advantage as they cope with resolving problems that face their nation.[10]

Whatever definition one prefers, the critical point is that espionage agencies engage in several activities to support the interests of their host nation. In the spirit of capturing this diversity of responsibilities, one can conclude that *national security intelligence consists of a cluster of government agencies that conduct secret activities, including covert action, counterintelligence, and, foremost, the collection and analysis of information for the purpose of illuminating the deliberations of policy officials by way of timely, accurate knowledge of potential threats and opportunities.*

Since intelligence activities are carried out by people in secretive government agencies, a closer look at intelligence as an organization is in order. Which institutions engage in crafting the final products – reports and oral briefings to decision-makers – that reside at the core of what is meant by national security intelligence; and which agencies and individuals engage in covert action and counterintelligence? Who in the intelligence bureaucracy responds to intelligence overseers? The configuration of the seventeen major spy organizations in the United States provides an illustration of what a nation's secret agencies actually do, and how.

Intelligence as a cluster of organizations: the American experience

A fundamental aspect of every nation's approach to spying is to recruit professional espionage officers and house them in buildings that are heavily fortified by fences, alarms, and armed guards. The American espionage establishment has grown into a sprawling bureaucracy – the largest ever devised by any society in history. Moreover, since the 9/11 attacks, the funding for intelligence in the United States has risen dramatically. For example, the NSA budget doubled between 2001 and 2006, reportedly reaching some $8 billion a year.[11] As displayed in Figure 1.2, the President and the National Security Council (NSC) stand at the apex of America's behemoth security apparatus. Beneath this National Command Authority (NCA) lie sixteen major intelligence agencies, led from 1947 through 2004 by a Director of Central Intelligence (DCI) and since 2005 by a new spymaster: the Director of National Intelligence

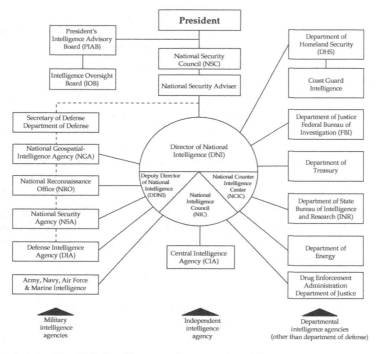

Figure 1.2 The U.S. Intelligence Community (IC) in 2016*

*From 1947 to 2005, a Director of Central Intelligence (DCI) led the IC, rather than a DNI.

(DNI), who is in charge of the Office of the DNI (ODNI) – often viewed as America's seventeenth intelligence agency – and responsible for the coordination of the entire intelligence establishment. An examination of organizational frameworks can be about as exciting as having hot porridge for breakfast on a summer's day; but knowing which agencies comprise the Intelligence Community, and what their duties are, is a necessary first step toward understanding the world of spies.

Military intelligence agencies

America's secret agencies have evolved into a cluster of organizations known, in a classic misnomer, as the "Intelligence Community" (IC). In reality, these agencies display the earmarks of rival tribes more than a harmonious community. Eight of the spy agencies are located within the framework of the Department of Defense (DoD), seven in civilian policy departments, and one – the CIA – stands as a civilian-oriented but independent organization. The military intelligence agencies include the National Security Agency (NSA), the nation's codebreaking, encrypting, and signals intelligence (sigint) organization, engaged primarily in telephone and email eavesdropping; the National Geospatial-Intelligence Agency (NGA), dedicated chiefly to taking photographs of enemy troops, weapons, and facilities ("imagery intelligence" or "geo-intelligence"), using cameras mounted on satellites in space, as well as on lower-altitude Unmanned Aerial Vehicles (UAVs or drones) and other reconnaissance aircraft; the National Reconnaissance Office (NRO), which supervises the construction, launching, and management of the nation's surveillance satellites; the Defense Intelligence Agency (DIA), which analyzes military-related subjects; and the intelligence units of the Army, Navy, Air Force, and Marines, each focused on the collection and analysis of tactical intelligence from places overseas – especially battlefields – where U.S. personnel serve in uniform.

Together, these military organizations account for some 85 percent of the total annual U.S. intelligence budget – an aggregate figure of some $80 billion in 2010 – and employ about 85 percent of the nation's intelligence personnel.[12] These military agencies absorb such a great portion of the yearly funding for espionage because of the high costs of the "platforms" they use for intelligence-gathering – especially large and expensive surveillance satellites, but also a global fleet of UAVs.

Funding for intelligence in the United States comes from two separate budgets: the National Intelligence Program (NIP), which supports the large national spy agencies, such as the NGA, the NRO, and the NSA, that have both military and civilian missions; and the Military Intelligence Program (MIP), which is devoted chiefly to tactical intelligence and related activities (TIARA). The boundary between the NIP and MIP, though, is "fluid, imprecise and subject to change," according to the Federation of American Scientists Project on Government Secrecy.[13] For instance, in 2006, the NGA received 70 percent of its funding from the NIP and 30 percent from the MIP; then, during the next year, the respective figures were 90 percent and 10 percent. In 2010, the respective percentages were approximately 66 percent and 34 percent.

In 2014, the NIP stood at $52.6 billion and the MIP at $19.2 billion, for a total of $71.8 billion. In 2016, the budget projections suggested a slight increase for the NIP, at $53.5 billion, and a decrease for the MIP, at $16.8 billion, or a total of $70.3 billion – a figure lower than the record spending in 2010, though an amount still vastly larger than America's aggregate spy budget before the 9/11 attacks (indeed, double the amount).

Civilian intelligence

Of the seven secret agencies embedded in civilian policy depart-ments, four have been part of the Intelligence Community for decades and three are newcomers. Among the older agencies, the FBI is located in the Department of Justice and assigned both a counterintelligence and a counterterrorism mission; the Office of Intelligence and Analysis is in the Department of Treasury, which includes among its duties the tracking of petrodollars and the hidden funds of terrorist organizations; the Bureau of Intelligence and Research (INR) is in the Department of State, the smallest of the secret agencies but one of the most highly regarded for its well-crafted and often prescient reports; and the Office of Intel-ligence and Counterintelligence is in the Department of Energy and monitors the worldwide movement of nuclear materials (uranium, plutonium, heavy water, nuclear reactor parts), while also main-taining security at the nation's weapons laboratories and nuclear weapons storage sites.

The three newcomer civilian agencies, all brought on board after the 9/11 terrorist attacks, include Coast Guard Intelligence; the Office of Intelligence and Analysis, in the Department of Homeland Security (DHS); and the Office of National Security Intelligence, in the Drug Enforcement Administration (DEA), which is part of the Justice Department. When admitted to the Intelligence Community in 2001, Coast Guard Intelligence initially had its own direct line to the nation's intelligence director on the organizational ("wiring") diagrams for America's spy establishment; but when the second Bush Administration created the DHS in 2003, Coast Guard Intel-ligence became an offshoot of this new Department, because of their common mission to protect the U.S. homeland and its coastline. The DEA, America's lead agency in the global struggle against illegal drug dealers, has been a part of the Justice Department for decades, but became a member of the Intelligence Community only in 2006.

The CIA

The last of the older agencies, and the eighth civilian intelligence organization, is the CIA, which is located outside the government's policy cabinet. During the Cold War, "the Agency" enjoyed special prestige in Washington, DC as the only espionage entity formally established by the National Security Act of 1947. Equally important for status and political clout in the nation's capital, it became the home office of the DCI – the titular leader of all the intelligence agencies. As noted earlier, since 2005 the DCI office has been replaced by a Director of National Intelligence or DNI, assisted by a set of deputies (DDNIs), a National Counterterrorism Center (NCTC), and a panel of top-flight analysts on the National Intelligence Council or NIC (see Figure 1.2). In the 1950s, the DCI moved with the CIA from a group of old Navy buildings in Washington, near the Mall, into new quarters located in Langley, Virginia, adjacent to the township of McLean. Today, the office of the DNI – the new leader of the American intelligence services – is located in an upscale building at Liberty Crossing, an urban neighborhood near the shopping district of Tyson's Corner, close to Arlington, Virginia, and some six miles away from CIA Headquarters at Langley.

As the names imply, the Central Intelligence Agency and the Director of Central Intelligence were originally meant to serve as a focal point for the U.S. intelligence establishment, playing the role of coordinators for the Community's activities and the collators of its "all-source" (that is, all-agency) reports, in an otherwise highly fragmented array of spy organizations. R. James Woolsey, who held the position of DCI during the early years of the Clinton Administration, has described the job of America's intelligence chief in this way: "You're kind of Chairman and CEO of the CIA, and you're kind of Chairman of the Board of the intelligence community."[14] He emphasized, though, that the Director does not have the authority to give "rudder orders" to the heads of the various intelligence agencies (Woolsey served for a time as Undersecretary of the Navy). Rather, he continued, "it's more subtle" – a matter of personal relationships, conversations, and gentle persuasion: the glue of trust and rapport rarely discussed in textbooks, but the essence of successful government transactions in DC and other national capitals.

As an example of the internal structure of an intelligence agency, the CIA's organizational framework during the Cold War is displayed in Figure 1.3. Admiral Stansfield Turner, who served as DCI during the Carter Administration (1977–81), has referred to the four Directorates within the Agency at the time – Operations, Intelligence, Science and Technology, and Administration – as "separate baronies," underscoring the notion that the CIA has several different cultures within its walls that are not always in sync with one another, or with the leadership cadre on the Agency's seventh floor.[15]

THE DO/NCS   As Figure 1.4 illustrates, during the Cold War the Directorate of Operations (DO), led by a Deputy Director for

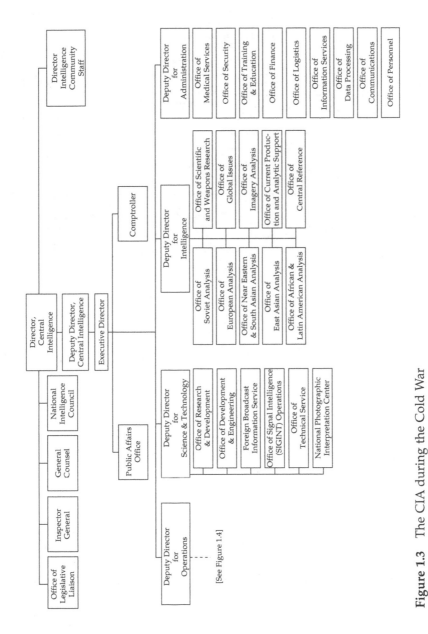

Figure 1.3 The CIA during the Cold War

Source: Fact Book on Intelligence, Office of Public Affairs, Central Intelligence Agency (April 1983), p. 9.

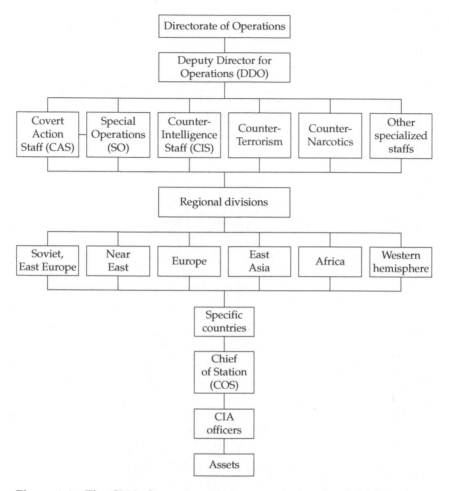

Figure 1.4   The CIA's Operations Directorate during the Cold War

Source: Loch K. Johnson, *America's Secret Power: The CIA in a Democratic Society* (New
York: Oxford University Press, 1989), p. 46.

Operations (DDO), was the arm of the CIA that extended overseas,
housed for the most part in "stations" around the world, along with
a few smaller "bases" within some nations or on some battlefields.
The stations have within their walls specially fortified rooms,
known as SCIFs (pronounced "skifs" – sensitive compartmented
information facilities), that are resistant to electronic eavesdropping and allow Agency personnel to conduct top secret meetings
overseas without fear of local counterintelligence officers or foreign
intelligence services listening in.

The DO went through a name change during the second Bush Administration, when it was known as the National Clandestine Service (NCS). During the Obama Administration it reclaimed its old DO tag. Its personnel abroad are referred to as "case officers," or, in a recent change of nomenclature, "operations officers." They are led by a chief of station, or COS, within each foreign country. The job of the case officer is to recruit locals (known as "assets" or "agents," who, if successful, are inducted into the Agency's service) to engage in espionage against their own countries, as well as to support the CIA's counterintelligence and covert action operations. To succeed, case or operations officers need to be gregarious individuals: charming, persuasive, and willing to take risks. For a foreigner to fall under their beguiling spell – or the attraction of the money the CIA may be offering – is to be "case officered" or "COed."

THE DI/DA   Back at CIA Headquarters, analysts in the Directorate of Intelligence (DI, now known as the Directorate of Analysis or DA) interpret the "raw" (unanalyzed) information gathered by operations officers and their assets, as well as by America's spy satellites and other machines. The CIA has the largest number of all-source analysts in the government. The job of the analysts – the Agency's intellectuals – is to provide insight into what the information means, and especially how it may affect the security and global interests of the United States.

THE DS&T AND THE DS   The Directorate of Science and Technology (DS&T) is the home of the CIA's "Dr. Q" scientists (a species of intelligence officer made famous by James Bond movies) and assorted other "techno-weenies" who develop equipment to aid the espionage effort, from wigs and other disguises to tiny listening devices and exotic weaponry. The Directorate of Support, or DS (known until recently as the Directorate of Administration or DA), is where the Agency's day-to-day managers reside. They meet payrolls, keep the hallways clean and hang art in the corridors at Langley, conduct polygraph tests on new recruits and (periodically) on employees, and maintain Headquarters security. Both the DS&T and the DS offer technical and security support to the Agency's operations abroad as well. During the Cold War, the Directorate of Administration also engaged improperly in spying against anti-Vietnam War protesters, triggering the Operation CHAOS scandal in 1974 and major investigations into the operations of the CIA and the other intelligence agencies.

Intelligence centers and task forces

To help overcome the fragmentation of America's intelligence apparatus, DCIs and now D/CIAs (Directors of the CIA) and DNIs have resorted to the use of "centers," "task forces," and "mission managers" that focus on particular topics and are staffed by personnel from throughout the Intelligence Community. For example, DCI John Deutch (1995–96) created an Environmental Intelligence Center to examine how intelligence officers and private-sector scientists could work together on the security and ecological implications of global environmental conditions, using spy satellites to examine such matters as the depletion of rain forests in Brazil, river water disputes in the Middle East, and the extent of melting ice floes in the Arctic Circle.[16] The year 2016 was the hottest in the history of recorded temperatures. The Environmental Intelligence Center would want to learn more about the effects of high temperatures on U.S. security and, more generally, on world affairs. Another DCI, William H. Webster (1987–91), established a special Iraqi Task Force to focus on the intelligence support needed for the First Persian Gulf War in 1990–91. More recently, DNI James R. Clapper, Jr. (2010–17) has relied on an Open Source Center (located at Langley, but reporting to the ODNI) to help integrate facts and figures available in the public domain with secret information acquired overseas.

Intelligence oversight boards

As Figure 1.2 displays, the Intelligence Community also has two prominent oversight boards: the President's Foreign Intelligence Advisory Board (PFIAB, shortened after the 9/11 attacks to the President's Intelligence Advisory Board, or PIAB), and the Intelligence Oversight Board (IOB). Since its creation in the 1950s, PFIAB/PIAB has had among its dozen or so members (the numbers vary from administration to administration) several prominent security, foreign policy, and scientific experts. The latter have given the panel a special niche: helping the President improve the science of espionage. Edward Land, the inventor of the Polaroid camera, is an example of a much-valued PFIAB member during the Eisenhower Administration. He significantly advanced the capabilities of America's spy cameras in space. Some presidents, however, have used membership on the Advisory Board not so much as a means for monitoring and improving U.S. intelligence but as a prestigious White House payoff to political allies who contributed money to their election campaign – a corruption of the original intent for the panel's existence.

The IOB, now folded into the PIAB as a subcommittee, is small, with only three or four members. Occasionally it has conducted a serious inquiry into charges of intelligence improprieties (such as the NSA metadata collection program); but it, too, has become largely an honorific assignment, more cosmetic than effective as a vigilant protector against the abuse of secret power. Not displayed in Figure 1.2, but nonetheless an integral part of the Intelligence Community, are the House and Senate intelligence committees, known more formally as the House Permanent Select Committee on Intelligence (HPSCI, pronounced "hip-see") and the Senate Select Committee on Intelligence (SSCI or "sis-see"). Their vital role in the Intelligence Community is examined in Chapter 5.

An iron pentagon

Added to this official complex of organizations are a plethora of smaller intelligence units in the federal government, as well as many private institutions that are hired by the U.S. intelligence agencies to help them with their missions – the "outsourcing" of intelligence. A special *Washington Post* inquiry in 2010 discovered the existence of 1,271 government organizations involved in intelligence work of one type or another, and an additional 1,931 private companies.[17] The most notorious example of the latter in recent years was the Blackwater firm (renamed Xe Services in 2009, then Academi in 2011), based in North Carolina. This group of security experts and paramilitary officers provided protection to American intelligence officials and diplomats in Iraq and Afghanistan during the recent U.S. interventions in those countries, among other locations. Blackwater reportedly even entered into the CIA's plans for executing terrorist leaders around the world – an idea that was scrubbed when this organization developed a reputation for overzealous operations overseas. For example, in 2007, Blackwater guards armed with machine guns and grenade launchers killed seventeen Iraqi civilians at Nisour Square in Baghdad.

In his famous farewell address, President Dwight D. Eisenhower warned the American people about a "military–industrial complex" – an expression of his concern that defense contractors might gain "unwarranted influence" over lawmakers, providing them with campaign contributions in exchange for appropriations to build an endless supply of new weaponry. Political scientists speak of this alliance as an "iron triangle" comprised of interest groups, bureaucrats, and politicians. In Eisenhower's description, the points of the triangle were the weapons manufacturers (Boeing, for instance), admirals and generals in the Pentagon, and key lawmakers on the Armed Services and Appropriations Committees. The alliance produced profits for the manufacturers; new planes, ships and tanks for the military brass; and defense jobs back home for the lawmakers. Presidents would come and go, but the iron triangle persisted – and often defied presidential leadership.

In more recent years, added to this venerable triangle are two more geometric points in the security establishment: outsource groups like Xe Services and the nation's weapons laboratories (where weapons systems are developed). This "iron pentagon" represents an even more potent and sophisticated security coalition than the triangle that Eisenhower found disconcerting in 1959. Accompanying the old lobbying efforts on behalf of new weaponry is an added corporate interest in lucrative intelligence dollars appropriated by Congress for spy platforms, such as the expensive satellites used by the NGA, the NRO, and the NSA, and the mass production of drones for the wars in Iraq, Afghanistan, and elsewhere. In addition, Xe Services and its proliferating counterparts, all with a lobbying staff, are attracted to funding for security, counterintelligence, and covert action support.

A flawed plan for U.S. intelligence

Like the intelligence organizations of other nations, the American espionage system has been built without any grand design, in response to a series of pressures: national emergencies; new technological developments (better eavesdropping capabilities, for example, have led to a greater emphasis on – and a larger staff and building for – sigint); the priorities of intelligence leaders (Allen Dulles in the 1950s concentrated on his favorite method of spying, human intelligence – the traditional use of agents recruited locally to spy on behalf of the United States); and the lobbying skills of bureaucrats (the master, J. Edgar Hoover of the FBI, built "the Bureau" into one of the most highly regarded – some would say feared and dangerous – organizations in Washington). The haphazard evolution of spy organizations in the United States can be seen in the history that led to the birth of the CIA in 1947.

The creation of the CIA: a Faustian bargain

The searing memory of one violent shock, and the potential for yet more violence, contributed to the establishment of the CIA. The initial shock occurred in 1941, when the Japanese attack against Hawaii pulled the United States into the Second World War. A potential for further violence loomed immediately after the end of the global war when, as early as 1945, the Soviet Union showed signs that it might attempt an armed expansion into Western Europe and Asia that could jeopardize America's global interests.

On December 7, 1941, Japanese warplanes swooped down on the U.S. Pacific Fleet anchored in Pearl Harbor at Oahu. In two waves of strafing and bombing just after sunrise, 350 planes from six Japanese carriers located north of Hawaii managed to demolish 187 aircraft on the ground, as well as eight battleships (five sank), three cruisers, three destroyers, and four auxiliary ships in the harbor. The assault killed 2,403 American service personnel, mostly Navy, and wounded another 1,178. One hundred civilians also died. In an address to Congress, President Franklin Roosevelt declared that the day of the attack would "live in infamy."

Eight separate panels of inquiry examined why the United States had been taken by surprise at Pearl Harbor. None of the investigations clearly fixed blame for the disaster, but one conclusion was indisputable: America's intelligence apparatus had failed to warn President Roosevelt that a Japanese war fleet was sailing toward Hawaii. Indeed, it was the most damaging intelligence failure in the nation's history, and would remain so until the horrific Al Qaeda terrorist attacks against New York City and Washington, DC in 2001.

In the lead-up to the Pearl Harbor tragedy, the fragments of data available here and there in the bureaucracy about the impending outbreak of war in the Pacific were never assembled, subjected to all-source analysis, and forwarded to the White House in a timely manner – the basics of what is known as the "intelligence cycle" (discussed in Chapter 2). This sequestering of information resulted in part from the intention of some intelligence officers to keep the existence of "MAGIC" (the breaking of the Japanese communications codes) carefully compartmented and secure. MAGIC might be compromised, they reasoned, if information from this source was shared outside the confines of a few Navy intelligence personnel. Yet, in concealing the secret decoding breakthrough from the Japanese, they managed to hide it from the President of the United States and his aides.

As a U.S. Senator from Missouri, Harry S. Truman was well aware of the significant loss of lives and matériel that had resulted from America's poor intelligence performance in 1941. During his three-month tenure as Vice President and upon becoming President with Roosevelt's death in April 1945, Truman experienced further dissatisfaction with the lack of coordination among America's few intelligence services throughout the remaining months of the Second World War. As one of Truman's top aides, Clark Clifford, recalled: "By early 1946, President Truman was becoming increasingly annoyed by the flood of conflicting and uncoordinated intelligence reports flowing haphazardly across his desk."[18] On January 22, 1946, he signed an executive order that created a Central Intelligence Group (CIG) for the express purpose of achieving a "correlation and evaluation of intelligence relating to the national security." The order allowed the CIG to "centralize" research and analysis and "coordinate all foreign intelligence activities."[19]

Truman's original intent was, in his own words, to avoid "having to look through a bunch of papers two feet high." Instead, he wanted to receive information that was "coordinated so that the President could arrive at the facts."[20] Yet the President never saw his objective fulfilled. From the beginning, the CIG proved weak. One of its primary tasks was to put together the *Daily Summary*, the precursor to today's *President's Daily Brief*. Intelligence units in the various departments balked, however, at handing over information to the CIG.

A central intelligence agency

Frustrated, the Truman Administration turned to the idea of establishing a strong, statutory espionage organization: a *Central Intelligence Agency*. It soon became evident to President Truman, however, that the creation of a truly focused intelligence system would come at too steep a price, in light of an even more urgent goal he desired: military consolidation. The Second World War had been rife with conflict between the U.S. military services, often interrupting the pursuit of battlefield objectives. Clifford remembered how the Administration had to slow down intelligence reform in favor of settling the "first order of business – the war between the Army and the Navy." The "first priority," he continued, "was still to get the squabbling military services together behind a unification bill."[21]

The creation of a new Department of Defense would provide an umbrella to bring the services closer together. The President wished to avoid complicating this core objective by carrying out at the same time a quest for intelligence consolidation that was bound to roil the military brass, who viewed a powerful new CIA as a threat to their own confederal and parochial approach to intelligence. As a top Agency official recalled, "The one thing that Army, Navy, State, and the FBI agreed on was that they did not want a strong central agency controlling their collection programs."[22] So Truman and his aides entered into a compromise with the armed services, in the hope that this would produce the desired goal of military unification. They tried to improve intelligence coordination to some extent, but without letting that sensitive subject anger the Pentagon and erase its support for the higher goal of military unity.

The result was a series of retreats from centralized intelligence, as exhibited in the diluted language on the CIA and the DCI in the National Security Act of 1947. This law provided for only an enfeebled DCI, along with a CIA that was hard to distinguish from the failed CIG. As Clifford conceded in understatement, the effort fell "far short of our original intent."[23] In this sense the Agency was from the beginning, as intelligence scholar Amy B. Zegart has remarked, "flawed by design."[24] The landmark National Security Act would mainly address the issue of military unification, and even on that subject with only moderate success. In the new law, the subject of intelligence was sharply downgraded.

The 1947 statute did set up a *Central* Intelligence Agency, at least in name; but it left the details vague on just how this new, independent organization was going to carry out its charge to "correlate," "evaluate," and "disseminate" information to policymakers when confronted with the powerful grip that extant departments held over their individual intelligence units. The portion of the 1947 law dealing with intelligence represented a delicate attempt to establish a CIA that, in the view of historian Michael Warner, would have to "steer between the two poles of centralization and departmental autonomy." As a result, the CIA "never quite became the integrator of U.S. intelligence that its presidential and congressional parents had envisioned."[25]

The rhetoric of "intelligence coordination" expressed in the law had a pleasant ring to it, but the reality of bringing about true jointness was another matter altogether. Genuine integration of the intelligence agencies required a strong DCI, with full budget and appointment powers. The word "community" was clearly a euphemism, coined in 1952 to describe America's loose aggregation of "stovepiped" espionage agencies, each with its own program director (a "gorilla," in intelligence slang) and allegiance to its own cabinet secretary (at Defense, Justice, and State). The powers of the DCI enumerated in the National Security Act of 1947 remained at best merely suggestions, leaving the spymaster in a position of having to cajole, persuade, plead, even beg for intelligence coordination, rather than demand unity through the threat of budget and personnel retaliation against the "gorillas in the stovepipes" who failed to comply with the Director's directives. As Warner concludes: "...a powerful statutory CIA never had a chance. From Day One,

War and Navy leaders strenuously opposed such a scheme. With no political capital to spare, the President went along."[26]

A DCI without authority

When Truman authorized the creation of the CIG by executive order in 1946, the Group's chief counsel, Lawrence R. Houston, soon complained that "we are nothing but a stepchild of the three departments [Defense, Justice, and State] we are supposed to coordinate."[27] Matters did not improve much with the more formal, statutory establishment of a CIA in the next year. Even twenty years after its creation, one of the Agency's deputy directors, Admiral Rufus Taylor (1966–69), referred to the Intelligence Community as still little more than a "tribal federation."[28]

An important aspect of U.S. intelligence history since the Truman Administration has been the series of efforts since 1947 to overcome the flaw in the CIA's original design: that is, to strengthen the DCI and the Agency in their roles as collator and disseminator of intelligence for the entire "Community." A series of commissions have all suggested the need for a more authoritative DCI to integrate the nation's fragmented intelligence agencies.[29]

The steam went out of each of these efforts, however, as soon as they confronted resistance from the community's gorillas, especially the 800-pound King Kong in the DoD – the Secretary of Defense, the DCI's rival over leadership of the eight military intelligence units and a cabinet secretary with redoubtable allies on the Armed Services and Appropriations Committees.[30] Nor were the other cabinet secretaries with a security portfolio exactly pushovers. "For the duration of the Cold War, the White House kept nudging successive Intelligence Directors to provide more leadership for the intelligence community," historian Warner writes. But a towering obstacle persisted: "Cabinet-level officials...saw no reason to cede power to a DCI."[31]

Redesigning the leadership of American intelligence

In the waning days of 2004, Congress finally addressed the need for intelligence reform. The key provision of the much amended 600-page law, entitled the Intelligence Reform and Terrorism Prevention Act (IRTPA), was an Office of Director of National Intelligence. The DNI, though, was still nowhere near dominant enough to draw the now sixteen intelligence agencies together into one cooperative harness. Despite the horrors of the 9/11 attacks, the far-reaching

mistakes related to the war in Iraq begun in 2003, and all the pub-
licity associated with the findings of the Kean Commission that
investigated the 9/11 failures, the best Congress seemed able to
achieve were half-measures that proved unable to knit together
the long-standing rents in the vast tent of the so-called Intelligence
Community.

The DNI would have to go on sharing authority with the Secretary of Defense (SecDef) over military intelligence – the same
situation faced by the DCI before the IRTPA was passed. This
meant that the 800-pound gorilla in the Pentagon, the SecDef,
would continue to dominate intelligence, maximizing support to
military operations while minimizing resources for global political,
economic, and cultural matters that might help curb the outbreak
of wars in the first place. As vaguely stated in the IRTPA law,
the new intelligence chief would be allowed only to "*monitor* the
implementation and execution" of intelligence operations. Tribal
warfare in the community would continue. Institutional diffusion
had trumped consolidation. On one point practically every observer
agreed: the statute was riddled with ambiguities and contradictions
that would have to be hammered out on the anvil of experience
over the coming years and strengthened by amendments. These
amendments never materialized.

A revolving door at the office of the DNI

With this new Intelligence Reform Act, Congress – under pressure
from the Pentagon – banned the DNI from having an office at the
CIA (over the objections of the White House).[32] It was payback time
against the Agency by supporters of the other intelligence services,
for all the CIA's slights and perceived arrogance over the years.

The first DNI appointee, Ambassador John D. Negroponte, even-
tually found space for his office in the Defense Intelligence Agency
Center (DIAC), the new DIA Headquarters Building at Bolling Air
Force Base, located across the Potomac River from National Airport.
The Ambassador brought with him a few analytic components from
the CIA and some other elements from around the Community.
Most of the CIA's analysts remained at Agency Headquarters in
Langley, however, a dozen miles away upstream on the other side of
the Potomac. Nesting at Bolling only temporarily (the DIA wanted
all its space back), intelligence managers and the White House set in
motion plans to build a new DNI facility at Liberty Crossing, near
Tyson's Corner in North Arlington, Virginia, ready for use in 2009.
The nation's intelligence director would still be miles away from

the CIA resources he needed if he wanted to be anything more than a shadow leader. Why not just move back to CIA Headquarters? That would require an amendment to the 2004 Intelligence Reform law. "That horse is out of the barn," concluded an experienced intelligence officer, waving aside any thoughts about revisiting that battle and taking on the Pentagon brass again.[33]

Ambassador Negroponte soon fled back to the Department of State, after serving for less than two years as DNI. His successor, former NSA director Admiral Mike McConnell, stayed in the Bolling office for the time being and continued to build up a staff. Both Negroponte and McConnell were talented, bright spy chiefs; but, nevertheless, the United States, in a search for greater cohesion in the Intelligence Community, had created instead (ironically) in the DNI an Intelligence Director even weaker than the old DCI – a leader with ambiguous authority, a small staff, and an office miles away from most of the government's reservoir of intelligence analysts at Langley. Just what the nation needed: an isolated spymaster and a new, hollowed-out seventeenth spy agency.

During the confirmation hearing for Admiral McConnell's appointment as DNI, the Chairman of the Senate Select Committee on Intelligence, John D. Rockefeller (D, West Virginia), raised serious questions about the weaknesses of the office. The Senator observed:

> We did not pull the technical collection agencies out of the Defense Department [one reform possibility] and we did not give the DNI direct authority over the main collection or analytic components of the community. We gave the DNI the authority to build the national intelligence budget, but we left the execution of the budget with the agencies. We gave the DNI tremendous responsibilities. The question is: did we give the position enough authority?[34]

For most observers – outside the DoD at least – the answer was a clear "no!" Even McConnell, after serving two months as DNI, could only offer a euphemistic description of a job that he had clearly found unwieldy. It was, in his words, a "challenging management condition."[35] In particular, he complained about his inability to dismiss incompetent people. "You cannot hire or fire," he told a reporter.[36] The Admiral soon announced a "100 Day Plan," in which he proposed a searching review of the DNI's authority and an ongoing effort to integrate the components of the Intelligence "Community." He vowed: "We're going to examine it; we're going to argue about it; we're going to make some proposals."[37] Appearing before the Senate in February 2008, he further testified: "Our current model...does not have operational control over the elements that conduct intelligence activities. The DNI also does not have direct authority over the personnel in the sixteen agencies in the community."[38]

At least the retired SecDef, Donald H. Rumsfeld, who opposed the DNI position to begin with, was no longer in Washington to stymie the development of an effective DNI Office. In Rumsfeld's place at the Pentagon had come Robert M. Gates, a former DI analyst and DCI, who understood intelligence probably better than any SecDef in the nation's history. Moreover, he had long been an advocate of a better working relationship between military and civilian intelligence agencies. Whether this happy alignment of the stars could overcome the DNI's inherent statutory weaknesses, though, was unlikely – especially with McConnell becoming more and more preoccupied with, and defensive about, the debate over controversial CIA torture methods and the NSA's use of warrantless wiretaps at the direction of the Bush White House (the latter a violation of the Foreign Intelligence Surveillance Act of 1978). In 2009, he resigned and was replaced by another former admiral, Dennis C. Blair, who would take up quarters in the new space for the DNI at Liberty Crossing.

Before long, Admiral Blair found himself embroiled in a squabble over who should appoint the top U.S. intelligence officer in each American intelligence station overseas, that is, the chief of station or COS. The outcome provides an illustration of how enfeebled the Office of the DNI is. Blair claimed the right as the nation's intelligence chief to make these appointments, even though they had been named traditionally by the head of the CIA (who was dual-hatted as DCI as well, prior to 2005). The DNI issued a memorandum announcing that, henceforth, he would select each COS. The next day, the Director of the CIA (D/CIA), former member of the House of Representatives Leon E. Panetta (D, California), countered with a memorandum of his own that ordered Agency employees to disregard the DNI's message. Panetta – prodded by the Director of the National Clandestine Service, who does the actual selection of station chiefs – reasoned that the CIA had traditionally named the nation's COSs for good reason: it was the Agency that had almost all the intelligence billets in each of the stations overseas, so its officers could recruit local spies – human intelligence, or humint – for the United States. These delicate relationships could be torn if suddenly the locals had to deal with new case officers who were not even led by the CIA; therefore, Panetta argued, it made sense to have Langley's officers remain in charge.

Both arguments had some merit. On Panetta's side, it is true that U.S. intelligence officers in most stations are there to recruit indigenous assets, the job primarily of the CIA. Yet, in some countries where signals intelligence is a forte – Britain and Australia, for example – America's intelligence officers serve chiefly as liaison personnel for sigint cooperation. In these cases, it made some sense for the COS to be from the NSA, America's sigint organization. Blair wanted to be able to make these distinctions, rather than simply have the CIA in charge everywhere. Moreover, if the Office of the DNI had been created in December 2004 to serve as America's intelligence chief, shouldn't Blair be calling the shots? He obviously thought so, but the White House eventually sided with Panetta in this dispute. President Barack Obama and his Vice President, Joseph R. Biden, Jr., may have bent naturally toward Panetta, a fellow pol and former member of Congress; and perhaps they were concerned, too, about a rumor circulating in Washington that Blair's gambit was an attempt by the military to further weaken the CIA, and that the DNI would soon name large numbers of senior military intelligence officers to COS positions around the world.

Blair, supposedly the CIA Director's superior on the organizational charts, was reportedly furious about what he perceived to be Panetta's insubordination. A *New York Times* reporter with an intelligence beat viewed the brouhaha as "further evidence that the intelligence overhaul five years ago did little to end longstanding rivalries or clearly delineate the chain of command within American intelligence bureaucracy."[39] The Admiral resigned in 2010 and President Obama replaced him with a seasoned intelligence official, former Air Force general James R. Clapper, Jr., mentioned previously, who had headed up both the DIA and NGA earlier in his career. In confirmation hearings, he vowed to establish better working relations with Panetta.

A dream still on hold

Would a strong DNI with full authority over the spy community solve America's intelligence woes and ward off future 9/11s? In itself, of course not. Improvements in intelligence must move forward across a broad front, a challenge explored throughout this book. The intelligence reform bill in 2004 represented, though, an important step toward the establishment of a genuine national intelligence chief. Here was a chance to have an intelligence leader with full authority over America's secret agencies, a spymaster who could overcome the twin banes of ineffective intelligence: interagency rivalry and parochialism. Yet a last-minute watering down of the reform legislation left the DNI enfeebled and separated from the National Intelligence Council and the rest of the vital corps of analytic "troops" who continued to be located in Langley at the CIA.⁴⁰ General Clapper, well aware of the weaknesses in the DNI office, nonetheless expressed a determination during his Senate confirmation hearings in 2010 to bring greater cohesion to the Intelligence Community. To enhance IC integration, he established a team of fifteen or so (the numbers varying from time to time) National Intelligence Managers or NIMs with specific portfolios related to world regions or specific issues (such as the counterproliferation of WMD). The NIM for the Western Hemisphere, for example, is expected to pull together all-source information from throughout the IC in preparing reports on America's neighbors to the north and south for the President and other top government consumers of intelligence.

Thanks to Clapper's half-century of experience in intelligence work, along with his widespread contacts among intelligence professionals, he had considerable success in managing the Intelligence Community. It will be difficult, though, for his successor to match these fortuitous advantages.

....

In trying to make espionage agencies more effective as a shield for the democracies – that is, less prone to failure and scandal – organizational reform at the DNI level of intelligence management is just part of the challenge. The mission of collection and analysis also cries out for improvements, as examined in the next chapter.

2 Intelligence Collection and Analysis

Knowing about the World

Early one morning in October 1994, Secretary of Defense William J. Perry – a tall, thoughtful man with a PhD in mathematics – greeted the Chairman of the Joint Chiefs of Staff, General John Shalikashvili, in the SecDef's spacious office at the Pentagon. Under his arm, the General carried a portfolio of satellite photographs of Iraq. He spread the images across a conference table. Using a pointer, Shalikashvili directed Perry's attention to a disturbing set of pictures. Improbable as it might have seemed, coming just three-and-a-half years after a U.S.-led coalition had knocked Saddam Hussein's army to its knees, elements of the Republican Guard (Saddam's elite troops), supported by mechanized infantry, armor, and tank units, were moving at a rapid clip southward toward Basra, a mere thirty miles from the Kuwaiti border. The force was aimed like an arrow at the Al Jahra heights overlooking Kuwait City, in an apparent repeat of the same maneuver that led to the Iraqi conquest of Kuwait in 1990 and the first Persian Gulf War. At its current rate of speed, the Republican guard would stream across the Kuwaiti border within a couple of days.

Perry quickly ordered a U.S. armored brigade stationed in Kuwait to the Iraqi border. With a mounting sense of uneasiness, the SecDef and the top Pentagon brass waited as young captains and lieutenants brought new batches of satellite imagery into Perry's office over the next twenty-four hours. Upwards of 10,000 Iraqi troops had amassed in an area near Basra. Steadily the number rose to 50,000, some camped within twelve miles of the border. The American brigade had arrived, but consisted of only 2,000 lightly armed Marines.

While the United States also had 200 warplanes in the area on standby alert, the Iraqi armored force dwarfed the American presence. President Bill Clinton ordered 450 more warplanes to Kuwait, along with the 24th Mechanized Infantry Division and a Marine contingent from Camp Pendleton in California. The aircraft carrier *George Washington* steamed at maximum speed toward the Red Sea from the Indian Ocean. None of these forces, though, would arrive in time to block an invasion of Kuwait. Perry and Shalikashvili faced the prospect of a rout that would quickly wipe away the small American brigade assembled at the border.

The two men waited nervously for the next set of satellite photographs. When they arrived, Perry and Shalikashvili breathed an audible sigh of relief. The Iraqi troops had suddenly stopped and some elements were already turning back toward Baghdad.

The good news was that imagery intelligence may have prevented the outbreak of another war in the Persian Gulf. Using these timely photographs to pinpoint the location of Iraqi troops, Perry had been able to place an American brigade as a barrier against Iraqi aggression. "Had the intelligence arrived three or four days later, it would have been too late," he told the Aspin–Brown Commission.

The episode revealed, however, troubling intelligence weaknesses as well. Even though vital information had arrived in time for the Secretary of Defense to put up some semblance of resistance at the Kuwaiti border, the thousands of troops in the Republican Guard could have overwhelmed the single Marine brigade. The best Perry could hope for was that the Marines might intimidate Saddam and make him think twice about another invasion. Fortunately, the bluff worked. Retrospective studies of the satellite imagery taken of Iraq before the crisis disclosed palpable clues that, for weeks, Saddam had been gathering a force near Baghdad for another invasion of Kuwait. The photos revealed trickles of Iraqi troops and armor moving toward Basra that would soon turn into a threatening flood of armed aggression. Intelligence analysts in the CIA's National Photographic Interpretation Center (NPIC, now a part of NGA) had missed these signs, as had everyone else at the Agency.

The problem had not been a lack of information: high-ranking government officials have access each day to enough imagery and other intelligence data to smother every desk in the Pentagon. Photos don't speak for themselves, however, and nobody had scrutinized them carefully enough, day-by-day, to notice the accretion of troop buildups that signaled the possibility of a gathering invasion force. "Had we analyzed the data better from techint [technical intelligence collection]," said Perry, looking back at the crisis, "we could have had a seven-to-ten-day earlier alert. Better humint [human intelligence – spies on the ground] might have given this alert, too."[1]

The message from the SecDef was clear: the U.S. Intelligence Community still had much room for improvement when it came to support for military operations and a host of other collection and analysis responsibilities. This chapter examines key strengths and weaknesses of this preeminent mission for the secret agencies of every nation – what a DCI once referred to as "the absolute essence of the intelligence profession."[2]

The intelligence cycle

The phrase "collection and analysis" is used here as shorthand to describe a complex process for the gathering, analysis, and dissemination of information to decision-makers. A convenient way of envisioning this flow is the theoretical construct known as the intelligence cycle (see Figure 2.1). Despite its oversimplification

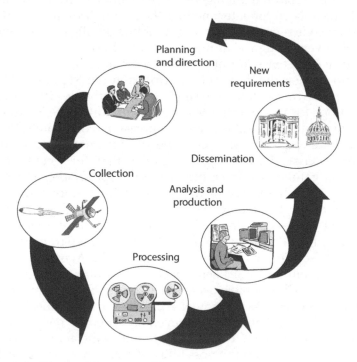

Figure 2.1   The intelligence cycle

Source: Adapted from *Fact Book on Intelligence*, Office of Public Affairs, Central
    Intelligence Agency (October 1993), p. 14.

of a complicated process with many stops and starts, the "cycle" captures the major phases in the life of an intelligence report.[3] The first phase is known as planning and direction.

Planning and direction

The beginning of the intelligence cycle is critical. Unless a potential target is clearly highlighted when officials gather to establish intelligence priorities ("requirements" or "tasks"), it is unlikely to receive much attention by those who collect information. The world is a large and fractious place, with some 200 nations and a plethora of groups, factions, gangs, cartels, and terrorist cells, some of whom have adversarial relationships with the democratic societies. A former DCI, R. James Woolsey (1993–95), observed after the Cold War that the United States had slain the Soviet dragon but "we live now in a jungle filled with a bewildering variety of poisonous snakes."[4] As noted in Chapter 1, some things – "mysteries" in the argot of intelligence professionals – are unknowable in any definitive way, such as who is likely to replace the current leader of North Korea. Secrets, in contrast, may be uncovered with a combination of luck and skill – say, the number of Chinese frigates, which are susceptible to satellite tracking.

At some point the degree of danger posed by foreign adversaries (or domestic subversives) becomes self-evident, as with the 9/11 attacks. Unfortunately, however, intelligence officers and government officials are (like other mortals) rarely able to predict exactly when and where danger will strike. As former Secretary of State Dean Rusk once put it, "Providence has not provided human beings with the capacity to pierce the fog of the future."[5]

Rwanda provides an example. Les Aspin recalled: "When I became Secretary of Defense [in 1993, at the beginning of the Clinton Administration], I served several months without ever giving Rwanda a thought. Then, for several weeks, that's all I thought about. After that, it fell abruptly off the screen and I never again thought about Rwanda."[6] The central African nation had become the "flavor of the month" for policymakers, as intelligence officers scrambled to find information about the genocidal civil war that had erupted there. Such unexpected "pop-up" intelligence targets are also known as the "ad hocs." Lowenthal notes how these international surprises can sometimes dominate the intelligence cycle and divert attention from the established formal targets of perceived danger or opportunity. He refers to this risky displacement as "the tyranny of the ad hocs."[7]

The Iranian revolution in 1979 offers a further illustration of the difficulties intelligence analysts face in anticipating future events. A top CIA analyst on Iran recalls that on the eve of the revolution,

> we knew the Shah was widely unpopular, and we knew there would be mass demonstrations, even riots. But how many shop-keepers would resort to violence, and how long would Army officers remain loyal to the Shah? Perhaps the Army would shoot down 10,000 rioters, maybe 20,000. If the ranks of the insurgents swelled further, though, how far would the Army be willing to go before it decided that the Shah was a losing proposition? All this we duly reported; but no one could predict with confidence the number of dissidents who would actually take up arms, or the "tipping point" for Army loyalty.[8]

A further example of a threat that was shrouded in ambiguity was the Soviet Backfire bomber during the Cold War. Analysts in the CIA concluded that the bomber was a medium-range aircraft, which its specifications seemed to indicate. Yet DIA analysts pointed out that if the Soviets operated the bomber in a certain manner, sending its pilots on a one-way, no-refueling, kamikaze mission, then clearly the range of the Backfire would be much longer. From the DIA's point of view, under these conditions the Backfire bomber was a weapon of strategic significance that could reach the United States, not one solely for tactical operations on the Soviet perimeter.

Sometimes differences in analytic conclusions seem driven by political considerations. For example, when North Korea failed to put a satellite into orbit in 2009, some analysts concluded that the country's technical capabilities were far less than Cassandras had warned. Other analysts, though, attempted to "hype the threat" of North Korean missiles in order to "scare people" – so observed Philip E. Coyle III, a former director of weapons testing at the Pentagon. Their goal, according to Coyle, was the promotion of the Pentagon's costly and controversial anti-missile program.[9]

In the United States, the job of evaluating the nature of threats to the United States and determining intelligence priorities is known as a "threat assessment." Experts and policymakers convene peri-odically to evaluate the perils that confront the nation, starting at the beginning of every incoming Administration in the January that follows the presidential election year. They establish a ladder of priorities from the most dangerous threats (labeled Tiers 1A and 1B in some administrations) to the least dangerous but still worthy of attention (Tier 4). A further Tier 0 is reserved for crisis situations that might entail the immediate use of military force.[10]

The Pentagon is always the most voracious consumer of intelligence, especially when wars involving the United States are under way. The combatant commanders (COCOMs) – the four-star officers who lead America's troops and sailors around the world – are always hungry, understandably, for information that will help to protect their forces and, in wartime, to advance America's battlefield objectives. This so-called SMO (support to military operations) tends to dominate the U.S. intelligence budget and target planning. The payoff can be substantial. America's secret agencies were far off the mark in predicting that the Saddam Hussein regime was developing a robust WMD program threatening to the United States in 2002; but once the U.S. invasion against Iraq began the following year, these agencies performed well. The U.S. forces benefited from full battlefield transparency, knowing the location of practically every Iraq tank, plane, boat, and even combat patrol. This dominant battlefield awareness (DBA, in Pentagonese) was remarkable in the annals of warfare. The same had been true during America's earlier invasion of Iraq in 1990–91. In both instances, the outcome was victory – coming quickly in the first war, though much more slowly in the second. Best of all, in both cases the United States suffered relatively few casualties compared with other major wars. America's military firepower was the most vital ingredient in these successes; but DBA played a significant role, too. For adversaries, fighting the United States in the post-Cold War era became equivalent to wearing a blindfold while confronting a superpower with seemingly omniscient vision – at least at the tactical level of the battlefield.

Some 80 percent of U.S. intelligence funding is related to military matters. This tilt of the Intelligence Community toward SMO has had its critics. They would prefer to see more funding for what might be called support to diplomatic operations, or SDO – gathering intelligence from around the world that might help to advance U.S. interests through diplomacy: a focus on peacemaking rather than war-fighting.

In addition to a threat analysis during the planning and direction phase of the intelligence cycle, important, too, are calculations about global opportunities. Intelligence is expected to provide a "heads up" regarding both dangers and chances to advance America's global interests. Whether related to threats or to opportunities, bias and guesswork enter into the picture, along with the limitations caused by the inherent opaqueness of the future. On which tier should policymakers place China? Iran? What about the Russian Federation, less hostile toward the United States than during the Cold War but still able to destroy every American metropolis in the thirty-minute witchfire of a nuclear holocaust? Or global climate change?

Around the Cabinet Room in the White House, or in the comparable forums of other nations, the arguments fly regarding the proper hierarchy of concerns. This is not an academic exercise. The outcome determines the priorities for multibillion-dollar spending on intelligence collection and analysis. It pinpoints locations on the world map where spies will be infiltrated; telephones and computers tapped; surveillance satellites set into orbit; reconnaissance aircraft dispatched on overflight missions; and potentially lethal covert actions directed. All too frequently in this process, intelligence officers are left in the dark about the "wish list" of policy officials, who assume that the secret agencies will somehow divine their needs. The solution: more regular discussions between the two groups – spies and the nation's leaders – to ensure that the secret agencies fully understand the top priorities of the nation's decision-makers.

Different nations are apt to have differing threat perceptions. Al Qaeda, ISIS, and other *jihadi* terrorist organizations, plus insurgents on the Iraqi and Afghan battlefields, global WMD proliferation, and state-sponsored cyberhackers, have recently been the top 1A intelligence targets for the United States and the United Kingdom. In many African nations, however, AIDS and poverty are the greatest threats to national security; in Brazil, crime is high on the list; in New Zealand, a top priority is the encroachment of Japanese fishing vessels into the Tasman Sea; for Norway, it is fishing rights in the Barents Sea, as well as Russian dumping of radioactive and other waste north of the Kola Peninsula. These variations in intelligence priorities can make it difficult for the secret services in the democracies to work together in sharing intelligence responsibilities.

A key question looms behind discussions of intelligence threats and opportunities. How much intelligence is enough? The answer depends on the chances a nation is willing to take about the future – how much "information insurance" its leaders desire. The relationship between intelligence and risk is depicted in Figure 2.2. The fewer the risks a nation is willing to take, the more intelligence it needs. At the same time, though, the more intelligence a nation gathers, the greater the costs become – and the greater the likelihood of information overload occurring, whereby a nation finds itself inundated with so much data that it is unable to analyze what it all means. Relevant, too, is the extent of a nation's global interests. Asked if the United States collected too much information, DCI William E. Colby (1973–76) replied: "Not for a big nation. If I

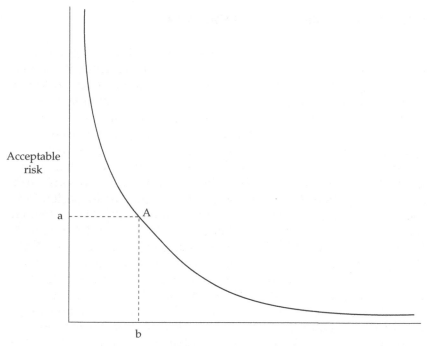

Figure 2.2 The relationship between a nation's sense of acceptable risk and its resources committed to intelligence collection and analysis

Source: Adapted from Loch K. Johnson, *Bombs, Bugs, Drugs, and Thugs: Intelligence and America's Quest for Security* (New York: New York University Press, 2000), p. 136.

were Israel, I'd spend my time on the neighboring Arab armies and I wouldn't give a damn about what happened in China. We are a big power and we've got to worry about all of the world."[11]

In 2003, during the tenure of DCI George Tenet, a National Intelligence Priorities Framework (NIPF) was created as a management tool for evaluating how well the Intelligence Community was meeting its goals of stating "requirements" (key targets), along with fulfilling all the other steps in the intelligence cycle that follow the planning phase. The list of targets generated by the threat assessment is reviewed annually by the President, as well as quarterly by the Intelligence Community – with updates made along the way as required by global events and conditions.

Intelligence collection and the "Ints"

The second phase in the intelligence cycle is collection: going after the information that policymakers have requested (plus items that the Intelligence Community presumes leaders will want to know, now or later). During the Cold War, the highest intelligence collection priority was to learn about the locations and capabilities of Soviet armaments, especially nuclear weapons. This was sometimes a dangerous endeavor, as underscored by the more than forty U.S. spy planes shot down by the Soviet Union and its allies. Intelligence-gathering during the Cold War – though important – was arguably less pressing than it is today, since at least the world understood then that the bipolar tensions between the superpowers defined international affairs. Now, as Joseph S. Nye, Jr., and William A. Owens have noted: "With the organizing framework of the Cold War gone, the implications are harder to categorize, and all nations want to know more about what is happening and why to help them decide how much it matters and what they should do about it."[12]

A recent analysis of worldwide ship and airplane movements suggests how difficult it is for the intelligence agencies in the Western democracies just to keep track of global transportation flows – a matter of some significance because ships might carry materials in violation of international sanctions against some countries, or, worse still, WMD bound for rogue nations or terrorist factions. Each year, "worldwide maritime activity includes more than 30,000 ocean-going ships of 10,000 gross tons or greater," noted a DNI report in 2009, and there are "over 43,000 fixed airfields worldwide with over 300,000 active aircraft."[13] On the counterterrorism front, just during the first half of 2010 the National Counterterrorism Center received 8,000–10,000 pieces of information related to global terrorist organizations, along with some 10,000 names of likely terrorists and more than forty specific threats and plots.[14]

In trying to understanding this more complicated world we live in since the Cold War ended in 1991, intelligence can provide "cat's eyes in the dark," in the British phrase, although even wealthy nations are unable to blanket the globe with expensive surveillance "platforms" designed for "remote sensing" – reconnaissance aircraft, satellites, and ground-based listening posts. The world is simply too vast and budgets are always finite. Still, satellite and airplane photography ("imagery" or, in the latest term for spy photography, "geoint," or geospatial intelligence) plays a vital role in a nation's defenses. Imagery eased the hair-trigger anxieties of the superpowers during the Cold War. Through the use of spy platforms, both ideological encampments – the superpowers – could watch one another's armies and a Pearl Harbor-like surprise attack became less likely. As DCI Colby observed, fear and ignorance were replaced by facts for decision-makers.[15] Before the United States had the capacity to accurately count Soviet bombers, ships, and missiles, Washington worried that Moscow was far ahead in armaments – the "bomber gap" and the "missile gap" that haunted America policymakers in the 1940s and 1950s. As a result of U-2 flights over the Soviet Union and, later, satellite surveillance over this vast territory with eleven time zones, the United States discovered that there were indeed bomber and missile gaps; but, contrary to conventional wisdom, they favored the United States. The Americans had outpaced the Soviets in weapons production.

George J. Tenet, who served Presidents Clinton and George W. Bush as DCI (1997–2004), referred early in his tenure to what he viewed as the basics of intelligence: stealing secrets and analyzing the capabilities and intentions of America's adversaries.[16] Every intelligence agency has its own set of methods ("tradecraft") for acquiring secrets. In the United States, these methods are referred to colloquially by the abbreviation "ints," short for "intelligence disciplines." Imagery or photographic intelligence becomes "imint," short for imagery intelligence – or, as mentioned earlier, in the new terminology, "geoint." Without the untrained eye of a professional photointerpreter, the white-and-black lines in this sophisticated photography can look more like the static of early television than landing strips and hangars on enemy bases. Signals intelligence becomes "sigint," an umbrella designation for a spate of operations that collect against electronic targets, such as telephone and other communications ("comint" for communications intelligence) and a variety of forms of electronic intelligence ("elint"), including data emitted by weapons during test flights ("telint" for telemetry) and additional emissions from enemy weapons and radar systems ("fisint" for foreign instrumentation signals). As already noted, human intelligence – the use of agents or "assets," as professionals refer to the foreign operatives who comprise their spy rings – becomes "humint."

Within each of the ints, intelligence professionals fashion ingenious techniques for purloining secrets from adversaries – say, the contents of a laptop computer owned by a foreign government scientist in charge of weapons engineering. The methods can range from sophisticated devices that track foreign military maneuvers through telescopic lenses on satellites orbiting deep in space, to the planting of miniature microphones in the breasts of pigeons trained to roost on the window ledges of foreign embassies. Best of all would be a reliable asset close to a senior official in another country, perhaps a staff aide, a chauffeur, or a lover.

A CIA U-2 photograph of Soviet missiles emplacements in Cuba, 1962.

Source: *Studies in Intelligence*, Central Intelligence Agency.

Another prominent int is "osint" or open-source intelligence: information gleaned from non-secretive sources, such as libraries or foreign media. Is there information in the public domain about whether the desert sands near Tehran are firm enough to support helicopters, or must an intelligence asset be deployed to find out the answer? This was an important matter in 1979, when the Carter Administration planned a rescue of U.S. diplomats held in the U.S. embassy in Iran. The DCI at the time, Admiral Stansfield Turner, had to send a special intelligence unit into Iran – a dangerous undertaking – to answer this question. The sand proved firm enough, but the mission eventually had to be aborted when U.S. military rescue helicopters collided in the desert before heading into Tehran. Today, the DNI's Center for Open-Source Intelligence studies what information is missing in the early drafts of intelligence reports that will have to be acquired through clandestine means.

Since the end of the Cold War, roughly 90 percent – some say as much as 95 percent – of all intelligence reports are made up of osint material, such as information from Iranian blogs on the Internet which can offer revealing glimpses into that secretive society. Based on this statistic, some critics have suggested that policymakers should obtain their information about world events from the Library of Congress and close down the secret agencies, saving the nation $50–$80 billion a year; yet the Library of Congress does not have agents around the world to gather the secret (and sometimes most important) "nuggets" of information that go into intelligence reporting; nor does it have the long experience of the secret agencies in analyzing foreign countries, putting together national security reports, and disseminating them in a timely manner to the right decision-makers around the bureaucracies in Washington, DC.

The newest and most technical int – measurement and signatures intelligence or "masint" – can be valuable, too. Run chiefly by the DIA, here the methodology involves testing for the presence of various materials, say, telltale vapors emitted by the cooling towers of foreign nuclear plants that might contain radioactive particles. These particles could indicate the presence of a "hot" reactor engaged in uranium enrichment. Other chemical and biological indicators might reveal the presence of illicit materials – perhaps waste fumes in a factory that point to the production of nerve gas. Between 1994 and 2008, for example, the intelligence unit in the U.S. Energy Department reportedly spent some $430 million on nuclear detection equipment at international border crossings, especially along Russia's frontiers.[17]

One of the most celebrated technical collection programs carried out by the CIA was an effort in 1974 to raise a disabled Soviet submarine from the bottom of the Pacific Ocean, an operation known as Project Jennifer. Officials in the Agency realized from satellite photography that the Soviet vessel, at the time skimming along on the ocean's surface, had experienced a fire on board, causing it to sink rapidly beneath the waves. Under orders from DCI William Colby, the Agency called upon Howard Hughes for assistance in retrieving the submarine. The eccentric billionaire was in the business (among other lucrative pursuits) of mining the ocean floors for valuable ore, such as magnesium. He owned a ship, the *Glomar Explorer*, capable of lowering wire cables deep enough into the Pacific to capture the submarine and pull it to the surface. Hughes agreed to help (in return for a tidy $350 million) and the recovery mission was under way. The dramatic attempt to raise the sub was only partially successful; half the prize fell back into the ocean, as the submarine was accidentally sliced in two by the *Glomar*'s wire jaws. Still, the Agency viewed the capture of half a Soviet submarine, which carried nuclear missiles and advanced communications equipment, as quite a coup. Unfortunately, the Project Jennifer operation was leaked to the media and a return trip to snare the rest of the ship was impossible once the Soviet Navy had been alerted to its position in the ocean. The actual contents of the captured half of the submarine remain classified, but insiders claim that the project was worth the costly price tag. Critics, though, questioned why the Agency decided to pay a king's ransom for access to an obsolete submarine.[18]

HUMINT VERSUS TECHINT   Intelligence professionals make a distinction between humint and technical intelligence ("techint") collection – the latter an acronym that lumps together all of the machine-based means of gathering information. The vast majority of funds spent on collection go into techint. This category includes geoint and sigint satellites; large, land-based NSA listening antennae; and reconnaissance aircraft, like the U-2 and A-12 spy planes in the United States, and their successor the SR-21, as well as the popular Predator, a UAV fielded over Afghanistan, Iraq, and other nations in the Middle East and South Asia following the 9/11 attacks. The Predator and its cousins, such as the larger Reaper and small (some even insect-sized) drones, are attractive to intelligence planners because of their mobility and their capacity to spy without endangering the life of a pilot. When the larger UAVs are equipped with missiles, they are able not only to spy but also to obliterate targets that appear in their camera lens. Awed by the technological capabilities of spy machines, nations spend sizable amounts of funds on their construction and deployment, prodded by the intelligence component of the "iron pentagon" lobby. One recent satellite program cost $9.5 billion, according to reliable newspaper reporting, and that amount was for one of the simpler types of satellites used only in daylight hours and clear weather.[19]

This fascination with intelligence hardware has continued into the Age of Terrorism, even though these platforms are apt to be less useful against ghost-like terrorists. Cameras on satellites or aircraft are unable to peer inside the canvas tents, roofed mud huts, or mountain caves in the Middle East, Southwest Asia, and Iraq where ISIS members meet to plan their deadly operations, or into the deep underground caverns where North Koreans construct atomic bombs. As an intelligence expert notes, often one "needs to know what's inside the building, not what the building looks like."[20] Another group of intelligence officers has emphasized that "technical collection lends itself to monitoring large-scale, widespread targets...."[21] This approach is less effective against discreet and carefully concealed WMD or terrorist cells.

Still, at times, techint can be a strong arm of counterterrorism – especially sigint telephone interceptions and spy cameras on low-flying drones. For example, in Afghanistan and Pakistan, Taliban and Al Qaeda leaders have been forced into hiding for fear of being spotted by U.S. geoint machines. As Richard Barrett notes: "This lack of face-to-face contact with their subordinates and the enemy is sapping their authority. Taliban leaders have also had to limit their telephone communications for fear of giving away their locations, and have had to find less reliable and efficient ways to discuss strategy and pass orders to the field."[22]

In contrast to techint spending, the United States devotes just a single-digit percentage of its annual intelligence budget to foreign humint. Moreover, within five years after the end of the Cold War, the CIA had experienced a 25 percent decline in case officers around the world, with fewer than 800 in the field. The FBI reportedly has more "special agents" (the Bureau's term for operational officers) in New York City than the CIA has counterparts across the globe.[23] On occasion, sigint satellites capture revealing information about adversaries – say, telephone conversations between international drug lords. The photography yielded by geoint satellites is of obvious importance on such matters as the whereabouts of Chinese naval vessels; trucks transporting ISIS soldiers into Iraq; the unloading of missile parts carried in the hulls of Chinese freighters steaming toward Karachi ports (despite official denials in Beijing and Islamabad); Hamas rocket emplacements in Gaza; or the construction of nuclear reactors in Iran. In the case of terrorism, though, a human agent well situated inside ISIS or Al Qaeda could be worth several costly satellites.

A category of humint tradecraft is the use of intelligence officers operating under deep or non-official cover, known as NOCs. In contrast to officers working from official U.S. government facilities with official cover (OC), a NOC exists outside in the local society – say, as an archaeologist, investment banker, or oil-rig operator. Acting as a NOC can be a difficult assignment. The intelligence officer must keep his or her cover during the day, then undergo a metamorphosis at night into a spy in search of local recruits. Further, the NOC often operates in remote locations where, as a senior CIA operative has put it, "diarrhea is the default setting."[24] Convincing middle- or upper-class Agency recruits to adopt a life of hardship over the comfort of working inside a U.S. facility overseas with fellow Americans under OC can be a hard sell. The NOC role can be dangerous as well, because an intelligence officer in this role operates without U.S. government immunity. If caught while engaged in espionage activities, he or she is likely to be arrested and imprisoned by local authorities and released to the United States only when – and if – an exchange of prisoners can be arranged.

Frequently, NOCs burn out from shouldering two jobs, one for cover and one for espionage. Or they may decide that the cover occupation is more remunerative than being a spy. For example, the CIA trained one NOC to serve as an investment banker overseas in a Third World capital. After almost a year of working long hours during the day as a banker, then donning his cloak and dagger in the evening, the NOC resigned, moved to New York City, and made four times his Agency salary, plus bonuses, from a well-known financial firm in Manhattan. The costly training of this individual reaped little payoff for the CIA.

For all these reasons, the Agency has shied away from the use of NOCs, although other nations have adopted this approach with great effectiveness – such as the Soviet Union in New York City during the Cold War, with a strong reliance on journalistic cover for its NOCs. Clearly an OC officer is not going to meet a member of ISIS at an embassy cocktail party, but a NOC operating in, say, Pakistan might have a chance of recruiting a local "cutout" (an intermediary asset) who can in turn attempt a recruitment pitch to an Al Qaeda or Taliban operative. Embassy parties, though, will remain a useful means for meeting potential recruits from major target countries, like Russia, as was the case during the Cold War.

Whether based on NOC or OC tradecraft, humint is no panacea. During the Vietnam War, for example, almost all of America's assets recruited to infiltrate the north were either killed or captured. Moreover, within closed societies like North Korea and Iran, local spies are difficult to recruit; and even if successfully recruited, they are often untrustworthy. Neither Boy Scouts nor nuns, they are known to fabricate reports, sell information to the highest bidder, and scheme as false defectors or double-agents. During the Cold War, all of America's assets in Cuba and East Germany proved to have been doubled back against the United States.[25]

A recent example of humint treachery is the German agent in 2002, Rafid Ahmed Alwan al-Janabi, prophetically codenamed "Curve Ball." A former Iraqi scientist, he persuaded the German intelligence service (the *Bundesnachtrichtendienst* or BND) that biological WMD existed in Iraq. The CIA took the bait through its intelligence liaison relationship with the Germans. Only after the war began in Iraq in 2003 did Curve Ball's bona fides fall into doubt among German and CIA intelligence officials; he was, it turned out, a consummate liar.[26]

Further, it takes a considerable amount of time to train a clandestine officer before he or she is ready to recruit foreign assets – upwards of seven years. A case officer must learn the delicate art of handling an asset, a "very close relationship" that requires motivating the foreign local to engage in espionage, continue to produce valuable information, and maintain a double life in risky circumstances.[27]

Despite these drawbacks, humint can provide extraordinarily helpful information, as did the Soviet military intelligence officer Oleg Penkovsky during the Cold War. He was not recruited by a U.S. clandestine officer but, rather, was a "walk-in" who volunteered to spy for the British and the Americans. To prove his bona fides, he tossed classified Soviet intelligence documents over the wall of the U.S. embassy in Moscow. The American officials feared, however, that he was a "dangle" meant to trick the United States, so his overture was initially rebuffed. He then tried the British embassy in Moscow and MI6 quickly determined that he was a legitimate volunteer. Subsequently, the Americans accepted his services, too. In 1962, information from Penkovsky helped the United States identify the presence of Soviet nuclear missiles in Cuba, based on his information that missile bases constructed by the USSR at the time were frequently configured in a six-pointed Star of David design.

Based on occasional successes like Penkovsky, the United States and most other countries persevere in their quest for reliable espionage assets. Following 9/11 and the WMD errors in Iraq, the Kean and the Silberman–Robb Commissions criticized America's lack of assets in important parts of the world. President George W. Bush authorized a 50 percent increase in the number of CIA operations officers, leading in 2004 to the largest incoming class of clandestine officers in the Agency's history.[28]

In an appraisal of humint, former DCI Colby observed: "It's one of those things you can't afford to say no to, because sometimes it can be valuable." He added: "You can go through years with nothing much happening, so then you cut off the relationship. Since nothing had happened there for ten years, we were in the process of closing the [CIA's] stations in El Salvador and Portugal – just before these countries blew up!" Colby's conclusion: "I think you'll always have some humint, and it'll pay off. And remember that the human agent is also available to somehow engage in the manipulation of a foreign government."[29]

Former DCI (1991–93) and later Secretary of Defense Robert M. Gates agrees that humint has been valuable. While acknowledging the contribution made by techint towards America's understanding of Soviet strategic weapons, he recalls that "a great deal of what we learned about the technical characteristics of Soviet conventional weapons we learned through humint."[30] He adds that when it came to probing into the Kremlin's intentions, not just its capabilities, humint provided important insights. Humint can address the matter of intentions in ways that are impossible for machines to achieve.

A well-placed asset might be in a position to pose the question to a foreign leader: "What will you do if the United States does X?" As former CIA officer John Millis has written: "Humint can shake the intelligence apple from the tree, where other intelligence collection techniques must wait for the apple to fall."[31]

THE CUBAN MISSILE CRISIS OF 1962 AS AN ILLUSTRATION OF INTELLIGENCE COLLECTION CHALLENGES   Pilots of the high-altitude U-2 reconnaissance spy plane, built in record time by the CIA, the U.S. Air Force, and Lockheed Corporation in the 1950s, had come to know the contours of Cuba well during the late 1950s and early 1960s. In an operation referred to inside the Agency as Project NIMBUS, overflights across the island from west to east and back again had become standard operating procedure in the spring of 1962.[32] Since the CIA's disastrous paramilitary attempt to overthrow Fidel Castro by way of the Bay of Pigs paramilitary invasion in May 1961, regime change in Cuba continued to be a high priority for the Kennedy Administration. Just as sabotage and assassination plots against Castro remained a part of Washington's secret agenda, so did America's surveillance of the island only ninety miles off the coast of Florida, which had become Moscow's favorite Marxist-Leninist showcase in the developing world – the only socialist revolution that had succeeded in Latin America. As rumors grew among the CIA's spies on the ground in Cuba about intensified Soviet activity on the island in late 1961 and early 1962, the frequency of the reconnaissance missions increased. By May 1962, a year after the Bay of Pigs, the number of monthly flights had doubled and would rise further as the year unfolded and the rumors continued. Most of the flights originated from Laughlin Air Force Base in Texas and Edwards Air Force Base in California. Designed to fly as high as 73,000 feet and equipped with high-resolution cameras, the U-2 was a major breakthrough in aerial surveillance, although the plane was thin-winged and fragile, difficult to steer, and vulnerable to turbulence.[33]

Reports from CIA intelligence sources in Cuba suggested the arrival of sizable numbers of Soviet troops on the island. More troubling still, the agents had spotted large cylindrical objects on the ground and new Soviet encampments being constructed in the palm forests of western Cuba. Senator Kenneth Keating (R, New York) had commented publicly about stories he had heard from some of his Cuban American constituents in New York, to the effect that the Soviets were importing missiles to the island. The CIA grilled its secret Cuban agents about these stories. The vast majority of the spies, though, were unreliable, offering conflicting and often fabricated reports – any "intelligence" to keep themselves on the Agency payroll.

Yet a few of the more trusted agents also claimed to have seen odd activities throughout the island, including the unloading of large objects from Soviet freighters in the port of Havana. In response to this humint, the Agency stepped up its U-2 surveillance flights. Bad weather intervened, though, and prohibited reconnaissance throughout most of August 1962. Even more important than the unpredictable weather was the political opposition in the Department of State to further U-2 surveillance of the island.[34] Secretary of State Dean Rusk and others thought the flights were too risky: a conventional surface-to-air missile (SAM) in Cuba might be able to down one of the reconnaissance aircraft and escalate the pressure in the United States from the Republican party to invade the island. Caution prevailed in the Kennedy Administration. Not until October 14 – after a full month of U-2 surveillance abstinence ordered by President Kennedy in deference to the State Department – did the spy aircraft take flight again over the island, snapping hundreds of photographs of the terrain below each day.

These fresh images were transmitted quickly to specialists in the CIA's National Photographic Interpretation Center. The black-and-white lines on the photos, difficult for the untrained eye to interpret, provided unmistakable clues to expert eyes: the Soviets were indeed constructing missile bases in Cuba. Shockingly, the photos ("imagery") revealed the presence of WMD. Agency analysts had forecast that the Soviet Union would never be so rash as to introduce such weapons into a country so near the United States – although the CIA's director at the time, John A. McCone, a successful California businessman turned spy chief, had predicted, on the contrary, that Moscow might attempt this provocative move. According to his reasoning, President Nikita Khrushchev of the Soviet Union might try to redress the lop-sided intercontinental ballistic missile (ICBM) advantage enjoyed by the United States at the time – an estimated 17:1 edge – by placing shorter-range nuclear missiles close to North America. Further, Khrushchev was apt to do what he could to protect a Marxist ally and protégé from a possible full-scale assault by the U.S. military, as foreshadowed by the Agency's Bay of Pigs operation.[35]

Ominously, the U-2 photographs taken on October 14 over Cuba showed a Star of David pattern on the ground near San Cristobal, just like the one Penkosky had warned about. The reality was both clear and disturbing: the Soviets had taken the fateful step of introducing missiles into their Caribbean satellite – and not just any rockets. These were medium- and intermediate-range ballistic missiles (MRBMs and IRBMs) capable of striking targets in the United States anywhere east of the Mississippi River, carrying nuclear warheads.

The next day, October 15, the CIA informed the White House about the presence of sophisticated Soviet WMD in Cuba. Now the U-2 surveillance trips over Cuba shot upwards in frequency, to several each day in the search for other missile sites. Low-level photography taken by Navy and Air Force aircraft complemented the U-2 imint and, together, they revealed more missile trailers, erectors, vehicles, and tent areas in the Star of David design.

The reconnaissance missions yielded thousands of feet of film, some of which President Kennedy later presented to the public as evidence in support of his allegations against the Soviet Union. Reports on the ground in Cuba from agents remained unreliable for the most part, but here was hard imagery of Soviet mischief – irrefutable empirical evidence in the form of photographs. The film pinpointed forty-two Soviet missiles in all, as well as the presence of Ilyushin-28 (IL-28) medium-range bombers, MIG-21 fighter aircraft, anti-aircraft missile batteries, and short-range battlefield rockets.

The U-2 photographs were a blessing to the President; it was a "moment of splendor," recalled a senior CIA analyst.[36] The images made it clear that the missiles would not be operational (that is, ready for firing) for some time – perhaps as long as a fortnight. Kennedy could now resist pressures from the Pentagon for a quick invasion; he had breathing room to consider other options. Had the United States, fearful that the Cuban rockets were ready for firing, sent in a land force in the early days of this crisis, the Pentagon and the White House would have discovered that – however vital it had been – the intelligence from the U-2 flights and agent reports had dangerous gaps. After the end of the Cold War, conferences on the Cuban missile crisis held with U.S. and Soviet participants disclosed that, unbeknownst to the CIA and the White House at the time, the Soviets had more than two hundred tactical nuclear warheads on the island; atomic bombs inside the cargo hatches of the IL-bombers; and five times more troops than estimated by U.S. intelligence (some 40,000 rather than 8,000). Moreover, early in the crisis, the Kremlin had given local Soviet commanders discretionary authority to use the tactical weapons and release the bombers for flight to the United States if an American army invaded the island.[37]

Reflecting back on these tense days, former Secretary of Defense Robert S. McNamara expressed his belief that an invasion would have triggered a nuclear war in Cuba, which would have led to a strategic response between the two superpowers – in other words, a thermo-nuclear Third World War that would have destroyed much of the United States and the Soviet Union.[38] The Cuban missile crisis was a fine example of how important intelligence can be to presidential decision-making, but it also stands as an illustration of how even saturated surveillance coverage of a target can miss significant information.

STRENGTHENING INTELLIGENCE COLLECTION "Many elements make up a decision," Secretary of State Rusk once told an interviewer. "First, though, one must grapple with the facts. What is the situation?"[39] In determining the situation overseas, no single int is sufficient. Success depends on all of the collection disciplines working together, just as an engine performs best when all of its cylinders are firing. Employing a different metaphor, intelligence officers sometimes refer to this synergism as the "Black & Decker" approach: every tool in the box is used in the search for useful information. Woolsey offers the example of North Korea: "That nation is so closely guarded that humint becomes indispensable to know what is going on. This humint then tips off sigint possibilities, which in turn may suggest where best to gather imint. These capabilities, ideally, dovetail with one another."[40]

At the end of the Cold War in 1991, efforts were made in Washington, DC to trim the defense and intelligence budgets. Some made the argument that intelligence capabilities associated with the various ints could be surged from one location to another, depending on where the latest crisis emerged. Others, though, maintained that intelligence had to have a global presence; only in this way could potential crises be anticipated. This surge-versus-presence debate led most participants to conclude that, yes, saving money was important and some technical collections systems could be moved (surged) from one hot spot to another; however, analysts were considered far less fungible. Moreover, operations officers who might have expertise in Latin American affairs, and were able to speak Spanish or Portuguese, could not perform effectively right away in Kabul or Islamabad. Thus, whereas the Intelligence Community needed global presence when it came to human assets, it could more easily surge drones, listening devices, and satellites.

Both survey data and case studies of collection operations indicate that humint can be particularly important when targeting terrorists, narcotics dealers, and weapons proliferators.[41] Much can be done, however, to improve both techint and humint. Technical intelligence collection must constantly overcome advances in deception and denial activities carried out by adversaries, such as the camouflaging of their weapons facilities and the encryption of telephone calls.[42] Humint, though, is most in need of reform.

Even observers sympathetic to this approach have serious reservations about its effectiveness. The United States has a "moribund Clandestine Service," concluded one experienced field officer; and the House Permanent Select Committee on Intelligence warned that humint is headed "over a cliff" as a result of poor management.[43]

An agenda for humint reform in the United States would embrace these initiatives:

- an increase in the number of case (operational) officers in key parts of the world, especially those under non-official cover (NOCs);
- the development of additional cover arrangements overseas, to reverse what DCI William E. Colby once referred to as the "melting ice floe of cover"[44] – that is, the increasing unwillingness of the State Department, U.S. newspapers and magazines, universities, and religious groups to provide shelter and false identification for U.S. intelligence officers, for fear of jeopardizing the safety of their own genuine employees (while the prohibition against using official media and academic cover continues to make sense in the democracies, other groups – especially U.S. businesses abroad – will have to shoulder more of this burden);
- the holding of more frequent tasking meetings between consumers and humint managers;
- a boost in the entrance requirements for operations officers, making this career as demanding and prestigious as a diplomatic career;
- the improvement of language training for operations officers – a challenge made all the more difficult because CIA managers have been unwilling to allow officers to concentrate on just one language with continual service in the country or countries where the language is spoken, preferring career pathways that place officers in a variety of locations around the world throughout their careers;[45]
- a more extensive study of the history and culture of other societies, which is limited by the career rotation policy mentioned above;
- the recruitment of more citizens with ethnic backgrounds relevant to the strategic "hot-spots" of the world, such as the Middle East and Southwest Asia, and the encouragement of diversity generally throughout the humint services;[46]
- the establishment of easier access to U.S. embassies abroad – which often look like forbidding fortresses – to encourage walk-ins (like Penkovsky), relying on perimeter physical searches and

metal detectors as a means for thwarting terrorist attacks against these facilities;

- a reduction in the size of the humint bureaucracy at headquarters, with increased reliance on a small, more nimble clandestine service that focuses on high-priority foreign targets;
- the basing of promotion decisions for case officers serving in particular hard targets (such as Russia and China) on the quality, not the quantity, of assets they recruit;
- the encouragement of closer cooperation between the CIA's Directorate of Analysis (DA) and the Directorate of Operations (DO) – a co-location experiment in partnership begun in 1995 (discussed later in this chapter) – with more rapid promotions as a reward for those who participate in this activity;
- an improved sharing of humint findings across the Intelligence Community;[47] and
- strengthened intelligence liaison relations, both humint and techint, among all regimes and international organizations that are determined to defeat terrorists, drug dealers, and other international criminals – although with a closer vetting by the United States of shared sources to avoid future "Curve Balls."[48]

The processing of intelligence

In the third phase of the intelligence cycle, the collected intelligence must be decoded if encrypted, interpreted if a satellite photograph, translated if in a foreign language, and generally put into a form that a president or a prime minister can readily comprehend. This is known as processing: the conversion of "raw" (unevaluated) intelligence, whether photographs or email intercepts, into a readable format.

Intelligence pours into the capitals of the larger nations like a fire hose held to the mouth, to use a simile made popular by a former NSA director, Admiral Noel Gayler. Each day, some four million telephone, fax, and email intercepts – often in difficult codes that must be deciphered or exotic languages that must be translated – flood the NSA. Hundreds of satellite photographs arrive at the NGA. This volume is unlikely to dissipate. Every minute, for instance, a thousand people around the world sign up for a new cell phone. A further problem is that nations are always short on translators, photo-interpreters, and codebreaking mathematicians. In response to a query about the major challenges facing U.S. intelligence, no wonder Vice Admiral J.M. "Mike" McConnell remarked when he was NSA director: "I have three major problems: processing, processing, and processing."[49] Most every intelligence expert agrees that the collection of information worldwide has far outraced the ability of intelligence services to process the data.

The day before the 9/11 attacks, the NSA intercepted a telephone message in Farsi from a suspected Al Qaeda operative. Translated on September 12 – a couple of days too late to help – the message proclaimed: "Tomorrow is zero hour."[50] Whether a more rapid translation might have led to a tightening of U.S. airport security procedures on the morning of September 11, thereby thwarting the attacks, is anyone's guess; but it may have. Today the vast majority of information gathered by intelligence agencies is never examined; it gathers dust in warehouses. An estimated 90 percent of what the U.S. Intelligence Community collects is never examined by human eyes (although "watch lists" are used to scan for key topics like "bombs," "Daesh," or "Al Qaeda"). As many as 99 percent of the telephone intercepts gathered by the NSA are never analyzed.[51] Here is a supreme challenge for the government's IT specialists: improving the nation's capacity to sift rapidly through incoming intelligence data, separating the signals from the noise, the wheat from the chaff.

In the United States, additional IT challenges present themselves. The computers in the seventeen intelligence agencies still need to be fully integrated, so collectors and analysts can communicate better with one another from agency to agency. Currently the connections are spotty. This data integration must also be carried down to the new intelligence "fusion centers" that have been developed for counterterrorism purposes at state and local levels, where officials stand on the front lines of counterterrorism and seek better intelligence from Washington. Further, as this organizational integration is pursued, steps must be taken to ensure that the channels of information-sharing are protected by firewalls that guard against cyber-intervention by hostile intelligence services. These are all tall orders for IT specialists, many of whom would rather make big money in Silicon Valley than work for government wages in Washington, DC.

Intelligence analysis

Analysis, the next phase, lies at the heart of the intelligence cycle: the task of bringing insight to the information that has been collected and processed. The method is straightforward enough: namely, hiring smart people to pore over all the information from open and secret sources, then present the findings to decision-makers in written reports and oral briefings. The *Washington Post* reported in 2010 that the Intelligence Community produces some 50,000 intelligence reports each year.[52] If these reports and briefings are unable to provide reliable insights into the meaning of the information gathered from around the world, then each of the preceding steps in the intelligence cycle is for naught.

Here's the bad news: intelligence analysts will always be taken by surprise from time to time, a fate guaranteed by the twin dilemmas of incomplete information and the uncertain light of the future.[53] Dean Rusk often advised DCIs during the Cold War that intelligence reports ought to start off with the honest caveat: "Damned if we know, but if you want our best guess, here it is."[54] Not all the news is bad, though. Western nations have taken long strides toward improving their intelligence capabilities against the enemies of democracy. The enormous amount of money spent on intelligence each year by the United States, for example, has allowed officials to deploy the largest and – at least in terms of spy machines – the most sophisticated espionage apparatus ever devised by humankind. This brings in a torrent of information, much of which improves the nation's safety.

Still, things go wrong. Perhaps nothing underscores this reality better than the surprise attacks of 9/11, followed by the intelligence misjudgment about WMD in Iraq. A look at the most prestigious intelligence products in the United States, the *President's Daily Brief* (*PDB*) and National Intelligence Estimates, illustrates the vulnerabilities of national security intelligence to human error.

THE *PDB*   From among the hundreds of classified reports prepared each year by the Intelligence Community, the *PDB* is the most prestigious document. Former DCI Tenet referred to the *PDB* as "our most important product"; and Thomas Kean, the Chair of the 9/11 Commission, dubbed it the "Holy Grail of the nation's secrets."[55]

The *PDB* is distributed by CIA couriers each morning to the President and a few top cabinet officials and aides. The number of recipients has varied from administration to administration, rising to as many as fourteen in the Clinton Administration and as few as five in the Reagan Administration, six in the second Bush Administration, and eight in the Obama Administration. The document often sets the agenda for early morning discussions in high councils – a "catalyst for further action," in the words of a NSC staff aide.[56]

The format of the *PDB* has varied over the years, though it has always had three core objectives: readability, logical reasoning, and fidelity to the Intelligence Community's sources. The document is normally fifteen to twenty pages long and printed in impressive four-color graphics, vividly displaying, say, global economic trends with multiple lines on a graph. The *PDB* – "the book," as it is known inside the CIA – is designed to grab the attention of busy policymakers and provide them with "current intelligence" about events that have just transpired around the world over the previous twenty-four hours, commenting perhaps on the health of an aging foreign leader or the deployment of a new Chinese weapon system. The *PDB*'s spiral-bound, glossy pages are attractive and easy to read. Further, the *PDB* focuses on topics known to be high on the President's agenda, rather than the daily smorgasbord offered readers by regular newspapers. The document attempts, as well, to integrate information gathered clandestinely from around the world by each of the secret agencies – the all-source fusion concept that permits "one-stop shopping" for information on global events.

The *PDB* comes with another important service unavailable to ordinary newspaper subscribers: follow-up oral briefings designed to answer specific questions posed by its VIP readership – six or sixty minutes of additional information, depending on the interest and patience of the policymaker. Here is a rare opportunity for a president or other official to talk back to their "newspaper" and actually get some immediate answers.[57] During a typical year of the Clinton Administration, for example, forty-two follow-up oral briefings took place in the offices of *PDB* recipients; and the CIA sent an additional 426 memoranda to those readers who requested more detailed written responses to their queries. About 75 percent of these follow-ups occurred by the next working day.[58] Thus, the *PDB* is more than a document; it is a process, allowing intelligence officers to interact with decision-makers and provide useful supportive information. As an NSC staffer noted during the Carter Administration, this interaction keeps "the CIA boys hopping, but, most importantly, it lets them know what is of interest at any given time to the President."[59]

Presidents and some other subscribers in the small "witting circle" of *PDB* recipients have sometimes complained about the quality of the document. George W. Bush, for instance, received the *PDB* and oral briefings during his first presidential campaign in 2000, along with other leading candidates, a service provided by the CIA since 1952 to presidential contenders.[60] He found them unhelpful and remarked: "Well, I assume I will start seeing the good stuff when I become President" – without realizing the Intelligence Community was already giving him its best material.[61] Yet when George Tenet was the senior intelligence director on the NSC staff in the mid-1990s, he observed that the *PDB* was "for the most part, a high-quality product. There are days when it's not earth-shattering; there are days when it's really interesting."[62]

The Aspin–Brown Commission's examination of whether the Chinese were selling M-11 missiles to Pakistan between 1989 and 1995 provides an example of the value added by the *PDB*. Reporting in public newspapers was filled with ambiguities about the alleged weapons sales.[63] The spy agencies, however, possessed geoint and sigint that moved the case from one of speculation to a level of reasonably strong evidence that the Chinese were indeed providing Pakistan with missile components. The sighting of "cylindrical objects" at the Sargodha Missile Complex in Pakistan and "unidentified, suspicious cargo" being unloaded in the Karachi harbor provided useful humint clues. When coupled with telephone intercepts between Pakistani and Chinese officials, "cylindrical objects" being unloaded from Chinese ships in Karachi harbors, and photographs of missile launchers at Sargodha, the President had more information about the weapons controversy in the *PDB* than he could have found in the public newspapers.

THE NIE   While the *PDB* is an example of current intelligence, a National Intelligence Estimate (NIE) concentrates on longer-range reporting, based on research intelligence. An NIE offers an appraisal of a foreign country or international situation, reflecting the coordinated judgment of the entire Intelligence Community. "Estimates," as NIEs are sometimes called (or "assessments" in Britain), are the outcome of an intricate gathering and evaluation of intelligence drawn from all IC sources, relying on each of the "ints."[64] They are not limited to the task of predicting specific events (which the *PDB* often attempts); indeed, their primary responsibility is to assist the President and other leaders by providing background research on foreign leaders, unfolding situations abroad, and the military and economic activities of other nations. Many NIEs set down on paper, and often rank, a range of possible outcomes related to developments inside a foreign nation or faction; or they will address the likely long-range pathway of a situation developing somewhere in the world that could threaten American interests or present an opportunity for the advancement of U.S. interests. An Agency official provides this definition of an Estimate: "a statement of what is going to happen in any country, in any area, in any given situation, and as far as possible into the future."[65]

A Range of NIE Topics   An Estimate sometimes begins with a formal request from a senior policymaker for an appraisal and prognosis of events and conditions in some part of the world. In an overwhelming majority of cases, however, the Intelligence Community itself generates NIE proposals – 75 percent in one recent year.

In this manner, the Community attempts to "push" intelligence toward the consumer, rather than wait (perhaps endlessly) for it to be "pulled" by the consumer. The potential subjects for an Estimate cover a wide front, as shown by these examples from the Carter Administration:

- the balance of strategic nuclear forces between the United States and the Soviet Union;
- the conventional military balance in Europe;
- the prospects for improvement in relations between the Soviet Union and China;
- the outlook for cohesiveness within the Atlantic Alliance; and
- the significance of the developing world's international debt problems.[66]

Preparing Estimates   In the preparation of an NIE, a panel of intelligence experts (known since 1980 as the National Intelligence Council or NIC – officially a part of the ODNI, but physically located at CIA Headquarters in Langley) initially examines the merits of each proposal in consultation with analysts throughout the Community, as well as with senior policy officials. If the decision is to move ahead, the NIC determines which segments of the IC can best contribute and then provides these agencies with an outline of objectives, asking them to respond with their facts and insights by a certain deadline. This outline is known as the Terms of Reference or TOR. A NIC document explains: "The TOR defines the key estimative questions, determines drafting responsibilities, and sets the drafting and publication schedule."[67]

In response to the TOR, data and ideas pour back to the NIC from around the Community and are shaped into a draft NIE by one or more of the senior analysts who comprise the NIC, in continual dialogue with experts further down the chain of analysts. Since 1973, the senior analysts on the NIC have been known as National Intelligence Officers or NIOs. These men and women are expected to have "the best in professional training, the highest intellectual integrity, and a very large amount of worldly wisdom."[68] The ten to sixteen or so NIOs (the number varies from time to time) are considered the *crème de la crème* of intelligence analysts, drawn from throughout the Community as well as from academe and the think-tanks. A recent set of NIOs consisted of four career intelligence officers; five analysts from academe and think-tanks; three from the military; and one from the legislative staff on Capitol Hill. The NIC also consults regularly with some fifty individuals across the country who hold security clearances. For the dozen NIOs in the

Clinton Administration, here is a listing of their "portfolios": Africa; Near East and South Asia; East Asia; Russia and Eurasia; Economics and Global Issues; Science and Technology; Europe; Special Activities (a euphemism for covert action); General Purpose Forces; Strategic and Nuclear Programs; Latin America; and Warning. The NIOs work closely with the DNI's National Intelligence Managers to bring about the kind of synergy in the Intelligence Community that leads to the ultimate goal of "all-source fusion" – a blend of all the findings from the ints into comprehensive intelligence reports for decision-makers.

To improve the intelligence product, the secret agencies will sometimes (although too infrequently) reach outside their walls to solicit the views of private-sector experts in academe and the think-tanks. Perhaps the most well-known of the Intelligence Community's efforts to consult with outsiders for a critique of an NIE came in 1976, by way of a "Team A, Team B" review of an Estimate on Soviet military intentions and capabilities.[69] The staff of the National Security Council selected the two teams. The CIA's own Soviet experts comprised Team A, and academics comprised Team B, led by Harvard University Russian historian Richard E. Pipes, known for his strongly hawkish views on the Soviet Union. Pipes and his panel were convinced the Agency had gone soft; its liberal "civilian" outlook, reinforced by naïve arms control experts in the scholarly community, had led to an NIE that downplayed the Soviet plan for world conquest. In the Team B view, the Soviets were subtly seeking – and could well achieve – a first-strike, war-winning strategy against the United States, rather than peaceful coexistence. Team B accused the CIA of miscalculating Soviet expenditures on weapons systems, thereby underestimating the formidable strength of the Red Army and its WMD. Team A, in turn, charged the Pipes panel with exaggerating the Soviet peril.

The upshot of this attempt at "competitive analysis" using outsider reviewers was that the CIA trimmed back on some of its more sanguine views about Moscow's intentions, adopting Soviet military production figures that were slightly more in line with the Team B projections. Nevertheless, a vast gulf between the two groups continued to exist on the subject of Soviet motivations: the more optimistic views of the Team A set against the pessimistic "hard-liners" like Pipes in Team B. The "debate" probably put a dent in the reputation of the Intelligence Community; the door had been opened to doubt about the wisdom of reliance on its internal judgments. Nonetheless, it was healthy for inside Agency analysts to have their views tested by outside experts, although the selection of an external review board known for a particular political stance

– a hard-line anti-Soviet perspective – was less useful than would have been a reliance on more neutral authorities.

During the NIE drafting process, the NIO in charge will send the first draft back to each of the intelligence agencies working on the study and so begins the process of interagency editing, as specialists from throughout the Community hammer the final document into shape. An analyst recalls this editing process in painful terms: "It was like defending a Ph.D. dissertation, time after time after time."[70]

The NIC makes the penultimate judgment on the appropriateness of the data and conclusions presented in each Estimate, then sends the document along to the National Intelligence Board for further review. The NIB is made up of the senior representatives of the Intelligence Community and is chaired by the DNI, who is also in charge of the NIC and has the last say on an Estimate before it is distributed to senior policymakers. In the past, intelligence directors have occasionally so disliked an Estimate produced by the intelligence bureaucracy that they have written one themselves on the topic in lieu of sending forward the NIC version. This practice is rare, however, and carries with it the danger of an Estimate becoming too personalized or even politicized.[71] Sometimes, though, intelligence chiefs can be correct and the bureaucracy wrong, as when DCI John McCone rejected the conclusion of an Estimate that predicted the Soviets would be unlikely to place missiles in Cuba in the early 1960s. The best approach, however, is to rely on well-trained and experienced analysts; then, if the Intelligence Director (or some other high official in the IC) disagrees with them, he or she can forward a dissent to policymakers as an addendum to the official NIO version.

The bulk of the NIE drafting resides in the hands of junior analysts within the IC – specialists who study the daily cable traffic from the country (or other topic) in question. The NIOs are expected to keep in touch with the various intelligence agencies that have contributed to the Estimate. Obviously, the tenor of the language in an NIE is all-important, especially the confidence levels evinced in the document (high, medium, or low). The NIOs must be careful not to claim more than the evidence can support, especially in the NIE's executive summary (called "Key Judgments" or KJs) found at the beginning of the document. This may be the only portion of an Estimate read by a harried (or sometimes perhaps lazy) policy official and it needs to convey the shades of gray, and the caveats, that serve as an antidote to overly assertive and simplistic conclusions.

The Question of Dissent   Especially tricky has been the question of how to represent dissenting views in an Estimate. The intelligence agencies sometimes have quite different perspectives on a world situation. Military intelligence organizations are notorious for their "worst-case" approach to estimating – a result, critics contend, of pressures on analysts applied by the Department of Defense and the military-industrial complex to justify larger military budgets by scaring the American people and their representatives in Congress with testimony about dire threats from abroad. Conversely, military intelligence officials often consider the CIA and INR as too "civilian" and unable to understand the true nature of foreign military threats.

The clash of differing views among intelligence agencies can be healthy, if driven by an objective weighing of facts rather than policy bias. Debate among analysts can provide policymakers with a range of views, instead of just the lowest common denominator. Sometimes Estimates are diluted to a tapioca consistency that robs policy officials of the nuances they need to understand. A NIC vice chair remembers that NIEs were "all too likely to produce a hedged and weasel-worded result."[72] Further, agency dissents have been relegated to obscure footnotes on occasion, if included at all. The best NIC managers have been careful to ensure that dissents are stated at some length in the text of the NIE, not hidden in a footnote – if only to avoid the resentment of dissenting agencies that have had their findings and judgments shunted aside. Some dissenting agencies insist that their contrary opinions be highlighted boldly in the text, often in a boxed format obvious to every reader, and placed as well in the KJ section of the document – a useful practice that encourages debate.

The Internal Liaison Challenge   An additional responsibility of intelligence managers is to ensure that NIOs and other designated intelligence analysts maintain good liaison relationships with consumers. "The difficulty lies not only in predicting the future, in a world of many variables, incomplete data, and intentional deception," writes an intelligence officer, "but in convincing policy makers that the prediction is valid."[73] Experience has shown that unless a policy-maker knows and feels personally comfortable with an NIO or other intelligence briefer, he or she is less likely to pay attention to an Estimate. Rapport between consumer and producer also provides analysts with a better understanding of the information needs of the policy departments, lowering the chances that intelligence reports will be irrelevant to current policy concerns and become merely "self-licking ice cream cones."[74] Too close a relationship, though, can undermine the objectivity of the intelligence process – the politicization danger.

Figure 2.3   Frequency of NIEs by year, 1950–2005

Source: Central Intelligence Agency, 2006.

The Timing and Frequency of NIES   An NIE can be written quickly, in two to four weeks (or less than a day in emergencies); in two to six months during normal times; or as long as three years on a slow track. Historically, Estimates have taken 215 days on average to produce: about seven months. Those studies readied on a fast-track basis during a crisis have their own name: a special NIE or SNIE (pronounced "snee"). During the Suez Canal crisis of 1956, the Intelligence Community produced a SNIE on Soviet intentions within a few hours. Analysts hope, though, to have at least three months to produce a thorough Estimate.

From 1947 to 2005, the IC produced 1,307 NIEs, averaging twenty-three a year.[75] The numbers have fluctuated over the years (see Figure 2.3), a reflection of the Intelligence Director's priorities and an administration's interest in receiving Estimates.[76] Added into the mix are changing world circumstances that may or may not require the preparation of new NIEs. In times of war, for example, policymakers are likely to be focused on current intelligence that reports on immediate battlefield exigencies, with NIEs pushed to a back burner.

NIE Hits and Misses   The dean of CIA analysts, Sherman Kent, commented on the goal of in-depth analysis. "The guts of the matter," he said, "is the synthesizing of the pieces and setting them forth in some meaningful pattern which everyone hopes is a close approximation of the truth."[77] Still, the end result remains something of a best guess, resulting from discussions among the top analysts in the Intelligence Community. As Kent once put it, "Estimating is what you do when you do not know." One enters "into the world of speculating."[78] However shrewd the forecasts, they still remain hunches. It is better than blind luck, because the judgments are based on expert research and knowledge; but they are a far cry from certainty.

At times, NIEs have been as accurate as an expensive Swiss watch; on other occasions they have been wide of the mark. Examples of successful predictions include: the likely conduct of the Soviet Union in world affairs (Moscow would try to expand, but would avoid the risk of general war);[79] the launching of the Soviet Sputnik in 1957; the Sino-Soviet split of 1962; the Chinese A-bomb test in 1964; the development of new Soviet weapon systems throughout the Cold War;[80] developments in the Vietnam War (1966–75); the Arab–Israeli War of 1967; the India–Pakistan War of 1971; the Turkish invasion of Cyprus in 1974; the Chinese invasion of Vietnam in 1978; the mass exodus from Cuba in 1978; the Soviet invasion of Afghanistan in 1979; the sharp deterioration of the Soviet economy just before the end of the Cold War (1984–89); the investment strategies of the Organization of Petroleum Exporting Countries (OPEC) consistently over the years; the rise and fall of political leaders around the world, including the breakup of Yugoslavia in the 1990s; the threat of "aerial terrorism" in 1995, presaging the 9/11 attacks (but, unfortunately, without details); and forecasting the difficulties of a post-invasion Iraqi society in 2002.

Most of the Intelligence Community's major mistakes during the Cold War were about what the Kremlin intended, not what weapons systems the communist empire possessed. The ability to track the numbers and capabilities of Soviet weaponry was vital during the superpower confrontation, and remains so today with Russia. Arms negotiations with the Russians and others still depend on the ability of the intelligence agencies to detect any significant violation of arms accords – a process known as verification. "Trust but verify" was a famous arms control slogan of the Reagan Administration during the 1980s.

Examples on the debit side of analysis include: the failure to predict the outbreak of the Korean War in 1950 or the placement of Soviet offensive missiles in Cuba in 1962; the reporting – especially by U.S. Air Force Intelligence – of a (non-existent) bomber and missile gap between the Soviet Union and the United States in the 1950s and early 1960s; underestimating during the Vietnam War the supplies coming to the Viet Cong through Cambodia; underestimating the pace of the Soviet strategic weapons program; faulty forecasts about the Soviet invasions of Hungary in 1956 and

Czechoslovakia in 1968, the Arab–Israeli war in 1973, and the fall of the Shah of Iran in 1979; and a lack of precise predictions about the collapse of the Soviet empire in 1989–91 – although the CIA tracked its economic decline and rising political turmoil more closely than critics concede.[81] More recently, mistakes regarding supposed WMD in Iraq in 2002 arose as a result of limited humint in the country, poor vetting of the few humint sources that were available (Curve Ball, for instance), and an overreaction to earlier underestimating of Iraq's weapons prowess in 1990.[82] Attacks by "lone wolf" terrorists have also taken the United States by surprise from time to time, as in San Bernardino, California (2015) and Orlando, Florida (2016).

In a nutshell, NIEs have been uneven in their capacity to provide officials with accurate forecasts about history's probable trajectory, especially when it comes to invaluable details. Long-range prognosticating is a skill that diminishes the farther one attempts to peer into the future. "The CIA Directorate of Science and Technology has not yet developed a crystal ball," Senator Frank Church (D, Idaho) cautioned. "Though the CIA did give an exact warning of the date when Turkey would invade Cyprus [in 1974], such precision will be rare. Simply too many unpredictable factors enter into most situations. The intrinsic element of caprice in the affairs of men and nations is the hair shirt of the intelligence estimator."[83] When it comes to predictions, Betts stresses as well that "some incidence of failure [is] inevitable." He urges a higher "tolerance for disaster."[84] The bottom line: information is usually scarce or ambiguous, and the situation in question may be fluid and changing. Former intelligence officer Arthur S. Hulnick advises that "policy makers may have to accept the fact that all intelligence estimators can really hope to do is to give them guidelines or scenarios to support policy discussion, and not the predictions they so badly want and expect from intelligence."[85]

This realistic sense of limitations is unhappy news for presidents and cabinet secretaries who seek clear-cut answers, not hunches and hypotheses; but such is the reality of national security intelligence. It bears repeating, though, that having intelligence agencies closely examining world affairs is better than operating blindly. As a CIA analyst writes, "There is no substitute for the depth, imaginativeness, and 'feel' that experienced, first-rate analysts and estimators can bring to the often semi-unknowable questions handed them."[86]

Even if NIEs are less than perfect instruments for forecasting future events, they have the virtue of gathering together in one place a dependable set of facts about a situation abroad. This frees up decision-makers to focus attention on sorting out the disagreements they might have over which policy options to choose. Former

NSA Director William Odom states this case: "The estimate process has the healthy effect of making analysts communicate and share evidence. If the NIEs performed no other service, they would still be entirely worth the effort."[87] Almost fifty years ago, Kent noted, too, that "the intelligence estimate will have made its contribution in the way it promoted a more thorough and enlightened debate.... "[88]

The Iraqi NIE Controversy   Caught up in the swiftly moving events that followed hard upon the 9/11 attacks in 2001, DCI Tenet never got around to ordering the preparation of an NIE on Al Qaeda or on suspected Iraqi WMD. Neither did the White House. Reportedly, advisers to President George W. Bush feared that a full-blown Estimate on the WMD question would reveal "disagreements over details in almost every aspect of the Administration's case against Iraq."[89]

The lack of an NIE on Iraqi WMD at the very time the United States was engaged in an important internal debate over whether to launch a war against Saddam Hussein's regime was unfortunate. Rumors about WMD in Iraq were rife and inflamed by references to "mushroom clouds" appearing on American soil, expressed by President Bush and National Security Adviser Condoleezza Rice.[90] Tenet has admitted his error: "An NIE on Iraq should have been initiated earlier, but at the time I didn't think one was necessary. I was wrong."[91]

Senators Richard Durban (D, Illinois) and Carl Levin (D, Michigan), both members of the Senate Select Committee on Intelligence (SSCI), believed at the time that a NIE would be important in the debate over a possible war against Iraq. They insisted on a formal written assessment and persuaded SSCI Chairman Bob Graham (D, Florida) to send a letter on September 10, 2002, to Tenet requesting that an Estimate on Iraq be prepared as soon as possible.[92]

Tenet replied that he would be unable to produce the kind of comprehensive NIE on Iraq that Graham sought, because of other pressing intelligence duties. Nevertheless, he promised to furnish, as soon as possible, an Estimate on the subject of WMD in Iraq.[93] The DCI ordered a "crash project" to meet SSCI's request. The ninety-page Estimate went to the Senate about three weeks after the request – too hastily prepared, in the view of critics. One reporter called it "the worst body of work in [the CIA's] long history."[94] The document arrived at SSCI's quarters in the Hart Office Building in early October and Tenet came to brief the Committee's members on its main points. In retrospect, Senator Graham feels that the DCI seemed to skate over dissenting views that downplayed the Iraqi threat.[95]

Senators Graham, Durbin, and Levin next sought to have the NIE declassified for public consumption, except for portions that might disclose sensitive sources and methods. They made the request on October 2, 2002, and two days later Tenet delivered an unclassified version of the longer document, this one twenty-five pages in length. The problem, from Graham's point of view, was that the new version "did not accurately represent the classified NIE we had received just days earlier."[96] Missing was the sense imparted in some passages of the longer, still-classified document that Saddam posed no immediate danger to the United States or his neighbors, if left alone. In Graham's opinion, Tenet had diluted the original document to keep in step with the opinion of the White House that Saddam was a great menace to the United States.[97] Republican Senator Chuck Hagel (Nebraska) concluded that the condensed NIE was "doctored" to suit the political needs of the White House.[98]

The "Key Judgments" section of the original NIE was not released until July 16, 2003 (the invasion of Iraq began four months earlier, on March 19, 2003). Only on June 1, 2004 – almost a year into the war in Iraq – did Tenet provide a more complete, but still redacted, version of the KJ section. In a report released in July 2004, SSCI concluded that the NIE's Key Judgments were, for the most part, "either overstated, or were not supported by the underlying intelligence reporting."[99] Only much later, in 2007, in a memoir published as war in Iraq lingered on, did Tenet acknowledge that "we should have said, in effect, that the intelligence was not sufficient to prove beyond a reasonable doubt that Saddam had WMD." The DCI said that he now believed "more accurate and nuanced findings would have made for a more vigorous debate – and would have served the country better."[100]

CURRENT VERSUS RESEARCH INTELLIGENCE   A vital question for any nation is how many resources should be devoted to the production of current intelligence, at the expense of preparing more deeply considered products of research intelligence like the NIE. In capitals around the world, most policy officials prefer to receive current rather than research intelligence. Indeed, policymakers in the United States recently rated NIEs eighth in value among the intelligence products they received.[101] Former CIA senior analyst Mark M. Lowenthal writes that, recently, the Intelligence Community has "put its greatest emphasis on shorter, more current products," a response to "a fairly consistent decline in policymaker interest in intelligence community products as they get longer and more removed from more current issues."

The upshot is that about 80–90 percent of the analytic resources of the U.S. Intelligence Community is now dedicated to clarifying for policymakers what happened today and yesterday, and what is likely to happen tomorrow – the essence of "current intelligence."[102] According to Lowenthal, the Intelligence Community has "gotten out of the knowledge-building business. Now it is: current, current, current."[103] A former CIA deputy director for intelligence points out, however, that "a bunch of research intelligence is done, not necessarily estimative – just everything we know about subject X. Then someone says, 'It's about time we do a formal Estimate.'"[104]

A YARDSTICK FOR INTELLIGENCE REPORTS   Whatever the type (more current or more research oriented), all intelligence reports should attempt to honor the basic canons of professional analysis. Among the major hallmarks of an outstanding intelligence report, the first requirement is to get the facts right.

Accuracy   In 1999, the American comedian Jay Leno quipped that "CIA" must stand for "Can't Identify Anything," after the Intelligence Community forwarded to a NATO bomber pilot coordinates for an arms depot in Serbia that turned out in fact to be the Chinese embassy. (The wrong map was actually sent to NATO by the National Geospatial-Intelligence Agency, not the CIA.) Several Chinese were killed in this accidental bombing and many Chinese continue to think the bombing was done on purpose. Obviously, the intelligence agencies must provide accurate information – within limits; no sensible policymaker expects IC clairvoyance about future world events.

Timeliness   Important, too, is the quality of timeliness. History runs on nimble feet, and if intelligence reports lag too far behind events, they are likely to be of little use to a decision-maker. The result may be the dreaded acronym "OBE" scrawled across an analytic report: "overtaken by events."

Relevance   Policymakers have no interest in receiving an intelligence report on local elections in Greenland when their in-box is filled with decisions that have to be made about events on the Horn of Africa. Sometimes intelligence analysts wish to write about their own interests or speciality – perhaps derived from their PhD dissertation topic, say, "Rural Politics in Outer Mongolia." If analysts are out of tune with the consumers they serve when it comes to topical focus, they may as well go on a fishing trip; consumers will have no time for their reports. The best intelligence reports are tailored to address the most pressing problems in a decision-maker's in-box. This reality underscores the value of close – yet non-political – ties between intelligence producers and consumers, brought about by forward liaison teams and periodic meetings between the two groups.

Readability   Considerable effort goes into making intelligence reports inviting to read: the four-color quality of the *PDB*, for instance, fully equipped with charts, graphs, and photographs – all on high-quality paper. It is not enough to write a solid intelligence assessment about some event or condition in the world; the report must be *marketed* as well, to catch the attention of busy policy officials. The language must be straightforward, too, even if the subject is economics and the temptation to use econometrics and jargon is great. Policymakers have a low tolerance for the obscure – and few of them have doctorates in economics.

Brevity   Like many overworked government leaders, the great Secretary of State George Catlett Marshall placed a premium on succinct reporting. When George F. Kennan became the first director of the Policy Planning Staff in the State Department, he asked Marshall what his instructions were. "Avoid trivia," the General replied. Prime Minister Winston S. Churchill of Great Britain felt the same way. In a compliment to one of his favorite policy advisers, Churchill referred to him as Lord Heart-of-the-Matter. Because of this emphasis on getting to the point quickly in our fast-paced society, praise descends upon those report writers and oral briefers who cut to the chase. It is also why the modern NIE will have to be trimmed down in length at least somewhat, although not to the degree of losing its in-depth research contribution to policy debates.

Imagination   The best analysts attempt to think imaginatively about how an adversary might try to harm the United States. Would a terrorist organization resort to aerial terrorism against the skyscrapers of New York City – a question insufficiently pondered before the 9/11 attacks would ultimately provide a tragic answer. What targets are most vulnerable inside the United States today? What are the likely strategic objectives of China in the South China Sea, or Russia on their border with Eastern Europe? What are the odds that a missile might strike the United States without anyone in Washington knowing who fired it? How likely is it that a pandemic might sweep from China or Africa toward the United States? To what extent is environmental degradation dangerous to U.S. security interests?

Jointness   The United States has seventeen intelligence agencies, plus a range of "ints," for a reason: the world is large and several approaches to intelligence-gathering are necessary to ferret out the information Washington leaders desire. Yet a fragmented flow of information to decision councils from seventeen different "hoses" would be overwhelming and confusing. Instead, presidents and other leaders want "all-source fusion" – a thoughtful blending of all the int findings into comprehensive reports ("jointness," in military intelligence jargon). This requires the sharing and integration of intelligence findings, which the Kean Commission inquiry found to be the weakest link in U.S. intelligence in the run-up to the 9/11 tragedy.

Objectivity   Intelligence reports must be free of political considerations and attempts to please decision-makers – a cardinal requirement. The Nazi Foreign Minister Joachim von Ribbentrop issued orders to his ministry that reports in contradiction to the views of Der Führer would be ill-advised, hinting further that anyone guilty of this offense would face an unpleasant outcome.[105] With these sorts of edicts traveling out from Berlin to the various bureaucratic entities of the Third Reich, the end result was predictable: Hitler and his retinue descended deeper and deeper into self-delusion, cut off from accurate intelligence about the progress of the war against Britain, Russia, and the United States. A strong sense of professional ethics keeps most intelligence officers in the democracies on the straight and narrow path of honest reporting. Occasionally, though, some individuals in the intelligence agencies have set aside this sense of ethics, as when DCI Allen Dulles failed to stand up to inflated DoD estimates on Soviet bomber production rates; or when DCI Richard Helms deleted a paragraph from an Estimate on Soviet missilery, under pressure from the Nixon Administration to paint a more frightening portrait of America's Cold War enemy.[106] This "politicization" of intelligence is much more likely to come, though, from the consumer side of the intelligence equation, as the less scrupulous of America's policymakers cherry-pick intelligence reports and otherwise bend and twist the findings to suit their political agendas.

Specificity   Finally, and most difficult of all, the best intelligence reports carry a sufficient degree of specificity to provide policymakers with an ability to take action. Intelligence officers are often able to monitor an increase in the flow of messages between members of an adversarial group or nation – say, the telephone conversations of ISIS lieutenants. This kind of "traffic analysis" that reveals an increase in enemy communications – more "chatter" – can be valuable to know, triggering a greater concentration of ints toward the target. Yet even more valuable would be a quick deciphering of the encoded messages and translation of them into English, which might point to an enemy's precise attack plans. In short, vague airport "orange alerts" about possible terrorist attacks provide little help; what is necessary are a terrorist organization's detailed and timely attack plans – actionable intelligence. The analyst must be explicit and honest about the limits of data in a report, conveying a sense of how confident he or she is about the findings.

This list of reporting attributes adds up to a lofty set of standards, on top of which comes the necessity of easy access to top policymakers. Given a lack of rapport at the level of intelligence dissemination, the intelligence will go unread or will fall on deaf ears. That is why the relationship between top intelligence managers – the DNI and the various agency directors – and senior policy officials is so important. DCI James Woolsey was rarely able to sit down with President Clinton and talk about intelligence findings; William Casey, despite his many deficiencies as DCI, enjoyed open access to President Reagan and, as a result, could return to Langley with full knowledge of the main foreign policy problems confronting the Administration – an indispensable ingredient for the achievement of relevant intelligence tasking. Often the Intelligence Community will fall short of these demanding standards, because of inadequate collection (during the war in Vietnam, for example, the CIA was never able to penetrate the North Vietnamese government with a spy[107]); the slow translation of foreign language and coded materials; flawed analyses; the political misuse of reports by policymakers; or a lack of access to the President and other top officials. Despite such challenges, the secret agencies must aim for the highest possible quality in intelligence reporting; policymakers must constantly resist the temptation to twist these reports for political purposes; and the producers and consumers of intelligence must develop bonds of trust in their common quest for better information to inform decisions.

As for NIEs, they often make a contribution in the mix of products for decision-makers, but improvements are necessary.[108] Estimates have to be more nuanced, with dissents – sometimes known by analysts as "footnote wars" – boldly presented ("flagged" – including both within the body of the text and in the Key Judgments or "executive summary" portion of the report). Their production levels ought to rise as well (in one year under DCI George H.

W. Bush, the community produced only five NIEs); they need to be shorter (thirty rather than one hundred pages long); and they should be completed in six months at the most – and much faster in emergencies. Moving the Office of the DNI to Langley would also make sense from the point-of-view of the NIE production process (and also the *PDB*). After all, the vast majority of the government's top strategic analysts are located in the CIA's Directorate of Analysis (DA) and the NIC, not in the Office of the DNI at Liberty Crossing, six miles away from Langley.

CO-LOCATION   Some reformers have long believed that analysis could be improved by having a closer relationship between operatives and analysts at the CIA. The operatives in the DO (formerly the NCA) enjoy "ground truth" about countries overseas, since that is where they serve under official or non-official cover. This gives them a certain inside knowledge, from café life to the nuances of local slang. The analysts are experts about foreign countries, too, and travel abroad, but for shorter periods of time. Their primary knowledge comes from study; they typically have a PhD that reflects their advanced book-learning and research on international affairs. Though quite different in their career paths and daily experiences, both groups can bring something to the table when a specific nation or region is the focus of U.S. attention. Yet traditionally operatives and analysts have been located in separate places at the CIA, behind doors with combination locks that bar any outsiders from entering. This can have unfortunate consequences.

For example, in the planning that went into the Bay of Pigs covert action in 1961, the DO operatives were enthusiastic and confident about the prospects of a relatively easy overthrow of Fidel Castro; the people of Cuba would supposedly rise up against the dictator once the Agency had landed its paramilitary force on the island beaches. In another part of the CIA, however, the analysts with expertise on Cuba understood that an uprising was highly unlikely; as they spelled out in a SNIE in December 1960, the people of Cuba adored their leader (Fidel Castro) and would fight a CIA invasion force door-to-door in Havana and across the island. The DO could have benefited significantly from rubbing shoulders with their colleagues in the DI (now called the DA); perhaps that interaction would have brought a stronger dose of realism to DO planning. Nor was President Kennedy made aware of the DI's views on the unlikely success of this scheme. The head of the Bay of Pigs planning, Richard Bissell, enthusiastic about the paramilitary operation and the advancement the successful overthrow of Castro might bring him personally in the CIA leadership hierarchy, had some corridor knowledge of the skeptical SNIE but elected never to bring it to the President's attention.[109]

Aware of this physical and cultural distance between the DO and the DI, John Deutch took steps as DCI in 1995 to improve the cooperation between the two at Langley by physically moving together elements of both Directorates. This experience in "co-location" has been uneven. Sometimes the two types of intelligence officers – the doers and the thinkers – have displayed personality clashes that get in the way of sharing information; still, on other occasions, the experiment has led successfully to the achievement of its goal: a blending of in-country experience with library learning to provide intelligence reports with more richly textured insights into world affairs. In 2009, the Director of the CIA, Leon Panetta, said that there would be "more co-location of analysts and operators at home and abroad" in the coming years, adding that greater fusion of the two groups "has been key to victories in counterterrorism and counterproliferation."[110] In 2010, he announced the formation of a CIA Counterproliferation Center to combat the global spread of WMD. In the Center, which would report to Panetta and further upward to the DNI's National Counterproliferation Center, operatives and analysts would work cheek-by-jowl in the spirit of "co-location."[111] Panetta's successor John Brennan, who assumed office in 2013, has pushed the CIA even further in the direction of co-location, with a major integration of operatives and researchers through the Agency's Headquarters Building at Langley.

Dissemination

Once prepared by analysts, intelligence reports are distributed to those who make decisions (and their top aides). This may seem easy enough, but even this phase of the intelligence cycle is rife with possibilities for error. For one thing, policy officials are often too busy to read documents provided to them by the IC. "I rarely have more than five minutes each day to read intelligence reports," an Assistant Secretary of Defense (a former Rhodes scholar and Harvard University professor) told the Aspin–Brown Commission in 1995.[112] That a nation may spend a king's ransom on the collection and analysis of national security intelligence, only to have the findings ignored by busy decision-makers, is a disquieting paradox. No wonder Betts concludes that "the typical problem at the highest levels of government is less often the misuse of intelligence than the non-use."[113] Misuse occurs as well, though – all too often, as when leaders cherry-pick the portions of a report they like and dismiss the rest.

Always of concern is the proper relationship between analysts and decision-makers. If a NIO becomes too cozy with those in power, the danger of politicization rises as the analyst may be tempted to bend intelligence in support of policy objectives – what is known as "intelligence to please." Yet if the NIO is too detached and unaware of the policy issues faced by a decision-maker, an intelligence report risks being irrelevant. The skillful analyst will carefully navigate between this Scylla and Charybdis, developing rapport with policy-makers to understand better their in-box pressures, while keeping a distance from the politics of an administration.

An important debate on this topic revolves around whether or not DNIs, D/CIAs, and other intelligence managers and analysts should enter into discussions with decision-makers about policy recommendations. Or should they maintain a strict no-cross zone between the presentation of facts – a universally acknowledged intelligence duty – and commenting on ideal policy directions. Richard Helms, DCI from 1966 to 1973, argued for neutrality; so did Sherman Kent, who thought a high wall should exist between intelligence and policy officers. As Helms put it:

> My view was that the DCI should be the man who called things the way he saw them, the purpose of this being to give the president one man in his Administration who was not trying to formulate a policy, carry out a policy, or defend a policy. In other words, this was the man who attempted to keep the game honest. When you sit around the table and the Secretary of State is propounding this and defending this, and the Secretary of Defense is defending this and propounding that, the President has the right to hear somebody who says: "Now listen, this isn't my understanding of the facts" or "That isn't the way it worked."[114]

Other intelligence officials, though, such as DCIs John A. McCone (1961–65) and William J. Casey (1981–87), have taken an active – often aggressive – role in debates over policy options.[115] McCone even strongly recommended a military invasion of Cuba in 1962. Whatever one's philosophy on this subject of intelligence activism versus neutrality, it might be difficult in practical terms to stay apart from the policy fray as an intelligence officer. As a senior analyst has noted, "When it's 8:30 at night and the Undersecretary of State says, 'What do you think I should do?', you can't say at that point: 'That's not my job, Mr. Secretary.' You just can't do that."[116] One solution followed by DCI Woolsey was to stay out of policy debates until after the formal meeting was over and the room cleared; then, if asked, he offered President Bill Clinton his personal views at that time. The most important obligation of an analyst or an intelligence manager is to resist political pressures from those in high office to twist intelligence in a manner that suits an administration's policy preferences, at the expense of the actual meaning of an intelligence report. Here is the soul-destroying sin of politicized intelligence – the gravest hazard of the intelligence cycle.

With respect to the Iraqi WMD controversy in 2002, the DCI at the time, George Tenet, had an obligation to spell out for President George W. Bush the weaknesses in the intelligence reporting. While it is true that thirteen of the sixteen U.S. intelligence agencies at the time concluded that WMD probably did exist in Iraq, every analyst knew how soft the data were (as personified by Curve Ball's unsubstantiated speculations). Neither Tenet nor the 2002 NIE adequately communicated this softness to the President, however, or to Congress and the public. Had these weaknesses been highlighted, responsible officials could have argued for a delay in the invasion plans until firmer data were acquired. Intelligence reports, based on flimsy evidence, had helped pave the way to war – although the Bush Administration may well have taken up arms against Saddam Hussein regardless of intelligence findings, so intent were its leaders on regime change.

Weaknesses in the Iraqi WMD data were improperly dealt with in Great Britain as well. The Prime Minister's communications director gave to the British people the impression that Iraq had WMD that could strike the British Isles, even though MI6's intelligence report on this subject noted only that Iraq probably had tactical WMD that might well be used against a British and American invasion force on the battlefield in Iraq. Neither the Prime Minister nor the Director of MI6 ever corrected the distorted record presented by the political leaders in the British government, which helped turn British public opinion more toward a pro-invasion stance out of fear that Saddam Hussein harbored nuclear (and perhaps chemical and biological) weapons that could hit London and other targets in the United Kingdom.[117]

The ongoing quest for better collection and analysis

Despite the well-intended efforts of many intelligence officers and policymakers to make the intelligence cycle function smoothly, serious questions remain about the usefulness of the information provided by the Intelligence Community. Even with the staggering amount of money spent gathering and analyzing national security intelligence each year, many consumers find its products lacking. "We never used the CIA stuff," recalls a former U.S. ambassador and assistant secretary of state. "It was irrelevant."[118] A survey of intelligence consumers conducted by the Senate Select Committee on Intelligence during the 1980s revealed widespread disdain toward the value of the Community's analytic work. Most widely reported was Senator Daniel Patrick Moynihan's sweeping indictment of the CIA for failing to predict the fall of the Soviet Union.[119]

In the months prior to the 9/11 attacks against the United States, the Agency and the FBI blundered repeatedly in their counterterrorism activities, from failing to investigate suspicious behavior by foreigners in the United States seeking flight training for large commercial airliners to mix-ups in tracking known terrorists who entered the nation in early 2001 and would join other 9/11 hijackers.[120] Then the intelligence mistakes multiplied in 2002 with the poor collection of information and faulty analysis related to suspected WMD in Iraq. Examples include gullibility over the trustworthiness of Curve Ball and other assets, as well as toward the pro-war lobbying in Washington of a self-serving Iraqi exile group; confusion over whether Saddam Hussein had purchased large amounts of yellow-cake uranium from Niger; facile conclusions reached about how Iraqi fire trucks spotted in the Iraqi desert indicated the presence of a biological weapons capability; how UAVs that the U.S. Air Force firmly believed were conventional surveillance aircraft were seen by others as carriers for WMD; speculation on the likely progress of an Iraqi WMD program based on extrapolation (and overestimation) to correct underestimating errors in 1990; taking at face value Saddam's blustering that he had WMD, rather than considering the possibility (which turned out to be true) that his rhetoric was a hollow attempt at a deterrence posture designed to frighten Iraq's archenemies in Tehran and keep them at arm's length. The list goes on.[121]

Yet, despite mistakes – and even an occasional scandal over the years (see Chapter 5) – the U.S. Intelligence Community has consistently provided valuable data and insights to policymakers about world affairs, from accurate specifications on Soviet and Chinese weaponry to advanced details on the negotiation positions of foreign diplomats. The Aspin–Brown Commission summarized some of the successes that had occurred just since the end of the Cold War in 1991:[122]

- discovering North Korea's nuclear weapons program;
- blocking the sale of radioactive materials to renegade nations;
- uncovering illegal WMD sales;
- supporting battlefield operations in the Middle East;

- backstopping many international negotiations with reliable information;
- helping to break up drug cartels, among them the Cali organization in Colombia;
- thwarting various terrorist activities, including the capture of Carlos the Jackal, as well as the ringleader of 1993 World Trade Center bombing and the leader of the Shining Path terrorist group in Peru;
- providing information that supported diplomatic peacekeeping initiatives around the world;
- disclosing and thus foiling assassination plots perpetrated by other countries overseas;
- revealing unfair global trade practices, thereby improving the chances of success for U.S. business enterprises in the developing world;
- pointing to countries that have violated trade sanctions, as well as alerting officials to approaching financial crises in foreign nations; and
- collecting information about human rights abuses around the world, as well as warning about ecological problems and humanitarian crises.

This is only a partial list from the years 1992–95; since then, America's intelligence agencies have recorded many additional successes, including capture or killing of a large number of Al Qaeda's leaders in Pakistan (Bin Laden among them) and ISIS members in Syria, Iraq, and Libya; the tracking and countering of other ISIS- and Al Qaeda-affiliated terrorist cells in such places as Somalia and Yemen; support for the wars in Iraq and Afghanistan; and surveillance assistance in the responses to a variety of natural disasters, not only abroad but (with special clearances from Congress and the White House) at home as well.

The United States and other democracies, as well as their adversaries, will continue to seek improvements in their knowledge of world events. On the collection side, this will mean spending more money on technical platforms and human agents to bring about greater transparency to the planet. On the analysis side, it will mean continuing to search for the brightest and most thoughtful citizens a government can find to work as analysts: smart, dedicated, patriotic individuals who can help decision-makers make better sense of history as it unfolds – especially those threats that could be dangerous for the democracies to overlook.

Vital for success will be cooperation among the intelligence services of the democracies through what is known as "foreign intelligence liaison" or "burden-sharing." The world is too vast for any one democracy alone to monitor for threats and opportunities; they need cooperation from one another. Intelligence burden-sharing arrangements can be dicey, however, as the Curve Ball example underscores. Each of the democracies will have to be cautious about vetting information from one another. Moreover, as the relationship between the United States and Pakistan illustrates, nations can have mixed agendas. Pakistan has been helpful in some instances in providing intelligence to Washington about Al Qaeda and Taliban activities in the mountainous border between Pakistan and Afghanistan. Yet the Pakistani intelligence service, Inter-Services Intelligence or ISI, has also attempted to run double agents against the United States; and some ISI officers are known to have close friendships and ideological ties with the Taliban and perhaps Al Qaeda.[123]

Despite the need for caution, the United States and the other democracies have much to gain from sharing their intelligence findings. The common foes of terrorism, illegal drug dealing, and other forms of international crime, as well as the proliferation of WMD, should provide adequate incentives for the open societies to share their collection and analytic capabilities.

3 Covert Action

Secret Attempts to Shape History

Two young men stood on either side of an easel that supported oversized charts. One man braced the charts, while the other occasionally moved a pointed marker up and down the slopes of red-colored trend lines.

Seated near them, a stout man in his fifties read from a typed statement. He spoke precisely, seldom looking up from the pages. His words fell in a dry monotone on the table before him. A gray ribbon of cigarette smoke curled slowly toward the high ceiling from an ashtray on the table. All three men wore starched white shirts with buttoned-down collars and Brooks Brothers ties. They might well have been marketing advisers tracing annual sales for the edification of a corporate board of directors.

The "board," however, showed remarkably little interest in whatever profits or losses the charts revealed. Nor was the room anything one might expect to find in a corporate headquarters. It was elegant, even stately. Doric pillars, carved from wood, embellished the rich walnut paneling on the walls. A grand chandelier sparkled at the center of the ceiling. Beyond the spacious windows, draped with regal purple curtains, was a courtyard where a fountain sprayed a column of water high into the frigid morning air. This was no industrial park; this was the venerable Russell Building of the United States Senate, named after the legendary Richard Brevard Russell, Jr., Democrat of Georgia, the most prominent national security expert in Congress for decades until he passed away in 1971.

A U-shaped bench dominated the hearing room, rising above the floor with its prongs facing the three men, as if they were trapped in a magnetic field. Within the concave space sat a stenotypist, her fingers dancing lightly on the keys of a machine. Two elderly lawmakers sat at the head of the bench, each a United States senator and a member of the secretive Subcommittee on Intelligence. They listened as the man at the table droned through his prepared statement on paramilitary, or warlike, activities of the CIA. As the Agency's Deputy Director of Operations (DDO), he was expected to present a report now and then to Congress. One of the senators rested his head in his arms and soon fell asleep. The other senator, the panel's chairman, stared blankly at the CIA briefer, nodded once in a while, and discreetly stole a glance at his wristwatch and then at the newspaper folded in front of him.

This was not the first time the DDO had experienced the distant look in the eyes of a lawmaker, or even the first time he'd seen one nod off. His job was to provide an update on the CIA's activities; how it was received on the Hill was not his problem. He cleared his throat and raised his voice for a moment, more to relieve his own boredom than to stir his small audience. "Paramilitary activities," he said, "have been an important part of our program since the early days of the Cold War."

The new inflection in the briefer's voice awoke the slumbering senator with a start. "Parliamentary activities?!" he bellowed. "You fellas can't go messin' round with parliaments. I won't have it!"

A silence fell over the room. The stenotypist's fingers stopped their dance. The deputy director pursed his lips and looked at the subcommittee chairman.

"Senator, this briefing is on *paramilitary*, not parliament, activity," the chairman said softly.

"Oh, well, uhruumph," replied the sleepy-eyed senator, clearing his throat. He paused and tugged at his ear. "Okay, but y'all stay away from parliaments, ya hear?" With that admonishment, he rose from his chair and shuffled out of the room. At a nod from the chairman, the deputy director resumed his statement.[1]

This tale from the 1950s continues to be told with glee at Langley. True or not, it is a fact that covert actions – and especially paramilitary activities – have often prompted concern and sometimes alarm on Capitol Hill, apparently even awakening octogenarian overseers. Of all the nation's intelligence missions, this one is the most likely to stir passions. Indeed, critics contend that covert action has done more to stain the reputation of the CIA – and, with it, the United States – than any other of the government's dark arts.

Covert action as an intelligence mission

Legal underpinnings

In the United States, covert action (CA) is sometimes referred to as the "quiet option" by officials inside the CIA, the organization normally called upon to plan and implement this approach to solving America's problems abroad. ("Active measures" is the Russian term.) The phrase is drawn from the questionable assumption that covert action is likely to be less noisy and obtrusive than a Marine brigade. While sometimes this is the case, there was nothing quiet about covert action at the Bay of Pigs in 1961 or against the Taliban regime in Afghanistan after the 9/11 attacks. Another label is the "third option," pointing to covert action as a choice that lies somewhere between diplomacy and overt warfare. As explained by Henry Kissinger, Secretary of State during the Nixon Administration: "We need an intelligence community that, in certain complicated situations, can defend the American national interest in the gray areas where military operations are not suitable and diplomacy cannot operate."[2] A favorite euphemism for covert action in more recent years, beginning with the Carter Administration, is the phrase "special activities."

In 1990, Congress provided, for the first time, a formal statutory definition of covert action as "an activity or activities of the United States Government to influence political, economic, or military conditions abroad, where it is intended that the role of the United States Government will not be apparent or acknowledged publicly."[3] Specifically excluded from the definition were intelligence collection and counterintelligence operations, traditional diplomatic, military, and law enforcement activities, or routine support to overt U.S. activities aboard. Stripped down further to the basics, covert action may be thought of as "those activities CIA undertakes to influence events overseas that are intended not to be attributable to this country."[4] Simpler still, "Covert action is influence."[5]

Prior to the specific legislative authority for covert action enacted in 1992, presidents relied on a boilerplate clause in the National Security Act of 1947 for legal justification. This founding statute for modern U.S. intelligence focused almost exclusively on the collection and analysis mission. Then, in a final section, the law (drafted mainly by one of President Truman's national security aides, Clark Clifford) provided authority for the Director of Central Intelligence and the Agency to perform "such other functions and duties related to intelligence affecting the national security as the President or the National Security Council may direct."[6]

Rationale

Behind this spongy legal language lies the reality that covert action is nothing less than a nation's attempt to change the course of history through the use of secret operations against other nations, terrorist groups, or factions – "giving history a push," as a senior CIA operative has put it.[7] During the Cold War, the main concern of the CIA's Covert Action Staff within the Operations Directorate (the CAS, now known as the Special Activities or SA Division) was, according to one of its chiefs, "the global challenge of communism...to be confronted whenever and wherever it seemed to threaten our interests."[8] With rare, albeit significant, exceptions (such as the Iran–*contra* affair), the CIA has been the implementer – not the instigator – of covert actions. Almost always, the White House has ordered such operations; and, since 1975, special committees of Congress have been in the reporting loop.

A Cold War DCI, William E. Colby (1973–76), reasoned that covert action was vital to counteract the political and subversive threat posed by the secret operations of the Soviet intelligence services (the KGB and the GRU) in Europe and around the world – just as NATO provided a critical line of military defense in Western Europe and the Marshall Plan erected a bulwark of foreign aid to counter Soviet economic encroachments. When threats arise to America's interests in the world, "it is better that we have the ability to help people in these countries where that will happen, quietly and secretly," Colby advised, "and not wait until we are faced with a military threat that has to be met by armed force."[9]

Thus, taking a stand against communism became the primary *raison d'être* for covert action during the Cold War. Whether such targets as Iran (1953), Guatemala (1954), Angola (1975), and Chile (1964–72) qualified as "truly important" (in Colby's phrase) is a matter of debate. With respect to Angola, a CIA official maintained that, "ultimately, the purpose was to throw the Soviets out, at which point we would leave, too." Critics, though, find these arguments unpersuasive. For example, with respect to Nicaragua during the 1980s, the German Nobel laureate in literature, Günter Grass, asked plaintively: "How impoverished must a country be before it is not a threat to the U.S. government?"[10] Senator Frank Church, who led a Senate inquiry into the subject of covert action in 1975, concluded that "our targets were leaders of small, weak countries that could not possibly threaten the United States."[11]

The implementation of covert action

The CIA has been the organization called upon by the President and the NSC to conduct covert actions. The Agency's covert action infrastructure ("the plumbing," in CIA-speak) consists of the DO; the SA Division and its paramilitary wing, the Special Operations Group (SOG); overseas stations and bases; personnel on loan from the military; and civilian contractors. For much of the Agency's early history, the role of the President in the approval of a covert action was meant to be tightly concealed, through the practice of "plausible deniability." According to this "doctrine," presidents should be as pure as Caesar's wife; the reputation of the United States had to be protected if a covert action ran amok and ended up on the front pages of the world's newspapers. Keeping the White House at a distance from unsavory activities would allow a president to say publicly: "I never authorized this inappropriate secret operation and I am taking measures to punish those who carried it out."

When the President is kept at arm's length from covert actions, however, the operations lack the proper accountability that comes with explicit White House approval. With no paper trail leading to the Oval Office, the danger arises that operations may be carried out without the President's approval or even knowledge. President Eisenhower rejected this approach in 1960, when the Soviets shot down a CIA U-2 spy plane over their territory on the eve of a Washington–Moscow summit. He chose to acknowledge responsibility publicly for the risky surveillance mission. The U-2 flight was a collection operation, not a covert action; nonetheless, for the first time, accountability had trumped plausible denial with respect to an intelligence activity. The implication was that presidents might henceforth take direct responsibility for covert actions, as well. The doctrine of plausible deniability proved more enduring than some anticipated, however. Not until the mid-1970s, in the midst of a spy scandal in the United States, did Congress at last decide to bury the doctrine. With the Hughes–Ryan Act of 1974, lawmakers passed legislation that required explicit presidential approval for all important covert actions. Such operations would now have to be authorized by the nation's chief executive and, in an even greater departure from tradition, the covert actions would have to be reported to special oversight panels on Capitol Hill.

In the aftermath of the 9/11 attacks and America's involvement in wars in Iraq and Afghanistan, another serious question arose about accountability in the implementation of covert actions. This new concern came about as a result of the Pentagon's Special Forces and CIA private contractors edging their way into this domain.[12] The improper use of organizations other than the Agency to conduct covert action had already produced a scandal of major proportions during the Reagan Administration: the Iran–*contra* affair. These covert actions, which involved a secret arms sale to Iran and escalating covert action in Nicaragua, were never properly reported to Congress, as required by the Hughes–Ryan Amendment and the Intelligence Oversight Act of 1980.[13] Further, the Reagan Administration violated the Boland Amendments – a series of increasingly restrictive laws, named after their chief sponsor, Edward P. Boland (D, Massachusetts), and passed in the early 1980s. These amendments expressly prohibited covert actions in support of the *contras* in Nicaragua, who were attempting to overthrow the left-leaning *Sandinista* regime.

Staff on the National Security Council (NSC), including two consecutive National Security Advisers, schemed to bypass the Boland restrictions and the other statutory limitations on covert action dealing with approval and reporting requirements. The NSC staff established its own secret organization outside the government, called "The Enterprise," and launched privately funded covert actions in support of the Nicaraguan *contras*. When this subterfuge eventually leaked to a Middle East newspaper in 1986 and played back into the United States, lawmakers realized Congress had been fooled and in 1987 they conducted a full-scale investigation. Congress instituted new legislative strictures related to covert action, including a more precise definition of its boundaries and a requirement that the President formally sign covert action approvals – not just say "yes" or offer a nod and a wink by way of approval.[14]

The methods of covert action

During the Cold War and since, covert action has taken four different forms, although they are often used together. The categories are: propaganda, political activities, economic disruptions, and paramilitary (PM) operations.

Propaganda

The most frequent form of covert action conducted by the United States has been various forms of propaganda, known more gently as "perception management" by Agency insiders. Nations have overt channels of information dissemination, of course, such as the United States Information Agency (USIA) or the White House use of press releases about presidential decisions; but governments frequently seek to reinforce these messages through hidden communications channels as well. These hidden channels are often more credible in other countries – say, Hans Beidenhofer (a fictional name used here for purposes of illustration) who writes op-eds for *Der Spiegel* and is widely read and trusted by Germans. If Herr Beidenhofer wrote during the Cold War that he liked the idea of U.S. intermediate nuclear missiles on German soil as a deterrent against a Soviet invasion through the Fulga Gap, that might have carried more weight with local readers than if the same idea were advocated by the U.S. secretary of defense. Foreigners who are newspaper reporters, magazine editors, television producers, or talk show hosts – anyone in a position to express a public point of view favorable to the United States as if it were their own – become fair game for recruitment by the CIA as a "media asset."

Whatever foreign policies or slogans an administration in Washington, DC might be touting in public – perhaps the danger of renegade nuclear aspirations pursued by Iran – the CIA pushes the same themes through its hundreds of covert media channels around the world. During the Cold War, some seventy to eighty secret media insertions were made each day by the Agency into different parts of its global propaganda system – a "Mighty Wurlitzer," as it was referred to proudly inside the Agency's Covert Action Staff.[15] Once released, however, propaganda can drift here and there, possibly back to the United States – a phenomenon known as "blow back" or "replay." When this occurs, information originally meant for the eyes and ears of audiences overseas (friend or foe) finds its way back home to influence – and perhaps inadvertently deceive – America's own citizens (see Figure 3.1). Most of America's covert propaganda, though, is truthful, a repeat of what officials are saying publicly in Washington. Yet sometimes, in 1–2 percent of cases, Agency propaganda is false ("black" or "disinformation") and these media placements abroad become a particularly disquieting form of blow back. A senior intelligence official, Dr. Ray Cline, conceded once that it "used to worry me a lot that false CIA propaganda about mainland China might fool China experts in the Department of State, skewing their analyses."[16]

An example of covert propaganda during the Cold War was the CIA's concealed sponsorship, until revealed by a leak in the early 1970s, of Radio Free Europe (RFE) and Radio Liberty (RL). These stations broadcast programming into the Soviet Union and its satellite nations, in an effort to break the communist government's biased grip on news, entertainment, and culture, as well as

Figure 3.1   Herblock on blow back

Source: "I SHOT AN ARROW INTO THE AIR…" – a 1956 Herblock Cartoon,
   copyright by The Herb Block Foundation.

to inculcate in listeners a favorable view of the United States and the
West. Similarly, the CIA routinely attempted to infiltrate Western
literature (books by Soviet dissenters and others, magazines,
newspapers) into the communist world. A high-ranking CIA official
offers this assessment of the Agency's propaganda program aimed
at the Soviet Union and its puppet allies: "This has maintained
several independent thinkers in the Soviet bloc, has encouraged the
distribution of ideas, and has increased the pressures on totalitarian regimes."[17] Even among more neutral observers, the Agency's
propaganda activities are generally credited with helping to sustain
dissident movements behind the Iron Curtain and subtly contribut-
ing to the eventual fall of the Soviet empire – although the effects
of this propaganda defy exact measurement.

  Of greater controversy during the Cold War was the Agency's
use of propaganda against the democratic republic of Chile. In
1964, at the direction of the Johnson Administration, the CIA spent

$3 million to blacken the name of presidential candidate Salvador Allende, in an effort to prevent his election for fear that he was a socialist with close ties to Moscow. An expenditure of this magnitude in the Chilean election was equivalent at that time, on a per capita basis, to about $60 million in a U.S. presidential campaign – a staggering sum that could shape an election outcome in either nation. Although defeated in the 1960s, Allende persevered and eventually won the Chilean presidency in 1970.

Under orders from the Nixon Administration, the CIA then ratcheted up its propaganda operations to undermine the Allende government, spending an additional $3 million between 1970 and 1973 in negative publicity against the regime. President Nixon and his top aides feared that the Soviet Union might use Chile as a base to spread communism throughout the Western Hemisphere. Allende might become the next Fidel Castro in Latin America. To help protect their own interests in Chile, the International Telephone and Telegraph (ITT) Corporation and other American businesses secretly offered the Nixon Administration $1.5 million to aid the anti-Allende covert actions, out of a concern that the Chilean President might decide to nationalize their holdings in Chile. According to Church Committee investigators in 1975, the forms of propaganda used by the CIA against Allende included press releases, radio commentary, films, pamphlets, posters, leaflets, direct mailings, paper streamers, and wall paintings. The Agency relied heavily on images of communist tanks and firing squads; and it paid for the distribution of hundreds of thousands of copies, in this Catholic country, of an anti-communist pastoral letter written years earlier by Pope Pius XI. The Allende government was overthrown in 1973.

Sometimes propaganda planners at the CIA seemed to be writing for the theater of the absurd. One scheme in the early 1960s envisioned the incitement of a coup against the Cuban regime, spurred by a flamboyant propaganda campaign. The idea was to have American submarines surface off the coast of Havana and fire starshells from their decks that would attract the attention of the islanders. Agency assets would then spread the word: "Christ has come! Rise up against the anti-Christ!" A DO officer explained to an investigative committee: "And this would be the manifestation of the Second Coming and Castro would be overthrown."[18] The CAS dubbed the plan "Elimination by Illumination." The Kennedy Administration had the good sense to reject the proposal before it went forward.

One of the most successful CIA propaganda operations took place in Central America in 1954. The purposes in this instance were twofold: first, to protect the investments in Guatemala of the

United Fruit Company, an American firm with a lucrative banana monopoly in Central America (America's spy chief, Allen Dulles, and his brother, the Secretary of State, John Foster Dulles, had both served on the board of directors for the United Fruit Company); and, second, to exhibit for world consumption the determination of the Eisenhower Administration to thwart any leader who might have some affiliation, however weak (or imagined), with the Soviet Union.[19] The Agency set up a radio station in the mountains of Guatemala, where local CIA assets began broadcasting the fiction that a full-fledged revolution was taking place, and that the masses were rising up against the supposedly pro-communist dictator Jacobo Árbenz. The skillful broadcasts led a nervous Arbenz to resign, in the belief that a mythical people's army of 5,000 was marching toward the capital.[20]

Political covert action

The quiet option sometimes takes the form of financial aid to friendly politicians and bureaucrats abroad – bribes, if one wishes to put a harsh light on the practice; or stipends for the advancement of democracy, if one prefers a rosier interpretation. Whatever one chooses to call this form of assistance ("King George's cavalry" is the amusing British MI6 expression), the record is clear that throughout the Cold War the CIA provided substantial sums of cash to a number of political groups and individuals overseas, including a host of pro-Western parties and factions in West Germany, Greece, Egypt, the Philippines, and Chile, to mention just some examples that have made their way into the public record. An important part of political covert action during the Cold War was funding for anti-communist labor unions in Europe, an objective of high priority soon after the end of World War II. One well-publicized case involved support for the Christian Democratic Party in Italy during the 1960s against its principal opponent, the Italian Communist Party. Providing money to the Christian Democratic Party openly may well have discredited its reputation, causing Italian voters to conclude that the party was just a puppet of the United States. The White House turned to covert funding as a means of avoiding this taint.

The CIA maintains a stable of "agents of influence" around the world: individuals, from valets and chauffeurs to personal secretaries and key ministerial aides, who presumably have sufficient access to high-ranking political figures to influence their decisions. The purpose, as with propaganda, is to convince important foreign officials to lean toward the United States and its allied democracies and away from the Soviet Union or, these days, Iraqi insurgents, extremists among the Taliban, Al Qaeda, ISIS, the government of Iran, and other anti-democracy adversaries in the Middle East, Southwest Asia, and anywhere else. As is the case with humint operations generally, the Agency seeks to expand its crop of agents of influence around the world – a goal made more difficult to achieve with the short tours of its operations officers and their limited foreign-language capabilities.

Economic covert action

The CIA has also attempted to slow or even destroy the economies of adversaries. In one instance during the Kennedy Administration (although apparently without the President's knowledge), Agency operatives planned to spoil Cuban–Soviet relations by lacing sugar bound from Havana to Moscow with an unpalatable, though harmless, chemical substance. At the eleventh hour, a White House aide discovered the scheme and had the 14,125 bags of sugar confiscated before they were shipped to the Soviet Union. The aide had concluded that the United States should not tamper with another nation's food supplies.[21] Other methods of secret economic disruption have reportedly included efforts to incite labor unrest; smuggling counterfeit currencies into the target nation to cause inflationary pressures; depressing the world price of agricultural products grown by adversaries (such as Cuban sugar cane); sneaking defective components into the construction materials for a foreign nuclear reactor; contaminating foreign oil supplies or computer parts; and – upping the ante – dynamiting electrical power lines and oil-storage tanks, as well as mining an enemy's harbors with explosive charges to harm ships and undermine the target nation's international trade relations.

The U.S. military tried to enter the covert action domain, too, against Castro during the early years of the Johnson Administration. In response to a presidential request for new ideas on how to deal with the Cuban leader, the Pentagon proposed "Operation SQUARE DANCE": the destruction of the Cuban economy by dropping from the cargo hatches of aircraft under the darkness of night a parasite known as Bunga that would attack the island's sugar cane plants. "The economic and political disturbances caused by this attack could be exacerbated and exploited," claimed a DoD memo, "by such measures as spreading hoof-and-mouth disease among draft animals, controlling rainfall by cloud seeding, mining cane fields, burning cane, and directing other acts of conventional sabotage against the cane milling and transportation system." The hoped-for end result, concluded the memo, would be "the collapse of the Castro regime." The military planners conceded that adoption of SQUARE DANCE "would introduce a new dimension into Cold War methods and would require a major change in national policy."[22] But they were ready to carry out these measures anyway, if the White House so desired. The National Security Adviser at the time, McGeorge Bundy (a former Harvard University professor and dean), was troubled, however, by such extreme options – even against the likes of dictator Fidel Castro. Bundy rejected the proposal. The DoD memo provides startling insight into America's capacity and, evidently at some levels of government, its willingness to engage in radical covert economic operations to achieve U.S. foreign policy goals.

As part and parcel of the attempts to undermine Allende before and after his run for the presidency, the CIA adopted various covert measures to undermine the Chilean economy. By heightening the level of economic dislocation and social unrest in Chile, the Nixon Administration hoped that local military forces would decide to strip Allende of his powers, since the Administration's initial covert actions had failed to prevent Allende's victory in the presidential election. The DCI at the time, Richard Helms, took handwritten notes at a White House meeting on September 15, 1970, about what could be done if Allende won the presidential campaign. Huddled in the Oval Office with President Nixon, Secretary of State Henry Kissinger, and Attorney General John Mitchell, Helms jotted in his notebook: "Make the economy scream." One method opted for this purpose by the Agency was to sow chaos in the nation's trucking industry, a ploy that dramatically impeded the flow of commerce from town to town. A decade later, attempts by the Reagan Administration to topple the *Sandinista* regime in Nicaragua would again turn to economic CAs, including the mining of the nation's harbors and the blowing up of power lines across the countryside.

Paramilitary covert action

Secret warlike activities, known as paramilitary covert actions or PM, are yet another arrow in the CIA's quiver – the most lethal of all. No covert actions have held higher risk or generated more criticism than large- and small-scale "covert" wars (as if wars can be kept secret for long). From 1950 to 1953, the Agency's covert action capabilities attracted high funding to support America's overt warfare on the Korean Peninsula – the first major use of this foreign policy tool by the United States. Henceforth, whenever the United States was involved in overt warfare somewhere in the world, the

Agency would be there as well to support the military with covert actions. Then, in 1953, the CIA provided support to pro-American factions that brought down the Iranian Prime Minister, Moham-med Mossadeq, and replaced him with some one more pliable, the Shah of Iran (Mohammed Reza Shah Pahlavi). The next year, the Agency succeeded with its plan to frighten the democratically elected Arbenz government out of office in Guatemala by a combi-nation of mainly CA propaganda, but also political, economic, and small-scale PM operations. Over the next two decades, the Agency mobilized its paramilitary capabilities for several secret military attacks against foreign governments, offering support (with mixed degrees of success) for anti-communist insurgents in such places as the Ukraine, Poland, Albania, Hungary, Indonesia, Oman, Malaysia, Iraq, the Dominican Republic, Venezuela, Thailand, Haiti, Greece, Turkey, and Cuba.

While the Bay of Pigs venture in Cuba exploded in the face of DO operatives, several other schemes experienced some degree of success – at least over the short run. For example, from 1962 to 1968, the CIA backed the Hmung tribesmen (pronounced with a silent "h"), sometimes referred to as the Meo tribesmen. The Hmung fought a war in North Laos against North Vietnamese puppets known as the Communist Pathet Lao. This war kept the Pathet Lao occupied and away from killing U.S. troops fighting next door in South Vietnam. The Hmung and the Pathet Lao struggled to a draw in Laos, until the United States withdrew from the ring to concentrate its efforts in Vietnam. Following this withdrawal, the Hmung lacked U.S. arms and advisers; they were soon routed, with some fortunate assets exfiltrated by the CIA for resettlement in the United States. The CIA redoubled its covert action operations against the North Vietnamese and their Viet Cong allies in South Vietnam, until the U.S. military retreated from Indochina in 1973.

Under President Ronald Reagan, the Agency pursued major para-military operations in a number of nations around the world, but with special emphasis in Nicaragua and Afghanistan – combined, the second most extensive use of covert action in the nation's history (slightly surpassing its emphasis in the Korean War; see Figure 3.2). While the Nicaragua involvement ended in the Iran–*contra* scandal, the Agency's support of *mujahideen* fighters against Soviet invaders in Afghanistan is considered one of the glory moments in the CIA's history. The Agency provided Stinger missiles to the *mujahideen*, which helped turn the tide of the war and sent the Red Army into retreat. Most recently, covert action has reached another high point in terms of emphasis by the United States – in fact, the nation's most pronounced use of this approach to foreign policy,

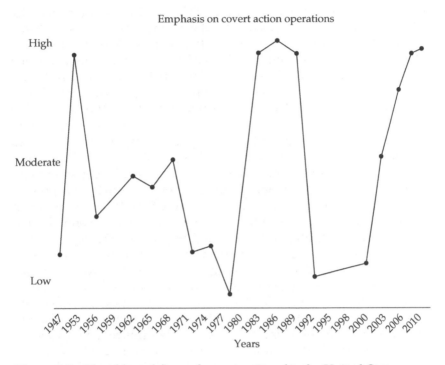

Figure 3.2   The ebb and flow of covert actions by the United States, 1947–2010

Source: The author's estimates based on interviews with intelligence managers over the years, along with a study of the literature cited in the notes of this chapter.

eclipsing by a narrow margin the adoption of "special activities" in both the Korean War and the Reagan Administration's covert wars in Nicaragua and Afghanistan. This time, in the wake of the 9/11 attacks, the purpose has been to support America's overt wars in Iraq and Afghanistan, along with operations directed against Al Qaeda, ISIS, and other terrorist organizations.

THE ASSASSINATION OPTION   Perhaps the most controversial form of PM covert action has been the use of assassination as a method to eliminate dangerous, or sometimes just annoying, foreign leaders. The Soviets referred to this option as "wet affairs," a method they adopted in 1940 to eliminate a regime critic, fellow communist Leon Trotsky, whom a Soviet intelligence operative killed with an ice pick during Trotsky's exile in Mexico. The CIA's involvement in murder plots came to light in 1975. In files discovered by presidential and congressional investigators (the Rockefeller Commission and the Church Committee, respectively), the DO referred to its attempts at dispatching selected foreign leaders with such euphemisms as "termination with extreme prejudice" or "neutralization." At one time the Agency established a special panel – the "Health Alteration Committee" – to screen assassination proposals. The CIA also developed a tiny dart the size of a sewing needle (a "nondiscernible microbioinoculator," in fanciful DS&T terminology), which could be silently propelled toward an unsuspecting target by an oversized .45 pistol equipped with a telescopic sight. Agency scientists considered the dart gun, which was accurate up to 250 feet and would leave no trace in the victim's body, the perfect murder weapon.

Fidel Castro attracted the full attention of the CIA's Covert Action Staff and its Special Operations Group during the Kennedy and Johnson administrations. The Agency emptied its medicine cabinet of drugs and poisons in various attempts to kill, or at least debilitate, the Cuban leader. Before escalating to the level of murder plots, the CIA in one operation placed depilatory powder in Castro's shoes when he traveled abroad; the substance was meant to enter his bloodstream through his feet and cause his famous charismatic beard to fall off his chin. The Agency also impregnated Castro's cigars with the hallucinatory drug LSD, as well as with a deadly botulinum toxin; dusted his underwater diving suit with Madura foot fungus; sneaked an agent into his kitchen, who tried (but failed) to place a poison capsule in his soup; and attempted to find someone with access to Castro who could inject the highly poisonous substance Blackleaf-40 into his skin, using a needle-tipped ballpoint pen. In this last plot, the CIA made contact with a promising agent on November 22, 1963, ironically the very day that America's own president was assassinated.

All these efforts cratered, for Castro was elusive and well protected by an elite security guard trained by the KGB (today known in Russia as the SVR or Foreign Intelligence Service). So the Agency turned to the Mafia for assistance: a Chicago gangster, Sam Giancana; the former Cosa Nostra chief for Cuba, Santo Trafficante; and the mobster, John Roselli. These men still had contacts on the island from pre-Castro days when Havana was a world gambling mecca. No doubt assuming the U.S. government would back off Mafia prosecutions in return for some help against Castro, the crime figures volunteered to assemble assassination teams of Cuban exiles and other hitmen, then infiltrate them into Cuba. None succeeded.

Starting with the Eisenhower Administration and continuing into the Kennedy years, another foreign leader targeted for death was Patrice Lumumba, the dynamic Congolese political leader. From

Washington's point of view, his error (like Castro's) had been to enter into ties with Moscow that seemed all too close. In the seemingly zero-sum context of the Cold War, both Castro and Lumumba had to go. Agency Headquarters sent to the COS in Congo an unusual assortment of items to achieve this objective: rubber gloves, gauze masks, a hypodermic syringe, and lethal biological material. The toxic substance would produce a disease that would either kill the victim outright or incapacitate him so severely that he would be out of commission. In 1961, a cable from DCI Allen Dulles sent to the Agency's COS in Congo underscored in capital letters that:

IN HIGH QUARTERS HERE IT IS THE CLEAR-CUT CONCLUSION THAT IF [LUMUMBA] CONTINUES TO HOLD HIGH OFFICE, THE INEVITABLE RESULT WILL AT BEST BE CHAOS AND AT WORST [IT WILL] PAVE THE WAY TO COMMUNIST TAKEOVER OF THE CONGO WITH DISASTROUS CONSEQUENCES FOR THE PRESTIGE OF THE UN AND FOR THE INTERESTS OF THE FREE WORLD GENERALLY. CONSEQUENTLY WE CONCLUDE THAT HIS REMOVAL MUST BE AN URGENT AND PRIME OBJECTIVE AND THAT UNDER EXISTING CONDITIONS THIS SHOULD BE A HIGH PRIORITY OF OUR COVERT ACTION.

The COS in Congo began to plan how he could carry out the specific directions from Agency Headquarters to inject the toxic material into something that could get into Lumumba's mouth – "whether it was food or a toothbrush," read the instructions. The COS informed one of his colleagues that there was a "virus" in a safe within the CIA's quarters at Leopoldville, the capital of Congo. The recipient of this hushed disclosure later conceded to investigators in dark humor that he "knew it wasn't for somebody to get his polio shot up-to-date." The plan, though, was never carried out. The CIA experienced problems getting near enough to Lumumba to inject the deadly toxin into an apple or toothpaste. Soon after, a rival Congo faction, fearful of Lumumba's popularity, snuffed out his life before a hastily arranged firing squad. A recent study of his death suggests that the CIA may have arranged to render Lumumba into the hands of his assassins and, therefore, may have finally and indirectly achieved its goal of his permanent demise.[23]

Rafael Trujillo of the Dominican Republic, Ngo Dinh Diem of South Vietnam, and General René Schneider of Chile were other national leaders murdered by assassins who at one time or another had connections with the CIA. The Church Committee concluded, however, that at the time each was murdered the Agency no longer had control over the assassins. The CIA also gave weapons to dissidents who dispatched President Sukarno of Indonesia and François

"Papa Doc" Duvalier of Haiti; but, once again, these plots seem to have gone forward without the Agency's direct involvement – though it is unlikely that officials at Langley or the White House shed many tears over the outcomes.

The CIA has been implicated, as well, in the incapacitation or death of lower-level officials. The most well-known operation of this kind was the CIA's Phoenix Program, carried out in South Vietnam as part of the U.S. war effort to subdue the influence of communists in the countryside (known as the Viet Cong or VC). According to DCI William Colby, who led the program for a time, some 20,000 VC leaders and sympathizers were killed – though 85 percent of these victims were engaged in military or paramilitary combat against South Vietnamese or American soldiers.

In 1976, soon after Congress revealed the CIA's involvement in international murder plots, President Gerald R. Ford signed an executive order against this practice. The wording of the order, endorsed by his successors, reads: "No person employed by or acting on behalf of the United States Government, shall engage in, or conspire to engage in assassination."[24] While honored most of the time, situations have occurred where administrations have bent this language to suit their own needs. For example, President Reagan ordered the bombing of President Muammar Qaddafi's house in 1986 as part of an air raid against Libya, on grounds that he had been aiding and abetting terrorism; and President George H. W. Bush ordered the bombing of Baghdad – including the palaces of Iraqi leader Saddam Hussein – during the first Persian Gulf War (1990–91). Indeed, this first Bush White House "lit a candle every night hoping Saddam Hussein would be killed in a bunker" during these bombings, recalls a DCI.[25] In these instances, the United States was involved in overt warfare against Libya and Iraq; under such conditions (ideally, authorized by Congress, although the attacks against Libya were not), the executive order on assassination is suspended.

More recently, as authorized by Congress, the United States has been involved in overt warfare in Iraq, Afghanistan, and against ISIS, as well as Al Qaeda and its supporters (most visibly, the Taliban in Afghanistan and Pakistan). Again, the executive order against assassination has been lifted, or at least loosely applied, in these struggles. Saddam was regularly a target in the Second Persian Gulf War that began in 2003; but, as in the First Persian Gulf War, he proved to be elusive. Eventually, in December of that year, U.S. troops discovered him hiding in a hole in the ground near his hometown. He was arrested, tried by an Iraqi tribunal, and hanged – all with the strong encouragement of the United States under President George W. Bush. Saddam had ordered an assassination attempt against the President's father and mother soon after Iraq's defeat in the first Persian Gulf War, when the Bushes were visiting Kuwait to celebrate the victory – a fact not lost on Bush the son.

Added to the current list of people to be captured or assassinated by the United States military and CIA paramilitary forces are extremist Taliban and Al Qaeda members in Afghanistan and Pakistan, as well as ISIS members in Syria, Iraq, Libya, and wherever else they pop up. The Obama Administration added Afghan narcotics dealers to the drone target list.

Since the end of the Cold War, the CIA (in cooperation with the U.S. Air Force) has developed and fielded its most deadly paramilitary weapon: UAVs, such as the Predator and its more muscular brother, the Reaper. Both drones are armed with Hellfire missiles and can easily fly across national boundaries. These systems are controlled remotely from sites in Afghanistan and Pakistan (for the takeoffs and landings) and at Langley, in Nevada, and other locations in the United States (for the targeting and killing phases of flight). Cruising at relatively low altitudes, the UAVs are equipped with sophisticated cameras that help operators in the United States identify distant targets before the missiles are released. Mistakes are still made, unfortunately, as Taliban and Al Qaeda terrorists hide in mosques and other locations where innocent civilians may be inadvertently hit by the missiles – although the CIA and the military go to great lengths to avoid this "collateral damage."

In an update on civilian casualties, the Obama administration told NBC News in 2016 that "only" 100 civilians had died in the nearly 500 U.S. drone strikes since 2009. Later that same year, the Administration clarified the numbers: between 64 and 116 civilians had died in 473 drone strikes. Independent groups countered, however, that the actual number of civilian deaths exceeded 1,000.[26]

At the time of writing, drone assassination initiatives are vetted by lawyers on the NSC working with their counterparts in the Intelligence Community. The initial step is a targeting recommendation prepared by attorneys in the IC or the Department of Defense. Next, the NSC Deputies Committee (consisting of those second in command at the recommending agency or the DoD), gives the proposal a thorough scrub, before passing it along to the DNI, D/CIA, and the SecDef on the Principals Committee. If the potential target is a U.S. citizen, the President must sign off as well and the congressional oversight committees are informed. In extraordinary cases, these steps can be short-circuited with the President alone providing authorization for the kill. Beyond these tightened procedures, the Obama Administration redoubled its efforts to avoid casualties among innocent civilians by improving intelligence reconnaissance before a drone attack takes place. Moreover, the guidelines fashioned by the Obama Administration require that drone assassinations can go forward only if the targeted individual poses a grave threat to the United States, and if there is a "near certainty" that no civilian casualties will result from the attack.

Several top officials at the Agency began to express their view publicly that covert action – and especially drone attacks – had become too dominant in the CIA's global operations, with intelligence analysts focused more and more on establishing GPS drone-targeting coordinates rather than on the production of assessments about world affairs.[27] At Langley, CIA Director John O. Brennan (who had served as an analyst throughout his career at the Agency) urged the restoration of traditional analysis as the top priority in the Agency's portfolio of responsibilities, with the CIA involved in drone strikes only in limited instances. In its final years, the Obama Administration started to shift more of the responsibility for counterterrorist drone attacks to the Pentagon and away from the CIA, in part because Brennan strongly opposed the idea of the Agency as a killing machine rather than an organization engaged chiefly in collection-and-analysis.

Earlier, during the Clinton Administration, the President called off two counterterrorist attacks by cruise missiles just as they were ready for firing from U.S. destroyers in the Red Sea against the Al Qaeda leader, Osama bin Laden. In one instance, Bin Laden was surrounded by his wives and children in a village and, in another, by princes from the United Arab Emirates (UAE, an American ally – of sorts) on a bird-hunting expedition. On another occasion, the missiles were fired from a U.S. Navy cruiser in the Red Sea at a suspected Al Qaeda gathering in the desert near the town of Khost in Paktia Province, Afghanistan, but Bin Laden had already departed before the warheads struck the encampment. He continued to evade U.S. assassination attempts, lying low somewhere (experts believed) in the mountains of Pakistan. In 2011, he was finally discovered and a U.S. Special Forces team shot him dead in a walled compound in the city of Abbottabad, just thirty-five miles from the capital Islamabad.

Exactly who should be on the "kill" list has been a controversial subject. Originally, the Patriot Act of 2001 stipulated that only those enemies involved in the 9/11 attacks were legitimate targets for retaliation. Since then – and without further legislative guidelines – the target list has widened. For example, a U.S. citizen hiding out in Yemen by the name of Anwar al-Awlaki was placed for consideration on an assassination list generated by the Obama Administration, even though it was never demonstrated to the public that he had actually been involved in plots against the United States. If he had been, al-Awlaki could be considered a legitimate target; however, if he had limited himself to making speeches against the United States, he would have been just one of hundreds of radicals in the Middle East and Southwest Asia who have advocated *jihad* against the West in recent years. Behind closed doors, attorneys in the Obama Administration eventually decided that Awlaki had participated sufficiently in terrorist activities to qualify as a legitimate assassination target. President Obama signed the death warrant and the Yemeni iman was blown to pieces by Hellfire missiles in 2011. He was not the first U.S. citizen to be killed by CIA drones. In 2002, a Predator fired a missile at an automobile in a Yemeni desert that carried six passengers suspected to be Al Qaeda members. All six were incinerated. One turned out to be an American citizen. Each of these events, and there have been others (including, by accident, Awlaki's son), raises serious questions about the relationship between due process and assassination.

At present, the procedures for developing assassination lists lack sufficient clarity and oversight. Reportedly, the decision to kill requires the approval of the U.S. ambassador to the target country, as well as the CIA chief of station, the DO director, and the D/CIA. As noted earlier, if the target is an American citizen, like Al-Awlaki, attorneys in the Justice Department and the President must also approve. Further, at least a few of the members of the congressional Intelligence Committees are briefed on the targeting, and some of their staff are invited to the White House Situation Room to follow the videos of the drone attacks. The idea is to demonstrate to overseers the great care that the Administration takes to avoid civilian casualties.

Despite some efforts to reassure congressional supervisors that the IC is doing its best to act prudently, the secret agencies have often drawn the ire of lawmakers who have viewed some post-9/11 spy operations as excessive. Examples include the use of harsh interrogation methods during the second Bush Administration, as well as the use of extraordinary renditions (subjects explored in more depth in Chapter 5). With these excesses in mind, critics have argued that a more formal congressional review should take place when it comes to drone assassinations. Critics have suggested that the courts should be part of this decision-making process, too. A new court could be established to issue warrants for assassinations. A precedent for special intelligence courts is the judicial panel set up by the Foreign Intelligence Surveillance Act (FISA) of 1978, where executive officials are supposed to seek warrants for telephone wiretaps against American citizens suspected of involvement in terrorist activities.[28]

In 2014 and after, the CIA flew no drone missile attacks against the ISIS target in Iraq and Syria, leaving this terrain to the Pentagon's UAV pilots. A new debate began in Washington about the CIA's remit. Should it step out of the Murder, Inc. business, handing over drone warfare exclusively to the Pentagon? A group of vocal dissenters opposed the views of the President and the D/CIA on shelving the Agency's drone capabilities. For one thing, argued top leaders on the Senate Select Committee on Intelligence (SSCI), Chairman Richard Burr (R, N. Carolina) and Ranking Minority Member Dianne Feinstein (D, California), sometimes the Pentagon was too slow in sending drones against known terrorist targets in Syria and Iraq, leading to "missed opportunities" once the CIA had spotted ISIS fighters. The CIA's drone commanders should be allowed to pull the trigger in those circumstances, they argued. Hiding behind this reasoning were two even stronger concerns on Capitol Hill. First, SSCI's leaders believed that the CIA was subject to greater congressional accountability than the Pentagon, because of the Hughes–Ryan reporting procedures, and therefore should remain in charge of most drone attacks – certainly those outside the official theaters of war. Those theaters continued to include Afghanistan and, with the spilling of ISIS terrorism from Syria eastward, Iraq as well – and, increasingly, Libya. Second, and unstated, the SSCI leaders (and those on the House Permanent Select Committee on Intelligence, or HPSCI, too) want to keep their jurisdiction over CIA drones, because it provided them with a heady closeness to the high circles of policymaking in the White House. Still others maintained, however, that Pentagon drone attacks were more accountable because they did not have to be clothed in as much secrecy as CIA operations.

Even when the United States has decided to "neutralize" (kill) an adversary overseas, the task has proved difficult to carry out. Castro reportedly survived thirty-two attempts on his life attempted by the Agency.[29] Efforts to take out the warlord Mohamed Ali Farrah Aidid of Somalia failed during America's brief involvement in fighting on the African Horn in 1993; Saddam Hussein proved impossible to find during the 1990s; and Bin Laden evaded detection for almost a decade after 9/11. Anwar al-Awlaki also proved elusive for years. Dictators are paranoid, well guarded, and elusive, as are high-ranking members of ISIS, Al Qaeda, and their terrorist brethren. Most troubling of all is the thought that assassinations carried out by the United States may encourage others to target, in return, the

American President and other leaders in Washington while they travel overseas.

The ebb and flow of covert action

Although out of favor with some administrations in the United States, others have spent enormous sums of money on covert action. Support for these operations during the Cold War accelerated from the very beginning of the CIA's history, moving from non-existence in 1947 to high prominence during the Korean War in 1950–53, falling back to much lower levels until a new spurt of major funding during the height of the Vietnam War in 1968–71, and then declining again for a decade before a dramatic resurgence during the Reagan years (see Figure 3.2 above). The war in Korea boosted the covert action mission in the Agency's infant days. As Ranelagh reports, funding "increased sixteenfold between January 1951 and January 1953," and personnel assigned to the mission doubled.[30] During this period, the budget for CA "skyrocketed," according to the Church Committee.[31] Successes in Iran (1953) and Guatemala (1954) encouraged the Eisenhower and Kennedy Administrations to rely further on the Covert Action Staff to achieve American foreign policy victories. Daugherty notes that the outcomes in Iran and Guatemala "left in their wake an attitude of hubris" at Langley and throughout the Eisenhower Administration's national security apparatus.[32]

Even the Bay of Pigs fiasco in 1961 created only a small and short-lived blip of skepticism about the use of covert action, before the Kennedy Administration turned again to the Agency for assistance in the resolution of international headaches. Throughout the 1960s and early 1970s, the DO and its allied mercenaries abroad waged a hidden World War III against communist forces – most notably in the jungles of Indochina. At times, covert actions absorbed up to 60 percent of the CIA's annual budget.[33]

A precipitous slide downward for the "quiet option" occurred in the early 1970s, induced by a souring of the war in Vietnam, government spending cuts pursued by the Nixon Administration, tentative overtures of détente with the Soviet Union, and a domestic spy scandal in 1975 that was accompanied by revelations about CIA assassination plots and attacks against the democratically elected government of Chile (the Allende regime). The covert action revelations, especially from the Church Committee, raised doubts among the American people and their representatives in Congress about the ethics and the value of special activities. Public reaction brought covert action "to a screeching halt," recalls a senior CIA official.[34] Interest in the "third option" (yet another euphemism for covert action) would resume during the presidency of Jimmy Carter – ironically, since he had campaigned in 1976 against the use of CA "dirty tricks" by the Agency. The most important catalyst for Carter's turn-around was the Soviet invasion of Afghanistan in 1979. The United States would have to fight back, the President decided (with strong nudging from his hawkish National Security Adviser, Zbigniew Brzezinski); and secret CIA operations would have to be the instrument of retaliation – since it would be mutually suicidal to initiate an overt war with the USSR, with its thousands of nuclear warheads atop ICBMs that could streak across the vast expanse of the northern polar region to strike cities from Los Angeles to New York City in less than a half-hour.

For proponents of covert action, the next decade – the 1980s – represented a Golden Age. The Reagan Administration recorded the historical high point of U.S. support for secret interventions abroad since 1947, although the current emphasis on covert operations – especially paramilitary activities with UAVs in the Middle East and Southwest Asia – surpassed this record during the Obama years. The 1980s were also the only time major attention was given to covert action by the United States without the nation's accompanying involvement in a major overt war. The more normal pattern is for covert action high points to occur within the framework of support to military operations (SMOs) during significant U.S. military interventions abroad: Korea, Vietnam, and, more recently, Iraq, Afghanistan, and the struggle against ISIS, Al Qaeda, and Taliban insurgents. The Reagan years demonstrated that, if an administration so chooses, it could commit to high levels of emphasis on covert action even during peacetime.

Thus, during the 1980s, the CIA's Operations Directorate would become the chief instrument for advancing the ideologically driven "Reagan Doctrine" of opposing communist-backed wars of liberation in the developing world, from El Salvador to Cambodia. The primary targets for the Reagan Administration were the *Sandinistas* in Nicaragua and the Red Army in Afghanistan. Funding poured into both operations, illegally so in the case of Nicaragua (and thus the Iran–*contra* scandal). The Nicaraguan intervention cast upon the CIA the darkest mark in the history of its use of covert action – worse even than the débâcle at the Bay of Pigs. The Iran–*contra* affair represented a fundamental assault on the U.S. Constitution, as the Reagan Administration (specifically, the NSC staff and elements of the CIA) attempted to bypass Congress and raise funds privately to advance covert actions against Nicaragua, even though these operations were prohibited by Congress (the Boland Amendments). In addition to its violations of U.S. law, the scheme also failed to topple the *Sandinistas*, whose leader, Daniel Ortega, continued to rule Nicaragua off and on in competitive elections (and is once again the President of Nicaragua today). In contrast, the Afghan intervention followed proper authorization, with appropriate adherence to the Hughes–Ryan CA reporting procedures at home; moreover, this use of covert action succeeded in helping to drive the Soviet military out of Afghanistan.

President George H. W. Bush has noted that he found covert action useful on occasion, but during his years in the White House (1989–92) the funding for special activities went into sharp decline, leveling out at around just below 1 percent of the U.S. intelligence budget – far below its heyday during the Reagan years.[35] From a place of prominence in the U.S.-led anti-communist crusades of the Cold War, the covert action mission had fallen into a state of near disregard by 1991. A senior DO officer looks back on these days ruefully:

> I feel that a lot more could be done in the broad area of covert action in support of policy with the proper resources allocated to the mission. I am not thinking in terms of going back to the days when CA was 60 percent of the CIA budget; but I do feel that less than 1 percent is below minimum. It is a mission that is legally and properly assigned to the Agency and, once we can get better understanding of it and clear up some of the controversies that surround it, I think it should have additional people if we are to carry out effectively what is the mission assigned to us by the president.[36]

During the Clinton Administration, DCI John Deutch observed: "Since the public controversies of the eighties over Iran–*contra* and activities in Central America, we have greatly reduced our capability to engage in covert action."[37] During Deutch's tenure (1995–96), funding for covert action turned modestly upward, as a means for aiding new democratic regimes against hostile forces (as in Haiti, for instance), as well as for thwarting the machinations of terrorists, drug dealers, and weapons proliferators (the latter rising to the level of the top 1A threat-assessment target during the Clinton years). Covert actions became more narrowly tailored – less global in nature – than during the Cold War.

With the election of George W. Bush, covert action at first remained at a modest level – until the 9/11 attacks. Then, with three wars fought simultaneously by the United States (in Iraq and Afghanistan, as well as against global terrorism), covert action underwent a renaissance, directed against targets chiefly in the Middle East and Southwest Asia. This rejuvenation brought the use, and the status, of covert action up to levels comparable to the earlier historical high points: those operations that had supported the war in Korea and the Reagan Administration's use of the third option in Nicaragua and Afghanistan. President Barack Obama first maintained the level of interest in covert action established by the second Bush Administration, then began to use this approach much more extensively in Afghanistan and Pakistan, reaching the record highs mentioned earlier (in terms of an administration's emphasis on CA). In 2011, President Obama also authorized covert action support to rebels fighting against the Qaddafi regime in Libya and, when that regime collapsed and Qaddafi was killed, against the new ISIS insurgency in this troubled North African nation.

A ladder of escalation for covert action

In 1965, strategist Herman Kahn of the Hudson Institute published an influential volume in which he offered an "escalation-ladder metaphor" for understanding the coercive features of international affairs. Kahn described his ladder as a "convenient list of the many options facing the strategist in a two-sided confrontation."[38] In a comparable ladder of escalation for covert actions (see Figure 3.3), the underlying analytical dimension traveling upward is the extent to which the options are increasingly harsh violations of international law and intrusions against national sovereignty. As the examples illustrate, covert actions can run the gamut from the routine on the lower rungs of the ladder to the extreme at the higher rungs.[39]

The lines of demarcation between high- and low-threshold covert actions can be indistinct, subject to debate and disagreement. Some members of the UN General Assembly's Special Committee on Friendly Relations argued in 1967, for instance, that covert propaganda and the secret financing of political parties represented "acts of lesser gravity than those directed towards the violent overthrow of the host government."[40] Other Assembly members rejected this perspective, especially those who wished to avoid legitimizing any form of covert action. As a result of the divided opinion, the Special Committee equivocated, neither supporting nor prohibiting covert propaganda and secret political funding. A perspicacious observer of the Committee's work concluded: "The texts that the General Assembly approved represent compromise formulations that are open to multiple interpretations."[41] What follows is also open to

Threshold Four: Extreme Options
29 Use of WMD
28 Major secret wars
27 Assassination
26 Small-scale coups d'état
25 Major economic dislocations; crop, livestock destruction
24 Environmental alterations
23 Pinpointed covert retaliations against non-combatants
22 Torture to gain compliance for a political deal
21 Extraordinary rendition for bartering
20 Major hostage-rescue attempts
19 Sophisticated arm supplies
Threshold Three: High-Risk Options
18 Massive increases of funding in democracies
17 Small-scale hostage rescue attempt
16 Training of foreign military forces for war
15 Limited arms supplies for offensive purposes
14 Limited arms supplies for balancing purposes
13 Economic disruption without loss of life
12 Modest funding in democracies
11 Massive increases of funding in autocracies
10 Large increases of funding in autocracies
 9 Disinformation against democratic regimes
 8 Disinformation against autocratic regimes
 7 Truthful but contentious propaganda in democracies
 6 Truthful but contentious propaganda in autocracies
Threshold Two: Modest Intrusions
 5 Low-level funding of friendly groups
 4 Truthful, benign propaganda in democracies
Threshold One: Routine Operations
 3 Truthful, benign propaganda in autocracies
 2 Recruitment of covert action assets
 1 Support for intelligence collection

Figure 3.3 A partial ladder of escalation for covert actions

Source: The author's estimates, based on interviews with intelligence managers and
 officers over the years, along with a study of the literature cited in the notes of
 this chapter. Adapted from Loch K. Johnson, *Secret Agencies: U.S. Intelligence in
 a Hostile World Order* (New Haven. CT: Yale University Press, 1996), pp. 62–3.

many interpretations, but the ladder metaphor does at least provide
the reader with a sense of the rising levels of severity that covert
action can entail.

Threshold one: routine options

At the lower end of the ladder for covert actions – Threshold One
– are arrayed such relatively benign activities as support for the
routine sharing of information (intelligence liaison, based on collection and analysis) between the CIA and friendly foreign intelligence
services about potential "hot spots," or rogue nations and groups,
in parts of the world that may warrant some form of covert action
in the future (Rung 1). Also at this threshold are attempts to recruit
covert action assets from native foreign populations, who are quite
often the same individuals tapped for overseas collection activities

(Rung 2). At this threshold, as well, is the limited dissemination of truthful, non-controversial propaganda themes (Rung 3) directed against closed, authoritarian societies (such as extolling to Yugoslavians the benefits of trade with the West in the early years of the CIA's covert propaganda programs). These low-rung activities are commonplace for most nations engaged in international affairs.[42]

Threshold two: modest intrusions

With Threshold Two, the degree of intrusiveness against another country or group begins to escalate beyond the routine, and the risks increase. This category would include the insertion of truthful, non-controversial propaganda material into the media outlets of democratic regimes with a free press (Rung 4) – U.S. covert action aimed at like-minded governments. Further, within this zone would be the payment of modest sums to political, labor, intellectual, and other organizations and individuals aboard who are favorably disposed toward, say, America's counterterrorist foreign policy objectives (Rung 5).

Threshold three: high-risk options

Threshold Three consists of controversial steps that could trigger within the target nation a response significantly damaging to international comity. Here, propaganda operations remain truthful and compatible with overt policy statements, but now the themes are contentious and are disseminated into media channels within both non-democratic (Rung 6) and democratic (Rung 7) regimes – say, reporting that Taliban soldiers have sprayed acid into the faces of young girls on their way to school in Afghanistan or killed international health-aid workers in Pakistan. At Rungs 8 and 9 (maintaining the distinction between non-democratic and democratic regimes), propaganda activities take a nastier turn, employing deception and disinformation that run contrary to one's avowed public policies – say, falsely blaming an adversary for an assassination attempt or fabricating documents to stain an adversary's reputation. Even propaganda operations against a nation without a free media are of concern here, because of the way in which blow back can deceive citizens in the democratic regimes.

Rungs 10 and 11 reflect first a large, and then a massive, increase in secret funding for political purposes within an autocratic regime. Rung 12 stands for an escalation based on relatively modest levels of secret funding to affect elections, but this time within a democratic regime – a much more questionable step. Damrosch underscores the distinction: "A political system that denies basic political rights is in my view no longer a strictly internal affair," but rather one properly subject to international interventions.[43]

At Rung 13, the use of covert action involves attacks against economic entities within a target nation. A power line is destroyed here, an oil depot contaminated there; a virus or "worm" is inserted into the computer infrastructures of a foreign government; labor strikes are encouraged inside an adversary's major cities. The measures are carefully planned to remain at the level of harassment operations, with a low probability that lives will be lost; nonetheless, a nation at this rung on the ladder has entered into a realm of more forceful operations.

A nation resorts to paramilitary operations at Rung 14, supplying arms to counter weapons previously introduced into the target nation by an adversary. Secret military training may accompany the arms transfers. This is a major step upward, for now an intelligence service has brought weapons into the equation. An intelligence agency might provide a modest arsenal of unsophisticated, but nonetheless deadly, arms to a favored rebel faction, as a means for balancing the correlation of forces in a civil war. At Rung 15, weapons are supplied to a friendly faction without the predicate of prior intervention by an outside adversary. Rung 16 goes further still, with the training of foreign armies or factions for the express purpose of initiating combat. A hostage rescue attempt is envisioned at Rung 17, one that could well lead to the loss of life – although designed to be small in scale so as to limit the potential for losses.

At Rung 18, massive expenditures are dedicated to improve the political fortunes of friendly parties within a democratic regime – perhaps $40 million in a small democracy and $100 million or more in a larger one. The objective is to bring that foreign faction into power that is the friendliest toward the United States. For some critics, this amounts to a troubling attempt to tamper with electoral outcomes in free societies; for proponents, it is simply an effort to make the world a better place by aligning nations along a compatible democratic axis. Attempts at covert influence against truly democratic elections – those in which the rights of political dissent and opposition are genuinely honored – represent a clear-cut violation of the non-interventionist norm (and related rules of international law) and have little claim to legitimacy, in contrast to lower-rung operations directed against self-interested autocratic regimes.

Threshold four: extreme options

With Threshold Four, a nation enters an especially dangerous and contentious domain of covert action: a secret foreign policy "hot zone." Here is where the lives of innocent people may be placed in extreme jeopardy. At Rung 19, the types of weapons provided to a friendly faction are more potent than at earlier rungs – say, Stinger and Blowpipe anti-aircraft missiles or UAVs armed with Hellfire missiles that enable the faction to take the offensive against a common adversary. At Rung 20, a nation might attempt an elaborate hostage-rescue operation that could well entail extensive casualties, even if that was not the intention. Rung 21 involves an extraordinary rendition – the kidnaping of a hostage. In this case, force is intended, carefully planned, and directed against a specific individual. Depending on the intent, this approach might fall into the bailiwick of a collection or counterintelligence operation; but if the purpose is to use the hostage as a pawn in secret negotiations toward some policy objective, then it becomes covert action. Rising up another step, a hostage might be tortured in an attempt to coerce compliance in a hostage swap or some other secret deal (Rung 22). On the next rung (23), acts of brutality are directed against lower-level noncombatants in retaliation for a hostile intelligence operation – say, the rendering and torturing of a terrorist's relative in a pay-back for a raid carried out by the terrorist cell (said to be a Russian speciality).

On the highest rungs, covert action escalates dramatically to include violence-laden environmental or economic operations, as well as paramilitary activities against targets of wider scope than is the case at lower levels on the ladder. Large numbers of non-combatants in the civilian population may become targets, whether planned or inadvertent. For example, the covert action may try to bring about major environmental alterations (Rung 24), from the defoliation or burning of forests to the contamination of lakes and rivers, the creation of floods through the destruction of dams, and operations designed to control weather conditions through cloud seeding in hopes of ruining crops and bringing about mass starvation. At Rung 25, the covert action aggressor attempts to wreak major economic dislocations within the target nation by engaging in the widespread counterfeiting of local currencies to fuel inflation and financial ruin; by sabotaging industrial facilities; destroying crops through the introduction of agricultural parasites (like Bunga) into the fields; or by spreading hoof-and-mouth disease or African swine fever among livestock.

Rung 26 has the covert action aggressor adopting even higher-stake operations: overthrowing a foreign regime, though with minimal intended bloodshed (as in Iran in 1953 or Guatemala in 1954). The next step, Rung 27, arrives at the level of the assassination plot against specific foreign leaders or terrorists and includes, in recent years, the use of Predators and Reapers as the instruments of murder – with all the risks these operations carry of incurring civilian casualties. At the top of the escalation ladder are two forms of secret warfare that inevitably affect large numbers of combatants and noncombatants: the launching of protracted, full-blown paramilitary warfare against an inimical regime. At Rung 28, the covert action perpetrator provides combat-ready intelligence officers to guide and arm indigenous rebel armies, comparable in scope to the CIA's "secret" war in Laos during the 1960s. Finally, at Rung 29, a nation introduces WMD into the covert action calculus – nuclear, biological, chemical, or radiological arms – meant to inflict widespread death in the population of the target nation.

Evaluating covert action

As the ladder of escalation suggests, covert action raises profound ethical questions about what kinds of operations should be acceptable and what is beyond the pale. How one assesses these questions will depend on how one views the place of morality in the conduct of a nation's foreign policy. "Do no evil though the world shall perish," admonished the eighteenth-century German philosopher Immanuel Kant. Taken to the extreme for covert action, a devotee of the Kantian school might well reject every rung on the ladder of escalation. In this spirit, a U.S. Undersecretary of State during the Cold War argued that America

> ought to discourage the idea of fighting secret wars or even initiating most covert operations [because] when...we mine harbors in Nicaragua...we fuzz the difference between ourselves and the Soviet Union. We act out of character...When we yield to what is, in my judgment, a childish temptation to fight the Russians on their own terms and in their own gutter, we make a major mistake and throw away one of our great assets.[44]

At the other end of the ethical spectrum is a point of view so nationalistic that the use of almost any form of covert action might be considered acceptable by some, if it would serve the national interest. The specific consequences of a covert action – the protection and advancement of the state – become more important than the means one adopts. According to this "consequentialist" perspective, in the light of the anarchic and hostile world environment in which we live, a nation must defend itself in every possible way, including the full range of dark arts available through the auspices of a nation's secret services. As the Hoover Commission advised America's leaders in 1954: "We must learn to subvert, sabotage, and destroy our enemies by more clever, more sophisticated and more effective methods than those used against us."[45]

Two former CIA officials have extolled this realist approach to covert action in the context of the Cold War (with logic that presumably applies to terrorism today). "The United States is faced with a situation in which the major world power opposing our system of government is trying to expand its power by using covert methods of warfare," argued Ray Cline, a senior analyst, referring to the Soviet Union. "Must the United States respond like a man in a barroom brawl who will fight only according to Marquis of Queensberry rules?"[46] G. Gordon Liddy, an Agency operative (and later a Watergate conspirator), stated the case more bluntly: "The world isn't Beverly Hills; it's a bad neighborhood at two o'clock in the morning."[47] The CIA would have to act accordingly.

One thing is certain: covert action is tricky in more than one sense of the word. For example, certain conditions must be present for success, such as an indigenous resistance movement supported by the CIA against an outside invader, as in the Afghanistan model during the 1980s. It helps, also, to have a willing partner in the region, as was Pakistan during the Afghanistan covert action during the Reagan years; or, in another example, the Northern Alliance of local Afghanis, who joined with the CIA soon after 9/11 in attacking the Taliban regime in Afghanistan, which had provided a safe haven for Bin Laden and other Al Qaeda leaders. Further, the more allies the better. Britain, China, Egypt, and Saudi Arabia joined with Pakistan and the United States in support of the *mujahideen*'s struggle against the Soviet invaders during the 1980s.[48]

Moreover, covert action outcomes can be highly unpredictable, for history is known to push back. Often there are long-range unanticipated, and detrimental, consequences that result from secret interventions. In the Guatemalan coup of 1954, for instance, the United Fruit Company was no doubt pleased at the outcome at the time – a result also sought by the U.S. Congress; but the impoverished citizens of that nation had to endure repressive regimes after the CIA intervention. As journalist Anthony Lewis writes, "The coup began a long national descent into savagery."[49] Not until 1986 did Guatemala enjoy a civilian government, in yet another change aided by the Agency. Moreover, following twenty-six years of repressive rule by the Shah of Iran (placed in power by the United States and the United Kingdom), the people of that nation rose up in revolt in 1979 and threw their support behind the nation's mullahs and a fundamentalist religious regime – one that remains at odds with the West.

Even the celebrated ousting of the Soviets from Afghanistan during the 1980s, which one experienced CIA operative has referred to as "the most effective [covert action] in the spy agency's history,"[50] had a down side. The Soviet defeat set the stage for the rise of the fundamentalist Taliban regime and its support for Al Qaeda during the build up for the terrorist attacks against New York City and Washington, DC in 2001. Moreover, the Stinger missiles and other CIA weaponry were never returned to Langley; they remained in the hands of Al Qaeda terrorists, Taliban extremists, and Iranians who purchased them on the open market from *mujahideen* warriors after the Soviets fled Afghanistan. "You get all steamed up backing a rebel group for reasons that are yours and not theirs," President Kennedy's National Security Adviser McGeorge Bundy once cautioned. "Your reasons run out of steam and theirs do not."[51]

The CIA's assassination plots against foreign heads of state eventually became known to the world and left an impression of the United States as a global Godfather. This was hardly the image most Americans desired in a Cold War contest with the communist nations to win the allegiance of people around the world. Moreover, say that Castro had been killed during the Kennedy years. He would have been replaced by his brother, Raoul, who was equally truculent toward the United States. Furthermore, to order the killing of foreign leaders is to invite retaliation against one's own chief of state – and in the democracies our leaders are much more accessible and vulnerable. Assassination plots open a Pandora's box. As a Yale University School of Law professor has written: "Assassination in any form presents a cascading threat to world order."[52] Such has been the history of assassinations between Israelis and Palestinians, with murder plots see-sawing back and forth endlessly between the two without any resolution to the major policy differences that divide them.

Of course, one person's perception of long-term negative effects may be countered by another's delight over short-term gains. Looking back on the Iranian coup, for example, DCI Colby argued that "the assistance to the Shah to return in 1953 was an extremely good move which gave Iran twenty-five years of progress before he was overthrown. Twenty-five years is no small thing."[53] He might have added that neither is a quarter-century of low prices for Americans at their gas pumps, which this allegiance with the Shah assisted.[54]

For Daugherty, the CIA's "finest hour" of covert action occurred in Poland near the end of the Cold War, when the Agency helped to prevent a Soviet invasion of that nation and aided its movement toward democracy, setting an example for the rest of Central Europe.[55] Another former DCI, Stansfield Turner (1977–80), points to the CIA's covert propaganda program aimed at communist regimes during the Cold War as a particularly effective use of covert action. "Certainly one thinks that the book programs [smuggling behind the Iron Curtain books and other reading materials that were critical of communism in general and the Soviet regime in particular], the broadcast programs, the information programs do good," he has said. "When you get facts into a country where the truth is not a common commodity, you're doing some good."[56]

Guidelines for covert action

As these illustrations suggest, special activities can be useful. This fact was demonstrated by the U.S. rout of the Taliban in Afghanistan immediately following the 9/11 attacks. The first U.S. casualty in that counterattack against Al Qaeda and its Taliban hosts was Johnny Michael "Mike" Spann of Winfield, Alabama, a CIA/SOG officer. America's combination of Special Forces, B-52 bombing, CIA paramilitary operations, and help from the local Northern Alliance in Afghanistan during 2001–02 provides a model of how covert action and overt force can be effectively intertwined to defeat enemies of democracy. Yet we know that the use of covert action can also be acutely embarrassing and damaging to a nation's reputation: witness the Bay of Pigs, the assassination plots, and the Iran–*contra* scandal. Hoping to avoid potential embarrassments caused by inappropriate CA activities, William H. Webster crafted a set of questions he posed to the Operations Directorate throughout his tenure as DCI (1987–91) each time its officers brought him a covert action proposal:

- Is it legal? [with respect to U.S. law, not necessarily international law]
- Is it consistent with American foreign policy and, if not, why not?
- Is it consistent with American values?
- If it becomes public, will it make sense to the American people?[57]

These questions make good sense and carry with them a set of principles that should be remembered by all covert action planners.

So should the admonition of former presidential adviser Clark Clifford, a drafter of the National Security Act of 1947. In his testimony before the Church Committee in 1975, he stressed that special activities should be adopted only in circumstances that "truly affect our national security." Cyrus Vance, who would become Secretary of State in the Carter Administration, advanced a similar thesis before the Committee. Covert action, he emphasized, should be used only when "absolutely essential."[58]

Planting propaganda in the media of fellow democracies and tampering with democratic elections hardly seem to qualify as acceptable practices under these standards. Indeed, one should be skeptical about all covert actions designed to manipulate fellow democratic regimes. Professor Roger Fisher of Harvard University's School of Law has it right. "To join some adversaries in the grotesque world of poison dart-guns and covert operations," he reasons, "is to give up the most powerful weapons we have: idealism, morality, due process of law, and belief in the freedom to disagree, including the right of other countries to disagree with ours."[59]

One should reject, too, special activities that target a nation's environment and food supplies; or those that involve lethal targeting against individuals – except in the case of terrorist leaders wanted for murder who resist arrest for purposes of a fair trial. Al Qaeda was responsible for the death of nearly 3,000 Americans on September 11, 2001, with additional killings in Iraq, Afghanistan, Syria, and elsewhere thereafter. Like ISIS, it hopes to bring about even larger casualties in the West. These terrorist groups are worthy targets for many of the covert action options presented in the ladder of escalation. The democracies of the world should coordinate their special activities against the enemies of open societies, just as they do their intelligence collection operations. Terrorists – with their agenda of suicide bombings, beheadings, mass executions, and savage attacks against schoolgirls, aid workers, and other innocents – have revealed themselves as barbarians. Even against such brutal adversaries, however, the West must avoid abandoning its own moral values by adopting the indiscriminate use of covert actions that reach beyond a pin-pointed targeting of Al Qaeda, ISIS, and related terrorist organizations.

Covert action will continue to have a significant role in the defense of the democracies against terrorist organizations, as well as in opposition to totalitarian and authoritarian regimes. In the practice of these dark arts, however, the democracies risk taking on some of the attributes of the very enemies they oppose; therefore, the conduct of covert action must be narrowly cast, closely supervised, and sparingly used.

4 Counterintelligence

The Hunt for Moles

In October and November 1969, the anti-war movement brought thousands of protesters to Washington, DC, in the largest mass demonstrations ever witnessed in the United States. Not only the draft-age youth of America, but the entire nation was obsessed with the war in Indochina. In turn, the Nixon Administration became obsessed with the rising tide of protests that ebbed and flowed along the Mall in Washington to within a stone's throw of the Oval Office. At one point, presidential aides encircled the White House grounds with DC Metro buses, as if the protesters were Apaches and the executive office buildings an imperiled wagon train in the western territories. As historian Theodore H. White recalled, "Perplexed by a street madness which seemed beyond the control of either his staff, his own efforts, or the FBI, [President Nixon] groped for solutions."[1]

Following riots by youthful protesters in April 1969, the President ordered one of his closest advisers, John Ehrlichman, to prepare a report on possible Soviet involvement in the financing of the student protest movement. Just as with President Lyndon B. Johnson before him, President Nixon could not believe that he or his policies could be so unpopular; there had to be a sinister foreign hand involved behind the scenes, inciting college radicals to turn against their own country by paying them off perhaps or by brainwashing them – maybe both. Ehrlichman turned to the Intelligence Community for answers, but they rejected the hypothesis of foreign involvement. There was simply no evidence to support the allegation. These were "credit card revolutionaries," as one intelligence officer put it, using their parents' credit cards to travel around the country demonstrating against a war they found illegitimate and unworthy of U.S. involvement.[2] Ehrlichman reported this conclusion to the President, but both men remained skeptical that the intelligence agencies had sufficiently probed the possibility that Soviet "active measures" might be the hidden hand behind the riots.

Two months later, in June 1969, Ehrlichman heard about a young White House aide on Pat Buchanan's speech-writing staff, a twenty-nine-year-old by the name of Tom Charles Huston. As an activist Republican and head of the Young Americans for Freedom (YAF, a right-leaning student association) while an undergraduate at Indiana University, Huston had gained first-hand experience in confronting anti-war campus protesters; he was articulate and impassioned about their lack of patriotism. He saw the protesters as unwashed, unruly, and disdainful of authority; they were, in his opinion, often bearded, shabbily dressed, and on the far left of the political spectrum, undermining the security of the United States by opposing the communist containment policy in Southeast Asia pursued by the Johnson and now the Nixon Administrations.

After college, Huston had joined the Army as an intelligence officer and was assigned to the Pentagon. During off-hours, he engaged in volunteer work for the Nixon presidential campaign. A bright, hard-working individual, he soon attracted attention among Nixon's senior assistants and, when his military tour came to an end, he had a job waiting for him in Buchanan's shop. Huston made clear to his new boss his deep-seated disdain for the tatterdemalion demonstrators marching through the streets of America. When Buchanan heard about the failure of the Intelligence Community to uncover a connection between the protesters and the Soviet Union, he shared the President's disbelief and suggested to Ehrlichman that Huston conduct a study of his own on behalf of the White House. After all, Huston wasn't much older than most of the protesters, had witnessed their tactics close-up at Indiana University, and knew more about radical ("New Left") student politics than anyone else in the White House. Buchanan informed Ehrlichman that his young aide shared the President's suspicions about Soviet ties to America's domestic unrest.

Ehrlichman called Huston into his West Wing office and, in the name of the President, charged him with the task of preparing a thorough report on the possibility of Soviet involvement in the funding of the anti-war movement in the United States. A brief pep talk in the Oval Office from the President followed. The young Indianan, slightly built with a finely boned face, spectacles, prematurely thinning hair, and little experience in Washington, suddenly found himself in a commanding position to carry on his opposition to the hippies who (he was convinced) were undermining American society. With a sense of zeal, he set out for the office of William C. Sullivan, the assistant director for domestic intelligence at the FBI – the number three official in the Bureau beneath the legendary J. Edgar Hoover and his deputy. Sullivan was the government's top counterintelligence officer, responsible for discovering and thwarting threats to the Republic from home-grown subversives, as well as from hostile intelligence services operating inside the United States – especially the Soviet KGB. His office was the place to begin in Huston's effort to stop KGB support for American student anti-war protests and protect the White House.

Huston informed Sullivan about his orders from Nixon and Ehrlichman. The President wanted to know everything about the anti-war movement, "especially," Sullivan remembers the youthful White House aide emphasizing, "all information possible relating to foreign influences and the financing of the New Left." Sullivan replied to Huston that the White House would have to put this request in writing to the redoubtable Mr. Hoover. At the time, the FBI Director was in his twilight years at the Bureau, past the official retirement age, and increasingly uneasy about any controversy that might strip him of his beloved position as head of the Bureau. Huston returned to his White House office and wrote a letter that informed the FBI Director – the nation's self-anointed foremost authority on the Red Menace – that U.S. intelligence about the influence of communists on the anti-war movement was "inadequate." The President wanted to know what intelligence gaps existed on this subject, as well as what steps could be taken to provide the maximum possible intelligence coverage of the street radicals who were tearing the nation apart. Huston sent a similar message to the leaders of the CIA (DCI Richard Helms), the NSA (Admiral Noel Gayler), and the DIA (General Donald Bennett) – all with a June 31 deadline for a written response back to the White House.

When the responses came back to Huston, among them was an argument from Sullivan that the FBI would need increased sigint authority to obtain the information the President wanted. Sullivan stressed that "increasingly closer links between [domestic radicals] and foreign communists in the future" remained a real danger.[3] The White House found the responses from the intelligence chieftains still lacking, however, in the search for a clear confirmation of its suspected link between Soviet intelligence and the hippie demonstrators.

Huston persevered. In the coming months, he developed a close working relationship with Sullivan, a man his father's age. Together, they worked out a plan to convince Hoover and the other leaders of America's secret agencies to lower the legal barriers that barred intelligence collection against domestic protesters inside the United

States. A year after he began this quest, Huston finally managed in June 1970 to arrange an Oval Office meeting between the President and the four intelligence leaders. Based on briefing notes provided to him by Huston, President Nixon told Helms, Hoover, Gayler, and Bennett that the demonstrators were "reaching out for the support – ideological and otherwise – of foreign powers," and that the radicals were trying to "destroy their country." He ordered the group to "insure that the fullest possible inter-agency cooperation is being realized and that all our resources are being utilized to gather the types of information which will enable us to halt the spread of this terrorism before it gets completely out of hand."[4]

Twenty days later, on July 25, 1970, following a series of intense work sessions with their top aides, the intelligence chiefs met again, this time in Hoover's office at FBI Headquarters in downtown Washington. They had gathered to sign the top secret (since declassified) forty-three-page "Special Report" that became known in the White House as the Huston Plan. The report provided a list of existing restraints on collection that the President should lift, thus enabling the Intelligence Community to spy on the war dissenters (see the examples in Figure 4.1). In a shocking episode

Communications Intelligence. Recommendation:
    Present interpretation should be broadened to permit and [sic] program for coverage by NSA of the communications of U.S. citizens using international facilities.

Electronic Surveillances and Penetrations. Recommendation:
    Present procedures should be changed to permit intensification of coverage of individuals and groups in the United States who pose a major threat to the internal security.
    ALSO, present procedures should be changed to permit intensification of coverage of foreign nations.... [the rest of this paragraph remains classified].

Mail Coverage. Recommendation:
    Restrictions on legal coverage [that is, examining the writing and postmarks on the outside of envelopes] should be removed.
    ALSO, present restrictions on covert coverage [that is, reading the message inside] should be relaxed on selected targets of priority foreign intelligence and internal security interest.

Surreptitious Entry. [that is, the break-in option] Recommendation:
    Present restrictions should be modified to permit procurement of vitally needed foreign [a still classified section] material.
    ALSO, present restrictions should be modified to permit selective use of this technique against other urgent and high priority internal security targets.

Development of Campus Sources. Recommendation:
    Present restrictions should be relaxed to permit expanded coverage of violence-prone campus and student-related groups.
    ALSO, CIA coverage of American students (and others) traveling or living abroad should be increased.

Use of Military Undercover Agents. Recommendation:
    Present restrictions should be retained.

Figure 4.1   Key recommendations in the Huston Plan, 1970

in the annals of American intelligence history, each of the intelligence leaders signed the document that authorized hitherto illegal operations inside the United States. Huston and his mentor, William Sullivan, had achieved their goal of enlisting America's secret services in the internal domestic struggle against the anti-war protesters.

As historian White has observed, the methods proposed in the Huston Plan reached "all the way to every mailbox, every college campus, every telephone, every home" in America.[5] A memorandum accompanying the Huston Plan, addressed to the President and written by Huston, raised – and quickly dismissed – questions about the legality of two collection techniques in particular: covert mail cover and surreptitious entry. "Covert [mail] coverage is illegal, and there are serious risks involved," he wrote. "However, the advantages to be derived from its use outweigh the risks."[6] As for surreptitious entries – break-ins, or "second-story jobs" in FBI lingo – Huston advised: "Use of this technique is clearly illegal: it amounts to burglary. It is also highly risky and could result in great embarrassment if exposed. However, it is also the most fruitful tool and can produce the type of intelligence which cannot be obtained in any other fashion."[7] With the provisions of this top secret document, the young White House aide was asking nothing less than for the President to sanction lawlessness inside the United States by the Intelligence Community – or, at any rate, four of its top agencies: the CIA, FBI, NSA, and DIA. The agencies themselves had worked with Huston to craft rationales for the use of these illegal operations. On July 14, President Nixon signed his approval of the recommendations. Chillingly, the Huston Plan was now secret presidential policy.

The plan, however, proved short-lived. The Attorney General, John Mitchell, learned of the President's authorization for the collection procedures and urged Nixon to reconsider, on grounds that the "risk of public disclosure...was greater than the possible benefits to be derived."[8] Hoover, too, began to have second thoughts. His feelings of job insecurity were magnified by the possibility that the Huston Plan might be publicly disclosed. He might be fired if any of these machinations leaked to the media. Hoover withdrew his support only days after signing off on the scheme, at which point the Huston Plan collapsed and the President rescinded his initial approval. The broad attack on American civil liberties aimed at the anti-war movement, whose members (except for a few criminal elements in the Weather and Black Panther factions) were simply exercising their First Amendment rights to protest a government decision, had been stopped short.

Or so it seemed. Five years later, the Church Committee would discover that the intelligence agencies had been involved in improper domestic spying both before the Huston Plan and after its rescission, all in the name of counterintelligence – protecting the nation against hostile (and, it turned out, virtually non-existent) Soviet influences among America's youth.[9] In 1975, the Church Committee called Huston as its chief witness for public hearings into the startling domestic spy caper. Five years after the fact, he expressed remorse for his role in the drafting of the plan that bore his name:

> The risk was that you would get people who would be susceptible to political considerations as opposed to national security considerations. Or would construe political considerations to be national security considerations, to move from the kid with the bomb to the kid with a picket sign, and from the kid with the picket sign to the kid with the bumper sticker of the opposing candidate. And you just keep going down the line.[10]

The case provides an important, indeed fundamental, lesson in counterintelligence: however vital this intelligence mission is – and there should be no doubt that the democracies have genuine enemies who must be identified and thwarted by a well-trained counterintelligence corps – one has to be on guard constantly against the use of this tradecraft to spy against the very law-abiding citizens whom the secret agencies have been established to shield in the first place. Sound security measures against genuine threats at home and abroad, yes; turning the democracies into Orwellian "Counterintelligence States," like North Korea, no.

The proper focus of counterintelligence as an intelligence mission

In the United States, an executive order offers this definition of counterintelligence (CI):

> Counterintelligence means information gathered and activities conducted to identify, deceive, exploit, disrupt or protect against espionage, other intelligence activities, sabotage or assassination conducted for or on behalf of foreign powers, organizations or persons or their agents, or international terrorist organizations or activities.[11]

Stated simply, the task of CI is to thwart hostile acts perpetrated against one's nation by foreign intelligence agencies, terrorist factions, and internal subversives.

Ambush at the agency

The dangers to the free societies from hostile regimes and terrorists are palpable – everything from attacking computers in the democracies (an electronic Pearl Harbor, as some specialists envision a massive, modern-day cyberattack) to murdering their citizens. Consider, for example, one dreadful January morning in 1993. At 8:00 a.m. on a work day, a long line of CIA employees queued up in their automobiles at a traffic signal on Dolly Madison Highway, preparing to make a left turn into the main entrance of the Agency's 213-acre, forested compound at Langley. Just another ordinary morning for commuters – until suddenly a strange noise became audible to those waiting at the stop light. Perhaps a fender bender had occurred somewhere in the queue. But the noise grew louder and sounded more like firecrackers popping. Then the source of the noise became all too clear.

Carrying an AK-47, a dark-haired man of stocky, medium build, dressed in brown, his face stone cold, his eyes unblinking, had walked up to the first of the idling cars, a Volkswagen, and fired into the open window, striking the driver in the back as he leaned away from the barrel. The assailant then started to trot toward the next car, and the next, spraying bullets into the windows at close range – some seventy rounds in all. As witnesses recall, glass shattered, car horns blared, and people screamed or prayed that the weapon would run out of ammunition.[12] The murderer, a Pakistani national by the name of Mir Aimal Kansi, raced back to the first car and finished off the driver as the wife of the dying CIA officer opened the door on the passenger side and ducked for cover. Kansi then ran to his brown station wagon parked nearby and sped away from the scene. Two Agency employees slumped against their steering wheels, blood seeping from bullet holes in their bodies. Down the line of cars, others moaned in the agony of their wounds.

Kansi escaped back to Pakistan, flying out of the United States that same day. His expired passport went unnoticed by airport security. It took four-and-a-half years for the CIA and the FBI to track him down at a small village in his homeland, but he was captured and returned to the United States for a trial. A day after his conviction in 1997, four American oil executives were killed in Karachi, Pakistan, in apparent retaliation. In 2002, Kansi was put to death by lethal injection at the Greensville Correctional Center in Jarratt, Virginia. Hours before, he said that he had carried out his attack to protest U.S. policies toward Muslim countries.

The Oklahoma City bombing

On April 19, 1995 – one of the most calamitous days in the nation's history – the United States suffered a different kind of assault, one that proved even more lethal. That morning in Oklahoma City, a rental truck sat parked at a curb downtown, near the entrance to the Alfred P. Murrah Federal Building. In the truck's storage space, a homemade bomb composed of fifty-five-gallon drums suddenly erupted in a powerful blast, fueled by a mixture of ammonium nitrate and nitromethane. The date marked the second anniversary of a fatal assault by the FBI on the Branch Davidian sect near Waco, Texas, which resulted in the death of seventy-six people – a symbol for some "patriot" groups of the growing danger posed by the federal government in Washington.

The Oklahoma City explosion, triggered by an alienated young military veteran, Timothy McVeigh, who seethed with anti-government rage, was the worst terrorist attack in the United States since a bomb exploded in front of the Morgan Bank on Wall Street, September 16, 1920, killing thirty-eight men and women.[13] In a letter written shortly before the bombing of the Murrah Building, McVeigh said that he had shifted from being an "intellectual" in the anti-government movement to being an "animal" determined to shed blood in honor of his cause.[14] The bombing left 168 people dead, including 19 children, and injured more than 500 other individuals.[15] Careless in his plans for escape (his car license plate was out of date, for instance), McVeigh was quickly captured as he fled Oklahoma City. Conviction and a death sentence soon followed.

One of the many questions raised by the Oklahoma City bombing was the extent to which the FBI had succeeded in placing counter-intelligence informants inside patriot groups of the kind to which McVeigh had belonged. A well-placed informant – a "mole," in counterintelligence spytalk – could have warned the Bureau of the planned attack.[16]

Treason inside the CIA and the FBI

Sometimes America's counterintelligence failures result not in the death of U.S. citizens at home, but in the targeting of its agents and operations abroad. The cases of Aldrich "Rick" Hazen Ames of the CIA and Robert Hanssen of the FBI, who began their spying for the Soviet Union at about the same time in 1984, are prime illustrations.[17] Ames was a senior counterintelligence officer within the Agency who had responsibilities for the Soviet Union. From that perch, he knew the identities of most CIA assets in the USSR and had knowledge of the Agency's collection activities, covert actions, and counterintelligence operations aimed at this most important of all the West's Cold War targets. A senior CIA counterintelligence officer, Paul J. Redmond, who helped uncover Ames's treachery, told the Aspin–Brown Commission in 1995 that the traitor had essentially ruined the CIA's ability to spy against the Soviets during the final years of the Cold War.[18]

Ames had engaged in espionage for the Soviets and then the Russians from 1984 to 1994, when his deceit was finally uncovered. Clues to his treasonous behavior had been there all along: questionable responses to the periodic polygraph tests given to all Agency employees (although he was given a pass by the examiners anyway); the absence of a mortgage on his $540,000 home in Arlington, Virginia; the purchase of a pricey new Jaguar automobile; expensive cosmetic dental work; a new wardrobe; increased foreign travel – all on a $70,000-a-year government salary. Yet Ames was hardly the only person at Langley to have a fancy house and car; the Agency has a number of well-to-do officers, individuals of independent wealth drawn through a sense of patriotism or a quest for adventure to a life of sleuthing on behalf of the United States.

Ames, though, stood out in other ways as well. The "corridor file" (rumors at Agency Headquarters) about him had been negative long before his misdeeds were uncovered. He was widely known as a drunkard. This fact, plus the surplus of money in his pockets significantly over a bureaucrat's salary, raised questions among some colleagues. When they inquired about the new Jag and the fancy home, however, Ames brushed them off with stories of his Colombian wife (who was his partner in espionage), who, he claimed, had recently inherited money from her family. Moreover, since Ames's father had been a well-regarded DO officer for decades (which provided the son with a halo effect), and because drunkenness was hardly page-one news at Langley, his colleagues accepted the explanations and moved on.

For Ames, the motivation for treason had been chiefly financial; an earlier divorce settlement had drained his bank account. Moreover, the challenge of evading detection became something of a fascinating game for him. The money wasn't bad: the Soviets and, after the Cold War, the Russians paid him more than $4.6 million for his handiwork. Redmond, the CI investigator, provided the Aspin–Brown commissioners with details about the painstaking detective work that finally exposed the Soviet mole ("walking back the cat," in counterintelligence terminology). It was an example of the CIA and the FBI effectively working together, which is not always the case. The damage assessment of Ames's spying revealed substantial setbacks for the United States. His sale of secrets to the KGB and its successor, the SVR, had led to the murder of at least ten Agency assets operating inside the government in Moscow. Further, the SVR's counterintelligence unit succeeded in rolling up more than 200 Agency intelligence operations against the Kremlin, based in part on Ames's tipoffs.

No one in Washington knew at the time that while the Aspin–Brown Commission was investigating the Ames case, his foul work was being complemented by another major Soviet asset inside the U.S. government: FBI agent Robert Hanssen, who had been working off and on for the KGB and the SVR throughout the previous two decades. Not until 2001 was the Bureau able to track down this Russian mole – thanks to a CIA agent inside the SVR who helped tag Hanssen and Ames (neither of whom knew about this particular Agency asset in Moscow). With a job high up in the FBI's Soviet counterintelligence division, Hanssen – like Ames – was well placed to inform the Kremlin about U.S. espionage activities against the Soviet Union and, subsequently, Russia. He reinforced many of the secrets that Ames had provided to his spymasters in Moscow; together, Hanssen and Ames managed to finger almost all of the CIA and FBI assets working against the Soviet and Russian targets. In addition, Hanssen told the SVR precisely where the Bureau had planted listening devices within the new Russian embassy (on Wisconsin Avenue in Georgetown) as it was being constructed; and he revealed to his handlers top secret information about exactly how American officials planned to continue emergency governance if a nuclear war broke out with Russia, as well as key information about U.S. underwater sigint capabilities for tracking enemy submarines.[19]

In Hanssen's case, the motivation for treason was less financial than had been the case with Ames, although Hanssen did request some payment in gems that were valued at $1.4 million (about a fourth of the payoff to Ames). Hanssen lavished these profits on a friend, an attractive stripper in DC, whom he had met at a bar. Professing to be a deeply religious Catholic, he spent little of these ill-gotten gains on himself and seemed primarily interested in a game of counterintelligence cat-and-mouse (could he evade his FBI and CIA counterintelligence colleagues?), as well as attempting to "save" his new-found barroom friend from her wayward life.

Sloppy tradecraft on both their parts, coupled with clues from the CIA's mole in Moscow, eventually gave Ames and Hanssen away, and now they are serving life sentences in U.S. federal penitentiaries.

The 9/11 attacks

The greatest counterintelligence failure in American history, though, came within the domain of counterterrorism – namely, the inability to stop Al Qaeda terrorists from striking the U.S. homeland on September 11, 2001. Certainly opportunities presented themselves for blocking the attacks. As early as 1995, the CIA's Counterterrorism Center (CTC) warned the White House and other government officials that "aerial terrorism" could strike inside the United States, with terrorists hijacking commercial aircraft and flying them into skyscrapers[20] – precisely what happened that heart-wrenching September morning. Recall from Chapter 2, though, that missing in this warning were any specifics about when and where such an event might occur – that is, actionable intelligence. Moreover, the warning about this danger was inserted into a list of many other threats, including chemical or biological attacks against urban areas by terrorists piloting crop-duster airplanes with anthrax or disease agents in their spray tanks; the contamination of U.S. water supplies with toxins; and the bombing of America's nuclear reactors.

The litany of dangers seemed to have the effect of paralyzing officials, preventing them from doing anything about any of the unsettling possibilities – although one would have thought the Clinton Administration would at least have shared this warning with the Department of Transportation (responsible for airport security) and the American Pilots Association. Another obstacle to action was no doubt the costs involved for defending against the eventuality of aerial terrorism, such as strengthening airport security, sealing cockpit doors, and hiring sky marshals – although each of these measures summed to a minuscule expense compared to dealing with the loss of life and the aftermath of the 9/11 attacks. Wishful thinking that aerial terrorism would never happen inside the United States trumped the political risks of advocating the spending of finite resources on events that might never take place. So did the press of daily events and the numbing effect that accompanied the thought of a wide range of other possible attacks – all expensive to deter.

The nation's experience with the devastation of Hurricane Katrina in 2005 points to a comparable scenario. If the political leaders and citizens of New Orleans had been willing to pay the billions of dollars necessary to strengthen the surrounding levees to withstand a Level 5 hurricane, the people of that great city would have been spared the catastrophic flooding that occurred, along with the immense costs and tragic deaths that came with the crisis.

Both the 9/11 attacks and the Katrina event point to a vexing public policy challenge: what should political leaders do when it comes to high-cost, low-probability contingencies?

With respect to the 9/11 attacks, better surveillance in California against two of the nineteen terrorists who hijacked the airplanes might have unraveled the plot as well. Instead, both the CIA and the FBI fumbled this assignment and worked together with all the good will and camaraderie of Kilkenny cats. The Bureau's headquarters personnel failed, as well, to respond to alerts from their own agents that suspicious flight-training activity was taking place in Phoenix, Arizona, and Minneapolis, Minnesota. In the context of the aerial terrorism report on 1995, these agent field reports should have set off multiple alarms at the J. Edgar Hoover FBI Building in downtown Washington – especially the case of the suspicious figure in Minneapolis, Zacarias Moussaoui, who had known connections to terrorists abroad.[21] Further, on the Hill, lawmakers on SSCI and HPSCI sat on their hands from 1995 to 2001, holding few hearings on terrorism, counterintelligence, or CIA–FBI surveillance cooperation.

Then, when, in January 2001, the Clinton Administration's chief of counterterrorism, Richard A. Clarke, warned the new National Security Adviser of the Bush Administration, Condoleezza Rice, that the NSC should act immediately to guard against an Al Qaeda attack aimed at the United States, it took Rice until September 4, 2001, to convene the first Council meeting of principals on this topic.[22] The counterintelligence errors seemed to metastasize like a terrible cancer in the decade preceding the attacks. Above all, the U.S. intelligence agencies lacked a mole inside the Al Qaeda organization, or even much historical understanding among its analysts of this terrorist organization.

A parade of traitors

While these cases are the most well known of the major counterintelligence and counterterrorism setbacks for the United States in recent years, they are hardly the only ones. Even during World War II, the United States was dealing with Soviet moles in the Manhattan Project. As Haynes, Klehr, and Vassiliev report, a British scientist by the name of Klaus Fuchs, affiliated with the Manhattan Project, worked secretly for the Soviets and managed to steal enough secrets about the construction of nuclear weaponry to save the Kremlin years of delay and millions of rubles in acquiring the atomic bomb – which it managed to do much more quickly than anticipated by the CIA.[23] The Soviets had other atomic spies, including David Greenglass, Russell McNutt, and Ethel Rosenberg – all part of the Julius Rosenberg spy ring. In the collection discipline of signals intelligence, the Soviets also recruited William Weisband, a sigint officer who informed the Soviets about America's ability to eavesdrop on their military communications (the Venona program). According to Haynes and his co-authors, the KGB was successful in suborning the influential left-leaning journalist I.F. Stone, too; and, according to most experts (although not all), Soviet military intelligence – the GRU – most likely recruited the senior State Department official Alger Hiss as a well-placed agent.

From the end of World War II through the 1950s, Haynes, Klehr, and Vassiliev calculate that the Soviets were able to entice some 500 Americans to spy on their behalf – chiefly private-sector engineers, not government officials. Many of these "spies" caused little damage to U.S. security and probably fooled their Kremlin handlers into thinking they were more valuable than they really were (a chronic problem for those in the business of recruiting agents for counterintelligence or intelligence collection). Clearly, though, a few individuals – like Fuchs and Weisband – were significant Soviet penetrations.

In another example of successful spying by the Soviet Union against the United States later in the Cold War, the Walker family pedaled U.S. Navy communications intelligence to Moscow during the 1960s. Among the items sold by the Walkers to the KGB was top-secret information about the U.S. Intelligence Community's underwater listening grid in the Atlantic Ocean that was able to track the movement of Soviet submarines. The Walkers also provided their handlers in Moscow with data on the firing codes for U.S. submarine-launched ballistic missiles (SLBMs), which in time of war would have given the Kremlin an opportunity to neutralize this important sea leg of America's nuclear deterrence. Had war erupted between the superpowers, the espionage carried out by the Walker family would have had much greater consequences than even the documents turned over to Moscow by Ames and Hanssen. In 1985, Barbara Walker, divorced and vengeful after being denied alimony payments, finally blew the whistle to the FBI on her former husband John, the leader of the spy ring.

The types of people who turn against their own country, and their motives, have varied over the years.[24] Some of the more prominent additional examples of betrayal by American intelligence officers and outside contractors include the following:

- Jack E. Dunlap worked at the NSA in the 1960s and spied for the Soviet Union, turning over to Moscow reams of useful sigint data.[25]

- Clyde Conrad, a U.S. Army non-commissioned officer, gave the KGB (via Czech and Hungarian "cut-out" – or intermediary – agents) information from 1975 to 1985 about Army operational plans and communications procedures, if war were to break out between the United States and the Soviet Union on the battlefields of Western Europe.[26]
- William Kampiles, a first-year CIA officer, sold the Soviets a manual on U.S. surveillance satellites for a pittance in 1977, hoping evidently – with wild reasoning (or simply a dumb excuse) – that the Agency would then use him as a double agent once he had developed his Soviet contacts.[27]
- William Bell, who worked for a defense contractor, tried to sell data on sensitive technologies to a Polish intelligence officer in 1981 and, instead, found himself in FBI handcuffs.
- Edward Lee Howard of the CIA signed up with the KGB in 1983 (a year before Ames) to sell secrets about the Agency's Moscow operations, then escaped to the Soviet Union when the FBI attempted to nab him.[28]
- Jonathan Jay Pollard and his wife, uncovered in 1985, gave U.S. Navy intelligence data to the Israeli government, because of their attraction to Zionism (although they didn't turn down the $30,000 yearly stipend they were provided by Israel for their ongoing kindnesses).[29]
- Ron Pelton, an NSA intelligence officer, gave highly classified sigint documents to the Soviets from 1980 to 1985, when he was finally arrested.
- Thomas Patrick Cavanagh, a scientist with a defense contractor, offered the Soviets information on advanced U.S. radar capabilities and was grabbed immediately by the FBI in 1985.
- James Hall III, an Army communications specialist, sold secrets to the KGB about U.S. sigint operations in Eastern Europe, until apprehended by counterintelligence investigators in 1988.
- A guard at the American embassy in Moscow, Corporal Clayton J. Lonetree (the first and only Marine ever convicted of espionage), was caught in a sexual entrapment – a "honey trap," in Soviet lingo – arranged by the KGB, which provided him and a few of his fellow guards access to beautiful Russian women ("swallows") in exchange for secret documents from the embassy's vaults, a relationship the guilt-ridden Lonetree finally confessed to in 1986.
- Harold J. Nicolson, the highest ranking CIA officer ever to be charged with treason, was busy spying for the Russians at the same time as Ames, Howard, and Hanssen, until he was caught in 1996 – thanks in part to the new, post-Ames procedures that

required intelligence officers to disclose information to their supervisors at Langley about their personal finances.[30]

- Earl Pitts, an FBI agent spying for the Russians, was detected in 1997.
- Robert C. Kim pled guilty to spying on behalf of South Korea in 1997.[31]
- Brian P. Regan, an Air Force master sergeant assigned as an analyst to the NRO, attempted to sell surveillance satellite data to the Iraqis, Libyans, and Chinese, but was discovered and sentenced to life in prison in 2003.
- A spate of American citizens of Chinese birth have either spied or offered to spy for China, including Larry Wu-tai Chin, a "sleeper agent" at the CIA – a mole-in-waiting, biding his time before he began to steal secrets for China (and who, like Ames, passed his polygraph tests) – caught in 1985; and Dongfan (Greg) Chung and Chi Mak, both California engineers working for defense contractors. Chung was arrested in 1979, and Mak in 2005.

Several of these traitors, along with a number of other minor miscreants, were discovered during the 1980s, and that is why this period is often referred to as "The Decade of the Spy." A high point in the number of captured moles in the United States during that decade was 1985, remembered by experts as "The Year of the Spy."

This rogues gallery sums to a depressing list of counterintelligence setbacks, leading a former CIA counterintelligence officer to concede that "the overall record of United States counterintelligence at catching spies is not good."[32] America, however, has hardly been alone in CI setbacks. Though of small comfort, Great Britain, France, and Germany suffered Soviet penetrations at even higher levels of government than occurred during the Cold War in Washington. Of greater succor perhaps is the fact that the West had its share of penetration successes against the Soviet empire.[33] Moreover, it should be underscored that these American traitors account for only a tiny fraction from among the millions of federal employees who have held sensitive positions in government over the years and have honored the public trust placed in them.

The motivations for treason

A central counterintelligence question is: why do citizens betray their country? Journalist Scott Shane has noted that the mnemonic MICE – for money, ideology, compromise (that is, being blackmailed after one is caught in a compromising circumstance), and ego (an

"I can beat the system" mentality, exhibited by Ames and Hanssen, among others) – sums up the standard answers from experts. He suggests that this rule of thumb should be updated with a new mnemonic: MINCES, adding to the mix that a deep-seated sense among some immigrants of a continuing devotion to their place of birth ("N" for nationalism) can lead them to spy for the "old country," plus "S" for the lure of sex.[34] For political scientists Stan Taylor and Daniel Snow, the reasons for treason by Americans during the Cold War can be broken down into several categories.[35] Greed (money) tops their list at 53.4 percent, followed by ideology at 23.7 percent. Much further down this hierarchy of motivations is ingratiation (5.8 percent), that is, efforts to fulfill a friendship or love obligation, impress a superior, or seduce a sexual partner; and disgruntlement (2.9 percent) – typically on-the-job anger over failure to advance in one's career. A final "other" category accounted for 12.2 percent and includes individuals who fantasized about possible James Bond escapades that might come from flirting with the KGB/SVR or some other foreign intelligence service (the "E" or ego group in MICE).

The capture of several American citizens of Chinese heritage acting for Beijing as moles points to a change in motivations for treason in the United States, at least as discerned in a study authored by Katherine L. Herbig, a Defense Department contractor.[36] Ideological causes were the driving influence for most traitors in the 1940s and during the early stages of the Cold War, according to her analysis. For example, with astounding naïveté about the intent of Joseph Stalin, Klaus Fuchs thought the Soviets would be able to advance world peace more effectively if the U.S.S.R. could match the United States in atomic weaponry. After the atomic spy cases of the 1940s and 1950s, though, Herbig (like Taylor and Snow) discovered that greed began to dominate the explanations for treachery until the end of the Cold War. In more recent years, she (like journalist Scott Shane) detects a trend toward naturalized Americans spying for their previous place of citizenship (China or South Korea, for example) out of a sense of devotion to their heritage. Many of these individuals have proclaimed loyalty to America, but to their nation of heritage as well – a duality that is obviously unacceptable when it leads to the unauthorized disclosure of sensitive national security information from the vaults of spy agencies in the United States.

Catching spies

Catching spies is not easy. Even super sleuth James Angleton, Chief of CIA Counterintelligence from 1954 to 1974, was taken in by the

Soviets in at least one significant instance.[37] A British MI6 liaison officer, Harold A. R. "Kim" Philby, befriended him in Washington while stationed there in the 1960s. The two met frequently for Georgetown lunches and other social events, and often compared notes on their counterintelligence experiences in battling the Soviet Union. Both were well educated (Yale and Harvard for Angleton, Cambridge for Philby), cultured and debonair, and seasoned CI specialists. Yet, all along, Philby was a Soviet mole, working with a number of other well-placed British intelligence officers who had been students with him at university (the so-called "Cambridge Spy Ring") and elected to spy against their own country. When investigators came close to uncovering his true loyalties, Philby fled to Moscow. Angleton had already begun to have suspicions about his British lunch-mate and was starting his own inquiries; nonetheless, his long ties with the MI6 officer were clearly an embarrassment to the Agency's CI Chief when Philby's true allegiances became known.[38]

Thereafter, Angleton turned even more paranoid, a natural occupational hazard for all counterintelligence officers. He redoubled his mole-hunting efforts inside the CIA, perhaps to compensate for his humiliation over the Philby surprise. Critics claimed that Angleton began to point the finger of guilt indiscriminately at colleagues, claiming they were possible Soviet agents without sufficient evidence to substantiate his charges – a form of McCarthyism inside the CIA. Critics complained, as well, that he had been far too passive in his attempts to penetrate governments in the Warsaw Pact (the Soviet satellites in Eastern Europe), since he believed such operations were futile as a result of probable existing penetrations within the CIA by KGB agents, who would immediately tip off the Kremlin.[39]

Angleton supporters retorted that he was just doing his job as a determined and indefatigable counterintelligence professional, one who would have caught Ames had he been CI Chief during the Decade of the Spy. Moreover, they argue, Angleton was hardly passive – indeed, he was the most energetic CI Chief the Agency has ever had, even running penetration and disinformation operations out of the CI Staff offices in the DO that sometimes looked more like covert action than counterintelligence, all with little supervision from the seventh floor at Langley. In one widely reported example, Angleton is said to have doctored the famous "secret speech" delivered by Nikita Khrushchev following the death of Joseph Stalin. By adding deceptive paragraphs to the document and circulating it in Eastern Europe, Angleton apparently hoped to stimulate uprisings against the Soviet regime by painting an even more venal portrait of the Stalinist era than did the unadulterated speech itself.[40]

A British journalist has captured part of the reason for the controversy over Angleton's tenure as CI Chief at Langley. Counterintelligence is "a murky world," he writes, "full of risks, dangers, personal jealousies and never-ceasing suspicions that the man in the office next to yours may be a Soviet agent. It is a situation that creates paranoia, corroding men's characters."[41] Adds political scientist Jervis: "There is no easy answer to the question of how much paranoia is enough."[42]

In 1974, as the accusations about Angleton's excesses swirled in the hallways at Langley, DCI William Colby fired him as CI Chief. The ostensible grounds were that he had too much control over the Agency's relations with Israeli intelligence, but the real reason was the rising number of complaints about his overzealous activities as CI Chief. Some even leveled the farfetched allegation that Angleton was himself a Soviet mole. Others, recklessly, thought that of Colby. No wonder Angleton often referred to counterintelligence as a "wilderness of mirrors."[43] It was hard to know in this surreal realm who was telling the truth and who was lying.

A seasoned CI officer has written: "Except temporarily in the aftermath of spy scandals and major operational failures, the CIA historically has put less emphasis on CI."[44] The judgment of a presidential commission was more blunt in 2005: "U.S. counterintelligence efforts have remained fractured, myopic, and only marginally effective."[45] Just as with the other intelligence missions, America's counterspy operations are far too decentralized ("stovepiped") and lacking in cohesive leadership. At least, though, the 2004 Intelligence Reform and Terrorism Prevention Act created a National Counterterrorism Center, with reporting lines to both the White House and the ODNI. The NCTC has helped to coordinate America's CT efforts against ISIS and other terrorist factions, although most observers view the Center as only partially successful in its attempts to bring "all-source fusion" into the counterintelligence domain.

In 1995, a senior Agency CI officer warned the Aspin–Brown Commission that "we're never going to stop people from 'volunteering' [that is, spying for the enemy]. We just have to learn how to catch them earlier, and to encourage people to report on those engaged in suspicious activities."[46] Catching spies relies on good CI tradecraft – the methods of mole-hunting.

CI tradecraft: security and counterespionage

Counterintelligence tradecraft consists of two complementary halves: security and counterespionage (CE). The former is the passive or defensive side of counterintelligence, while the latter is the offensive or aggressive side.

Security

In Renaissance Venice, a method of security used by the all-mighty Council of Ten was the Lions' Mouths. Marble lions were placed throughout the city with their mouths agape, so "Venetians could inform the Council anonymously of their suspicions of their neighbors" by simply stuffing a hand-written note into the mouth of the beast to finger the threat to society.[47] There were no public trials and no appeals. A favorite punishment was to bury the accused upside-down in the Piazzetta, legs protruding. Happily, those days are passed – although ISIS has its own medieval forms of counterintelligence. In 2016, when one of its senior leaders was killed by a U.S. drone strike in northern Syria, the ISIS counterintelligence unit conducted a witch hunt in an attempt to find informants within the ranks of the terrorist organization. The possession of a mobile phone or an Internet connection could be enough to have a suspected Western spy beheaded, burned alive, or lowered into a vat of acid.

In the more humane democratic societies, counterintelligence relies instead on the maintenance of good security at an intelligence agency, which entails putting in place static defenses against hostile operations aimed at one's country. Such defenses include the screening and clearance of personnel, along with the establishment of programs to safeguard sensitive information, such as extensive investigations into the backgrounds of job candidates.

Other security checks come into play. Polygraph examinations are administered to all new recruits at the CIA, for example, and periodically for those intelligence officers who are already employed. The polygraph is hardly foolproof, though, as the Ames example illustrates. Even before the Ames era, several traitors at the NSA underwent periodic polygraph tests, but their spying for the Soviet Union never came to light.[48] The unreliability of the polygraph can sometimes ruin the reputations of individuals who are innocent but who react poorly when wired up to the machine. In the words of a three-time COS officer at Langley, "[The polygraph] has done great harm to our personnel system and agent base."[49] On occasion, however, lie-detector tests can disclose genuinely suspicious behavior. For example, one prospective Agency employee blurted out during a polygraph "flutter" (CIA slang for the test) that he had murdered his wife and buried her in the backyard – a guaranteed disqualification for a security clearance. On the whole, however, polygraph tests should be weighed with some degree of skepticism.

Additional security measures include electric fences; armed guards accompanied by dogs; Jersey barriers, razor wire, and bollards; locks on vaults and doors; ID badges; education sessions on how to maintain security; a close accounting of sensitive documents by way of sign-in and sign-out systems; computer, email, fax, and telephone monitoring by internal security officers; a censorship of materials written by intelligence officers for public consumption; camouflage; and the use of encoded messages.

Security concerns extend overseas, too. Embassies must protect their personnel and classified documents, for instance. Further, U.S. intelligence officers often find themselves in hostile regions of the world. In 1983, a hashish-drugged terrorist drove a truck filled with explosives into the entrance of the American embassy in Beirut, killing hundreds of Marines and several intelligence officers. In 2000, Al Qaeda terrorists in Yemen attacked the Navy destroyer USS *Cole* moored in the harbor of the capital city, Aden. Seventeen American sailors died in the suicide bombing. In 2009, a double agent – a Jordanian physician by the name of Humam Khali Abu-Mulal al-Balawi, pretending to work for the CIA against Al Qaeda – detonated a bomb concealed beneath a suicide vest while standing near a cluster of Agency officers, gathered to meet with him for a strategy session in Khost, Afghanistan. Among the CIA officers who perished was the COS for Afghanistan, Jennifer Matthews. In each of these instances, tighter security could have prevented the tragedies. For example, at a minimum, prior to the Khost attack, al-Balawi's bona fides should have been more completely vetted by counterintelligence specialists, and he should have been thoroughly searched (as a matter of routine) before the meeting took place.[50]

THE CYBER DIMENSION OF SECURITY   Also vulnerable to hostile assault in recent years are computer systems in democratic regimes, doubly so since the 9/11 attacks and ensuing efforts by the United States and others to share information more effectively via computers that connect their intelligence services and, to some extent, foreign intelligence liaison computers. In the United States, attempts are underway to link up the computers of the seventeen major intelligence agencies, as well as the computers used by state and local counterterrorism authorities. While this improved sharing is vital, it creates a counterintelligence nightmare, with the possibility of a future Ames or Hanssen not only stealing from their own corners of the Intelligence Community but having access to the full IC computer system. "Even as we've greatly expanded information sharing since 9/11," warns a U.S. counterterrorism official, "you still have to think about security and the sensitivity of certain data."[51] Experts in the intelligence agencies and outside IT consultants are laboring intensively to establish reliable firewalls to prevent an all-source Ames from happening. Soon after the end of the Cold War, a senior CIA/CI manager referred to this problem as the No. 1 challenge facing counterintelligence officers; and DNI James Clapper has often referred to cybersecurity as America's foremost intelligence challenge.[52]

As important as cybersecurity is, the efforts by the United States to organize its defenses (and offenses) in this domain remain in a preliminary state. Confusion about lines of authority and responsibility is rampant within a collection of government cyber entities characterized more by their fragmentation than by their unified efforts to protect America against hackers and even more aggressive cyberattacks. Every security agency has its own cyber capacity without sufficient integration with one another – the old "stovepipe" problem in a new setting. Progress is being made on the defensive side of the cyber equation, as stronger firewalls are erected and important steps are taken against future "inside threats" similar to the theft by government contractor and whistle-blower, Edward J. Snowden, of highly classified documents in 2013; but much more thought must go into the offensive side, especially related to the feasibility and the ethics of U.S. cyberattacks as an evolving form of covert action-electronic sabotage.

Additional aspects of computer counterintelligence are the issues of cyber-espionage and cyber-warfare. Cyber-espionage involves attempts to steal U.S. national security or commercial information from the Internet carried out by foreign governments (notoriously, Russian intelligence, as well as China's Ministry of State Security and its Peoples Liberation Army); terrorist organizations (ISIS has exhibited remarkable computer skills in its dissemination of propaganda and the recruitment of young would-be *jihadists*); and mischievous teenage hackers. Cyber-warfare goes a step further and seeks to disrupt or destroy computer networks – a form of cyber covert action. Corporate, stock exchange, and government computers, airport control towers, and subways, as well as American power grids, are among the potential targets for those engaged in cyber-espionage or cyber-warfare. Experts have warned, for example, that China "is in full economic attack" when it comes to cyber-espionage, although the evidence is virtually non-existent – so far – that Beijing has turned to cyber-warfare against the United States. Indeed, China is a country so heavily invested in Wall Street that it would, in a sense, be equivalent to attacking itself.

Clearly, though, China has mounted a full-court press when it comes to cyber-espionage operations, with its top U.S. targets being commercial companies (in search of technical secrets) and the military (weapons blueprints). In addition, China seeks through cyber-operations to retaliate against individuals or groups in the United States who may be placing anti-Chinese commentary on the Internet. The Chinese also manufacture and market computers for worldwide sales, and they often leave in these products a "back door" for electronic access by the government in Beijing – a practice periodically adopted as well by other nations selling computers in the world marketplace.

Despite the logic that China, Russia, and the United States would be better off improving their political and trade relations rather than spying on one another, 160 espionage agents working for China were uncovered in the United States between 1985 and 2016, as well as 161 deployed by Russia during this same period. Economic espionage cases under FBI investigation shot up 53 percent from 2014 to 2015. The targets of these foreign spies have included such companies as U.S. Steel, Alcoa, General Electric, and Westinghouse Electric, among others. The cyber-spies relentlessly search for data on such matters as the construction blueprints for U.S. fighter jet engines and drones. Chinese hacking into the personnel files held by the Office of Personnel Management in Washington, DC captured for Beijing records on 22 million U.S. government workers – valuable information for Chinese counterintelligence officers seeking to spot and recruit agents in America. In one ray of good news on the CI front, Reuters reported in 2016 that Chinese cyber-espionage had fallen by 90 percent in the wake of negotiations between Washington and Beijing over improved trade relations.[53]

Counterintelligence problems have arisen, too, because of the emphasis in the post-9/11 world on sharing data from agency to agency, including better cooperation between the intelligence agencies and law enforcement officials. Often, though, the two groups – spies and cops – fail to see eye-to-eye. Spy-catchers want to secretly follow suspected foreign agents to find out who else belongs in their ring, what their objectives are, and how they operate; in contrast, law enforcement officials tend to think more in terms of immediate arrests and convictions.

In 2010, law enforcement officials in Washington revealed the presence of a Russian spy ring in the United States and arrested its known members, who were deported back to their homeland (where they were greeted as heroes). Counterintelligence officials at the CIA would have much preferred to continue watching their activities for a period of time to learn more about the ring's objectives; but in this case they agreed with FBI law enforcement officials about the need to arrest these agents, because they feared that

Russian intelligence officials were about to close in on an Agency mole in their midst – a "Colonel Shcherbakov" – who had tipped off the CIA about the activities of the Russian network within the United States. The Colonel and his family needed to be exfiltrated and absorbed into American society with new identities before they were captured and the Colonel executed. Despite this congruence of policy among U.S. cops and spies in this instance, much tension and only limited cooperation between the two groups remain the rule.[54]

Counterespionage

The identification of specific adversaries and the development of detailed knowledge about the operations they are planning, or already conducting, are the starting points for successful counter-espionage (CE), which Redmond defines as "the detection and neutralization of human spies."[55] Personnel engaged in CE attempt to block these operations by infiltrating the hostile service or terrorist faction with a mole of their own, an operation known as a penetration, and (alternatively or jointly) by using sundry forms of manipulation to mislead the adversary.

THE PENETRATION   The penetration operation transcends all other counterintelligence tradecraft in its potential value.[56] Since the primary goal of CI is to contain the intelligence services and saboteurs of the enemy, it is desirable to know the enemy's intentions and capabilities in advance; the best way to achieve this objective is through a highly placed infiltrator – a mole – inside the adversary's intelligence service or government, or inside a terrorist cell. In the words of John A. McCone, a DCI from the Kennedy era: "Experience has shown penetration to be the most effective response to Soviet and Bloc [intelligence] services."[57] More recently, DNI Dennis C. Blair observed in 2009 that "the primary way" the Intelligence Community determines which terrorist organizations pose a direct threat to the nation is "to penetrate them and learn whether they're talking about making attacks against the United States."[58] Furthermore, a well-placed mole may be better able than anyone else to determine whether one's own service has been infiltrated by an outsider. Recall, too, that Ames and Hanssen may have escaped detection far longer if the CIA had not had the benefit of an asset inside the Kremlin, unbeknownst to the two traitors, who helped pinpoint their identities.

THE AGENT-IN-PLACE   The methods used for infiltrating an opposition's intelligence service take several forms. Usually the most effective and desirable penetration is the recruitment of an agent-in-place, sometimes called a defector-in-place. He or she is already in the employment of an enemy intelligence service or a terrorist organization and, therefore, close to the documents the United States would like to steal.

THE DOUBLE AGENT   The double agent is another standard method of infiltration, whereby an individual pretends to spy for the intelligence service of his or her own country, but in fact is working all along for the adversary. This approach is costly and time-consuming (some genuine documents need to be given to the agent for passage to the adversary, as a means for supporting his or her bona fides), as well as risky because the loyalty of the agent is often ambiguous and double-crosses are commonplace. Is the double agent really working for the United States or still for the other side? Or perhaps playing both sides for twice the profit? Further complicating matters in the double-agent business is the fact that they can become triple agents. Welcome to Angleton's dizzying maze of mirrors.

THE DEFECTOR   Almost as good as the agent-in-place, and less troublesome to manage than the double agent, is the defector who can bring with him or her a deep knowledge of an enemy's intelligence service or the internal operations of a terrorist group. An agent-in-place is ultimately preferable to the defector, though, because of the former's continuing access to useful information from inside the enemy's camp about the latest plans and capabilities; however, quite often, the agent-in-place is reluctant to stay in place too long, for fear of being caught. This is especially true in nations like Iran and North Korea. or the ISIS terrorist group, where security in each case is sophisticated and the execution of traitors is swift and often brutal. At some point, most agents-in-place plead for exfiltration, as their nightmares increase about the cold barrel of a pistol pressed against the back of their skull by a local counter-intelligence officer or, in the case of ISIS, the awaiting vat of acid.

At times in the United States, the avowed credentials of a defector have remained in dispute for years – sometimes forever – and from time to time this has poisoned relations between the CIA and the FBI. During the 1960s, for example, a disagreement over whether a Soviet defector was genuine or a "false defector" led to the exchange of sharp rebukes between counterintelligence officers in the two agencies. Even DCI Richard Helms and FBI Director J. Edgar Hoover refused to talk to one another for many months as a result of the bad feelings that arose between their organizations.

Four decades later, DCI George Tenet referred to poor CIA–FBI relations as the most serious weakness in the U.S. counterintelligence shield in the lead-up to the 9/11 attacks.[59]

Many of the best assets acquired by the United States, such as Oleg Penkovsky, have been agents-in-place; others have been genuine defectors who initially contacted a U.S. embassy overseas as "walk-ins." They either literally walk into the embassy and volunteer as spies, or perhaps toss classified documents over an embassy wall to make contact (as did Penkovsky, though as an agent-in-place, not a defector). Then, if the CIA accepts their candidacies as spies for America (recall how Penkovsky was rejected at first by the Americans, but not the British), they may be relocated to the United States for debriefing and a new identity, if a defector, or remain inside their original espionage organizations as agents-in-place (the Penkovsky model – which he eventually regretted, no doubt, when he was discovered and executed by the KGB).

Soon after the assassination of President Kennedy, the CIA granted asylum to a Soviet defector by the name of Yuri Nosenko, who offered a central message in his debriefings once inside the United States: the Soviets had nothing to do with the assassination of the President – even though the accused murderer, Lee Harvey Oswald, had temporarily defected to the USSR before the assassination. After an extensive questioning of Nosenko, the FBI concluded that his story was true and signed off on his bona fides; however, James Angleton, the Agency's CI Chief, refused to side with the Bureau's judgment after extensive interrogation sessions with Nosenko at the Agency's training facility in rural Virginia (conducted by the Agency's Office of Security, not Angleton – although he was kept closely informed). The Office of Security held Nosenko for 1,277 days at the facility, in Spartan conditions. Eventually, most of the Intelligence Community – including most of his Agency interrogators – accepted Nosenko as a dependable ally in the struggle against the Soviet Union. He resettled in the Washington, DC area and served as a CIA consultant. Angleton never believed in him, though, or in his core message.

DECEPTION AND DISINFORMATION   Another CE method is to give the enemy a false impression about something, causing him to take actions contrary to his own best interests. As Jervis observes: "Counterintelligence and deception are closely intertwined. Most obviously, the state must fear that the other side is using its agents to convey a false picture. The other side of this coin is that the state can use the other's intelligence service in order to propagate its own deceptions."[60] More mirrors with multiple images and reflections.

Fooling the Germans into believing that D-Day landings would occur in the Pas de Calais, rather than at Normandy, is a classic example of a successful joint American and British deception operation during a turning point of the Second World War. Jervis emphasizes the potential importance of this deception: "Had [Hitler] known that the landings were coming at Normandy or had he released his reserve divisions as soon as the Allied troops hit the beaches, he could have pushed the invaders into the sea."[61]

SURREPTITIOUS SURVEILLANCE AND PROVOCATIONS Counterespionage practitioners are expert as well in tracking suspected moles through the use of audio, mail, physical, and "optical" (photographic, imint, or geoint) surveillance techniques. In 1975, a local terrorist group known as September 17th gunned down a CIA chief of station in Athens, Greece. When his body was flown home for burial at Arlington National Cemetery, Eastern European "diplomats" (actually counterintelligence officers) slipped into the throng of media attending the service and began taking pictures of CIA officers in attendance, as well as recording their automobile license plate numbers.

Since the focus of offensive counterintelligence is the disruption of the enemy service, provocation operations can be an important element of counterespionage. Here the objective is to harass an adversary, perhaps by suppressing or jamming broadcasts emitting from enemy radio and television stations, or by interrupting social media communications. Other methods involve the public disclosure of the names of an enemy's agents or by sending a trouble-making false defector – a "dangle" – into an adversary's midst, someone who is in reality an *agent provocateur* on a short-term mission to sow confusion and dissension, then escape. Some counterintelligence specialists thought this was exactly the mission of SVR Colonel Vitaliy Sergeyevich Yurchenko, who "defected" to the United States in 1995, only three months later to spring from his table while at a Georgetown restaurant with his CIA handler and race up Wisconsin Avenue to the Russian embassy, where he re-defected (as do about half of all defectors). Postmortems on this case remain torn over whether Yurchenko was a dangle all along, or if he became fearful that Russian intelligence officers would harm his family in Russia and thus decided to return home and cooperate with authorities. The fact that Yurchenko was never killed, or even imprisoned, by the Russians lends credence to the hypothesis that he was a false defector engaged in finding out what he could about Agency CI methods (although while in the hands of the CIA he did give up some useful information about Russian spy operations against the United States).

Another case involving a defector, this time from Iran, which was reported in the *New York Times* in August 2016, demonstrates what often happens to defectors who change their minds and return to their homes. In 2009, the CIA recruited a young Iranian nuclear scientist by the name of Shahram Amiri to spy as an agent-in-place on his country's burgeoning WMD program and especially its efforts to build an atomic bomb. When Agency officials grew concerned that Iranian intelligence was on to Amiri, they relocated him in Tucson (and gave him a $5 million bonus). But from the start, Amiri found himself missing his son, who had remained in Iran with the scientist's estranged wife, to such an extent that he took the risky step of returning to Tehran (despite CIA warnings to him of the danger). Once back in Tehran in 2010, he told Iranian counterintelligence officials that he had refused to cooperate in any meaningful way with the Americans and wanted to resume life with his son in Iran. A different outcome awaited Amiri than that enjoyed by Yurchenko. In 2015, a spokesman for Iran's Justice Ministry announced in Tehran that, after spending five years in prison for espionage, Amiri had been hanged "for revealing the country's top secrets to the enemy."

RENDITIONS AND INTERROGATIONS   Perhaps the most controversial forms of counterintelligence tradecraft since the Huston Plan have been the use of extraordinary renditions and harsh interrogations by the CIA. During the Administration of President George W. Bush, it came to light that the Agency had rendered (kidnaped) suspected terrorists in Europe and flown them in CIA aircraft to places – Cairo was a favorite or the Agency's own secret prisons ("black sites") in Central Europe and elsewhere – where they could be interrogated, and sometimes tortured, in an attempt to learn more about the activities of Al Qaeda. These renditions were ordered by the Bush Administration and loose guidelines from the Justice Department led to excesses.[62] By allowing detainees to be taken to another country that had no concerns about the niceties of U.S. constitutional protections, government officials somehow deluded themselves into believing that the United States had thereby evaded responsibility for any unethical activities that might occur during the interrogations. After all, it was not the Agency itself applying electrodes to the bodies of the victims. Sometimes mistaken identities led to the rendering of the wrong individuals; other times, victims told their tormentors whatever they thought they wanted to hear – anything to stop the pain – then they later recanted.

In 2003, for instance, the CIA captured Khalid Sheikh Mohammed (given the acronym KSM for short by Agency handlers) in Pakistan. He was the suspected, and later confirmed, mastermind of the 9/11 attacks against the Pentagon and the World Trade Center. When KSM was captured, the media speculated that he might be mistreated, even tortured, by his Agency interrogators. Officials at Langley responded that no brutal force would be used, not least because psychological pressure was considered more effective than physical pain. He might be subjected to sleep deprivation, perhaps; but, if he cooperated, he would be given rewards: good food, cigarettes, books, rest, a television set. Agency officials conceded, though, that the captured terrorist might be forced to sit or stand in stressful positions for hours at a time – but there would be no stretching on the rack. Only subsequently did it become known that KSM was waterboarded more than 130 times, a form of torture that simulates drowning.

Another top Al Qaeda operative, also captured in Pakistan, Abu Zubaydah, was on painkillers because of a pistol shot to the groin. Until he began to cooperate, interrogators held back his full medication. The report on torture issued by SSCI's Democratic staff in 2015 indicates, further, that Al Qaeda members were chained, naked and hooded, to the ceiling of interrogation rooms; routinely kicked to keep them awake; and shackled so tightly that blood flow to their limbs was halted. Most alarming are charges that two prisoners identified as Al Qaeda members were killed during interrogations at a U.S. military base in Afghanistan, beaten to death with blunt instruments.[63] It remains a matter of dispute as to whether such methods produced valuable intelligence gains (most experts say no), but one conclusion is widely accepted: in the court of world opinion, the use of torture has harmed American's reputation for fair play and ethical behavior – a significant attribute in the global contest for the allegiance of other nations and their citizens.[64]

The line between acceptable and abject CI interrogation techniques was poorly defined during the second Bush Administration and, in light of the barbaric 9/11 attacks, this line was likely smudged further by interrogators angry about 9/11 and anxious about the possibility of sudden new strikes against the United States. Intelligence had to be extracted quickly from the subject, according to this "ticking time-bomb" scenario. In the wake of the terrorist attacks against the United States, Cofer Black, the head of the CIA's Counterterrorism Center (CTC), declared: "There was a before 9/11 and there was an after 9/11. After 9/11, the gloves came off."[65] Yet when the gloves come off, all too often the Constitution is thrown out of the window.

Secrecy and the state

Among the responsibilities of counterintelligence officers is the protection of state secrets from leaks, either intentional or inadvertent. Early in the history of the Republic, none other than General George Washington commented on the importance of secrecy during the Revolutionary War:

> The necessity of procuring good Intelligence is apparent and need not be further urged. All that remains for me to add is that you keep the whole matter as secret as possible, for upon Secrecy Success depends in most enterprises of the kind, and for want of it, they are generally defeated, however well-planned or promising of favorable issue.[66]

Recently, in an unprecedented public speech, MI6 chief John Sawers in London commented on the importance of secrecy in the democracies: "Secrecy is not a dirty word. Secrecy is not there as a cover-up. Without secrecy there would be no intelligence services, or indeed other national assets like our special forces. Our nation would be more exposed as a result."[67] An ongoing challenge for the open societies is to protect good secrets from the enemies of democracy without hiding bad secrets – improper government activities – from the public.

Good secrets and bad

The democracies have secrets that are legitimate, which must be kept even from their own citizens for fear that adversaries would also be informed. These secrets include such matters as the sailing dates and destinations of troop ships during time of war; the sophisticated technology of advanced weapons systems, such as the radar-elusive Stealth bombers; the sensitive technology associated with techint, whether sigint listening methodology or the specifics of geoint resolution; the names of humint assets overseas; and the bargaining positions of U.S. negotiators at trade or arms control talks.

Yet the argument for secrecy frequently rests on less firm grounds. Officials in the executive branch sometimes prefer to conduct their activities in secret simply to avoid the necessity for defending their policies before lawmakers, judges, the media, and the American people. National Security Adviser Vice Admiral John M. Poindexter testified during the Iran–*contra* inquiry that he avoided keeping Congress informed about covert actions in Iran and Nicaragua because he "did not want any outside interference." In response, the co-chairman of the investigative committee, Lee H. Hamilton (D, Indiana), said: "You compartmentalized not only the President's senior advisers [neither Secretary of State George P. Shultz nor Secretary of Defense Casper Weinberger knew of "The Enterprise"], but, in effect, you locked the President out of the process."[68]

Lawmakers and the people they represent have become wary of secrecy claims, because of the many instances when they have been misled by officials: President Johnson's often contradictory reports on the progress of war in Indochina; President Nixon's lies about the Watergate break-in; the revelations of intelligence intrigues abroad, and even at home, disclosed by the Rockefeller, Pike, and Church panels in 1975–76; more lies about the Iran–*contra* affair in 1986–87; and, recently, revelations about secret CIA prisons abroad, the use of torture and rendition, and the second Bush Administration's bypassing of the warrant requirement for national security wiretaps (revealed by Snowden – a subject taken up in the next chapter). Over the years, open debate – the very anchor of democracy – has often been abandoned. As the thoughtful television commentator and author Bill Moyers observed during the Cold War, the abandonment of traditional American values,

> out of fear, to imitate the foe [communism] in order to defeat him, is to shred the distinction that makes us different. In the end, not only our values but our methods separate us from the enemies of freedom in the world. The decisions we make are inherent in the methods that produce them. An open society cannot survive a secret government.[69]

Regardless of the lessons drawn from recent scandals and the strong democratic arguments in favor of openness (with the exceptions mentioned above), secrecy continues to hold an almost irresistible temptation for officials in the executive branch. An example is the frequent evocation of the "executive privilege doctrine" by a series of White Houses.

Executive privilege

In the eyes of executive branch officials, a central attraction of America's secret agencies is the opportunity they afford to chart a foreign policy course with little or no public debate. In its covert shipment of arms to Iran during 1985–6, for example, the Reagan Administration carried the goal of exclusion to an extreme, not only refusing to inform the Congress but keeping the operation strictly within the limited confines of a few NSC staffers, some field operatives, and a narrow slice of the CIA – beyond the purview of even the President and the NSC's other principal members.

Often this goal of exclusion is achieved through the proclamation of executive privilege – an assertion by the President of constitutional authority to withhold information from the legislative and judicial branches of government. Appearing before the Ervin Committee, established by the Senate in 1973 to investigate the Watergate scandal and chaired by Sam Ervin, Jr. (D, North Carolina), President Nixon's Attorney General, Richard Kleindienst, claimed that "the constitutional authority of the President in his discretion" allowed the White House to withhold information in the President's possession "or in the possession of the executive branch" if the President concluded that disclosure "would impair the proper exercise of his constitutional functions." This implied that Congress could be prohibited from speaking to any of the millions of employees in the executive branch.

President Nixon went even further, claiming that not only could current members of his staff refuse to appear before congressional committees, including the Ervin panel, but so could past members – an unprecedented expansion of the executive privilege doctrine, which some senators immediately labeled "the doctrine of eternal privilege." Nixon said, too, that all of his "presidential papers," which he defined magisterially as "all documents, produced or received by the President or any member of the White House staff in connection with his official duties," were immune from congressional probes. Conveniently for the White House, this definition included White House tape-recordings sought by Ervin Committee investigators to see if they contained conversations about the Watergate scandal (which, indeed, they did – the "smoking gun" that led to the impeachment proceedings against President Nixon). "What do they eat that makes them grow so great?" Senator Ervin asked in reference to the President and his staff. The Senator continued: "I am not willing to elevate them to a position above the great mass of the American people. I don't think we have any such thing as royalty or nobility to let anybody come down at night like Nicodemus and whisper something in my ear that no one else can hear. This is not executive privilege. It is executive poppycock."

In 1974, the Supreme Court also disagreed with the President's broad interpretation of executive privilege and, in the case *United States* v. *Nixon* [418 U.S. 683], a majority of the judges required that the tape-recordings be turned over to Senator Ervin.

Subsequently, the Ford Administration stretched the cloak of executive privilege to another extravagant length. At issue was

Operation SHAMROCK, a secret program designed to intercept cables and telegrams sent abroad or received by Americans. Initially at the request of the Truman Administration, the corporations RCA, Global, and ITT World Communications began to store their international paid message traffic on magnetic tapes, which were then turned over to the NSA. Concerned that the operation may have been in violation of a federal law that protects the privacy of communications, a House subcommittee decided in 1976 to investigate the matter and called the corporation presidents to testify as witnesses. The CEOs turned to the White House for guidance and President Gerald R. Ford, through his Attorney General, Edward H. Levi (former dean of the Law School at the University of Chicago), claimed that the corporations were immune from congressional appearances in this case, because SHAMROCK was a sensitive, top-secret project ordered by the White House. The doctrine of executive privilege had now been extended to the private sector.

Members of the House subcommittee were dismayed by this response. "The Attorney General is without any authority," declared Representative John E. Moss (D, Utah), a respected, long-serving lawmaker. "It is the most outrageous assumption, the most arrogant display by the Attorney General I have seen. Some damn two-bit appointee of the President is not the law-making body of this country."[70] The subcommittee voted for a contempt of Congress citation against any witness who failed to appear for the hearings. When the gavel came down to begin the hearings a few days later, all three CEOs – now having second thoughts about following General Levi's recommendation to stay at home – were in their assigned chairs in front of the subcommittee members, ready to answer questions. The hearing proceeded without sensitive NSA methods being discussed, but with the rightful airing of the improper White House and corporate violation of U.S. privacy laws.

Delay and deceit

Such major confrontations between the branches over secrecy provisions are rare. More commonly, the executive branch simply resorts to "stonewalling" and "slow-rolling" – attempts to avoid sharing information with lawmakers by the methods of delay. Professor Raoul Berger of Harvard University's School of Law, an expert on executive privilege, observed that "bureaucrats engage in interminable stalling when asked for information."[71] This occurred, in just one of thousands of examples, with the secrecy surrounding the harmful effects of nuclear waste at government facilities, concealed since the dawning of the Nuclear Age in 1945 by officials more concerned with nuclear weapons production than with public health.[72] Berger spelled out the implications:

> At bottom, the issue concerns the right of Congress and the people to participate in making the fateful decisions that affect the fortunes of the nation. Claims of presidential power to bar such participation, or to withhold on one ground or another the information that is indispensable for intelligent participation undermine this right, sap the very foundations of democratic government.[73]

Prior restraint

As a further attempt to bottle up information within the executive branch despite the right of the people in a democracy to know about almost all of their government's activities, officials sometimes try to curb the publication of materials deemed sensitive. This withholding by the government of the right to publish information is often referred to as "prior restraint." Understanding that truth and transparency are the *sine qua non* for successful democracy, courts in the United States have been loath for the most part to permit the enforcement of prior restraints. "Any system of prior restraints of expression comes to this Court bearing a heavy presumption against its constitutional validity," declared the Supreme Court in the celebrated case *New York Times v. United States* (1971), better known as the *Pentagon Papers* case.

In this case, the Nixon Administration failed to convince a majority of Supreme Court justices that prior restraint was necessary to prevent publication of a secret Department of Defense history of the Vietnam War. Administration lawyers maintained that publication would be harmful to U.S. foreign policy. The man responsible for the leak, DoD analyst Daniel Ellsberg, believed the contrary to be true: that Americans deserved to know the facts about their nation's combat involvement in Indochina. This knowledge would make the national debate over further warfare in that remote part of the world more meaningful and accurate. Ellsberg was convinced that no secrets of real significance were in the documents; rather, the materials were being kept secret because officials wished to hide from the public a record of various mistakes that had been made, leading the United States deeper into the war. In sharp contrast, Ellsberg's critics saw his decision as being close to treason, because he had revealed classified information without proper authorization – a major counterintelligence taboo.

Ellsberg leaked the documents to the *New York Times* and the *Washington Post*. In response, the White House moved to stop further publication of the papers by bringing an injunction against the *Times*, which was the first paper to print excerpts from the documents. Given the great importance of the issue and the key figures involved, the case moved quickly to the nation's highest court. Mr. Justice Potter Stewart expressed the majority view in the six to three decision against prior restraint:

> We are asked, quite simply, to prevent the publication by two newspapers of material that the Executive Branch insists should not, in the national interest, be published. I am convinced that the Executive is correct with respect to some of the documents involved. But *I cannot say that disclosure of any of them will surely result in direct, immediate, and irreparable damage to the Nation or its people.* That being so, there can under the First Amendment be but one judicial resolution of the issues before us. I join the judgments of the Court.[74]

In 2010, another major leak case would capture the attention of democracies around the world. Out of London, a whistle-blowing group named WikiLeaks managed to acquire more than 400,000 classified documents on the conduct of the U.S. wars in Iraq and Afghanistan – probably the most massive unauthorized disclosure of classified information in American history prior to the Snowden blizzard of documents in 2013. WikiLeaks defended the action by claiming the right of citizens to know the full truth about the wars, including the much higher rate of civilian casualties in the regions. The Obama Administration began a criminal investigation against the group. WikiLeaks lost much of its public credibility when it was discovered that the leaked documents revealed the names of U.S. intelligence assets, sure to be targeted for death by Taliban and Al Qaeda fighters.[75]

Then, in 2013, the Edward Snowden revelations about NSA's warrantless wiretaps and its collection of "metadata" on the communications patterns of American citizens proved as controversial a leak as the Pentagon Papers had been. As examined further in the next chapter, Snowden provided the media with more than a million classified documents, which he stole from NSA computers.

Secrecy and democracy

A proper counterintelligence concern for the protection of certain information within the executive branch makes sense. No American wants to endanger the lives of public servants in the U.S. intelligence agencies, the assets they recruit overseas, or the FBI's informants at home; and no thoughtful person would countenance the revealing of other "good" secrets. The record indicates that these secrets have been fairly well contained. Former Secretary of State Dean Rusk said repeatedly that he knew of no national security leak that truly damaged America's major interests.[76] Similarly, according to a prominent senator in 1976:

> Secrets that ought to be kept are being kept. For example, with the single exception of the book by Philip Agee [a CIA officer who defected and wrote an account of his experiences inside the Agency, which revealed the names of some of his fellow officers overseas]...there has been little or no disclosure of CIA sources or methods, or of the confidentiality of sensitive negotiations, such as preceded the partial test ban treaty, SALT I, and the release of the Pueblo crew [a U.S. spy ship captured by North Korea during the Cold War].[77]

The most egregious security breaches have come from within the executive branch itself, not from the media, lawmakers, or other "outsiders." For example, the Department of State leaked highly classified information to a writer preparing a favorable profile on then-Secretary of State Henry Kissinger, with no legal action taken against the leaker. Further, as this chapter has documented, the CIA and other intelligence agencies have had personnel who sold secrets to America's enemies, such as Edward Lee Howard, the Walker family, Ames, and Hanssen. Improved counterintelligence within the executive branch would do more to protect the "good" secrets than measures taken against the First Amendment rights of reporters and other scribblers.

Still, the publication of agent identities by WikiLeaks clearly goes beyond the pale. So does the massive leakage of classified documents by Snowden, including detailed intelligence budget data that had nothing to do with his plausible ethical and legal objections to the NSA's metadata program. A further objection to the Snowden leaks is the fact that he could have taken his grievances to SSCI or HPSCI and would have been given an audience by staffers and lawmakers – some of whom agreed with his criticism of the metadata program. Instead, he chose to pass his stolen documents to the media, before racing off to China and on to Russia. A majority of the members of SSCI and HPSCI may have rejected his criticism of the metadata program; if so, that is part of the democratic process. He could have continued to lobby his position quietly within the Intelligence Community and with the oversight committees – and may well have had success eventually, as lawmakers further considered the implications of the NSA's sigint programs aimed at U.S. citizens.

Clearly troubling has been the mountains of information improperly kept from the public, harming the ability of citizens to judge the merits of foreign policy decisions. The Pentagon Papers held out little prospect for genuine damage to the United States, but did serve to inform Americans about the course of U.S. involvement in Indochina. Other government secrets have been equally dubious, such as the files on illegal FBI activities (COINTELPRO), improper CIA operations (CHAOS and, more recently, the torture program), and NSA domestic wiretaps (SHAMROCK and MINARET, as well as its more recent metadata program and warrantless wiretaps). Other examples of inappropriate government secrets over the years have included the Watergate tape transcripts; internal Pentagon reports on atrocities committed by American soldiers in Vietnam (the My Lai village massacre, for instance, or the use of torture at Abu Ghraib in Iraq by military intelligence and in secret overseas prisons by the CIA); secret bombing missions in Cambodia during the 1960s – the list goes on. This form of secrecy, usually clothed in the name of "national security," has been designed more to keep a "meddlesome" public and their representatives in Congress out of the policy process, and to assure executive domination over the government – sometimes at the agency level against even the will of the President. As historian Arthur M. Schlesinger, Jr., has written: "By the 1960s and 1970s, the religion of secrecy had become an all-purpose means by which the American Presidency sought to dissemble its purpose, bury its mistakes, manipulate its citizens, and maximize its power."[78]

Over the years, the executive branch has developed to a high art various methods of evading legislative and public scrutiny over its conduct of foreign affairs. Senator Daniel Patrick Moynihan (D, New York) concluded in 1992 that:

> [The Iran–*contra* affair] could not have happened without the secrecy system. Millions on millions of secret documents every year – some seven million to be semi-exact, for the number itself is a secret. The effect is to hide things from the American people that they need to know. And within the executive branch to hide things from each other...
>
> It's over, you could say. But it's not. A set of captains and kings has departed. Issues are different. But the secrecy system is still in place: the oldest, most enduring institution of the Cold War.[79]

In 1995, when Moynihan led a special commission of inquiry into excessive secrecy, he concluded that the government was continuing to classify improperly hordes of documents – some 85 percent of the total.[80] Disclosures in the WikiLeaks papers indicate that the system of secrecy and deception continued to thrive. In 1998, Congress enacted the Intelligence Community Whistleblower Protection Act to make it easier for those within the IC to raise questions about intelligence activities they find dubious; however, as the Snowden case illustrates (as well as others less well known), whistle-blowers – even those with the best intentions – remain wary of this law's procedures. The law requires them to go through their home-agency channels, thus immediately jeopardizing their intelligence careers. Reformers continue to wrestle with how to make whistle-blowing less career wrenching, while at the same time maintaining necessary controls over classified information. The onus rests with SSCI and HPSCI, as well as the Intelligence Oversight Board at the White House, to develop improved avenues of legitimate dissent for whistle-blowers.

Counterintelligence and accountability

Experience shows that counterintelligence can drive secret agencies toward overzealous operations that can include even spying against law-abiding citizens in their own homeland, as underscored by the Huston Plan and the domestic spy scandal of the 1970s in the United States (CHAOS). Other disturbing examples include COINTELPRO, as well as the CIA's uses of rendition and torture, and the NSA's casual approach to the wiretap restrictions in the United States and Europe.

The United States and North Korea

In the midst of the Cold War, the CIA generated a data bank on 1.5 million American citizens engaged in lawful protests against the war in Vietnam. Many had their mail read, their telephone conversations listened to, their day-to-day lives secretly watched. Further, the FBI carried out 500,000 investigations of so-called "subversives" (mostly Vietnam War dissenters and civil rights activists), without a single court conviction.[81] During this period, Bureau agents wrote anonymous letters meant to incite violence among African Americans. J. Edgar Hoover's counterintelligence program, labeled Operation COINTELPRO, involved not only spying on, but also the harassment of, civil rights activists and anti-war protesters in an attempt to fray or break family and friendship ties and stop both movements – all in the name of counterintelligence. The unchecked pursuit of CI objectives imperiled the very foundations of American democracy, casting aside basic U.S. laws and the constitutional right to free expression. Only when the CIA's transgressions leaked to the media in 1974, triggering the first significant congressional inquiry into U.S. intelligence operations, did these illegal activities cease – at least for a while.

National security letters and warrantless wiretaps

The proper balance between security and civil liberties faced another test after the 9/11 attacks, when the Bush Administration initiated the use of national security letters (NSLs) by the FBI and ordered warrantless wiretaps against American citizens by the NSA. The adoption of NSLs required the recipient to turn over documents and data requested by the FBI. The recipient had to remain silent about having received the letter – essentially a gag rule that strips the hapless citizen of basic rights to a legal defense. The number of NSLs rose from just a few annually in 1978 to 19,000 in 2005.

The resurrection of warrantless wiretaps – a clear violation of law – in the aftermath of the 9/11 attacks is more troubling still. In December 2005, the *New York Times* reported that President George W. Bush had authorized the NSA (by secret executive order) to eavesdrop on Americans without first acquiring a judicial warrant. Critics maintained that the hush-hush program violated the intent of the Foreign Intelligence Surveillance Act (FISA), passed by Congress in 1978 to establish a special FISA Court to review FBI, CIA, and other agency requests for wiretap warrant authority. The FISA statue stemmed from the findings of the Church Committee that the NSA had participated in widespread surveillance of Americans. The NSA's Operation SHAMROCK monitored every cable sent overseas or received by U.S. citizens from 1947 to 1975; and its Operation MINARET swept in the telephone conversations of an additional 1,680 citizens. The effects of such spying, according to a prominent member of the Church Committee, Walter Mondale (D, Minnesota), was to "discourage dissent in this country." Not a single one of these cable interceptions or wiretaps underwent judicial review. When Senator Mondale asked the NSA deputy director in public hearings whether he was concerned about the program's legality, the official replied (with a look of embarrassment): "That particular aspect didn't enter into the discussions."[82]

The FISA Court has been made more effective by reforms adopted in 2013 by the Obama Administration – at congressional insistence through its enactment of the USA Freedom Act – such as requiring the presence of a public-interest attorney to raise objections against questionable arguments made by the intelligence agencies before the FIS Court, and preventing the NSA from storing telephone and social media logs regarding the communications patterns of American citizens. When the Bush Administration decided that the FISA law requiring wiretap warrants needed improvements to meet the requirements of counterterrorism in the aftermath of the 9/11 attacks, then the proper remedy would have been for the President to ask Congress to amend the law. Instead, in secret the White House simply bypassed the law, without allowing SSCI and HPSCI an opportunity to fully review the ramped-up use of questionable NSA eavesdropping capabilities.

In the instances when secret agencies have overreached in their counterintelligence operations, the nation has been reminded again of James Madison's warning, now etched in marble on the walls of the Library of Congress: "Power, lodged as it must be in the hands of human beings, is ever liable to abuse." A free society cannot remain free for long without a reliable counterintelligence capability; yet, nor can it remain free for long without effective accountability over CI operations. Democracies are no longer democracies when a kid with the picket sign or the bumper sticker of the opposing candidate becomes, in the distorted vision of overzealous CI specialists, equivalent to a kid with a bomb.

5 Safeguards against the Abuse of Secret Power

On December 6, 1977, the House Permanent Select Committee on Intelligence (HPSCI) convened to hear Admiral Stansfield Turner, DCI for President Jimmy Carter, present his first briefing on a presidential covert action approval. The Committee had only recently come into existence, in response to congressional investigations in 1975–76 that revealed widespread violations of domestic law by the Intelligence Community. Moving more quickly, senators across the Hill had already put in place their own new intelligence oversight committee in 1976: the Senate Select Committee on Intelligence (SSCI). Comporting with congressional tradition, each panel was known informally by the name of its chair, the Boland Committee in the House (after Edward P. "Eddie" Boland, D, Massachusetts) and the Inouye Committee in the Senate (after Daniel K. Inouye, D, Hawaii).

A sixty-five-year-old bachelor with a legendary baritone singing voice that in the right Irish pub softened his otherwise stern disposition, Chairman Boland was a force to be reckoned with in the House of Representatives. He was a former roommate and close confidant of the Speaker, Thomas "Tip" O'Neill (another Boston Democrat equally at home in Irish pubs), and a senior member of the almighty Appropriations Committee. Boland eschewed the arrogance of many of those in lofty positions in Washington, but he was in the habit of getting his way. On this morning in HPSCI's suite of offices near the Capitol Rotunda, well guarded by police, Boland rose to greet Admiral Turner as he entered the low-ceiling, bunker-like hearing room accompanied by aides. It was the DCI's first trip to HPSCI's quarters. Seven of the panel's thirteen members had shown up for the session, plus the three Committee staffers allowed to attend this particularly sensitive meeting. All were curious to meet the President's spy chief. The other six members evidently had duties they deemed more pressing than this opportunity to participate in the Committee's first top secret covert action briefing. As the staff director of HPSCI's Oversight Subcommittee, I was one of the staff aides at the meeting.

Turner carried himself with an air of supreme confidence. It was rumored that he had worn a Superman costume to an NSC meeting as a joke, early in the Carter Administration. Not everyone on the Council was amused. Ruggedly handsome, stocky, and silver-haired, Turner had been a pugnacious middle guard on the Naval Academy football team, had won a Rhodes Scholarship in his senior year, and then raced through the naval ranks to an admiralty. The position of Chief of Naval Operations was said to be his prime objective, after this interlude at the CIA, a post for which he had been recruited by an admiring classmate, Jimmy Carter.

The DCI nodded cordially to the Chairman and the other Committee members who were seated around a thick mahogany bench in front of a table that awaited the Admiral and his entourage. After an exchange of pleasantries and some mild grumbling about DC traffic congestion, Turner pulled a prepared statement from his briefcase and took less than five minutes to present the basics to the Committee about President Carter's recent approval (a "finding") for a covert action – a briefing required by law ever since the passage of the Hughes–Ryan Act in December 1974.

Once Turner had completed his brief statement, silence filled the room, disturbed only by the hum of neon lights behind a latticework of wooden slats on the ceiling. The lawmakers at first assumed the DCI was just pausing for a drink of water, but instead Turner looked around the room at the members and grinned. "That's it," he said.

Representative Roman Mazzoli, a short, feisty Democrat from Kentucky, cleared his throat and proceeded to pick apart the covert action from A to Z. The target was an insignificant country; the operation cost too much; the briefing had been vague. Turner stared at the notebook on the table in front of him. He clenched his teeth and flexed the muscles that lined his jaw. When Mazzoli finished, the DCI offered a spirited defense of the operation. The Kentuckian remained skeptical and presented another round of objections.

Chairman Boland interceded. "I'd like to have a serious debate," he said, "but this is not the place." One could only wonder why this was not the place. After all, was this not a closed meeting within the inner sanctum of the HPSCI offices, guarded by Capitol Hill's finest and periodically "swept" to ensure that no listening devices were present? Was it not the duty of the new Committee to review the activities of the nation's secret espionage organizations, perhaps especially covert actions?

"I don't want any adversary proceedings between this Committee and the intelligence agencies," Boland added, with furrowed eyebrows and the implicit suggestion that the Admiral had done his duty and could now depart. A lowly junior member of the Congress, Mazzoli sank back into his chair, with a mixture of shock and vexation registering on his face. A few of the Committee members looked at Boland in dismay, but none came to Mazzoli's rescue. This was, after all, Edward P. Boland, a man who could make or break a career for anyone who sought funding for their district from the House Appropriations Committee – in other words, every member of Congress. Crossing swords with a committee chairman could be unhealthy, and doubly so when he was the Speaker's best pal and someone highly placed on the House money committee. Boland adjourned the session and Admiral Turner left the room wreathed in smiles.

The HPSCI Chairman had objected to Mazzoli's cross-examination because of the experience that the House of Representatives had recently endured with the Pike Committee, led by Otis Pike (D, New York). In 1975, the House established the Pike Committee as a counterpart to the Senate's Church Committee, both created to examine charges of CIA domestic spying. A former Marine aviator and a likable, fair-minded individual, Pike nonetheless proved unable to control his investigative panel and it self-destructed, pulled in a dozen different directions by a politically diverse membership and an overzealous staff. The Committee alienated other House members, who ultimately refused to endorse its final report or even release it to the public in a sanitized (declassified) form. In a blatant breach of security provisions, some still unknown person (or persons) leaked the top secret report to the journalist Daniel Schorr, who in turn passed it along to the *Village Voice*, a left-leaning New York City newspaper. Whatever remaining shred of respectability the Pike panel still possessed was now obliterated.

Two years following this egregious leak, Edward Boland was determined to demonstrate that the House could be trusted with classified information and could work in harmony with the DCI and other components of the Intelligence Community. Congress and the nation's spies would have a new, cooperative relationship. Debates with the DCI, if necessary, would be conducted by Boland in the confines of his office, not before the full HPSCI membership. As Boland and the Speaker agreed, this was no longer a time for heated rhetoric and confrontation; this was a time for peace between the branches. Comity would trump conflict. The Boland Committee would not be Son of Pike. While it was understandable that the HPSCI Chairman had no intention of seeing his new committee discredited as the Pike panel had been, Boland's passive attitude

toward the role of the House in supervising intelligence operations was bound to signal to the DCI and every other intelligence
officer that the new watchdog lacked teeth and wouldn't even bark.
Here were shades of the slumbering senator in the introduction to
Chapter 3, who opposed "parliamentary activities" in the 1950s.

Boland's philosophy was about to be tested more rigorously,
however, by a few members of his Committee. Admiral Turner
returned to the HPSCI hearing room a few weeks later with another
covert action finding signed by President Carter. On this occasion,
the DCI found on the premises a congressional transcriber, known
on the Hill as a "recorder." This individual, carefully screened by
the FBI and given a top secret clearance (as were the Committee's
three aides in the room), was in attendance to keep a verbatim
record of what was said by the Intelligence Director and his aides
during the briefing, as well as by the lawmakers in attendance.
Turner began his briefing, but kept his eye on the recorder. After
only two minutes, the Admiral abruptly stopped his review of the
covert action, having concluded – as he told Boland and the rest
of the Committee (eleven members strong this time) – that, after
further thought, he had decided that to allow a verbatim record of
the briefing would be a breach of security. He would discontinue the
briefing until the recorder had departed. For almost a full minute,
only the hum of the neon lights could be heard in the tomb-like
quiet of the room.

Boland finally interrupted the silence. "All right," he said, "we'll
dispense with the recorder."

As the recorder began to gather his equipment for an exit, one of
the HPSCI aides slipped a note to Les Aspin (D, Wisconsin), a junior
member of the Committee. "We *must* have a record of these briefings," emphasized the note. "How else are we going to have any
memory of what the DCI said, and whether – a year from now – the
CIA is living up to his assurances? It'll be the Agency's recollection
against ours." The aide was suggesting that Aspin walk the plank,
with Captain Boland glowering from the bridge. Aspin, though,
understood the importance of a written record for holding officials
to account, and he also had something of a swashbuckling streak.
He spoke up immediately against dismissing the reporter. Boland
looked down the table in his direction with a scowl on his face.
When Mazzoli seconded Aspin's request, Boland's countenance
grew darker.

With the grim look of a headmaster about to frogmarch two
disobedient schoolboys from the classroom, Boland repeated that
a recorder was unnecessary. In support of the Chairman, Admiral
Turner said that he would leave behind a copy of the short

presidential statement of approval. Aspin insisted, however, that the finding itself – a highly abbreviated synopsis of the target and the scope of the covert action – was insufficient. (For a rare example of a published finding, see Figure 5.1.) Far more important was the DCI's follow-up explanation about the operation's goals, methods, costs, and risks. Unimpressed by the young upstarts Aspin and Mazzoli, Chairman Boland again ordered the hapless recorder, caught in the middle of this exchange, to leave the premises.

At this point, Aspin thrust his head and shoulders across the green baize bench top and stared along its curvature toward Boland. "I call for a vote on this matter, Mr. Chairman," Aspin said coldly.

I hereby find that the following operations in foreign countries (including all support necessary to such operations) are important to the national security of the United States, and direct the Director of Central Intelligence, or his designee, to report this Finding to the concern committee of the Congress pursuant to law, and to provide such briefings as necessary.

SCOPE

Central America

PURPOSE

Provide all forms of training, equipment and related assistance to cooperating government throughout Central America in order to counter foreign-sponsored subversion and terrorism. [Still-classified section omitted here.] Encourage and influence foreign governments around the world to support all of the above objectives.

Figure 5.1   An example of a statement accompanying a presidentially approved covert action: the *contra* portion of the Iran–*contra* finding, 1981

Source: "Presidential Finding on Central America, N16574," *Public Papers of the President: Ronald Reagan* (Washington, D.C.: U.S. Government Printing Office, 1986). The President approved the finding on March 9, 1981. Originally top secret, it was partially declassified during hearings into the Iran–*contra* scandal in 1987. The "purpose" section is succinct, leaving considerable leeway for the CIA to fill in the details during implementation. When Congress passed the Boland Amendments to prohibit further covert actions in Nicaragua, the Reagan Administration moved underground and created "The Enterprise" to carry on these operations without the knowledge of Congress.

A crisp "second" came from Mazzoli. Boland's face changed color from a dark hue to a deep shade of crimson as he pushed his chair back from the bench in anger and disgust. He ordered the Committee clerk to call the roll. In the boxing ring of House politics, Les Aspin and his sidekick Roman Mazzoli had just bloodied the nose of a House heavyweight champion.

The Committee clerk slowly read the names of those Committee members present. When the tally came to an end, by a margin of a single vote – six to five – Aspin had won the right for HPSCI to have a verbatim record of the full DCI briefing on a covert action proposal. By implication, this principle would apply as well to any other briefing the Committee deemed important enough to require an accurate, written account. Against his will, Eddie Boland had been forced into a more serious form of intelligence oversight, one that would allow HPSCI lawmakers and their staff to monitor the ongoing performance of the secret agencies in light of promises made by the DCI during committee hearings. Word of this confrontation soon made its way to the other side of the Hill and members of the Senate Intelligence Committee demanded to have their own recorder to ensure a reliable memory for senators about promises from the nation's spy chief during briefings.

When a new administration came to town led by President Ronald Reagan, the Intelligence Community changed leaders from Stansfield Turner to William J. Casey, a businessman and former national presidential campaign manager for the new President. A curmudgeon who carried no brief for the idea of congressional intelligence accountability, Casey – soon to be the father of the Iran–*contra* scandal – quickly locked horns with Boland and his Senate counterpart, the arch-CIA defender Barry Goldwater (R, Arizona), the SSCI Chairman. Thanks largely to Casey's pitbull personality, Boland soon came to appreciate the merits of vigilant intelligence oversight as propounded by Aspin and Mazzoli. To everyone's amazement – perhaps even his own – so did Senator Goldwater, who at one time had been even more willing than Boland to place the goal of warm relations with the secret agencies high above any attempt at a rigorous review of their operations.

The evolution of safeguards against intelligence abuse in the United States

The Era of Trust (1787–1974)

The approach toward intelligence accountability chosen by Chairman Boland in his early years as HPSCI Chairman – that is, a

Figure 5.2   Auth on the relationship between Congress and the CIA
            prior to 1974

Source: Auth, *Philadelphia Inquirer* (1976). Used with permission.

posture of benign neglect – had prevailed throughout the long
sweep of American history from the nation's founding in 1787
until the domestic spy scandals of 1974. Cartoonist Auth of the
Philadelphia Inquirer depicted the "footsie" relationship between the
CIA and lawmakers during the early decades of the Cold War (see
Figure 5.2). Throughout this Era of Trust, intelligence was set apart
from the rest of the government. The dominant attitude among
members of Congress was that the honorable men and women in
the intelligence agencies would have to be trusted to protect the
United States against dangerous and unscrupulous forces at home
and abroad. "No, no, my boy, don't tell me," a leading Senate overseer, John Stennis (D, Mississippi), told DCI James R. Schlesinger in
1973 when the Director attempted to provide a full accounting of
the CIA's operations abroad. "Just go ahead and do it, but I don't
want to know."[1]

While most of the nation's intelligence officers have indeed been
honorable men and women, the writers of the Constitution could
have predicted that eventually power – perhaps especially secret
power – would be misused. Resonating this bedrock principle of
government accountability, Supreme Court Justice Louis Brandeis
reminded Americans in a 1926 opinion that the purpose of the

Constitution had been "not to promote efficiency but to preclude the exercise of arbitrary power. The purpose was not to avoid friction, but, by means of the inevitable friction incident to the distribution of the governmental powers among three departments, to save the people from autocracy."[2]

Yet this sound doctrine often gave way to the exigencies of fighting against enemies of the state, whether the Barbary pirates of yore, communists of the Cold War, or terrorists in the contemporary setting. The United States, the world's first democracy, would follow the practice of regimes around the world and throughout history; it would set its secret agencies outside the framework of checks and balances that is the hallmark of open and free societies. A hostile world demanded no less; efficiency would have to take pride of place over civil liberties.

This is not to say that the U.S. intelligence agencies were devoid of all vestiges of accountability. During the Cold War and since, most of their activities were and continue to be approved by officials in the White House and the National Security Council (NSC). Further, from time to time, the CIA would report (or at least try to report) to lawmakers – though often only to find deaf ears like those of Stennis, or closed eyes like the sleeping senator in the introduction to Chapter 3. Now and then, as in the aftermath of the Bay of Pigs fiasco, the embarrassing U-2 shoot-down over the Soviet Union in 1960, and the controversy surrounding CIA subsidies for the National Student Association in 1968, a few lawmakers would call for inquiries and intelligence reform; but there were never enough reformers in Congress to bring about significant change. While David M. Barrett correctly maintains that the devotion of lawmakers to intelligence oversight has been underrated in the scholarly and popular literature, congressional approval of intelligence programs seems nonetheless to have been highly discretionary during the Era of Trust. For the most part, presidents and lawmakers provided DCIs and other intelligence managers with broad authority to conduct secret operations at home and abroad as they saw fit.[3]

In the autumn of 1974, this neglect of adequate intelligence supervision would change, beginning with a spy scandal and accelerating into the most thorough investigation ever made of the U.S. intelligence agencies. Soon, 1975 would become known as the "Year of Intelligence."

The Era of Uneasy Partnership (1974–86)

Belief in intelligence exceptionalism underwent radical revision in the United States when the *New York Times* reported in 1974 that the

Agency had been engaged in domestic espionage.[4] The Bay of Pigs, the U-2 shoot-down, and CIA student subsidies were one thing, but spying on American citizens – voters back home – quite another. In the context of this stunning revelation, concurrent *Times* reporting on Agency covert actions against the Allende regime in Chile – a democratically elected government – took on added weight and drew further criticism of the CIA's secret operations. Reacting with rare alacrity, Congress set up panels of inquiry in January of 1975: first the Church Committee in the Senate (led by Frank Church) and what eventually became the Pike Committee in the House (chaired by Otis Pike). Not to be left behind, the Ford Administration established a presidential investigative commission, led by and named after Vice President Nelson Rockefeller (R, New York).

The Church Committee, on which the author served as assistant to the Chairman, dug deeper than the other panels, spending sixteen months on its investigation and issuing a set of public reports that stood over six feet high (as well as other reports another six feet high that remain classified).[5] The Church Committee confirmed that the *Times* was correct about CIA surveillance within the United States, as well as covert action against the democratic government of Chile; but the panel found that the newspaper accounts had only scratched the surface of wrongdoing by America's intelligence organizations. The investigative findings demonstrated, for example, that the CIA had opened the mail to and from selected American citizens, which generated 1.5 million names stored in the Agency's computer bank (Operation CHAOS). Moreover, Army intelligence units had compiled dossiers on 100,000 U.S. citizens during the Vietnam war era; and the vast computer facilities of the NSA had monitored every cable sent overseas, or received from overseas, by Americans between 1947 and 1975 (Operation SHAMROCK), and had engaged as well in questionable wiretapping within the United States (Operation MINARET).

Among the most chilling of the Church Committee findings emerged from the vaults of the FBI: Operation COINTELPRO. The Bureau had created files on over one million Americans and carried out more than 500,000 investigations of "subversives" from 1960 to 1974 – without a single court conviction. As Senator Walter Mondale (D, Minnesota), a member of the Church Committee, recalled: "No meeting was too small, no group too insignificant" to escape the FBI's attention.[6] From 1956 to 1971, the Bureau carried out secret smear campaigns against thousands of groups and individuals, simply because they had expressed opposition to the war in Vietnam or criticized the slow pace of the civil rights movement. The Klu Klux Klan made the Bureau hit list as well – as did seemingly any group that failed to fit into J. Edgar Hoover's Norman Rockwell image of a loyal American. Target Number One for Hoover, though, was the civil rights leader Martin Luther King, Jr., the victim of many campaigns of lies and innuendo perpetrated by the Bureau, including a blackmail attempt in 1964 that sought to push Dr. King into suicide on the eve of his acceptance speech for a Nobel Peace Prize.

Historian Henry Steele Commager correctly observed that "perhaps the most threatening of all the evidence that [stemmed] from the findings of the Church Committee" was "the indifference of the intelligence agencies to constitutional restraint."[7] As a result of the *Times* reporting and the congressional and the Rockefeller inquiries, lawmakers vowed to change this indifference through the institution of laws, regulations, and, above all, a new philosophy of meaningful and consistent legislative review of intelligence activities. It was time to say goodbye to the earlier era of benign neglect.

The law works: that was the central conclusion reached by the Church Committee. Each of the security objectives sought by presidents and their aides during the Cold War could have been achieved without descending into the dark realms of COINTELPRO, CHAOS, SHAMROCK, MINARET, and other questionable operations adopted by the intelligence agencies. The United States could fight the totalitarian states without becoming one itself. Liberty and security had to be kept in balance if America were to stay true to its democratic values and traditions.

The *Times* reporting and the investigations of 1975 led to a sea change in attitudes within the United States, and soon after within other democracies around the world as well, about the need for better supervision of the secret services. Even before the establishment of the Church and Pike Committees, Congress passed the Hughes–Ryan Act in late December 1974. This law was revolutionary in concept. It required the President to explicitly approve ("find" – therefore, the approval is called a "finding") all important covert actions. By requiring a statement of purpose about the covert action, endorsed by the commander in chief, this first step effectively ended the doctrine of plausible deniability. Next, the finding had to be reported to Congress in a "timely manner." Since 1976 and 1977, the reports have been presented orally in executive session to SSCI and HPSCI (as with the examples that began this chapter).

The Hughes–Ryan law did not go so far as to require congressional *approval* of covert actions, but it did set up an opportunity for lawmakers to influence these operations. After a covert action briefing, nothing would stop members of SSCI and HPSCI (meeting separately for the briefings) from expressing their opposition – or even having a vote on the merits of the covert action. Neither the opinions nor the vote would be legally binding, but a Committee that was riled up over what members considered an ill-advised operation could only be ignored at political risk by the DCI (or, today, the D/CIA and the DNI) and by the President. The nature of the opposition would matter. If it were only a junior member or two, the President might choose to ignore the criticism. If the opponents included powerful members of SSCI and HPSCI – say, the chairs – that would be a different story and a president would probably want to reconsider going forward with the covert action. Backing away might be prudent, as well, for a president facing majority opposition in both Committees. So while Hughes–Ryan provided no formal legal authority for Congress to stop a covert action in its tracks, it did require reporting on these operations to legislative overseers, and that sets the stage for political opposition within the sheltered confines of the oversight committees (SSCI and HPSCI) to form against moving forward with the proposal.

Further, if SSCI and HPSCI opposed a covert action, but a president ignored this "suggestion," members of the two Committees could convene a secret session of Congress and vote up or down to shut off money for the operation – an extreme contingency, but exactly what Congress did with the Boland Amendments to stop covert action in Nicaragua during the 1980s. Constitutionally, an irate set of lawmakers could (but never have so far) even bring impeachment proceedings against a president considered out of control in his or her conduct of a particularly questionable covert action.

Short of these more extreme responses, members of Congress could vote against replenishment of the CIA's Reserve for Contingency Fund, through which lawmakers annually provide seed money for covert actions so the White House can move swiftly if necessary in ordering the use of the "third option" in emergency situations. Just as one should think twice about pulling on the tail of a tiger, so does a president and a DNI think twice about entering into a dispute with a congressional committee. This sense of executive branch prudence gives to the Hughes–Ryan Act an added unwritten dimension of power, even if the law is devoid of explicit authority for lawmakers to approve or disapprove these decisions.

One of the continuing problems of the findings process has been the occasional authorization from the President for so-called "generic" or "worldwide" findings – broad statements that endorse vague covert actions. For example, without elaboration, the wording of the finding might say: "The President finds in favor of using lethal force against terrorists worldwide." This would be an ambiguous prescription for unleashing assassins and drones against any number of targets abroad, including American citizens who may be preaching *jihad* against the West from Yemen (as in the case of Anwar al-Awlaki, killed by a U.S. drone in 2011) or other nations. Especially when assassination is involved, critics advocate the use of more specific findings for each target, so that lawmakers and others in the covert action decision loop can review the merits of each case.

Other statues designed to define the boundaries of probity for the secret agencies would soon be passed in the wake of Hughes–Ryan, such as the important Foreign Intelligence Surveillance Act (FISA) in 1978, which banned warrantless national security wiretaps. Two years later, Congress enacted a far-reaching law to further tighten supervision over America's secret agencies. Although only two pages in length, this Intelligence Oversight Act of 1980 bore sharp teeth, requiring prior (not just timely) notice to SSCI and HPSCI, and on all (not just CIA) important intelligence operations – collection and counterintelligence, too, in addition to covert action.

Beginning with the Hughes–Ryan Act and carrying on until the Iran–*contra* scandal of 1987, lawmakers, presidents, and DCIs attempted during this experimental Era of Uneasy Partnership to fashion a workable relationship between democratic openness, on the one hand, and effective espionage, on the other hand – that is, between liberty and security. The result was a dramatic increase in attention on Capitol Hill to intelligence activities. When it comes to intelligence supervision by lawmakers and their staff, the difference between pre-1974 and post-1974 is as stark as night is to day. The Iran–*contra* affair would demonstrate, however, that this New Oversight was far from foolproof.

An Interlude of Distrust (1986–91)

Efforts by the NSC staff and a few CIA officers during the Reagan years to bypass Congress and conduct covert actions against the *Sandinista* regime in Nicaragua – even though prohibited by the Boland Amendments – displayed a disquieting failure of the New Oversight that had been established in 1974–80.[8] Even when SSCI and HPSCI leaders directly questioned NSC staffers, including National Security Advisers Robert C. McFarlane and Vice Admiral John M. Poindexter, about the rumored super-secret organization, "The Enterprise," created by the NSC staff to carry out the covert actions, the lawmakers were deceived. The NSC's top staff simply lied to members of Congress about these illicit operations.

Following their investigation into the scandal, lawmakers enacted new legislation to further tighten executive and legislative supervision over the secret agencies. The Inspector General (IG) Act of 1989 established a meaningful IG office at the Agency, confirmed by the Senate and with a mandate to keep the members of Congress regularly and fully informed of any improper activities at Langley. In addition, the Intelligence Oversight Act of 1991 clarified the meaning and the limits of covert action and required formal written approval by the President in a finding, not just a slippery verbal assent. With these measures, the government would make another attempt at making the experiment in intelligence accountability work.

The Era of Partisan Advocacy (1991–2001)

A product chiefly of redistricting decisions across the country that produced an abundance of safe congressional districts, along with a harsh take-no-prisoners form of political rhetoric advocated by a new GOP Speaker, Newt Gingrich (Georgia), the post-Iran–*contra* atmosphere in Washington proved poisonous to constructive bipartisan support for intelligence within SSCI and HPSCI. This sudden partisan divide on the oversight panels was a startling departure from the past.[9] Except for some acrimony and split votes generated by disagreements over whether to allow CIA covert actions in Nicaragua during the Reagan years, the Committees had almost always registered unanimous votes as they decided on intelligence policies, with members from both parties guided by a sense that intelligence matters were especially sensitive and ought to be placed above the normal partisan fray in Washington.

Yet in the period after the Republican takeover of the Hill in the 1990s, notes Aberbach, a new mood emerged, one that was "hostile not only to the intent and behavior of political appointees, but to the missions of many federal programs and agencies."[10] Both HPSCI and SSCI proved vulnerable to this rising partisan storm. Knott attributes the growing polarization, in part, to a Republican wariness toward President Bill Clinton's foreign policy, as well as to a "simple partisan payback for years of perceived Democratic hectoring of Republican presidents."[11] Acrimonious partisan politics swirled around the nomination of Robert M. Gates for DCI in 1991 – his second try, this time successful by the narrowest vote margin of any DCI nominee before or since. By 1997, the politics of intelligence had become as vituperative as any other policy domain. The candidacy of Anthony Lake, the incumbent Democratic National Security Adviser for DCI, in 1996 led to a deeply bitter struggle between Democrats and Republicans in Congress, with Lake finally withdrawing his name from consideration. The hearings, described by an observer as "vitriolic," were punctuated by the most heated public exchanges across the aisle in SSCI's history.[12]

In a continuation of the political in-fighting, SSCI – under the leadership of Senator Pat Roberts (R, Kansas) – would soon vote along party lines to reject a proposed investigation of the second Bush Administration's decision in the aftermath of the 9/11 attacks to bypass the procedures of the FISA and engage in the warrantless surveillance of the international communications of American citizens. The SSCI Vice Chairman, John D. Rockefeller IV (D, West Virginia), pronounced the panel "basically under the control of the White House, through its chairman [Roberts]." Chairman Roberts was equally adamant that the Committee's Democrats were merely trying to score points against President Bush.[13] "Got'ya" oversight became the standard practice for both parties on each of the intelligence oversight panels.

The Era of Mass Surveillance (2001–12)

Partisan squabbling over intelligence continued to roil SSCI and HPSCI after the Al Qaeda attacks against the United States in 2001. Indeed, according to a keen observer of Congress, the bickering grew even more heated. "One could only marvel at the degree to which partisanship had come to infect the work of the two committees," writes L. Britt Snider, former SSCI counsel (as well as a former CIA inspector general). "Once held up as models of how congressional committees should work," he further observed, "they now seemed no different from the rest."[14] Added to this internal political stress on the Intelligence Committees was a new ambivalence among their members toward the nation's secret agencies, displayed when the lawmakers merged temporarily into a Joint Committee to probe the tragic 9/11 intelligence and policy failures. Some members of the Joint Committee scolded the intelligence agencies for their errors leading up to terrorist attacks against the United States. Even SSCI's chair, Senator Roberts, once an arch-defender of the CIA, bemoaned in 2004 that not a single official in the Intelligence Community had been "disciplined, let alone fired" for the mistakes related to 9/11, or for the faulty prognosis about WMD in Iraq. In dismay, he concluded that the "community is in denial over the full extent of the shortcomings of its work."[15]

Although Roberts had developed a new love–hate relationship with the nation's intelligence agencies, he abandoned none of his partisan disdain for lawmakers across the aisle. He issued a spate of intelligence reform proposals that were endorsed by all but one of the SSCI Republican members, but he never shared any of his plans with the Democratic members of the Committee. The Roberts initiatives – a quixotic scheme to disperse the elements of the CIA into the Intelligence Community's other agencies – perplexed Congress-watchers. Once viewed as an unalloyed advocate of the intelligence status quo, Roberts no longer fit the Procrustean bed. Yet he didn't stray too far away from his underlying devotion to the secret agencies. The SSCI Chairman could be counted on by the DCI to grant the funding he and other agency managers requested, even if Roberts wished to shift around the organizational boxes on the Intelligence Community's wiring diagram.

While Roberts and a few other once reliable champions of the intelligence agencies occasionally displayed flashes of ambivalence and rebellion, for the most part SSCI and HPSCI members fell into an oversight stupor. They forgot the warnings of Madison and the wisdom of the Constitution. Oversight came to mean rallying behind the President and the Intelligence Community to support the fighting that ensued in Iraq, Afghanistan, and against global terrorism. This was an amplification of a trend visible even before 9/11. Prior to the terrorist attacks on the American homeland that day, SSCI had held only a couple of hearings on the subject of Al Qaeda. On the House side, the oversight record was just as dismal. Members of HPSCI held only two hearings on terrorism from 1998 to 2001 – the fewest of any conducted by a security or foreign affairs panel on Capitol Hill in the period leading up to the 9/11 attacks.[16] In another measure of their relative inactivity, from 1976 to 1990 the two Intelligence Committees averaged fewer than two public hearings a year. Zegart found a low number of intelligence hearings in later sessions of Congress as well.[17] Even when hearings are held, the attendance can be poor. Lawmakers on SSCI and HPSCI could easily hold more public hearings than they do presently, without jeopardizing national secrets. Moreover, attendance records for closed hearings could be published, so constituents could know whether their representatives were taking seriously the task of monitoring and improving America's secret agencies.

"We really don't have, still don't have, meaningful congressional oversight [of the intelligence agencies]," observed a GOP leader, Senator John McCain (R, Arizona), in 2004.[18] That same year, the 9/11 Commission concluded that "congressional oversight for intelligence – and counterterrorism – is now dysfunctional."[19] A former staff member of the Church Committee noted further in 2009 that, "unfortunately, the process of congressional oversight of intelligence, including covert action, so carefully crafted in the 1970s, is now regarded as something of a joke in Washington."[20]

When news broke in December 2005 about warrantless wiretaps secretly carried out by the second Bush Administration, some SSCI and HPSCI members complained publicly about the FISA violations, but they never did much about it. According to a seasoned reporter with an intelligence beat, the relationship between the oversight committees and the Intelligence Community had "degenerated into a mutual admiration society for secret agencies."[21] Lawmakers seemed to have concluded that it was time to rally behind the spy organizations, even if some (like Roberts) felt occasional twinges of ambivalence toward the secret agencies because of the disturbing intelligence failures that had occurred from 2001 to 2003.

The Era of Rebalancing (2013–)

THE NSA METADATA PROGRAM   In 2013, a controversial "metadata" surveillance program was disclosed through the most significant breach of classified information in American history. That year, the NSA temporarily hired from the private sector (the Booz Allen Hamilton corporation) a computer expert by the name of Edward J. Snowden, who had also worked for the CIA. Snowden was appalled by what he viewed as an excessive gathering of information by the NSA about the communication patterns of American citizens, including the names and contact numbers of anyone in the United States using a telephone or social media (though not the actual content of their communications). Snowden leaked information to the media about this program, codenamed "215," in contrast to Operation PRISM that targeted sigint communications without first obtaining a FIAS warrant (which the *New York Times* had revealed in December of 2005). He also provided the media with thousands of other secret documents that included highly classified, detailed budget data for the intelligence agencies. Snowden fled overseas and, in an odd landing for someone professing devotion to democratic principles, he took up residence in Russia.[22]

The Snowden documents on the NSA's metadata program, along with the FISA violations disclosed earlier by the *Times*, vividly revealed how the fear and anger generated by the September 2001 terrorist attacks had caused the United States to turn rapidly toward an emphasis on security over liberty. This tilt toward unfettered intelligence-collection operations – even at home – would experience a reversal beginning in 2013, however, as a result of the public's reaction to the Snowden revelations about the NSA intelligence fishing expedition. Questions arose as to whether the second Bush

Administration and the NSA had gone too far in targeting the communications logs of American citizens, the overwhelming number of whom had nothing to do with global terrorism.

Yet even in the face of a strong public reaction to the NSA's bulk collection activities, only a pair of SSCI members voted against its continuation: Ron Wyden (D, Washington) and Mark Udall (D, Colorado), who joined forces in a failed attempt to declassify the program. "What happens when you get on [the SSCI]," Wyden has observed, "right away the Intelligence Community sweeps in and basically starts the process of trying to kind of say, 'Well, these are tough issues.' And, in effect, only one point of view gets conveyed." He continued: "It's our job to do vigorous oversight and not just get caught up in the culture that makes you, in effect, something more like an ambassador [for the IC] than a vigorous overseer."[23] For another leading Republican Senator, John McCain, what happened in the metadata case was simple: "Clearly, [the members of SSCI] have been co-opted. There's no doubt about that."[24] A study by the Brookings Institution (a think-tank in Washington, DC) found that "the Snowden revelations exposed a profound failure by Congress to understand and deliberate about the government's massive collection of phone and email records. It dealt with the need for secrecy by leaving the decisions entirely to the president or the intelligence agencies themselves, while pretending to maintain statutory standards."[25]

The number of SSCI and HPSCI members in support of the metadata program started to shrink, though, as more details came to light – especially when an Obama-appointed study panel (the President's Review Group), led by Professor Geoffrey Stone of the University of Chicago Law School, issued a strongly critical analysis.[26] Another prominent law professor, Jack Goldsmith at Harvard University, said that "the program was an example of the Administration going it alone, in secret, based on inadequate legal reasoning and flawed legal opinions."[27] With the criticism mounting, President Obama started to have second thoughts about his unquestioning adoption of the Bush Administration's electronic surveillance programs.

For many on Capitol Hill and elsewhere, the demand from the Bush and Obama Administrations for actionable intelligence about terrorism had trumped basic American values of privacy and liberty. Shock, fear, uncertainty, and revenge had comingled to erase the established legal standards for surveillance (especially as embodied in the FISA of 1978). After 9/11, the Bush Administration adopted a vacuum-cleaner approach to electronic surveillance, rather than (as advocated by civil libertarians) a more pinpointed targeting of individuals based on a standard of reasonable suspicion that they might be involved in terrorist activities.

As the public debate continued to roil over the NSA's bulk data program, Congress passed the USA Freedom Act. The bill, designed to overhaul the Patriot Act of 2001 (about to expire on June 1), passed in 2015 by a vote of 338 to 88. The new law sought to trim back the reach of the Patriot Act and the NSA's metadata activities. In the same month, the U.S. Court of Appeals for the Second Circuit in New York declared metadata collection illegal, a judicial decision that bolstered the efforts of privacy-oriented lawmakers on Capitol Hill to rebalance the equilibrium between security and liberty.

President Barack Obama continued to endorsed some aspects of the NSA metadata program, but he instituted improved safeguards. Since the USA Freedom Act adopted his proposed added privacy protections, President Obama signed the bill. The key provisions of the new law and the President's new approach included an emphasis on limiting metadata collection to just two communications linkages from an initial terrorist suspect, along with the storage of this more constricted data in the files of the telephone companies – rather than within the NSA's massive computer storage banks in Utah. Further, the data could be kept for no more than five years. With a proper FISA warrant, the NSA could access these files to examine the intelligence as it related to terrorist suspects. In addition, the FISA Court would be encouraged to have a public-interest attorney present during its hearings about intelligence agency requests for wiretap warrants and for access to the metadata held by private telephone companies (like Verizon).

The decision of the New York federal court and the enactment of the USA Freedom Act strongly signaled a change in attitudes about the proper balance between national security and individual privacy – both vital for any viable democracy. "I'm not going to vote for an extension of a law [the Patriot Act] that has recently been declared illegal by a federal circuit court," declared Senator Chris Coons (D, Delaware); and Senator Rand Paul (R, Kentucky) asked his colleagues on the Senate floor: "Are you really willing to give up your liberty for security?"[28] Now the pendulum was swinging against the nation's national security hawks and back toward its civil liberty doves. As *New York Times* analysts put it, in motion on Capitol Hill was a shift away "from a singular focus on national security at the expense of civil liberties to a new balance in the post-Snowden era."[29] The coalition in favor of an intelligence rebalancing was made up of Democrats and libertarian Republicans who brought, the *Times* reported, "a changing tide in post-Sept.

11 America, where privacy concerns have become as important as national security interests for many people."[30]

Further complicating this ongoing debate between proponents of security and defenders of civil liberties was a ruling by the FISA Court, in the summer of 2015, that the NSA did indeed have a right to continue its metadata program – regardless of the New York Second Circuit opinion – at least until Congress made clear exactly what the boundaries were going to be for the NSA's surveillance practices. "Second Circuit rulings are not binding" on this panel, declared Michael W. Mosman, a FISA Court judge.[31] Judge Mosman had become persuaded that a metadata program, had one existed in 2001, might have stopped the 9/11 attacks; however, other reports pointed to the fact that the CIA had lots of information about two of the eventual terrorists hiding out in San Diego fully two years before the attack, but never shared this information with the FBI, which is responsible for domestic counterintelligence. "There was no need for a metadata collection program," concluded a thoughtful commentator. "What was needed was [CIA] cooperation with other federal agencies."[32]

Congress would no doubt have to deliberate further on the long-term fate of the NSA's collection operations involving American citizens as targets, although not until the 2016 presidential election had run its course. Had these NSA intelligence operations unequivocally led to successes in curbing terrorist attacks, the argument in favor of their continuation would have been persuasive; in fact, though, the NSA and the White House were unable to offer instances compelling enough to quell the defenders of civil liberties – just as was the case with the CIA's use of torture against suspected terrorists.

THE SENATE TORTURE REPORT   Immediately after the 9/11 attacks, President Bush gave the CIA authority to capture, detain, and, when necessary, kill Al Qaeda operatives around the world; then, the following year, he waived Common Article 3 of the Geneva Conventions that prohibited "cruel treatment and torture." (The United States had also ratified the Convention Against Torture in 1988, signed by President Ronald Reagan.) Further, in 2002, the head of Justice's Office of Legal Counsel (OLC) provided the CIA with additional after-the-fact authority to engage in harsh interrogation techniques.[33] Jane Mayer writes that "unthinkable cruelty" was becoming official U.S. policy.[34]

The CIA Reacts to 9/11   In September of 2002, the CIA finally briefed a few members of HPSCI and SSCI about their interrogation activities. The Chair of the Senate Committee, Bob Graham (D, Florida), requested additional information; the Agency slow-rolled and stonewalled him, however, knowing that he was about to retire from the Senate in a few months. One nonpartisan outside observer concluded that the Agency's approach to SSCI and HPSCI during this time was one of "disdain and evasiveness."[35]

In 2005 the Agency's interrogation program began to unravel. During November of that year, reporter Dana Priest of the *Washington Post* revealed the existence of CIA prisons aboard; and, soon afterward, the Deputy Director of Operations (DDO, the top covert action officer at the Agency), destroyed videotapes of the torture sessions, despite earlier admonitions from SSCI and HPSCI that these tapes had to be preserved.[36] It took two years, though, before the *New York Times* learned about and reported on the destruction of the tapes. "There is only one reason why [the videotapes] were destroyed: because certain people wanted that information never to be available," concluded SSCI Chairwoman Dianne Feinstein (D, California), who had expressed support for the NSA's controversial sigint operations as a counterterrorism tool but decidedly did not approve of torture. She believed that the destruction of the torture tapes had all the earmarks of a cover-up.[37]

During the fall of 2006, the plenary SSCI membership was briefed on the interrogation program for the first time, five years after its initiation. General Michael V. Hayden, the CIA's Director (and the former NSA Director who had initiated the metadata program), gave the briefing in his typically self-assured and pugnacious style. He vouched for the effectiveness of the interrogation methods and, in one of his more egregious moments of peddling fiction on Capitol Hill, he claimed that they were actually quite benign: merely "tummy slapping," as Senator Feinstein recalls him saying.[38] Feinstein later remembered that Hayden had presented "the entire set of techniques as minimally harmful and applied in a highly clinical and professional manner. They were not."[39]

While these events were evolving, SSCI decided in March of 2009 – at long last, critics would complain – to initiate a staff investigation into the Agency's interrogation practices. Prodded by public calls for a "truth commission" to examine "torture" and other rumored harsh inflictions against detainees, as well as reeling from the unauthorized destruction of the interrogation videotapes, the SSCI voted fourteen to one in favor of a formal inquiry. The lone holdout was Senator Saxby Chambliss (R, Georgia), the Committee's Vice Chairman.[40]

The GOP members of SSCI soon abandoned the inquiry, however, on grounds that it had become politicized. The Democrats pressed on and, after more than five years of research, writing, and wrangling with the CIA and SSCI Republicans, they sent a draft report to the Agency and the White House for a classification review. Several more months went by. Finally, a fatigued SSCI voted by a margin of eleven to three (with one abstention) to give up on publication of the full report and settle for the release of just an executive summary – if it could even achieve that. The three senators voting no, all Republicans, did not want to see even the public release of a declassified executive summary.

After an agonizing eight more months of tug-of-war over declassification decisions, SSCI finally gained permission from the Obama Administration near the end of 2014 to publish the executive summary. (At no point during or after this process did President Obama ever say a word to Senator Feinstein about her Committee's findings.) Even in its truncated form, the executive summary of the report was a lengthy and searing document: 499 pages long and with 2,725 footnotes.

Reaction to the Torture Report   When the GOP members of SSCI bailed out of the torture inquiry, the Democratic members authorized six of their professional staffers to move forward in trying to determine the authorization for the Agency's use of torture. The staff also examined the nature of the around-the-clock interrogation techniques, which ran from waterboarding three detainees (183 times, in the instance of detainee Khalid Sheikh Mohammed, the suspected mastermind of the 9/11 attacks, known by Agency interrogators as KSM) and rectal feeding, to mock executions and sleep deprivation lasting for days (seven-and-a-half days in one case). Some of the detainees were confined to cramped, coffin-like boxes. According to the SSCI report, one of the waterboarded detainees, Abu Zubaydah, "became completely unresponsive, with bubbles rising through his open, full mouth."[41] The report said that one ploy used by the CIA was the "hard takedown," whereby five Agency people would jump a detainee, hood him, cut away his clothing, punch him, and drag him down a hallway.

The Director of the CIA, John Brennan, has said that the Senate report is full of exaggerations and errors – an incomplete and selective picture of what occurred. Republicans on SSCI echoed this judgment in a minority report. Yet, in 2016, the chief military prosecutor at Guantánamo, General Mark Martins, read the full classified document and commented publicly that the facts were accurate, based on his knowledge of the interrogation program.[42]

The investigators studied, as well, the question of whether these methods had elicited useful information that shielded the United

States from further terrorist attacks. Brennan eventually acknowledged: "We have not concluded that it was the EITs [enhanced interrogation techniques, in spytalk] within that program that allowed us to obtain useful information from the detainees subjected to them." Ultimately, though, in his opinion, the question of whether torture had been useful was "unknowable."[43] In contrast, the conclusions reached by SSCI investigators were that the methods used by the CIA to extract information from detainees were far more barbaric than the Agency had claimed (one partially naked detainee, who had been apprehended in a case of mistaken identity, died of hypothermia in 2002); and that the effectiveness of this approach had been grossly exaggerated by General Hayden and everyone else at the CIA, the White House, and the Justice Department.

Many observers of this debate pointed out that the more important matter had to do with the damage the use of torture had done to America's reputation around the world for fair play and dedication to human rights. As President Obama said about the SSCI report, it "reinforces my long-held view that these harsh methods were not only inconsistent with our values as a nation, they did not serve our broader counterterrorism efforts or our national security interests... upholding the values we profess doesn't make us weaker, it makes us stronger."[44] The Senate Torture Report raised vital questions about whether secret agencies had overreached in the direction of security by adopting counterterrorism measures alien to America's fundamental ethical principles.

CIA Attacks the SSCI Staff   Also in 2014, in the context of the SSCI torture investigation, the Agency further contributed to the growing sense in the United States that the time had come to rebalance the security–liberty equation. In a move that set a new standard of brazenness and disdain toward congressional overseers, CIA officers hacked into computers – four times – that the SSCI staff had used during the torture inquiry. The Agency's cyber-warriors removed 870 documents during one hit, and 50 on another occasion.[45] Director Brennan claimed – falsely, it turned out, although perhaps he thought his statement was correct at the time – that SSCI staffers had first hacked into the Agency's computers. In fact, the Agency had accidentally sent to the SSCI staff computers the CIA's own internal examination of its interrogation practices – the so-called Panetta Review, named after then CIA Director Leon Panetta, who had ordered an internal review into the Agency's uses of torture. Amazed and pleased to stumble across this unknown study, which the CIA should have shared with SSCI in the first place, the Committee staff was gratified to find that this in-house study closely paralleled its own findings.

Unhappy that the Senate investigators now had inadvertently been provided with the Panetta Report, some people in the Agency, including Brennan, tried to turn the tables on their Hill tormentors by claiming that the SSCI staff had stolen the document by way of illegal hacking. The tradecraft of the CIA abroad often includes the use of deception and manipulation; these dark arts were now turned against "Sissystan," as Agency officers had nicknamed SSCI. The Senate Intelligence Committee had become, essentially, just another foreign country targeted for covert action. Even Senator Chambliss, one of the Agency's top cheerleaders in Congress, blanched at these accusations from the D/CIA. "John [Brennan] didn't handle that right," Chambliss managed to say in mild rebuke.[46] Another SSCI member observed at the time: "It's WWIII between the CIA and Senate."[47]

Feinstein wrote to Brennan, reprimanding the Agency for its search into SSCI's computers, which she said might well have violated the separation of powers doctrine that lay at the heart of the Constitution (not to mention the CIA's founding law in 1947, which clearly prohibited Agency operations inside the United States). The Director took weeks to respond. A Senate colleague of Feinstein's told the SSCI Chairwoman that Brennan's intentions on behalf of the CIA were "to intimidate, deflect, and thwart legitimate oversight."[48] Subsequently, Brennan would concede in testimony before the full Committee that a "trust deficit" had opened up between SSCI and the Agency, and he apologized to Feinstein and Chambliss for the hacking transgression.

The CIA engaged in other forms of harassment against the Committee's investigators, too. Its Acting Chief Counsel went after the SSCI staff with a vengeance, perhaps distressed by the fact that his name had come up more than 1,600 times in the SSCI Torture Report (each of which he managed to have deleted during the White House declassification wars). He referred the names of the SSCI staffers who wrote the Torture Report to the Justice Department for investigation.

In the light of these activities, the Agency's understanding of and allegiance to the existing laws and rules on accountability became a subject of deep concern on Capitol Hill and in the media. Senate Majority Leader Harry Reed (D, Nevada) warned Feinstein: "Look, you can't stand by anymore! The CIA is leaking stuff. They're making your staff out to be the bad guys!"[49] The Agency's efforts to spy on SSCI staffers was an unprecedented violation of the oversight relationship – an operation carried out with impunity, despite the strong, even angry complaint delivered by Senator Feinstein in a press conference.

Brennan appointed a panel to look into the charges. Three of the five members of this group were CIA officers, and the other two were outside individuals known to be friendly toward the Agency. After a brief "investigation," the CIA absolved itself of any blame and announced, with its practiced skills of agitprop, that the whole episode had been just a "misunderstanding."[50] In sharp contrast, the CIA's own Inspector General had reported earlier that the Agency's hacking into SSCI computers was improper, as was the effort by the CIA Acting General Counsel to file a crimes report with the Department of Justice against Committee's staffers. The Agency's IG, David Buckley, soon found himself discredited and ostracized inside the CIA. He resigned, as his own organization – the brother-hood – closed ranks against him.

Despite this opposition from Langley, in 2015 the findings of the SSCI Torture Report significantly influenced the Senate vote of seventy-eight to twenty-one in favor of banning America's use of any interrogation techniques in the future that were not specifically authorized in the list of less draconian methods printed in the U.S. Army Field Manual.

A Mixed Record   A former SSCI Chair, Jay Rockefeller (D, West Virginia), summed up the CIA's response to the interrogation inquiry as an "active subversion of meaningful congressional oversight."[51] To some degree, however, SSCI and HPSCI bear blame for allowing the CIA torture and the NSA metadata programs to move forward for so long before they took a closer look at them. Accepting at face value Hayden's "tummy slapping" remarks (as happened, too, with National Security Adviser Robert McFarlane's assurances in the 1980s about the non-existence of the Enterprise during the Iran–*contra* episode) proved to be a painful mistake. Overseers must learn to be more skeptical and tenacious – using hearings to dig for the truth, with witnesses sworn under oath, as well as resorting to subpoena powers to obtain access to key documents and witnesses – until they are reasonably sure that all the facts are on the table.

Further, as several CIA directors noted in an op-ed, once they were finally informed by the executive branch about the interroga-tion activities, SSCI and HPSCI "missed a chance to help shape the program – they couldn't reach a consensus. The executive branch was left to proceed alone, merely keeping the committees informed."[52] Journalist David Ignatius concurs. He accepted the SSCI report as "immensely valuable," but tagged the oversight committee for never properly addressing "Congress's own failure to oversee these activities more effectively." Ignatius wondered: "Did the members of Congress push back hard, as we now realize they should have? Did they demand more information and set stricter limits? Did they question details about the interrogation techniques that were being used?" His correct response: "They did not."[53] Legal scholar Michael Glennon asks: "Where was SSCI while all this was going on?"[54] He might have added: And where was HPSCI? Neither Committee visited any of the CIA's controversial black sites overseas, for example.

At the same time, SSCI earns high marks in persevering with its inquiry into the interrogation program, despite great adversity and insufficient cooperation from the executive branch (for instance, the White House, at the CIA's instigation, blocked 9,000 pages of documents from going to SSCI during its investigation, on grounds of executive privilege). The Torture Report is no doubt flawed. It would have been especially good to have more bipartisan participation, at the staff and member levels. The Republicans could have made this happen, but deserted the effort as an early means of trying to slow down and discredit the inquiry. The GOP members would have had plenty of opportunities along the way to insert their dissenting views into the report, setting the record straight when they thought the Democrats were off-mark. In this sense, the Republican strategy did the CIA a great disservice. Only courageous Olympia Snowe (R, New Hampshire) displayed a bipartisan spirit on SSCI and a willingness to search for the truth with her colleagues across the aisle.

Critics have charged the Democratic staff who worked on the report with allowing their ethical objections toward torture to trump a dispassionate weighing of the program's effectiveness. The staffers deny this, arguing that their purpose was to lay out the facts.[55] At any rate, the facts did indicate that the CIA's resort to torture was not very effective, just as the value of the NSA's controversial sigint programs were routinely exaggerated by intelligence officials – and even by Senator Feinstein.[56]

Senator Feinstein, the accountability hero throughout this doleful episode, captured the Torture Report's normative sentiments: "We're not Nazi Germany. We don't torture people. We don't waterboard them 183 times until they nearly stop breathing. We don't put them in coffins and attach them to walls for, like, 100 hours."[57] Hayden dismissed her views as "emotional," but she was not alone in her outrage. Senator McCain for one, himself a victim of torture at the hands of ruthless North Vietnamese interrogators during the war in Vietnam, said that "this question is not about our enemies; it's about us."[58]

A shock theory of intelligence accountability

As this look at the different phases of intelligence accountability suggests, the oversight performance of SSCI and HPSCI has fluctuated widely during the Cold War and since. Several observers have commented on these ups and downs. Writing about oversight in the years before the Church Committee investigation, for example, Ransom noted that intelligence accountability had been "sporadic, spotty, and essentially uncritical."[59] Even after the introduction of the New Oversight in 1975, students of the subject have discerned little serious attention to this responsibility in recent years.[60] The chief cause of the inattentiveness derives from the nature of Congress: lawmakers seek re-election as their primary objective and they usually conclude that passing bills and raising campaign funds is a better use of their time than the often tedious review of executive branch programs. This is especially true for intelligence review. The examination of secret operations must take place in closed committee sanctuaries, outside of public view. Absent public awareness, the chances for credit-claiming – vital to a lawmaker's re-election prospects – become difficult.[61]

An examination of intelligence accountability in the United States since the Year of Intelligence in 1975 indicates a cyclical pattern of stimulus and response. A major intelligence scandal or failure – a shock – transforms the perfunctory performance of oversight into a burst of intense program scrutiny. This burst is followed by a period of reasonably attentive oversight activities that yields remedial legislation or other reforms designed to curb inappropriate intelligence operations in the future. Then comes the third phase of the shock cycle: a return to a middling practice of oversight. Political scientists McCubbins and Schwartz offer the useful metaphor of "police patrolling" and "firefighting" to highlight these differences in commitment by lawmakers to oversight responsibilities.[62] Patrolling consists of steadily checking up on the executive bureaucracy: the shining of a flashlight into darkened windows, jiggling the lock on the door, walking the streets with a keen eye. In contrast, firefighting requires an emergency reaction to a calamity after it occurs. Lawmakers qua firefighters jump on the fire truck when the alarm sounds and try to put out the conflagration. A prominent member of Congress has recently used the policing analogy. "There has been no cop on the beat," said Representative Henry A. Waxman (D, California), chair of the House Oversight and Government Reform Committee, who accused Republicans of abandoning their oversight responsibilities. "And when there

The Patterns

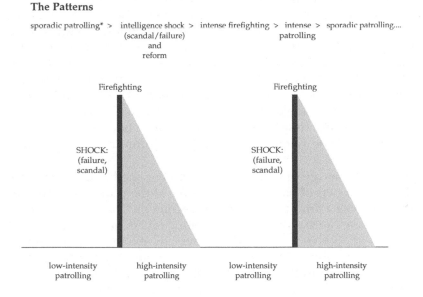

sporadic patrolling* > intelligence shock > intense firefighting > intense > sporadic patrolling....
                       (scandal/failure)   patrolling
                            and
                           reform

* A result of insufficient opportunities for credit-claiming and the enhancement of re-election prospects, which in turn produce an inattentiveness to oversight duties and a concomitant ripening of conditions for scandal or failure.

Figure 5.3   The cycle of intelligence shock and reaction by congressional overseers, 1975–2006

Source: Loch K. Johnson, "A Shock Theory of Congressional Accountability for Intelligence," in Loch K. Johnson, ed., *Handbook of Intelligence Studies* (New York: Routledge, 2007), pp. 343–360; figure at p. 344.

is no cop on the beat, criminals are more willing to engage in crimes."[63]

Sometimes the high-intensity police patrolling that follows firefighting can last for months and, if the original shock was strong enough to produce extended media attention, even years. Once the firestorm (an intelligence failure or scandal) has subsided and reforms are in place, however, lawmakers return to a state of relative inattentiveness to intelligence activities – low-intensity, or perhaps even non-existent, police patrolling. This pattern is depicted in Figure 5.3.

To reach the level of a shock (or "fire alarm"), an allegation of intelligence failure or impropriety has to have sustained media coverage, with at least a few front-page stories. In 1974, for example, the *New York Times* had an unusually high run of reporting on the CIA from June through December: some 200 articles. In December alone, nine stories on the Agency made the front page – unprecedented at the time. Here was a steady drumbeat of chiefly negative reports, setting the stage for a strong public – and, therefore, congressional and presidential – reaction to the most explosive of these news items: Operation CHAOS, the CIA domestic spy scandal. On the eve of the next major intelligence scandal, the Iran–*contra* affair the *Times* carried eleven front-page stories in both October and November 1986 about possible intelligence abuses related to a covert war in Nicaragua. The number jumped to eighteen front-page stories in December, setting the stage for the Joint Committee investigation into the scandal in 1987.

Congress has greater authority than the media to investigate intelligence operations – from the power of the purse to the power of the subpoena and, ultimately, impeachment. The media, though, seem to have more will-power to conduct oversight, driven in part by a profit motive to sell newspapers by exposing government scandals and failures. Intense media coverage may not be enough in itself to bring out the firefighters on Capitol Hill. The warrantless wiretaps and the CIA torture practices during the second Bush Administration, for instance, garnered considerable media attention but no major congressional inquiry. The nation continued to feel under the threat of possible terrorist attacks and, in this climate of fear, investigations into these shocking revelations were never pursued. Such considerations as the personalities of congressional overseers – especially the attitudes of the SSCI and HPSCI chairs – and the existence of divided government can play a role, too, in determining whether an intelligence shock leads to a major firefighting episode.[64]

The intelligence shocks

Since Congress began to take intelligence oversight seriously, near the end of 1974, lawmakers have devoted about six years of their time to intensive investigating (firefighting), stimulated by five major intelligence controversies or shocks (alarms), presented in the text below and in Table 5.1. The rest of the time – the vast majority – has been spent in police patrolling. Sometimes this patrolling has been vigorous (the Senate Torture Report is a conspicuous example, at least for the Democrats on SSCI); but, for the most part, it has been carried out in a perfunctory manner.

MAJOR ALARM NO. 1: THE DOMESTIC SPY SCANDAL (1974) The government of the United States responded to news allegations of CIA domestic spying (Operation CHAOS) with the Church, Pike,

Table 5.1 Type of stimuli and oversight responses by lawmakers, 1974–2016

Year	Stimulus	Oversight response	Purpose of response
1974	FA (#1)	Hughes–Ryan Act	Controls over covert action
1976–7	FA (#1)	Est. SSCI, HPSCI; critical reports	More robust accountability
1978	FA (#1)	FISA	Warrants for electronic surveillance
1980	FA (#1)	Intel. Oversight Act	Tightening oversight rules
1980	P	Intel. Information Procedures Act	Ease intel. judicial proceedings
1982	P	Intel. Identities Act	Protect intel. officers/agents
1984	P	CIA Information Act	Limits on FOIA requests
1987	FA (#2)	Critical report	Improve intelligence oversight
1989	FA (#2)	CIA Inspector General Act	Improve internal CIA oversight
1991	FA (#2)	Intel. Oversight Act	Further tightening oversight rules
1996	FA (#3)	Est. DCI assistants; critical reports	IC management improvements; strengthening CI
1997	P	Intel. Authorization Act provision	Controls on CIA use of journalists; improving
1998	P	Whistle-blowers Protection Act	procedures for whistle-blowing
2001	FA (#4)	USA Patriot Act; authorization of war against Al Qaeda and Taliban regime, AUMF; increases in counterterrorism funding	Surveillance of suspected terrorists; paramilitary counterattacks against Al Qaeda and Taliban
2004	FA (#4)	Critical reports	Improving humint and analysis
2004	FA (#4, #5)	Intel. Reform & Terrorism Prevention Act (IRTPA)	Strengthening CT, IC coordination, est. Director of National Intel.
2008	P	FISA Amendments Act	Supporting NSA metadata program
2015	P	USA FREEDOM Act	Safeguards for NSA operations

Abbreviations:
FA = fire alarm (#1 = domestic spying; #2 = Iran-contra; #3 = Ames; #4 = 9/11; #5 = WMD in Iraq)
P = patrolling
humint = human intelligence
IC = Intelligence Community
FISA = Foreign Intelligence Surveillance Act [P.L. 95-511; 92 Stat. 1783 (Oct. 25, 1978)]
DCI = Director of Central Intelligence
CI, CT = counterintelligence, counterterrorism
AUMF = Authorization of the Use of Military Force

and Rockefeller inquiries. The findings of these panels led to the creation of SSCI and HPSCI, the FISA warrant requirements of 1978, and the Intelligence Oversight Act of 1980 with its dramatic requirement of prior notice to Congress for all important intelligence operations.[65]

MAJOR ALARM NO. 2: THE IRAN–*CONTRA* SCANDAL (1986)　The Inouye–Hamilton Committee, which examined the Iran–*contra* allegations, revealed unlawful intelligence operations carried out by the NSC staff and a few CIA officials.[66] Its findings led to enactment of the CIA Inspector General Act of 1989, creating an IG with responsibilities to keep Congress informed of Agency improprieties; and the Intelligence Oversight Act of 1991, which clarified covert action definitions and tightened its approval procedures.

MAJOR ALARM NO. 3: THE AMES COUNTERINTELLIGENCE FAILURE (1994)　In response to the discovery of Aldrich Ames's treachery, the Congress created a presidential–congressional panel of inquiry, known as the Aspin–Brown Commission and led by former Secretaries of Defense Les Aspin and Harold Brown. A U.S. intelligence failure on the Horn of Africa, leading to the deaths of several American soldiers, contributed to the sense in Washington that a major investigation into intelligence practices was warranted. The Commission published a report calling for reforms across the board of intelligence activities, but with special emphasis on the need for a stronger DCI and for revealing to the public the annual aggregate intelligence budget figure.[67]

MAJOR ALARM No. 4: THE 9/11 ATTACKS (2001)　The failure of the intelligence agencies to warn the nation about the catastrophic terrorist attacks against the American homeland in 2001 led Congress to form a joint committee of inquiry (the Graham–Goss Committee) and, subsequently, to urge the creation of an even more comprehensive presidential investigative panel (the Kean Commission) to probe further into the disaster.[68] Moreover, HPSCI released to the public a critical evaluation of the CIA's humint activities around the world, stressing the lack of good assets in key locations.[69]

MAJOR ALARM No. 5: THE ABSENCE OF WMD IN IRAQ (2003)　In light of an incorrect intelligence judgment about the likely presence of WMD in Iraq, expressed in a National Intelligence Estimate of October 2002, Congress supported the creation of a presidential commission on intelligence (the Silberman–Robb Commission) to investigate this analytic failure.[70] Moreover, SSCI undertook a parallel but separate probe into the faulty WMD estimate. The Committee focused on the CIA's errors, but elected not to examine questions about the poor use of warning intelligence by the Clinton and second Bush White Houses.[71]

Major alarms – No. 6, followed by No. 7 – might normally have occurred in the wake of the NSA sigint collection controversies (warrantless wiretaps, metadata) and the CIA torture program, respectively; but the impulses toward intelligence inquiries (firefighting) by lawmakers and the White House were dampened down by the ongoing potential danger of future terrorist attacks. A sense prevailed among many (although not all) key officials in Washington that security considerations would have to supersede matters of liberty and privacy – at least for a while.

As shown in Table 5.1, Congress embraced eighteen significant intelligence reform initiatives during the time span from 1974 to 2016. Eleven of these stemmed from major investigations (firefighting), and seven occurred outside the context of a response to a major fire alarm (police patrolling). Of these seven, the first made it easier for the Intelligence Community to shelter its secrets during legal proceedings in a judicial court, by permitting in camera (private) review by judges of any classified documents involved in a law suit involving the Intelligence Community. The second, the Intelligence Identities Act of 1982, was the result of a conclusion reached by members of Congress that a law was needed to provide stiff penalties against anyone who revealed, without proper authorization, the name of a U.S. intelligence officer or asset.[72] The third consisted of placing limits on Freedom of Information Act (FOIA) requests to the secret agencies in some instances, especially related to CIA covert actions. The fourth and fifth initiatives dealt, respectively, with ensuring that the Intelligence Community reported to Congress any use of U.S. journalists in intelligence operations, and with improving whistle-blowing procedures.[73] The final two police-patrolling initiatives (six and seven) contributed to the passage of laws that supported some key features of the NSA metadata program (the FISA Amendments Act of 2008), while, subsequently, also providing new safeguards for privacy from NSA intrusions (the USA Freedom Act of 2015). While these police-patrolling influences were important, they fell short of the more sweeping changes wrought by the five fire-alarm events: such reforms as the Hughes-Ryan Act, FISA, and the Intelligence Oversight Acts of 1980 and 1991. These major reforms – the outcome of specific shocks – highlight a number of fundamental issues related to the effective conduct of intelligence accountability. These issues are explored next.

Key issues of intelligence accountability

Who should be informed?

Several prominent issues have dominated the ongoing debate over how legislative oversight should be conducted with respect to the intelligence agencies. The first issue is who should be kept informed on Capitol Hill. Before 1974, the answer was just a few lawmakers on the small intelligence subcommittees of the Armed Services and Appropriations Committees – if indeed the DCI deigned to tell them anything, or if the lawmakers were (unlike Senator John Stennis) willing to listen. Today the "witting circle" on the Hill has widened to include members of SSCI and HPSCI, as well as (on some topics) selected members who serve on the appropriations, armed services, foreign affairs, and judiciary committees – with the top four leaders of Congress (two from each party) also informed on some emergency occasions. Intelligence officials, though, are not beyond playing games with these reporting rules, sometimes attempting to whisper only in the ear of a committee chair – DCI Turner's ploy with Eddie Boland early in their relationship, until Boland began to wonder how much he could really peer into the activities of the intelligence agencies while locked in a bear hug by the DCI.

On other occasions, intelligence managers may seek to limit their briefings on a finding, or some other key intelligence decision, to a "Gang of Eight" (the top four congressional leaders and the top four SSCI and HPSCI leaders from both parties); or even a "Gang of Four," by limiting the witting circle to only the leaders of the two Intelligence Committees (or sometimes the phrase is used to refer to the four top congressional leaders).[74] The Gang of Four concept is strictly an invention of the executive branch, used from time to time by presidents of both parties since 1980, as during the attempts by the second Bush Administration to inform only a few lawmakers about the NSA metadata program and the CIA's adoption of torture. Nowhere is the Gang of Four provision allowed by statute; and the Gang of Eight is a group, it should be emphasized, that was supposed to be used only in times of emergency. Yet, in 2002, the second Bush Administration briefed – all too briefly, according to recipients – just the Gang of Eight for its questionable use of warrantless wiretaps, an operation revealed by the *New York Times* in 2005.

In another bit of trickery, intelligence managers often do their best to make sure that no staff are present for briefings on covert action to the Gang of Eight or the Gang of Four. It is a clever strategy, relying on the fact that members of Congress usually don't have enough time or expertise to question an operation deeply, while experienced staff aides might raise serious objections for the members of Congress to consider. As Kathleen Clark notes, the executive branch will inform the Gang of Eight *sans* staff support, then claim that it had the support of Congress for an operation – as if eight lawmakers represented all of SSCI and HPSCI, let alone the full Senate and House.[75] Sometimes the staff on SSCI and HPSCI are partisan, inexperienced in the procedures of oversight, or have limited knowledge about intelligence. Good staff are vital, because the members are often too busy to address the details of intelligence initiatives advanced by the CIA and the other secret agencies. "The staff has to take the lead," concludes a former CIA officer who has observed Agency–Hill relations for many years. "You ultimately must choose the right people and pay them well to stay."[76]

Clark has concluded that "the Obama Administration has continued the Bush administration practice of resisting robust intelligence disclosure to Congress."[77] The Obama Administration, for example, sometimes refused to report to Congress on covert actions beyond the Gang of Eight. It bears repeating that the intent of Congress in the 1980 and the 1991 Intelligence Oversight Acts was to allow a Gang of Eight just in emergencies, after which ("in a few days" – interpreted to mean forty-eight hours) the privileged Eight were expected to ensure that the full complement of SSCI and HPSCI members were properly briefed. Here is the standard to which the Congress should return, insisting at the same time that if there is a genuine need for a Gang of Eight briefing, then a few senior and knowledgeable staffers will be included in the session and the entire SSCI and HPSCI membership will be informed that the Gang of Eight provision has been temporarily evoked.

Sometimes the favorite number of lawmakers to brief on Capitol Hill has been zero – a "Gang of None" – as was clearly the case with Operation CHAOS, COINTELPRO, SHAMROCK, MINARET, and the CIA assassination plots. The longest-serving DCI, Allen Dulles (1953–61), once said that he felt obliged to tell the truth only to one person: the President – if he asked.[78] On another occasion Dulles widened the circle by one. "I'll fudge the truth to the oversight committee," he said, "but I'll tell the chairman the truth – that is, if he wants to know."[79]

In bold contrast, the intent of the 1980 and 1991 Intelligence Oversight Acts was to have all the members of SSCI and HPSCI briefed (along with a few staff in attendance), not just some subset. The Committees, though, must insist on this approach or intelligence managers will sidestep the full-briefing rule.[80] Certainly the two oversight committees have demonstrated their trustworthiness over the years, with virtually no major leaks from them – far fewer than the flood from the executive branch. Further, during its long history Congress has never had any "plumbers in the basement" – unlike the executive branch during the Nixon Administration with its Watergate conspirators.[81]

A well-known controversy regarding reporting to Congress by a DCI occurred during the tenure of Richard Helms. In 1973, while appearing before a Foreign Relations subcommittee in the Senate, he was asked whether or not the Agency had been involved in secret efforts to overthrow the Allende regime in Chile. He said no, but that was not a truthful answer. When lawmakers complained about this misleading response, the Justice Department tried the DCI for perjury. In plea bargaining, Helms agreed to a misdemeanor charge and was fined $2,000, evading a two-year prison sentence. He continued to believe that he had acted appropriately before the subcommittee, because (in his view) the CIA had not been involved so much in a *coup d'état* as in an effort to prevent Allende's election in the first place; moreover, Helms maintained, he was simply honoring the secrecy strictures placed on him by President Nixon. Yet the end result was that members of Congress were misled (although some knew the truth from other briefings). Rather than lie to lawmakers, Helms could have said that, as is always the case with allegations about covert action (whether real or imagined), he was unable to discuss such matters in public, but that he would be happy to meet with members in a closed session to set the record straight on Agency operations in Latin America or anywhere else.

When should reporting to Congress occur?

Another central issue has been the question of when intelligence managers should inform lawmakers about their activities. Before 1974, the answer was: whenever – and if – the managers felt like it. With respect to the Hughes–Ryan Act, the answer for covert actions evolved into an understanding that the briefing would take place "in a timely fashion," defined during the floor colloquy that preceded the vote on this law to mean within twenty-four hours. The 1980 Intelligence Oversight Act – short in length, but long in reach – changed the formula powerfully to mean "prior notice" (except in an emergency, which allowed reporting – recall – to just the Gang of Eight for a day or two, after which full briefings to SSCI and HPSCI were expected). *Ante facto* reporting had won out over *ex post facto* reporting and, in the process, intelligence oversight acquired much greater strength. Lawmakers were now in a position to object to an operation before it was already under way. For example, HPSCI chairman Peter Hoekstra (R, Michigan) once protested to President George W. Bush directly about a specific covert action and the President reportedly modified the operation based on this criticism.[82]

The 1991 Intelligence Oversight Act retained this reporting requirement, but clarified during floor colloquy before the vote on the proposal that the emergency delay provision (which permitted reporting only to the Gang of Eight) could be used by the executive branch for a full forty-eight hours – but no longer. At that point, the Gang of Eight was expected to report to the rest of the SSCI and HPSCI membership.[83] During confirmation hearings, the (successful) DCI nominee Robert M. Gates testified that he would strongly consider resigning from office if a delay in reporting to Congress went beyond just a few days at the most.[84]

What information should be reported?

The question of what kind of information should be reported is obviously important, too. Again, before 1974, this decision was left to the discretion of the DCI. The Hughes–Ryan Act then required reporting on important covert actions. The far-reaching Intelligence Oversight Act of 1980 made it clear that Congress wished to be kept informed of "all" important intelligence activities, which remains the gold standard – although one the executive branch has periodically ignored.

Which agencies are expected to report?

Further debate has surrounded the topic of which of the sixteen intelligence agencies must report to lawmakers (or seventeen, if one includes the ODNI as a agency, rather than an administrative office). Before 1974, the answer was: the reporting, however infrequent, would be carried out by the CIA, since the DCI was housed in its headquarters building at Langley. After 1974 (Hughes–Ryan), the answer was modified to include the White House along with the CIA – at least when it came to covert actions, which henceforth required a presidential finding. Then the 1980 Oversight Act stressed that all government agencies and other "entities" would be expected to keep the oversight panels on Capitol Hill informed, if they were engaged in intelligence activities. The broad language included the NSC staff, a matter that became controversial during the Reagan Administration when that staff chose to ignore this provision as it launched its super-secret Iran–*contra* covert actions. The staff (including the NSC's lawyers) argued that the Council was not an official member of the Intelligence Community and, therefore, was immune to the provisions of the 1980 Intelligence Oversight Act – an interpretation never intended back in 1980 and rejected in 1987 by a majority of the lawmakers involved in the Inouye–Hamilton inquiry into the scandal.

How long should lawmakers serve?

The question of committee term limits has been of significance, too, in understanding the lack of effective oversight on Capitol Hill. At the time of its creation in 1977, HPSCI limited its members to four terms (eight years), although the chairman and ranking minority member were allowed to stay on for ten years. The theory behind these restrictions is that high turnover among members would keep them from becoming co-opted by the intelligence agencies – a phenomenon all too common on Capitol Hill in other policy domains. Driven by the same theory, SSCI had similar term limits, until 2005, when its members decided that greater longevity among members – and therefore greater experience and knowledge – trumped the earlier concentration on countering co-optation. In recent years, HPSCI also jettisoned term limits. Now intelligence overseers in both chambers of Congress have a longer period of time in which to become genuine experts on the arcane aspects of espionage – or to be co-opted.

Who should enact legislation?

The normal passage in Congress of authorization bills, followed by appropriations bills to pay for the policies, has sometimes fallen apart in the intelligence domain. Often the Appropriations Committees strike their own deals with intelligence managers, despite what SSCI and HPSCI have recommended. For example, the Intelligence Committees have been scorching in their criticism of some recent satellite programs, yet the Appropriations Committees – lobbied effectively by intelligence managers in an end run – have funded them anyway.[85] More disquieting still is the fact that SSCI and HPSCI, caught up in partisan wrangling, proved unable to pass an authorization bill for several years during the early 2000s because of strong disagreements over policy between Republican and Democratic lawmakers on the panels. This polarization raised serious questions about the ability of SSCI and HPSCI to perform as responsible intelligence overseers. Given this state of affairs on the Intelligence Committees, the Senate leadership assigned the Government Affairs Committee (rather than SSCI) to reform the Intelligence Community after the 9/11 Commission concluded in 2004 that intelligence oversight had become dysfunctional on the Hill – "the low point in the history of the [Intelligence] Committees," according to a seasoned observer.[86] In more recent years, both Committees have been able to pass annual authorization bills, but considerable partisan strife continues within their confines, as dramatically displayed during the wrestling over SSCI's Torture Report. The most obvious remedy to this dilemma is for the congressional leadership to select SSCI and HPSCI chairs and ranking minority members who can get along with one another in a spirit of bipartisanship – no mean feat in this unfortunate and ongoing time of partisan warfare in Washington, DC and across the country.

Who is in charge?

Finally, the lines of authority for intelligence on Capitol Hill have been a jumble. Each of the following committees in both houses claim intelligence jurisdiction: Appropriations (money), Foreign Relations and Foreign Affairs (international affairs), Judiciary (FBI and the FISA Court), Armed Services (tactical military intelligence), Homeland Security (domestic security), and, of course, SSCI and HPSCI (which presently have sole authority only over the CIA and the ODNI). This many committees is a sure prescription for confusion, as well as a major surcharge on the time and energy of intelligence managers, be they the DNI or program managers at the agency level. In the old saw: when everyone is in charge, no one is in charge. Intelligence programs can be overlooked by lawmakers because they think one of the other committees is responsible. Zegart reports, for example, that the FBI counterterrorism reforms in the late 1990s fell between the stools of SSCI and HPSCI, on the one hand, and the Judiciary Committees, on the other hand, as each counted on the other to examine these new proposals.[87]

The ideal solution would be for SSCI and HPSCI to have more extensive jurisdiction over most aspects of intelligence, aided by the staff of the Government Accountability Office (GAO, an arm of Congress), as well as an outside oversight panel (a proposal discussed in Chapter 6). In conjunction with SSCI and HPSCI, the Judiciary Committees could still review FBI and FISA matters, given their close relationship to domestic legal considerations. On the whole, though, the other committees presently involved in intelligence reviews have more than enough work on their plates already when it comes to government oversight, without the added burden (which they often ignore anyway) of responsibilities for the secret agencies.[88] Moreover, several lawmakers on SSCI and HPSCI also serve on the other national security panels in Congress; they can report back to Armed Services and the other committees on intelligence developments as they see fit.

The placement of more intelligence activities within SSCI and HPSCI would require strong congressional leadership, however, and, some would say, divine intervention as well. Nevertheless, in 1975–77 powerful forces opposed the creation of SSCI and HPSCI in the first place and these forces were defeated by a feeling in the nation and on Capitol Hill that intelligence oversight had to undergo fundamental change. Reform – so badly needed – can happen again, if the will is there.

The roles played by lawmakers as intelligence supervisors

These years of experimentation in the United States from 1974 until now about how to maintain a proper balance between efficient spy agencies, on the one hand, and the sanctity of civil liberties, on the other hand, have been turbulent, see-sawing between intensive oversight at times (in reaction to major alarms) but, more often, a lackadaisical approach to standing guard against the abuses of secret power. In dealing with their intelligence oversight duties since 1974, members of Congress have adopted one of four major roles: that of the ostrich, the cheerleader, the lemon-sucker, or the guardian, with fluctuations by some lawmakers between the different roles according to the circumstances and personalities of the time.

One can imagine other roles that intelligence overseers could assume. During the Aspin–Brown Commission inquiry, for example, a member of that panel, Senator James Exon (D, Nebraska), rarely bothered even to attend meetings and hearings, let alone read draft reports, interview witnesses, travel to inspect U.S. intelligence programs overseas, or engage in other tasks carried out by his colleagues on the Commission. Exon showed up for the first session; once more midway through the inquiry when a celebrity witness came before the Commission in secret session (former Secretary of State Henry Kissinger); and, finally, when the panel's report was finished and the commissioners were invited to brief President Clinton and Vice President Gore on their findings in the Oval. In terms of role types, one could invent the "prairie dog" just for Exon, for he poked his head out of his underground hole every now and then to see what was going on, only to disappear quickly if it looked like work was on the horizon.

Another role might be the "sleeping watch dog," based on the CIA tale of the congressional response to the paramilitary briefing in the 1950s; or perhaps a "junkyard dog," reminiscent of when Representatives Aspin and Mazzoli clamped their teeth around the ankle of DCI Turner. A former seasoned CIA officer, who once served as an Agency liaison officer to SSCI and HPSCI, suggested to the author some additional role types. "How about 'grandstander,' for the politician who bashes intelligence for political gain?" he proposed, only partially tongue-in-cheek, continuing: "or 'weasel' – a member of Congress who evades responsibility by being ostensibly shocked by matters on which they were full briefed?"

For the purposes here, though, the four roles that follow – ostrich, cheerleader, lemon-sucker, and guardian – suggest a range of oversight involvement that members of SSCI and HPSCI have tended to display.

The ostrich

The first type of intelligence overseer is the "ostrich." Here is the lawmaker who embraces a philosophy of benign neglect toward the intelligence agencies (see Figure 5.4). This view characterized almost all members of Congress before the domestic spy scandal of 1974. A classic illustration of the ostrich is Senator Barry Goldwater, who became chairman of SSCI in 1981. He had previously served as a member of the Church Committee. While on that Committee, Goldwater voted in 1976 against the creation of SSCI, the very panel that, ironically, he would come to lead. He also opposed most of the other ninety-eight reforms recommended by the Church

		Responsibility for intelligence support	
		Low	High
Responsibility for intelligence evaluation	Low	1 The ostrich	2 The cheerleader
	High	3 The lemon-sucker	4 The guardian

Figure 5.4   A typology of roles assumed by intelligence overseers in the U.S. Congress

Committee, including closer judicial scrutiny of wiretapping operations inside the United States and more extensive congressional hearings on CIA covert actions. Goldwater was content with the system of oversight that existed before 1975: an occasional review of secret activities by a few subcommittees on intelligence housed within the Armed Services and the Appropriations Committees.[89]

The cheerleader

The second type of intelligence overseer is the "cheerleader." In this instance, the member of Congress has removed his or her head from the sand, but only for the purpose of cheering more loudly on behalf of the intelligence agencies. The cheerleader is interested primarily in the advocacy of spy activities, the support of intelligence budgets, and the advancement of clandestine operations at home and abroad against suspected enemies of the United States. During hearings, the cheerleader specializes in "softball" pitches – easy questions gently tossed so that intelligence managers called as witnesses can slug them over the center-field fence.[90] In press conferences, the cheerleader acts as a defense attorney for America's secret agencies, hinting at their behind-the-scenes, "if you only knew" successes; lauding the heroism of intelligence officers and agents; castigating journalists for printing leaked secrets that imperil the nation; and warning of threats at home and abroad that could lead to another 9/11 if the intelligence agencies are hamstrung by kibitzing lawmakers and their staffs. Such statements by cheerleaders are often true: intelligence officers do have successes, they are occasionally heroes, sometimes they do prevent terrorist attacks. Yet the cheerleaders are one-sided in their perspective, lacking a critical eye for intelligence inadequacies that cry out for reform. Recall how Representative Boland assumed the role of cheerleader when he became the first chair of HPSCI in 1977. He often swallowed his personal skepticism about specific covert operations and expressed his support for the government's secret bureaucracy, determined to show that his Committee could be trusted as a responsible supervisor of intelligence operations on Capitol Hill.

The lemon-sucker

A third role type is the "lemon-sucker" – a term used by President Bill Clinton to describe economists who exhibited a sour disposition toward a government policy. This approach is as one-sided as the cheerleader, only at the opposite extreme. For the lemon-sucker, nothing the intelligence agencies undertake is likely to be worthwhile. From this point-of-view, the secret agencies are inherently immoral: opening and reading other people's mail, eavesdropping on telephone conversations and social media, stealing documents, overthrowing governments, perhaps even killing people with drone missiles or poisons. The skeptical lemon-suckers also charge the spy agencies with incompetence, pointing to the CIA's inability to dispatch foreign leaders on its hit list (despite many attempts) during the Eisenhower and Kennedy Administrations, the failure to anticipate either the fall of the Soviet Union or the 9/11 attacks, and the absence of predicted WMD in Iraq in 2002.[91] For the most extreme skeptic, there is but one solution: shut down the CIA and the other secret agencies. In 1996, for example, a well-regarded member of SSCI, Senator Daniel Patrick Moynihan (D, New York), dismayed by the CIA's inability to anticipate the collapse of the Soviet empire, called for the Agency's abolition.[92]

The guardian

The fourth type of intelligence overseer is the "guardian." This role conforms best with the hopes expressed by legislative reformers during the Year of Intelligence in 1975. Representative Lee Hamilton (D, Indiana), HPSCI chair from 1985 to 1987, has argued that the ideal intelligence overseers are both "partners and critics" of the secret agencies.[93] Another HPSCI member, Norm Dicks (D, Washington), has said that "overseeing the intelligence community is like being a good parent: you have to encourage and discipline."[94]

As intelligence "partners," lawmakers must educate the American people on the virtues of maintaining an effective intelligence capability for the sake of America's security. Without defenders on Capitol Hill, the spy agencies are at a major disadvantage in gaining public support for their secret activities and sizable budgets. Yet, to be an effective overseer, a lawmaker must also be a critic: someone who searches for, acknowledges, and corrects programmatic flaws. This challenging role requires the ability, above all, to be objective and to speak out against questionable activities (in closed hearings on those occasions when operations are too sensitive for public review). Lee Hamilton has come as close to this ideal as any member of SSCI or HPSCI. When he was head of HPSCI, he regularly convened committee meetings, paid close attention to memos and reports from his staff and the intelligence agencies, followed up on media allegations of intelligence wrongdoing or mistakes, and spent long hours reviewing budgets and talking to intelligence professionals.

Yet remember how even Hamilton faltered during the Iran–*contra* scandal in the mid-1980s. When staffers on the NSC assured him they were not involved in these illegal operations, Hamilton, along with other SSCI and HPSCI leaders, accepted these assurances at face value[95] – always a mistake when rumors to the contrary are rampant and highlight the need for a more formal probe.

The dynamic nature of intelligence accountability

During their tenures, individual members of SSCI and HPSCI have sometimes displayed more than one approach to intelligence supervision. An illustration of this migration of lawmakers between the four oversight roles is displayed in Figure 5.5. Representative Boland, for example, felt it necessary to be a strong supporter of the intelligence agencies in 1977–80, thereby offsetting the bad impression left by the Pike Committee's strident criticism of the CIA. As the 1980s progressed, however, Boland began to drift away from the posture of cheerleading to assume a more balanced stance as a guardian. By 1982, he had become increasingly concerned about DCI Casey and his use of covert action to advance the *contras* against the *Sandinista* Marxist regime in Nicaragua. Boland, joined by a majority in the Congress (controlled by Democrats at the time), concluded that the mining of Nicaraguan harbors and the blowing up of power lines – along with other extreme paramilitary operations – were excessive responses to the minimal threat posed by the President Daniel Ortega and his *Sandinista* regime. Boland

Ostrich	Cheerleader
Goldwater (1981-83)	Boland (1977-80)
Shelby (1997-98)	Goldwater (1985)
	Graham (2001)

Skeptic	Guardian
Goldwater (1984)	Boland (1981)
Boland (1982-85)	Aspin (1977-82)
Shelby (1999-04)	Mazzoli (1977-82)
Graham (2002-04)	Robinson (1977-82)
	Hamilton (1985-87)

Figure 5.5   Illustrations of role migration and stability among intelligence overseers in Congress, 1977–2004

introduced and guided to passage seven eponymous amendments, each progressively restricting the use of paramilitary and other extreme CA operations in Nicaragua.

By the time his tenure as HPSCI Chairman had come to an end in 1985, Boland's relations with DCI Casey had substantially deteriorated. Boland had undergone a metamorphosis from cheerleader to guardian, then to a full-fledged lemon-sucker. As illustrated in Figure 5.5, he began in cell two, traveled to cell four for a brief period, and then settled in cell three. In Boland's case, the stimuli for these changes were twofold: first, what he perceived as the Reagan Administration's overheated response to events in Central America; and, second, a new, aggressive, and arrogant DCI (Casey) who did nothing to hide his disdain toward the notion of congressional intelligence oversight. Casey once explained his "theory" of intelligence oversight in this manner: "The job of Congress is to stay the f— out of my business."[96] First, policy (paramilitary operations in Nicaragua), then personality (Casey's irascibility and his negative view of Congress) transformed Chairman Boland's approach to intelligence accountability dramatically from cheerleader to skeptic or lemon-sucker.

Senator Goldwater went on a similar, though even more tortuous, odyssey within the SSCI. With his head mostly in the ground during the first few years of his SSCI chairmanship (1981–83), Goldwater initially played the role of ostrich, deferring to DCI Casey and the intelligence agencies. He reasoned that the intelligence bureaucrats should be trusted to do a good job in the trying circumstances of the Cold War – the same guiding philosophy of "the good old days" of intelligence oversight (pre-1975).

Then, in 1984, William Casey managed to do the seemingly impossible: he single-handedly turned the Intelligence Community's most reliable ostrich, Goldwater, into one of its most vocal lemon-suckers. The catalyst in this dramatic transformation was Casey's misleading testimony during an appearance before Goldwater's Committee. When asked by a SSCI member whether the CIA was mining harbors in Nicaragua, the DCI offered an adamant "no" in response. Only later did it become clear that Casey was relying on a technical point: the Agency was not mining *harbors*; it was mining *piers* within the harbors. This attempt to toy with the SSCI angered its Chairman, his institutional pride trumping his former feelings of blind deference toward the Intelligence Community – at least temporarily. Goldwater fired off a letter to one of the best venues in the nation's capital for venting: the *Washington Post*. Castigating Casey for his attempts at legerdemain on Capitol Hill, the letter said in part: "It gets down to one, little, simple phrase: I am pissed off!"[97]

As Goldwater's ire over Casey receded, however, the Chairman drifted into a cheerleading role (though not an ostrich) for the remainder of his tenure on SSCI through 1985.

Additional illustrations about the sometimes fluctuating nature of oversight roles come from the period just before and right after the 9/11 terrorist attacks against the United States. Richard C. Shelby (R, Alabama) initially came to Congress as a Democrat in 1987 and eight years later joined most of his Southern colleagues in a switch to the GOP as conservatism deepened in Dixie. He led SSCI from 1997 to 2001. Initially, Shelby oscillated between the roles of ostrich and cheerleader, apparently seeing few imperfections in the work of the Intelligence Community during his first years in the Committee's wheelhouse. This sanguine outlook would soon begin to fade, however. In 1998, after India tested a nuclear bomb – an event that the CIA forecasted would not happen – Shelby questioned DCI George Tenet over the telephone about the intelligence failure. "Senator, we were clueless," replied the DCI, a troubling response that reportedly initiated doubts in Shelby's mind about the competence of the Intelligence Director.[98]

Subsequently, on April 26, 1999, Tenet failed to invite the SSCI Chairman to the christening of the new George H. W. Bush Center for Intelligence (named by Congress after the only DCI to become president). The Shelby–Tenet relationship circled down the drain in the aftermath of that perceived slight. Finally, after the 9/11 attacks, Shelby came to the conclusion that Tenet had failed to warn the nation sufficiently about the Al Qaeda terrorist peril. The DCI needed to go.[99] Thereafter, the SSCI Chair waxed ever more critical of Tenet and the intelligence agencies during the rest of his time on SSCI (where he remained for an additional three years as the ranking minority member when his chairmanship came to an end as the Democrats took over the Senate). In the case of Richard Shelby, the perceived 9/11 failure, combined with a sense of personal insult over being excluded from the Bush Center ceremonies, again transformed a cheerleader into a lemon-sucker.

The next SSCI Chairman (2001–02), Bob Graham, likewise moved from cheerleader on the Senate Committee (in 2001) to a lemon-sucker (from 2002 to 2004), as a result of yet another confrontation between a SSCI chair and a DCI (Tenet again). In this instance, Graham's pique stemmed from procedural slaps in the face, some of which the Chairman (like Shelby) took as a personal affront.[100]

After the 9/11 attacks, Graham became co-chair (along with HPSCI leader Porter Goss, R, Florida) of a special Joint Committee that temporarily combined SSCI and HPSCI to investigate the 9/11 intelligence failures. Once hearings began, Graham and Tenet soon clashed over the Committee's authority and procedures. When Graham asked the DCI to be brief in his introductory remarks before the panel, Tenet instead went on at length and, according to a newspaper report, in a "somewhat defiant tone."[101] With a preternatural obstinacy when challenged, Tenet also refused to declassify some intelligence documents that Graham thought important for the public record. Further, the DCI frequently caused havoc in the Committee's proceedings by denying access to basic intelligence documents related to the 9/11 attacks, refusing at the last minute to allow scheduled intelligence officers to testify before the Committee, and even canceling his own appearance scheduled for a closed hearing. Tenet's script seemed to have consisted solely of the words of King Lear on his daughter Cordelia's death: "never, never, never, never, never."

This is not the way senators, particularly committee chairs, like to be treated. As the DCI stonewalled and slow-rolled the Joint Committee, Graham started his transition from cheerleader to lemonsucker. After Tenet's continued disruptions and disrespect, Graham finally exploded and accused the intelligence chief of "obstructionism" and "unacceptable" behavior.[102] His anger increased further when the executive branch refused to declassify a section of the Joint Committee report (twenty-eight pages) that, according to the Senator, spelled out troubling ties between the 9/11 terrorists and the government of Saudi Arabia.[103]

In search of guardians

The time and study required to become an effective legislative supervisor for the spy agencies, plus the lack of credit back home for engaging in intelligence oversight, sums to an unattractive formula for lawmakers concerned about re-election. They usually conclude that their time is better spent raising campaign funds and pursuing legislative goals that are more closely reported on by the media – especially in their home state. Yet what about future intelligence failures that could lead to even more drastic attacks against the United States than those experienced by the nation on 9/11? What if lawmakers could have prevented the failures of 9/11, or the invasion of Iraq based on the faulty assumption that Saddam Hussein had WMD, by way of a more robust review of intelligence procedures, the effectiveness of information-sharing arrangements among the agencies (especially between the CIA and the FBI), and the quality of intelligence collection and analysis on such topics as Al Qaeda and Iraq? What member of Congress wants to explain to constituents why he or she was too busy fundraising to improve, through serious hearings and budget reviews, the readiness of America's intelligence agencies?

The role of guardian was widely accepted by intelligence reformers on Capitol Hill in 1975 as the ideal, because it balanced support for intelligence with a determination through persistent program review to avoid future agency failures and scandals. In pursuit of this objective, how can members of Congress be encouraged to spend more time on serious program evaluation? What incentives can be introduced into the culture of Capitol Hill to make intelligence accountability a more valued pursuit?

Some initiatives to encourage better intelligence oversight could include greater recognition of lawmakers who perform with distinction as overseers. This recognition could take the form of increased perks, such as improved office space and parking opportunities in Congress, along with augmented funds for travel and staff support dispensed by party leaders to lawmakers known for their oversight tenacity and fairness. Closer media coverage of oversight activities would help, too, as well as the bestowing of "Overseer of the Year" awards by civic groups to acknowledge the hard work of those members of Congress who devote time and energy to intelligence oversight hearings and budget reviews.[104] Further, academic researchers and teachers at all levels of education could pay more attention to this neglected responsibility of Congress, explaining to rising citizens the importance of accountability.

One might think that enough oversight incentives already exist. In the first instance, the quality of intelligence accountability could well determine the degree of protection afforded the American people against domestic spy scandals. Moreover, another powerful incentive should be the desire of lawmakers to improve America's intelligence shield, thereby helping to ward off future terrorist attacks against the United States; or to avoid further faulty conclusions about unconventional weapons abroad of the kind that helped draw the United States into war with Iraq in 2003 and could lead the nation into war again. Former DCI Robert M. Gates has well stated the case for intelligence oversight on Capitol Hill:

> Some awfully crazy schemes might well have been approved had everyone present [in the White House] not known and expected hard questions, debate, and criticism from the Hill. And when, on a few occasions, Congress was left in the dark, and such schemes did proceed, it was nearly always to the lasting regret of the presidents involved.[105]

Regardless of these compelling reasons for a lawmaker to assume the guardian role of a dedicated intelligence overseer, most observers agree that members of Congress continue to perform far below their potential when it comes to the supervision of the nation's spy agencies. As former Senator Gary Hart (D, Colorado), a member of the Church Committee in 1975, has emphasized: "Public interest and insistence is necessary for reform."[106] Intelligence oversight is a neglected responsibility on Capitol Hill and will remain so, until the citizens of the United States demand otherwise.

6 National Security Intelligence

Shield and Hidden Sword of the Democracies

This volume has examined the three core dimensions of national security intelligence: organization, mission (collection and analysis, covert action, and counterintelligence), and accountability. Each is vital to the success of the democracies in their ongoing struggle against global forces anathema to the principles of a free and open society.

National security intelligence is by no means the only, or even the most important, ingredient for success in this struggle. That distinction would go to the armed might of the democracies: the possession of weaponry – firepower – capable of repelling the dark forces arrayed against freedom, be they the Barbary pirates in America's early history, autocrats and monarchs from the 1600s to the 1900s, the totalitarian threat posed by Germany, Italy, and Japan during the first half of the twentieth century, the communist challenge of the Cold War, or the terrorists of the present age.[1] Important, as well, in the defense of the democracies is an effective program of public diplomacy: the soft power that exerts an attraction on the would-be democracies of the world that comes from living a life worthy of emulation through the nurturing of an unfettered media, just trials, competitive elections, and fair play in international affairs. Accompanying the basic requirement of setting a good example for other countries is the need to help the poor nations of the world develop economically, through foreign aid, joint ventures, trade agreements, and the sharing of technological know-how. Important, too, is rejecting torture, extraordinary rendition, secret prisons, and illegal or highly unsavory intelligence operations that erase the difference between the democracies and their adversaries.[2]

National security intelligence, though, has a significant part to play as a shield for the democracies, and sometimes through the use of a hidden sword – covert action and counterespionage – on their behalf. It can provide information that improves the chances of victory on the battlefield against anti-democratic forces, as at Midway during the Second World War or in the recent Persian Gulf wars. It can detect moles burrowing inside the open societies, as with Ames and Hanssen in the United States (though with a more rapid detection of traitors in the future, one can hope). It can fool opponents, as with the deception operations preceding the Allied invasion of Europe at Normandy. It can offer insights that smooth the way to more effective diplomacy and more equitable trade relations. It can discover and prove human rights violations, from the horror of mass graves spotted by satellites to the reports from agents who have infiltrated human trafficking cells.

Often referred to as the "first line of defense," national security intelligence is that and more. Beyond the eyes and ears of the democracies, it is a measure of their hearts, a test of whether open societies can stand strong against the enemies of freedom and still keep their constitutional principles intact – the accountability side of national security intelligence. This brief closing chapter offers an overview of these core dimensions and highlights the central challenges that lie ahead to ensure that the intelligence shield and sword serve as a reliable complement to armed defense, public diplomacy, and economic statecraft in the protection and advancement of democratic governments around the world.

National security intelligence as organization

The democracies have no use for an intelligence service that is splintered into separate baronies and fails to provide policymakers with the holistic "all-source fusion" of information that is so necessary for good decision-making. Nor do they want an all-powerful intelligence czar who stifles competitive intelligence and dissent, or rises above the reach of overseers. The organizational ideal is a well-integrated intelligence service with a director able to hire and fire, and to coordinate community-wide budgets and programs; but, at the same time, a spy chief who is appropriately held in check by the internal safeguards of serious-minded review by intelligence overseers in all three branches of government in the United States.

A cosmetic DNI

The America model falls far short of this ideal. Its Director of National Intelligence is weak, with limited authority over the nation's sixteen intelligence agencies – a "leader" without sufficient personnel or budget controls. Other than improving its accountability practices, no reform measure in the United States is more pressing than a more effective integration of the nation's intelligence services. This would require the establishment of a genuine DNI to replace the cardboard cutout fashioned for the nation by a misguided Congress during the failed intelligence reform movement of 2004.

Horizontal and vertical integration

An additional organizational challenge in the democracies is to carry forward the integration of their national intelligence agencies not only "horizontally" – that is, melding the training, the computers, and the sharing of findings among the intelligence services in the service of the federal government – but "vertically" as well, downward from the federal government to the states and localities. At these lower levels of governance, counterterrorist and law enforcement officials are on the front lines of likely terrorist targets: the cities and transportation facilities of the world's democracies. Yet, presently in the United States, these state and local officials are rarely provided with the timely, high-quality intelligence they need, even though tentative steps have been taken toward developing "intelligence fusion centers" in the nation's major metropolitan areas, where federal and local analysts gather to share their data and insights on potential terrorist and other criminal activities against the United States.[3]

Liaison relationships

Challenging, as well, is the development of better liaison connections of two kinds: the first is internal to each of the democracies, and the second is among the democracies. Internal liaison refers to the crafting of improved professional (non-political) ties between decision-makers in the policy departments and the analysts in the intelligence services who serve them with timely and relevant information and insight. Frequently, the left hand (decision-makers) lacks coordination with the right hand (information-providers in the IC). The increased placement of intelligence liaison officers inside government departments would allow them to provide their home agencies each day with an accurate, up-to-date understanding of what information needs are of highest priority among decision-makers. Otherwise, an intelligence officer risks becoming irrelevant, instead of a valuable partner in decision-making who brings to the table reliable facts and assessments.

Liaison among the democracies poses an even more difficult problem, since it must address the security and cultural barriers that are inherent in relations between nations. The principle of "foreign liaison" or "burden-sharing" is compelling, though. The world has changed in important ways that we sum up with the term "globalization" – an unparalleled integration of nations across the latitudes, brought about by new communications and transportation technologies. Along with this globalization has come the potential rapid spread of threats that can have an effect far beyond their local origins: crime from Nigeria, heroin from Afghanistan, weapons proliferation from North Korea, terrorism from the Al Qaeda mountain hideouts in Pakistan, disease from Central China and the jungles of Africa, ecological changes caused by acid rain in the regions of Europe, Asia, and the United States. What used to be someone else's problem is now everybody's problem. No single country has all the answers, all the information, or all the resources to respond to these challenges to freedom; however, by working together and sharing intelligence, as well as participating in more aggressive intelligence operations – covert action and counterespionage – against the world's dark forces, the democracies can improve their chances for success.

The United States, the United Kingdom, and other nations have shown that intelligence can be shared effectively within the framework of the United Nations and NATO.[4] Further, Europe has exhibited some success in its ongoing experiment to develop a Euro intelligence service. These are hopeful signs that the secret services can help unite the democracies through intelligence-sharing, in their common quest to subdue the world's violent and anti-democratic forces – be they war-prone autocracies, drug dealers, human traffickers, environmental polluters, or terrorist organizations.

Security intelligence as a set of missions

Challenges abound for each of the three intelligence missions: collection and analysis, covert action, and counterintelligence.

Collection and analysis

PLANNING AND DIRECTION   Frequently, intelligence producers are left in the dark about what manner of information those in high office need to address the problems they confront in their in-boxes. The organizational remedy of improved internal liaison ties – the building of information bridges between the policy and the spy agencies – is a necessary condition for a better understanding between the two camps, but it is not sufficient. One must also have much more direct dialogue between consumers and producers of intelligence, with more frequent meetings devoted to the discussion of the nation's intelligence priorities. Valuable, as well, would be more regular informal get-togethers to nurture the ties of friendship, trust, and rapport that are essential for a smooth working relationship between decision-makers and intelligence officers – although each side must maintain its objectivity in dealing with facts and assessments related to world threats and opportunities.

COLLECTION   Too often the techint side of tradecraft, with its dazzling machines and tangible data, attracts a preponderance of resources from budget planners – prodded by the lobbying efforts of satellite and drone manufacturers (now part of the military-industrial complex that President Dwight D. Eisenhower warned of in his "Farewell Address" of 1959). This focus on technical intelligence often comes at the expensive of humint and osint. Yet the array of world targets demands adequate funding for each of the "ints" – the Black & Decker approach whereby all the tools in the box are put to use. The idea is to have synergistic, all-source fusion, to meet the goal of acquiring as complete a portrait of the world as possible each day, derived from all of the secret agencies employing their int specialties in close coordination with one another. Crying out for more humint resources are non-official (NOC) positions overseas, which provide a better opportunity for meeting and recruiting the non-traditional enemies of the democracies – terrorists in particular – than do embassy cocktail parties.

PROCESSING   Perhaps no feature of intelligence in the democracies is more conspicuous than the outpacing of data collection over what the secret agencies are able to absorb, translate, and understand. Every four to six hours, the NSA collects a volume of material equivalent to the entire holdings of the Library of Congress.[5] The democracies face the proverbial search for the needle in the haystack, with the needles and the haystacks growing exponentially in number. The solution will come only with breakthroughs in information sorting, as the democracies become smarter about what to collect and faster at finding the needles in the haystacks (the "signals" rather than the "noise"). These advances depend on improvements in information technology (IT), as well as better methods for producing accurately translated foreign language texts and messages.

ANALYSIS Vital to better performance in the cerebral domain of analysis is the recruitment to the intelligence services of the best brain-power the democracies can muster: men and women well trained in the array of university curricula relevant to understanding world affairs – which, today, includes courses in just about every academic discipline. As with case officers responsible for asset recruitment, especially valuable will be individuals proficient in the world's so-called "strategic languages" spoken in hot spots around the world from North Korea to Iraq, such as Arabic, Farsi, and Pashtun.

As a way of encouraging all-source fusion, a greater commitment to the joint training of analysts from different agencies will help to engender the kinds of lasting collegial bonds that result in better interagency communications and data-sharing throughout the Intelligence Community. So will more regular transfers of personnel between agencies – circulating the intelligence workforce – as a part of any successful officer's career advancement. While these steps have already been initiated, they remain too limited in their reach. Further, within agencies, "co-location" deserves more support (as the CIA has recently understood and moved to adopt more energetically): knocking down the barriers between operatives and analysts so they can work more closely together to create accurate assessments of foreign events and conditions that draw upon both their "ground truth" and "library" knowledge. Also of high priority must be the encouragement of critical reviews of intelligence draft reports, through the use of Team A–Team B exercises and other critiques of preliminary assessments that can provide an acid bath by objective, outside experts in academe and the think-tanks. Moreover, analytic dissent needs to be clearly flagged for the attention of decision-makers. As the "slam dunk" experience with DCI George Tenet and President George W. Bush illustrates, the virtues of dissent are sometimes discarded in Washington in a rush for good news and group consensus.

DISSEMINATION Then comes one of the toughest assignment of all for the intelligence officer: in the midst of building the rapport so necessary for access to policymakers and to enhance the flow of information from the field into the mind of the decision-maker, the analyst, the liaison officer, the *PDB* and NIE briefer, the D/CIA, the DNI – whatever the intelligence position – must remain absolutely neutral in providing data and insights. Rapport, yes, even friendship; but the intelligence officer must maintain an ability to step back from Washington politics, to understand the importance of the bright line of honesty and neutrality that should exist between the producer and the consumer of intelligence. Crossing that line can transport the intelligence officer into the domain of politicization – the "cooking" of intelligence to please the political objectives of an administration. Staying on the proper (non-policy) side of this demilitarized zone is the cardinal rule of intelligence. When that line is crossed, the guilty intelligence officer becomes simply another policy advocate – of which there is already an abundance in the democratic capitals of the world.

COVERT ACTION   As American decision-makers ponder the adoption of covert action methods, they should keep former DCI William H. Webster's set of guidelines close at hand. In Judge Webster's prescription (Chapter 3), these controversial secret operations should honor an adherence to U.S. law, remain consistent with foreign policy objectives and traditional values, and – should they become public – make sense to the American people. Further, in congruence with the spirit of a democratic alliance against the enemies of open societies, covert actions should not be directed against fellow democratic regimes. In the same spirit, the democracies should join together when possible for covert actions against common threats.

Above all, the democracies should move up the ladder of covert action escalation toward highly intrusive operations only with the greatest circumspection, mindful that wise observers over the years have counseled that the "third option" should be adopted only when absolutely essential – as a last measure when every other policy option has been found lacking. Leaders in the democracies should be sensitive to the fact, too, that the highest rungs on the ladder are anathema to the values extolled by the open societies, threatening the great moral advantage enjoyed by the democracies over the "anything goes" attitude of terrorists and dictators who fear the ethical standards raised high by the open societies. Only ISIS, Al Qaeda, and the most intransigent of the Taliban armies should be targets of high-rung covert actions, and even then the democracies should reject operations that risk the death of innocent civilians, destroy animal and plant life, or cause Western intelligence officers – whether interrogators or paramilitary soldiers – to descend into the kind of barbaric behavior displayed by the terrorists.

COUNTERINTELLIGENCE   Success in the world of counterintelligence depends on the vigilance of fellow workers inside the secret agencies. Intelligence officers and their managers can best spot suspicious activities, excessive drinking, or lavish lifestyles among their colleagues that might be a tip-off to outside funding by a foreign intelligence or terrorist organization. The Americans and the Europeans have learned a great deal from CI failures over the past several decades and have taken steps to tighten their defenses, such as more careful monitoring of the bank accounts of employees in the aftermath of the Ames treachery at the CIA. Although no doubt there will be another Ames or Kim Philby some day, what one hopes for is that – as a result of greater attention to security and counterespionage – future traitors will be quickly detected.

National security intelligence and the importance of accountability

The experiment in intelligence accountability is here to stay in most, if not all, of the democracies; but it has displayed unsettling signs of backsliding. In the United States, one could see this most obviously in the Iran–*contra* affair; in the failure of Congress to examine the preparedness of the Intelligence Community to discover and thwart a terrorist attack in the years leading up to 9/11; in the warrantless wiretapping, metadata collection, and torture techniques adopted by the second Bush Administration after the terrorist attacks; and in the lethargy that settled over the SSCI and HPSCI oversight panels during the first decade of the twenty-first century. The cycle of shock and reaction repeated itself time and again, without sufficient attention by members of Congress to the dedicated, high-intensity police patrolling on Capitol Hill that might have served as a circuit-breaker. Nevertheless, even though the New Intelligence Oversight has sometimes proved disappointing in practice, the level of congressional (as well as executive and judicial) accountability over intelligence operations still remains vastly superior to what existed before 1975.

In the United States, a starting place to correct a drift backwards toward weak intelligence accountability is to straighten out the tangled lines of jurisdictional responsibility among the oversight committees on Capitol Hill. The committees on the Judiciary, Foreign Relations, Armed Services, and Appropriations already have full plates; SSCI and HPSCI should be given sole jurisdiction for almost all intelligence activities (with the Judiciary Committees helping out with the FBI and the FIS Court). The outcome would be clearer lines of responsibility.

The greatest challenge, though, is to bring out the guardian instincts of lawmakers serving on SSCI and HPSCI. This feat will require a fresh set of incentives on the Hill that reward the serious practice of guardianship with the perks of office, as well as greater recognition and praise for oversight work. The public, however, will be the ultimate arbiter of whether lawmakers pay attention to their oversight duties. If citizens direct their votes toward candidates who are dedicated to the guardian role; if journalists cover sterling acts of oversight by lawmakers; if academicians teach about the central place of oversight in America's form of government, as spelled out in the *Federalist Papers*; if presidents and DNIs explain how accountability actually strengthens national security intelligence by engendering debate within the hidden councils of government, then lawmakers will be more likely to gravitate toward the guardian role.

These steps toward genuine intelligence accountability may prove quixotic. Perhaps there is just not enough gumption on Capitol Hill to make the necessary changes. Perhaps money has such a grip on the American system of government that fundraising for re-election, along with lobbying by the military-industrial-intelligence complex, will keep lawmakers frozen in the posture of an "ostrich" or uncritical "cheerleader." Perhaps a cycle of feckless police patrolling, followed by vigorous firefighting, is the fate of the United States and the other open societies. Ultimately, it is up to the citizens of the democracies to demand more of their public servants.

A citizens intelligence advisory board

The challenges examined in this volume demand a renewed sense of determination by the democracies to strengthen their national security intelligence capabilities (see Table 6.1), including improved accountability procedures. Congress, like the parliaments in the other democracies, needs help in supervising the spy agencies. This is not to say that lawmakers have abjectly failed in their efforts to hold the secret agencies accountable. Since the days of the Church Committee, as we have seen, members of Congress have managed to craft several laudable oversight laws and guidelines. It is the case, however, that those in Congress are unable to fully handle the duties of intelligence accountability by themselves; the pressures for re-election simply make too large a surcharge on their time. Despite these campaign pressures, members of SSCI and HPSCI have displayed a respectable (though uneven) record of accomplishment; still, the Intelligence Community is too large, and its activities too complicated and dispersed, for lawmakers to monitor these agencies unaided. Those serving on SSCI and HPSCI need a helping hand from a newly created, independent, and permanent intelligence review board.

Table 6.1 National security intelligence: a reform agenda for the
United States

Focus	Primary proposals
Organization	*Provide the DNI with full budget and appointment powers*; expand internal intelligence liaison services; expand bilateral and multilateral liaison among the democracies; expand "co-location" practices
Missions	
Collection and analysis	
Planning	Improve formal and informal dialogue between producers and consumers of intelligence
Collection	Expand humint, especially NOCs
Processing	Improve "horizontal" interagency computer compatibility, as well as "vertical" connections to state and local law enforcement and intelligence officials; improve data shifting
Analysis	Establish more competitive analysis; highlight dissent (including within the executive summaries or Key Judgments); increase production of research intelligence
Dissemination	Market intelligence more effectively; focus on niche intelligence; educate analysts and managers about the dangers of *politicization* and call attention to its practice wherever spotted
Covert action	Practice greater discrimination, adopting this approach only when absolutely essential; avoid operations against fellow democracies; reject extreme options
Counterintelligence	Pay more attention to this neglected mission; redouble emphasis in training, at the time of recruitment and steadily thereafter; constantly upgrade computer firewalls against cyberattacks; tighten security checks for all personnel
Accountability	Improve incentives for "guardians" engaged in intensive "patrolling"; insist on full and timely (normally, *ante facto*) reporting to SSCI and HPSCI on all important intelligence activities (as stipulated in the 1980 Intelligence Oversight Act)

The Senate Intelligence Committee has divided its duties into four categories: responding to daily events, confirmation hearings, drafting legislation, and taking on major reviews and investigations. The members and staff of SSCI and HPSCI can cope with the first three obligations, even though lawmakers are torn by their other legislative duties and fundraising sirens. Where the Committees need an oversight partner is with the fourth category: major reviews and investigations, time-consuming special inquiries like the Joint Committee probe into 9/11, or the extensive research associated with the Senate Torture Report.

In the United States, a Citizens Intelligence Advisory Board (CIAB) could provide the necessary extra oversight assistance.[6] Such a board could have, say, nine members, aided by a staff of a dozen specialists. The members could be chosen in this fashion: two by SSCI (one by the majority party, one by the minority party, each of whom would also continue to serve on SSCI); two from the House (under comparable arrangements); two private citizens selected by the Supreme Court (one chosen by the Chief Justice and one by the senior judge appointed by the opposite party from that of the President who appointed the Chief Justice); two selected by the President; and a staff director picked by a majority vote of the deans at the top five ranked schools of international and public affairs in the United States (with the balloting supervised by the Intelligence Oversight Board in the White House). The term of service for each CIAB member could be five years, with the possibility of an additional five-year term. The Board would be coordinated by a chair elected from among, and by, CIAB members.

The CIAB membership positions would be full time – except for the four lawmakers, who would serve part time as they fulfilled their responsibilities in Congress as well. The congressional members would have to be a special breed with an abiding interest in intelligence matters to sustain this double duty – an Aspin, Hamilton or Mazzoli – and from a reasonably safe constituency. Congressional participation in CIAB activities would be important, as a means of providing a connection and continuity to the organization that funds the Intelligence Community: the U.S. Congress. Nothing so attracts the attention of intelligence bureaucrats as the congressional power of the purse.

The CIAB, SSCI, and HPSCI, along with the Government Accountability Office, would work together as an intelligence oversight team. The CIAB chair along with the SSCI and HPSCI chairs, would serve as the Board's managing triad. The purpose of the CIAB would be to supplement the work of the Intelligence Oversight Committees, not to duplicate or interfere with their agendas; and when SSCI and HPSCI are, at certain times in their history, captured by ostriches and cheerleaders, the Citizens Intelligence Advisory Board – a neutral, nonpartisan entity – could take up the slack in intelligence guardianship.

The CIAB would issue annual reports to the public, as well as classified reports to SSCI, HPSCI, the congressional leadership, and the White House. It would also hold hearings (with at least a few each year in open session); conduct formal inquiries when necessary (with full subpoena powers, along with the leverage of contempt citations that accompany them); take on special research projects that SSCI and HPSCI do not have time or inclination to consider (say, an analysis into the appropriateness of various kinds of intelligence reporting mandated by Congress, which the Committee itself may be unable to evaluate fairly); and disclose to the public any espionage activities that violate the laws of the United States or taint the nation's societal norms.

The CIAB may sound like an elaborate structure, but liberty and privacy in the United States are worth careful protection. Should operations like CHAOS, COINTELPRO, SHAMROCK, and MINERET, as well as torture and unbridled metadata programs, be stopped in their tracks before they begin? Should the likes of the Bay of Pigs and other questionable covert actions have been subjected to closer scrutiny? How about the poor analysis associated with the 9/11 attacks and the question of WMD in Iraq? In each case, clearly the answer in a democracy is a resounding yes. This will simply not happen, though, with SSCI and HPSCI acting alone, however well intended and hard working its members and staff may be. The proposed CIAB should not be an overly complex new system that would excessively burden the Intelligence Community, but rather a way of separating out from SSCI and HPSCI the extraordinarily demanding tasks of special reviews and investigations – tasks that frenetically busy lawmakers are ill-equipped to handle.

Citizen responsibilities

Students often say, "I don't care if the government spies on me; I have nothing to hide." They – and every American citizen – need to reevaluate that philosophy of governance, so anathema to the founding principles of this nation. All of us must remember Operation CHAOS, COINTELPRO, SHAMROCK, MINARET, and the more recent examples of overreach displayed in post-9/11 operations of the NSA, as well as the CIA's embrace of harsh interrogation methods. These overzealous intelligence initiatives should impress upon every American citizen that even our democratic government has in the past, and could in the future, use its secret agencies to counter lawful protest, possibly ruining the lives of citizens because some bureaucrat (in the case of COINTELPRO, J. Edgar Hoover) doesn't like the way they look, or what they say or write – the content of their political belief, moving, as Tom Charles Huston put it, "from the kid with the bomb to the kid with a picket sign, and from the kid with the picket sign to the kid with the bumper sticker of the opposing candidate." Part of the responsibility of living in a democracy is to take an active role in demanding the protection of fundamental constitutional freedoms, electing only those presidents, senators, and representatives who vow to take seriously the question of intelligence accountability. Americans, as well as citizens in other democracies, must either fight for their liberty – or see it vanish.

Notes

Preface: Roadmap to a hidden world

1 See Richard W. Aldrich, *The Hidden Hand: Britain, America and Cold War Secret Intelligence* (London: John Murray, 2001), p. 5; and Michael Herman, *Intelligence Power in Peace and War*. Cambridge, UK: Cambridge University Press, 1996.

2 For the 2009 survey, see Peter Monaghan, "Intelligence Studies," *Chronicle of Higher Education* (March 20, 2009), pp. B4–B5; and for the more recent appraisal that finds a dramatic growth in the discipline since the survey, see Loch K. Johnson, "The Development of Intelligence Studies," in Robert Dover, Michael S. Goodman, and Claudia Hillebrand, eds., *Routledge Companion to Intelligence Studies* (London and New York: Routledge, 2014), pp. 3–22.

3 See Peter Gill, Stephen Marrin, and Mark Phythian, eds., *Intelligence Theory: Key Questions and Debates* (New York: Routledge, 2009). Also: Peter Gill and Mark Phythian, "What Is Intelligence Studies?" *International Journal of Intelligence, Security and Public Affairs* 18/1 (2016), pp. 5–19; Loch K. Johnson and Allison M. Shelton, "Thoughts on the State of Intelligence Studies: A Survey Report," *Intelligence and National Security* 28 (February 2013), pp. 109–20; Stephen Marrin, "Improving Intelligence Studies as an Academic Discipline," *Intelligence and National Security* 31/2 (March 2016), pp. 266–79; and Damien Van Puyvelde and Sean Curtis, "'Standing on the Shoulders of Giants': Diversity and Scholarship in Intelligence Studies," *Intelligence and National Security* 32/1 (February 2017).

4 See R. Gerald Hughes, Peter Jackson, and Len Scott, eds., *Exploring Intelligence Archives: Enquiries into the Secret State* (New York: Routledge, 2008); and Loch K. Johnson, ed., *Strategic Intelligence, Vol. I: Understanding the Hidden Side of Government* (Westport, CT: Praeger, 2007).

Chapter 1   National security intelligence: the first line of defense

1   This reconstruction is based on the evidence presented in *The 9/11 Commission Report: Final Report of the National Commission on Terrorist Attacks Upon the United States* (New York: Norton, 2004) – the Kean Commission, led by Thomas H. Kean, Chair, and Lee H. Hamilton, Vice Chair.

2   Carl von Clausewitz, *On War*, translated by Michael Howard and Peter Paret (Princeton, NJ: Princeton University Press, 1989), p. 117.

3   Letter from John Emerich Edward Dalberg-Acton (Lord Acton) to Bishop Mandell Creigton, dated April 5, 1887, quoted in John Bartlett, *Familiar Quotations*, 14th edn (Boston: Little, Brown, 1968), p. 750a.

4   In a speech given on July 8, 1975, Senator Frank Church (D, Idaho, for whom the author served as a speech-writer at the time) suggested that Lord Acton's famous admonition should be rephrased: "All secrecy corrupts. Absolute secrecy corrupts absolutely."

5   Merle Miller, *Plain Speaking: An Oral Biography of Harry S. Truman* (New York: Berkley Publishing, 1973), p. 420.

6   Loch K. Johnson, ed., *The Oxford Handbook of National Security Intelligence* (New York: Oxford University Press, 2010), pp. 3–32.

7   For example: Hans Born, Loch K. Johnson, and Ian Leigh, eds., *Who's Watching the Spies? Establishing Intelligence Service Accountability* (Washington, DC: Potomac Books, 2005).

8   From a book review of Loch K. Johnson, ed., *Strategic Intelligence*, Vols. 1–5 (Westport, CT: Praeger, 2007), in *Intelligence and National Security* 25 (April 2010), pp. 245–7, quote at p. 247. For examples of credible attempts to appraise national security intelligence across national boundaries, see Born et al., eds., *Who's Watching the Spies?*; Ada Bozeman, "Statecraft and Intelligence in the Non-Western World," *Conflict* 6 (1985), pp. 1–35; Thomas C. Bruneau and Florina Cristiana (Cris) Matei, "Intelligence in the Developing Democracies: The Quest for Transparency and Effectiveness," in Johnson, ed., *Oxford Handbook of National Security Intelligence*, pp. 757–73; Peter Gill, *Intelligence Governance and Democratisation: A Comparative Analysis of the Limits of Reform* (Routledge: London, 2016); John Keegan, *Intelligence in War* (New York: Knopf, 2003); and Walter Laquer, *A World of Secrets* (New York: Basic Books, 1985).

9   *Fact Book on Intelligence*, Office of Public Affairs, Central Intelligence Agency (September 1991), p. 13. An experienced foreign policy practitioner, Secretary of State Dean Rusk, liked to think of the purpose of intelligence simply as "informing policymakers about what is going on in the world": see his *As I Saw It*, as told to Richard Rusk and edited by Daniel S. Papp (New York: Norton, 1990), p. 555.

10   The quote is from Peter Gill and Mark Phythian, *Intelligence in an Insecure World*, 2nd edn (Cambridge, UK: Polity, 2012), p. 19. On intelligence and the idea of decision advantage, see Jennifer E. Sims,

"Decision Advantage and the Nature of Intelligence Analysis," in Loch K. Johnson, ed., *The Oxford Handbook of National Security Intelligence* (New York: Oxford University Press, 2010), pp. 389–403. A legendary British intelligence officer (and academician), R. V. Jones, explained intelligence simply by noting that "a sensible nation will seek to be as well informed as possible about its opponents, potential or otherwise, and – for that matter – about its friends. It will therefore set up an intelligence organization": "Intelligence in a Democracy," lecture, Department of State, Washington, DC (December 4, 1975), p. 8. Even seemingly small matters can be important when it comes to intelligence. The great American general George Marshall recalls this memory from the Normandy invasion during the Second World War: "[Army intelligence] never told me what I needed to know. They didn't tell me about the hedgerows, and it was not until later, after much bloodshed, that we were able to deal with them"; quoted in Andrew Roberts, *Masters and Commander: How Four Titans Won the War in the West, 1941–1945* (New York: HarperCollins, 2009), p. 490.

11   Siobhan Gorman, "NSA Has Higher Profile, New Problems," *Baltimore Sun* (September 8, 2006), p. A1.

12   Both 85 percent figures are from *Preparing for the 21st Century: An Appraisal of U.S. Intelligence*, Report of the Commission on the Roles and Capabilities of the United States Intelligence Community (the Aspin–Brown Commission) (Washington, DC: Government Printing Office, March 1, 1996), p. 49. The $80 billion figure is based on a first-time disclosure by the government, in October 2010, of both the National Intelligence Program (NIP, composed of the CIA and the large collection agencies) and the Military Intelligence Program (MIP, composed of the Defense Department's tactical collection operations), as summarized by Walter Pincus, "Intelligence Spending at Record $80.1 Billion in First Disclosure of Overall Figure," *Washington Post* (October 28, 2010), p. A1. This spending was a record high and represented a 7 percent increase over the year before, and a doubling of the aggregate intelligence budget from pre-9/11 levels. In 2009, a DNI said publicly that the Intelligence Community in the United States employs 200,000 people: Dennis C. Blair, Director of National Intelligence, media round table, Washington, DC (September 15, 2009). For purposes of contrast, the British intelligence budget is reported to be about $3.6 billion a year: Philip Johnston, "GCGH: Licensed to Eavesdrop," *Daily Telegraph*, London (August 27, 2010), p. A1.

13   Steven Aftergood, "DOD Releases Military Intel Program Budget Docs," *Secrecy New* 79 (October 5, 2009), p. 1. For a perspective on Intelligence Community spending over time in recent decades, see the Report of the Commission on the Roles and Capabilities of the United States Intelligence Community (the Aspin–Brown Commission), *Preparing for the 21st Century: An Appraisal of U.S. Intelligence* (U.S. Government Printing Office: Washington, DC, March 1, 1996).

14   R. James Woolsey, author's interview, CIA Headquarters, Langley, VA (September 29, 1993).

15 Admiral Stansfield Turner, author's interview, McLean, VA (May 1, 1991). For a vivid description of the Admiral's difficulties in trying to manage the CIA, let alone the larger Intelligence Community, see his *Secrecy and Democracy: The CIA in Transition* (Boston: Houghton Mifflin, 1985).

16 See Loch K. Johnson, *Bombs, Bugs, Drugs, and Thugs: Intelligence and America's Quest for Security* (New York: New York University Press, 2000), Ch. 3.

17 Dana Priest and William M. Arkin, "A Hidden World, Growing Beyond Control," *Washington Post* (July 19, 2010), p. A1. On espionage outsourcing, see Tim Shorrock, *Spies for Hire: The Secret World of Intelligence Outsourcing* (New York: Simon and Schuster, 2008).

18 Clark Clifford, with Richard Holbrooke, *Counsel to the President: A Memoir* (New York: Random House, 1991), p. 166.

19 Michael Warner, "Central Intelligence: Origin and Evolution," in Michael Warner, ed., *Central Intelligence: Origin and Evolution* (Washington, DC: Center for the Study of Intelligence, Central Intelligence Agency, 2001), reprinted in Roger Z. George and Robert D. Kline, eds., *Intelligence and the National Security Strategist: Enduring Issues and Challenges* (Washington, DC: National Defense University Press, 2004), p. 43. See, also, Michael Warner, *The Rise and Fall of Intelligence: An International Security History* (Washington, DC: Georgetown University Press, 2014).

20 Miller, *Plain Speaking*, p. 420 note.

21 Clifford, with Holbrooke, *Counsel to the President*, pp. 168, 169.

22 Ray S. Cline, *The CIA under Reagan, Bush, and Casey* (Washington, DC: Acropolis Books, 1981), p. 112.

23 Clifford, with Holbrooke, *Counsel to the President*, p. 169.

24 Amy B. Zegart, *Flawed by Design: The Evolution of the CIA, JCS, and NSC* (Stanford: Stanford University Press, 1999).

25 Warner, "Central Intelligence," pp. 45, 47.

26 Warner, "Central Intelligence," p. 38.

27 Clifford, with Holbrooke, *Counsel to the President*, p. 168.

28 Quoted by Victor Marchetti and John D. Marks, *The CIA and the Cult of Intelligence* (New York: Knopf, 1974), p. 70.

29 Phyllis Provost McNeil, "The Evolution of the U.S. Intelligence Community – An Historical Perspective," *Preparing for the 21st Century: An Appraisal of U.S. Intelligence*, Appendix A; Warner, "Central Intelligence"; and Larry Kindsvater, "The Need to Reorganize the Intelligence Community," *Studies in Intelligence* 47 (2003), pp. 33–7.

30 Johnson, *Bombs, Bugs, Drugs, and Thugs*.

31 Warner, "Central Intelligence," p. 49.

32 Charles Babington and Walter Pincus, "White House Assails Parts of Bills," *Washington Post* (October 20, 2004), p. A10.

33 William M. Nolte, remark, International Studies Association meeting (March 27, 2008).

34 Senator John D. Rockefeller, *Confirmation Hearings*, John M. McConnell, Select Committee on Intelligence, U.S. Senate, 110th Cong., 1st Sess. (February 1, 2007).

35   Quoted by Mark Mazzetti, "Intelligence Chief Finds That Challenges Abound," *New York Times* (April 7, 2007), p. A10.
36   Bloomsberg News, "Director Wants More Authority in Intelligence," *New York Times* (April 5, 2007), p. A13.
37   Quoted by Mark Mazzetti, "Intelligence Director Announces Renewed Plan for Overhaul," *New York Times* (April 12, 2007), p. A13.
38   Admiral Mike McConnell, testimony, "DNI Authorities," Hearings, Select Committee on Intelligence, U.S. Senate, 110th Cong., 2nd Sess. (February 14, 2008).
39   Mark Mazzetti, "White House Sides With the CIA in a Spy Turf Battle," *New York Times* (November 13, 2009), p. A12.
40   See Loch K. Johnson, *The Threat on the Horizon: An Inside Account of America's Search for Security after the Cold War* (New York: Oxford University Press, 2011).

Chapter 2   Intelligence collection and analysis: Knowing about the world

1   Loch K. Johnson, *The Threat on the Horizon: An Inside Account of America's Search for Security after the Cold War* (New York: Oxford University Press, 2011), pp. 219–20; this account draws on this source. See also *Report of the Secretary of Defense to the President and the Congress* (Washington, DC: Government Printing Office, 1996).
2   Richard Helms, with William Hood, *A Look over My Shoulder: A Life in the Central Intelligence Agency* (New York: Random House, 2003), p. 234.
3   On the oversimplification of the cycle, see Arthur S. Hulnick, "What's Wrong with the Intelligence Cycle?" in Loch K. Johnson, ed., *Strategic Intelligence, Vol. 2: The Intelligence Cycle* (Westport, CT: Praeger, 2007), pp. 1–22.
4   R. James Woolsey, testimony, *Hearings*, Select Committee on Intelligence, U.S. Senate, 103rd Cong., 2nd Sess. (March 6, 1993).
5   Dean Rusk, remark to the author, Athens, GA (February 21, 1988).
6   Les Aspin, remark to the author, Washington, DC (July 14, 1994).
7   Mark M. Lowenthal, *Intelligence: From Secrets to Policy*, 6th edn (Washington, DC: CQ Press, 2014), p. 76.
8   Author's interview (August 28, 1984), Washington, DC.
9   See William J. Broad, "The Rocket Science of Missile Threats," *New York Times* (April 26, 2009), p. Wk. 3.
10   Douglas F. Garthoff, *Directors of Central Intelligence as Leaders of the U.S. Intelligence Community, 1946–2005* (Washington, DC: Center for the Study of Intelligence, Central Intelligence Agency, 2005), p. 240.
11   William E. Colby, remark to the author, Washington, DC (January 22, 1991).
12   Joseph S. Nye, Jr., and William A. Owens, "America's Information Edge," *Foreign Affairs* (March/April 1996), p. 26.

13   Office of the Director of National Intelligence, *The Inaugural Report of the Global Maritime and Air Communities of Interest Intelligence Enterprises* (November 2009), cited in "Federation of American Scientists Project on Government Secrecy," *Secrecy News* 89 (November 9, 2009), p. 2.

14   *Questions & Answers on the Intelligence Community Post 9/11*, Office of the Director of National Intelligence (July 2010), p. 3.

15   Remarks to the Aspin–Brown Commission, author's notes (April 28, 1995). The author served as Aspin's assistant during the Commission's inquiries.

16   Remarks in a speech cited by intelligence scholar Richard L. Russell, "Low-Pressure System," *The American Interest* 2 (July/August 2007), pp. 119–23, quote at p. 120.

17   Michael Bronner, "When the War Ends, Start to Worry," *New York Times* (August 16, 2008), p. A27.

18   On the *Glomar Explorer*, see David H. Sharp, *The CIA's Greatest Covert Operation: Inside the Daring Mission to Recover a Nuclear-Armed Soviet Sub* (Lawrence: University Press of Kansas, 2012). When the operation leaked to the media in 1975, Senator Frank Church (D, Idaho) said: "If we are prepared to pay Howard Hughes $350 million for an obsolete Russian submarine, it's little wonder we are broke." His Senate colleague Barry Goldwater (R, Arizona) had a different view: "Frankly, if they hadn't gone out and raised that sub, I'd be mad" (both quoted in the *Boston Globe*, March 20, 1975). Generally on the "ints," see Mark M. Lowenthal and Robert M. Clark, eds., *The 5 Disciplines of Intelligence Collection* (Los Angeles: Sage and CQ Press, 2016).

19   Douglas Jehl, "New Spy Plan Said to Involve Satellite System," *New York Times* (December 12, 2004), p. A1.

20   Steven Emerson, *Secret Warriors: Inside the Covet Military Operations of the Reagan Era* (New York: Putnam, 1988), p. 35. Recently released documents from the Carter Administration era included this revealing observation from NSC staffer Paul Henze about the limits of technical intelligence collection: "While we now enjoy nearly real-time photography from satellites...we are not much closer than we were thirty years ago to knowing what goes on in the minds of the top men in Moscow or Madrid, Peking, Algeria or Brasilia, what Arab leaders say to each other when they get together or how French elections are going to come out": *Organization and Management of Foreign Policy: 1977–80*, Department of State, Vol. 28 (2016), document 63, p. 321.

21   Richard Kerr, Thomas Wolfe, Rebecca Donegan, and Aris Pappas, "Collection and Analysis on Iraq: Issues for the US Intelligence Community," *Studies in Intelligence* 49 (2005), pp. 47–54, quote at p. 50.

22   Richard Barrett, "Time to Talk to the Taliban," *New York Times* (October 19, 2010), p. 25.

23   See John L. Millis, staff member, House Permanent Select Committee on Intelligence, "Our Spying Success Is No Secret," letter, *New York*

Times (October 12, 1994), p. A27; and Steve Coll, *Ghost Wars: The Secret History of the CIA, Afghanistan, and Bin Laden, From the Soviet Invasion to September 10, 2001* (New York: Penguin, 2004), p. 317.

24 Interview conducted by Amy B. Zegart (June 2004), cited in her *Spying Blind: The CIA, the FBI, and the Origins of 9/11* (Princeton, NJ: Princeton University Press, 2007), p. 93. Given the hardships and risks involved in the life of NOCs in remote locations, the pay scale will have to be higher than the usual salary for intelligence officers if good recruits are to be attracted to this important challenge. According to several authoritative reports, those intelligence officers under official cover (OC) enjoy the comfort and safety of working under the auspices of the State Department overseas, as part of the embassy "country team" led by the ambassador. See, for example, William Colby and Peter Forbath, *Honorable Men: My Life in the CIA* (New York: Simon and Schuster, 1978), p. 336; John Ranelagh, *The Agency: The Rise and Decline of the CIA* (New York: Simon and Schuster, 1987), p. 20; Lowenthal, *Intelligence: From Secrets to Policy*, 6th edn, p. 129; and Mark Mazzetti, "White House Sides With the CIA in a Spy Turf Battle," *New York Times* (November 13, 2009), p. A12, as well as his "Pakistan's Public Enemy," *New York Times Magazine* (April 14, 2013), p. 33.

25 See Robert M. Gates, *From the Shadows* (New York: Simon & Schuster, 1996), p. 560; and Bud Shuster, "HiTech vs. Human Spying," *Washington Times* (February 11, 1992), p. F3.

26 CBS News, "Faulty Intel Source 'Curve Ball' Revealed," *60 Minutes* (November 4, 2007).

27 See Joseph W. Wippl, "The CIA and Tolkachev vs. the KGB/SVR and Ames: A Comparison," *International Journal of Intelligence and Counterintelligence* 23 (Winter 2010–11), pp. 636–46; and a fictional account of the complicated relationship between assets and their handlers, Joseph Weisberg, *An Ordinary Spy* (New York: Bloomsbury, 2008), referred to in a blurb by a former DDO as "stunningly realistic."

28 See, respectively, the Kean Commission's report, entitled *The 9/11 Commission Report: Final Report of the National Commission on Terrorist Attacks upon the United States* (New York: Norton, 2004), p. 415; the Silberman–Robb Commission on the Intelligence Capabilities of the United States Regarding Weapons of Mass Destruction, *Final Report* (Washington, DC: Government Printing Office, 2005), pp. 410–11; and George Tenet, with Bill Harlow, *At the Center of the Storm: My Years at the CIA* (New York: HarperCollins, 2007), p. 24.

29 Author's interview with William E. Colby, Washington, DC (January 22, 1991). Former Secretary of State Dean Rusk, who served in both the Kennedy and the Johnson Administrations, has observed: "I regret our relying so heavily on technical intelligence, which produces limited information, at the expense of the old-fashioned spy on the ground who steals information, infiltrates groups, and eavesdrops on conversations": see his *As I Saw It*, as told to Richard Rusk and edited by Daniel S. Papp (New York: Norton, 1990), p. 560.

30   Author's interview with Robert M. Gates, Washington, DC (March 28, 1994).
31   John L. Millis, speech, Central Intelligence Retirees Association, Arlington, VA (October 5, 1998), p. 6.
32   Max Holland, "The 'Photo Gap' that Delayed Discovery of Missiles in Cuba," *Studies in Intelligence* 49 (2005), pp. 15–30, see especially p. 15.
33   On the U-2, see Gregory W. Pedlow and Donald E. Welzenbach, *The CIA and the U-2 Program, 1954–1975* (Washington, DC: Center for the Study of Intelligence, Central Intelligence Agency, 1998), with a section on the aircraft's use during the Cuban missile crisis (at pp. 199–210). On the missile crisis of 1962, see also Graham Allison and Philip Zelikow, *Essence of Decision: Explaining the Cuban Missile Crisis*, 2nd edn (New York: Longman, 1995); and James G. Blight, Bruce J. Allyn, and David A. Welch, *Cuba on the Brink: Castro, the Missile Crisis, and the Soviet Collapse* (New York: Pantheon, 1993).
34   Holland, "The 'Photo Gap.'"
35   John Lewis Gaddis, *We Now Know: Rethinking Cold War History* (New York: Oxford University Press, 1997), p. 262.
36   Sherman Kent, "A Crucial Estimate Relived," *Studies in Intelligence* (Spring 1964), pp. 1–18, quote at p. 15.
37   Gaddis, *We Now Know*, p. 267; James G. Blight and David A. Welch, eds., *Intelligence and the Cuban Missile Crisis* (London: Cass, 1998); and Raymond L. Garthoff, *Reflections on the Cuban Missile Crisis*, rev. edn (Washington: Brookings Institution, 1989), pp. 35–6.
38   Author's interview with McNamara (January 24, 1985), Athens, GA.
39   Dean Rusk, interview conducted by Professor Eric Goldman (January 12, 1964), Rusk Papers, Russell Library, University of Georgia, Athens, GA. See, also, Rusk, *As I Saw It*.
40   R. James Woolsey, author's interview, CIA Headquarters, Langley, VA (September 29, 1993).
41   Loch K. Johnson, "Evaluating 'Humint': The Role of Foreign Agents in U.S. Security," *Comparative Strategy* 29 (September–October 2010), pp. 308–33.
42   See Jeffrey T. Richelson, "The Technical Collection of Intelligence," in Loch K. Johnson, ed., *Handbook of Intelligence Studies* (New York: Routledge, 2007), pp. 105–17.
43   Respectively: Reuel Marc Gerecht, "A New Clandestine Service: The Case for Creative Destruction," in Peter Berkowitz, ed., *The Future of American Intelligence* (Stanford: Hoover Press, 2005), p. 128; and *Intelligence Authorization Act for Fiscal Year 2005*, Report 108–558, Permanent Select Committee on Intelligence (the Goss Committee), U.S. House of Representatives, 108th Cong., 2nd Sess. (June 21, 2004), p. 24.
44   "The CIA and the Media," *Hearings*, Subcommittee on Oversight, Permanent Select Committee on Intelligence, U.S. House of Representatives, 96th Cong., 1st Sess. (1979), p. 7.
45   Fewer than 10 percent of America's college students study a foreign language as part of their curriculum. An experienced former CIA

officer notes: "CIA operatives are not particularly well prepared; they seldom speak foreign languages well and almost never know a line of business or a technical field": Michael Turner, *Why Secret Intelligence Fails* (Washington, DC: Potomac Books, 2005), p. 92. A risk associated with the placing of intelligence officers in the same foreign country for long periods of time is "clientitis" – that is, an intelligence officer "going native" and losing the capacity to appraise objectively the nation where he or she is serving. The solution is for CIA managers to remove an intelligence officer from another country when signs of this malady occur, not eliminating the opportunity for all intelligence officers across the board to learn foreign languages inside-out through more extensive periods of service in a single country or region. Another reason for longer service in one country: the recruitment and development of a local asset takes time.

46 See Robert Callum, "The Case for Cultural Diversity in the Intelligence Community," *International Journal of Intelligence and Counterintelligence* 14 (Spring 2001), pp. 25–48. In September 2009, the new D/CIA, Leon Panetta, traveled to Dearborn, Michigan, to recruit intelligence officers in the Detroit suburb known for its large enclave of Arab Americans; David Carr, "Investment in a City Of Struggles," *New York Times* (September 21, 2009), p. B1.

47 On the FBI's failure to share counterterrorism data in the lead-up to 9/11, see Daniel Benjamin and Steven Simon, *The Age of Sacred Terror: Radical Islam's War against America* (New York: Random House, 2003), p. 304.

48 Foreign liaison can be tricky. Some of the liaison services abroad with which the United States has a relationship must be kept at arm's length, because they are embedded in authoritarian regimes with suspect motives and behavior; and even those that reside in friendly democracies must be dealt with gingerly, because they may have been compromised – as the CIA discovered during the Cold War when top-level MI6 officers proved to be Soviet assets (among them, Kim Philby, a case examined in Chapter 4).

49 Author's interview with a senior NSA official who quoted the NSA Director, Washington, DC (July 14, 1994). McConnell would later serve as the nation's second DNI (2007–09).

50 Bob Woodward, *Plan of Attack* (New York: Simon & Schuster, 2004), p. 215.

51 Millis, speech (see note 31). A leading expert on the NSA and sigint has noted that this agency collects from intercepted Internet traffic alone "the equivalent of the entire textual collection of the library of Congress 2,990 times every day. Of this amount, according to NSA, only 0.025 percent of the intercepted Internet material is selected for review by the agency's analysts." Even that amount is equivalent to "119 times the size of the entire collection of the Library of Congress": Matthew M. Aid, "Prometheus Embattled: A Post-9/11 Report Card on the National Security Agency," in Loch K. Johnson, ed., *Essentials of Strategic Intelligence* (Santa Barbara, CA: Praeger, 2015), p. 436.

52   Dana Priest and William M. Arkin, "A Hidden World, Growing Beyond Control," *Washington Post* (July 19, 2010), p. A1.
53   See Richard K. Betts, *Enemies of Intelligence: Knowledge & Power in American National Security* (New York: Columbia University Press, 2007).
54   Rusk, *As I Saw It*, p. 553.
55   Tenet, with Harlow, *At the Center of the Storm*, p. 30; the Kean quote is from Linton Weeks, "An Indelible Day," *Washington Post* (June 16, 2004), p. C1.
56   Author's interview (November 19, 1984), Washington, DC.
57   A DDI study during six months in 1994–95 indicated that policymakers had asked 1,300 follow-up questions after reading a *PDB*. In 57 percent of the cases, the questions were answered at the time of the briefing; and in 43 percent of the cases, the CIA was queried later and provided answers within a day or two.
58   Author's interviews with Clinton Administration officials throughout 1992–97, Washington, DC.
59   Quoted in Loch K. Johnson, *America's Secret Power: The CIA in a Democratic Society* (New York: Oxford University Press, 1989), p. 90.
60   See John L. Helgerson, *Getting to Know the President: CIA Briefings of Presidential Candidates, 1952–1992* (Washington, DC: Center for the Study of Intelligence, Central Intelligence Agency, undated – but apparently released in 1995 by the CIA).
61   Quoted by Russell, "Low-Pressure System," p. 123.
62   Author's interview with George Tenet, Senior Director for Intelligence, National Security Council, Old Executive Office Building, Washington, DC (June 17, 1994).
63   See Tim Weiner, "C.I.A. Chief Defends Secrecy, in Spending and Spying, to Senate," *New York Times* (February 23, 1996), p. A5.
64   See Loch K. Johnson, "Glimpses into the Gems of American Intelligence: The *President's Daily Brief* and the National Intelligence Estimate," *Intelligence and National Security* 23 (June 2008), pp. 333–70.
65   Lyman B. Kirkpatrick, "United States Intelligence," *Military Review* 41 (May 1961), pp. 18–22, quote at p. 20.
66   Stansfield Turner, *Secrecy and Democracy: The CIA in Transition* (Boston: Houghton Mifflin, 1985), p. 243.
67   National Intelligence Council, National Intelligence Estimate, *Iran: Nuclear Intentions and Capabilities* (November 2007), cited by CNN News (December 2, 2007).
68   Sherman Kent, *Intelligence for American World Policy* (Princeton: Princeton University Press, 1949), pp. 64–5.
69   See Anne Hessing Cahn, *Killing Détente: The Right Attacks the CIA* (University Park: Pennsylvania State University Press, 1998).
70   Chester Cooper, retired CIA analyst, interviewed by Ron Nessen, "Intelligence Failure: From Pearl Harbor to 9/11 and Iraq" (television transcript), *America Abroad Media* (July 2004), p. 11.
71   For examples of DCI-penned NIEs, see the discussion of DCI Stansfield Turner in Garthoff, *Directors of Central Intelligence*, p. 153.

72   Gregory F. Treverton, "Intelligence Analysis: Between 'Politiciza-
      tion' and Irrelevance," in Roger Z. George and James B. Bruce, eds.,
      Analyzing Intelligence: Origins, Obstacles, and Innovations (Washington,
      DC: Georgetown University Press, 2008), p. 102.
73   Arthur S. Hulnick, review of Harold P. Ford, *Estimative Intelligence:
      The Purposes and Problems of National Intelligence Estimating* (New
      York: University Press of America, 1993), *Conflict Quarterly* 14 (Winter
      1994), pp. 72–4, quote at p. 74. President Lyndon B. Johnson once
      vividly explained why some policymakers are reluctant to hear from
      intelligence officers. "When I was growing up in Texas," he recalled
      at a private dinner party in Washington, DC, "we had a cow named
      Bessie. I'd get her in the stanchion, seat myself and squeeze out a pail
      of fresh milk. One day, I'd worked hard and gotten a full pail of milk,
      but I wasn't paying attention and old Bessie swung her s——smeared
      tail through that bucket of milk. Now, you know, that's what these
      intelligence guys do. You work hard and get a good program or
      policy going, and they swing a s——smeared tail through it"; quoted
      in the memoir by former DCI Robert M. Gates, *From the Shadows*
      (New York: Simon and Schuster, 1996), p. 566.
74   The metaphor comes from a CIA analyst, quoted in Johnson, *The
      Threat on the Horizon*, p. 92. See also Johnson, "Analysis for a New
      Age," *Intelligence and National Security* 11 (October 1996), pp. 657–71.
      This article argues in favor of placing more intelligence liaison offic-
      ers in policy departments, so the officers can return to their agencies
      each day to inform analysts about what topics the departments are
      focused on – a vital method for making intelligence more relevant
      to the information needs of decision-makers. Sometimes those on
      the policy side of the government are inclined to discount the value
      of the Intelligence Community and its products. Poking fun at this
      aspect of government – at the expense of an example drawn from
      the United Kingdom – a former Director of INR, Thomas Hughes,
      quotes an analyst in the Research Department of the British Foreign
      Office who served from 1903 to 1950. "Year after year the worriers
      and fretters would come to me with awful predictions of the outbreak
      of war," said the UK analyst. "I denied it each time. I was only wrong
      twice." Hughes observes that, using this methodology, the analyst
      "can curl up in the luxury of a freebooting negativism. No reputation
      is staked, no career endangered"; Thomas L. Hughes. *The Fate of Facts
      in a World of Men: Foreign Policy and Intelligence Making*. Headline
      Series, No. 233 (Washington, DC; Foreign Policy Association), 1976,
      p. 48. Former Secretary of State Dean Rusk recalls that some U.S.
      intelligence officers dealt with the risk of intelligence failure by fore-
      casting danger everywhere. "The CIA predicted eight out of the last
      three crises," recalled Rusk, looking back on his tenure as Secretary
      from 1961 to 1969; author's interview with Rusk (October 5, 1979),
      Athens, Georgia.
75   The author is grateful to the CIA for providing these statistics, which
      come independently from two different sources within the Agency.

76   The data came to the author by year, not by DCI tenure; the decision rule here was to award all of the Estimates in a given year to the Intelligence Director who served the most time in that particular year.

77   Letter from Sherman Kent to Frank Wisner (dated November 18, 1963), found by the author (October 16, 2005) in the Sterling Library Collection, Yale University, Series I, Box 18, Folder 390.

78   Sherman Kent, "Estimates and Influence," *Foreign Service Journal* (April 1969), p. 17.

79   British intelligence came to the same conclusion. One of its leaders has written that "identifying Soviet strategic caution [was] perhaps the most important single judgement of the [Cold War] period": Percy Cradock, *Know Your Enemy* (London: John Murray, 2002), p. 292.

80   In 1975, Senator Frank Church (D, Idaho) noted: "In the last twenty-five years, no important new Soviet weapons system, from the H-bomb to the most recent missiles, has appeared which had not been heralded in advance by NIEs": *Congressional Record* (November 11, 1975), p. S35787.

81   See Loch K. Johnson, *Secret Agencies: U.S. Intelligence in a Hostile World* (New Haven, CT: Yale University Press, 1996).

82   See George and Bruce, eds., *Analyzing Intelligence*; James P. Pfiffner and Mark Phythian, eds., *Intelligence and National Security Policy-making on Iraq: British and American Perspectives* (Manchester, UK: Manchester University Press, 2008); and Robert M. Clark, *Intelligence Analysis: A Target-Centric Approach*, 3rd edn (Washington, DC: CQ Press, 2010), pp. 314–19.

83   Church (see note 80), p. S35786.

84   Richard K. Betts, "Analysis, War and Decision: Why Intelligence Failures Are Inevitable," *World Politics* 31 (October 1978), pp. 61–89, quote at p. 78. See also Betts, *Enemies of Intelligence*.

85   Hulnick, review of Ford, *Estimative Intelligence*, p. 74.

86   Harold P. Ford, *Estimative Intelligence: The Purposes and Problems of National Intelligence Estimating* (New York: University Press of America, 1993), p. 49.

87   William E. Odom, *Fixing Intelligence for a More Secure America*, 2nd edn (New Haven, CT: Yale University Press, 2004), p. 81.

88   Kent, "Estimates and Influence," p. 17.

89   Barton Gellman and Walter Pincus, "Depiction of Threat Outgrew Supporting Evidence," *Washington Post* (August 10, 2003), p. A1, quoting a senior intelligence official.

90   Gellman and Pincus, "Depiction of Threat Outgrew Supporting Evidence."

91   Tenet, with Harlow, *At the Center of the Storm*, pp. 321–2.

92   Tenet, with Harlow, *At the Center of the Storm*, pp. 322–3.

93   Senator Bob Graham, with Jeff Nussbaum, *Intelligence Matters: The CIA, the FBI, Saudi Arabia, and the Failure of America's War on Terror* (New York: Random House, 2004), p. 180.

94   Tim Weiner, *Legacy of Ashes: The History of the CIA* (New York: Doubleday, 2007), p. 487.
95   The NIE was entitled *Iraq's Continuing Program for Weapons of Mass Destruction* (NIE 2002–16HC). On the timing and Tenet's briefing, see Graham, with Nussbaum, *Intelligence Matters*, pp. 179–80.
96   Graham, with Nussbaum, *Intelligence Matters*, p. 187.
97   Graham, with Nussbaum, *Intelligence Matters*, pp. 185–9.
98   Interviewed by Wil S. Hylton, "The Angry One," *Gentleman's Quarterly* (January 2007), p. 21.
99   *Report on the U.S. Intelligence Community's Prewar Intelligence Assessments on Iraq*, Senate Select Committee on Intelligence (Washington, DC: Government Printing Office, July 7, 2004), p. 14.
100 Tenet, with Harlow, *At the Center of the Storm*, p. 338.
101 Author's notes on remarks by Mark M. Lowenthal, Canadian Association for Security and Intelligence Studies (CASIS) Conference, Ottawa (October 27, 2006).
102 The 80–90 percent figure comes from the author's interview with a senior CIA manager in the Agency's Intelligence Directorate, Washington, DC (August 28, 1997).
103 Lowenthal, CASIS Conference (see note 101).
104 John L. Helgerson, remarks to the author, International Symposium, The Hague, Holland (June 8, 2007).
105 Michael Bloch, *Ribbentrop* (London: Abacus, 2003), p. 167. At one point Ribbentrop vowed that he would personally shoot, at the person's office desk, any official who dissented from Hitler's worldview (p. xix).
106 See, respectively, Stansfield Turner, *Burn before Reading: Presidents, CIA Directors, and Secret Intelligence* (New York: Hyperion, 2005), p. 77; and Johnson, *America's Secret Power*, pp. 63–4. Mark Lowenthal, a former CIA analysis, notes that a "subtle and difficult skill to master is cultivating the intelligence consumer without politicizing the intelligence as a means of currying favor": *Intelligence: From Secrets to Policy*, 6th edn (Washington, DC: CQ Press, 2014), p. 161.
107 Helms, with Hood, *A Look over My Shoulder*, p. 318.
108 On improving analysis, see Clark, *Intelligence Analysis*; George and Bruce, eds., *Analyzing Intelligence*; Robert Jervis, *Why Intelligence Fails* (Ithaca, NY: Cornell University Press, 2010); Johnson, ed., *Strategic Intelligence: Vol. 2: The Intelligence Cycle*; Richard L. Russell, *Sharpening Strategic Intelligence* (New York: Cambridge University Press, 2007); and Timothy Walton, *Challenges in Intelligence Analysis* (New York: Cambridge University Press, 2010).
109 See Peter Wyden, *Bay of Pigs: The Untold Story* (New York: Simon & Schuster, 1979); and Arthur M. Schlesinger, Jr., *Robert Kennedy and His Times* (Boston: Houghton Mifflin, 1978), p. 453.
110 Quoted by Greg Miller, "CIA to Station More Analysts Overseas as Part of its Strategy," *Washington Post* (April 30, 2010), p. A1.
111 Kimberly Dozier, "CIA Forms New Center to Combat Nukes, WMDs," Associated Press Report (August 18, 2010).

112   Joseph S. Nye, Jr., remarks, Commission of the Roles and Capabilities of the United States Intelligence Community, Washington, DC (June 1, 1995).

113   Richard K. Betts, "The New Politics of Intelligence: Will Reforms Work This Time?" *Foreign Affairs* 83 (May/June 2004), pp. 2–8, quote at p. 7.

114   Author's interview with Richard Helms, Washington, DC (December 12, 1990), in Loch K. Johnson, "Spymaster Richard Helms," *Intelligence and National Security* 18 (Autumn 2003), pp. 24–44, quote at p. 27.

115   See also, Willmoore Kendall, "The Function of Intelligence," *World Politics* 1 (1948–49), pp. 542–52.

116   William M. Nolte, remark, panel on intelligence analysis, International Studies Association annual meeting, San Francisco (March 2008).

117   See the findings of the Butler Report, which are discussed in R. Gerald Hughes, Peter Jackson, and Len Scott, eds., *Exploring Intelligence Archives: Enquiries into the Secret State* (New York: Routledge, 2008), Ch. 12.

118   Former U.S. diplomat Martin Hillenbrand, remarks to the author, Athens, GA (January 21, 1987). President Ronald Reagan's Secretary of State, George P. Shultz concluded acidly in his memoirs: "I had no confidence in the intelligence community…I had been misled, lied to, cut out." This reaction went beyond the Iran-*contra* scandal to include his view that "CIA analysis was distorted by strong views about policy": see George P. Shultz, *Turmoil and Triumph: My Years as Secretary of State* (New York: Scribner's, 1993), p. 864.

119   Daniel P. Moynihan, "Do We Still Need the CIA? The State Dept. Can Do the Job," *New York Times* (May 19, 1991), p. E17.

120   See *The 9/11 Commission Report*, as well as Graham, with Nussbaum, *Intelligence Matters*; Jane Mayer, *The Dark Side* (New York: Doubleday, 2008); and Zegart, *Spying Blind*.

121   See Hughes et al., *Exploring Intelligence Archives*; Jervis, *Why Intelligence Fails*; and Loch K. Johnson, "A Framework for Strengthening U.S. Intelligence," *Yale Journal of International Affairs* 2 (February 2006), pp. 116–31.

122   *Preparing for the 21st Century: An Appraisal of U.S. Intelligence*, Report of the Commission on the Roles and Capabilities of the United States Intelligence Community (Washington, DC: Government Printing Office, March 1, 1996).

123   See, for example, Adam Goldman and Matt Apuzzo, "CIA and Pakistan Locked in Aggressive Spy Battles," *Associated Press* (July 6, 2010).

Chapter 3   Covert action: secret attempts to shape history

1   This scenario is drawn from Loch K. Johnson, "It's Never a Quick Fix at the CIA," *Washington Post* (August 30, 2009), Outlook Section, p. A1.

2   Henry Kissinger, remark, "Evening News," NBC Television Network (January 13, 1978).
3   The Intelligence Authorization Act of 1991 (50 U.S.C. 503 (e); Pub. L. No. 102–88, 105 Stat. 441, August 14, 1991); this statute amended the National Security Act of 1947, repealed the Hughes–Ryan Amendment of 1974, and codified into law Executive Order 12333.
4   John Deutch, DCI, speech, National Press Club, Washington, DC (September 12, 1995).
5   William J. Daugherty, *Executive Secrets: Covert Action & the Presidency* (Lexington: University Press of Kentucky, 2004), p. 12.
6   The National Security Act of 1947, Pub. L. No. 80–253, 61 Stat. 495; 50 U.S.C. 403–3(d)(5).
7   Author's interview with a senior CIA official in the Operations Directorate, Washington, DC (February 1986).
8   B. Hugh Tovar, "Strengths and Weaknesses in Past U.S. Covert Action," in Roy Godson, ed., *Intelligence Requirements for the 1980s: Covert Action* (Washington, DC: National Strategy Information Center, 1981), pp. 194–5.
9   William E. Colby, "Gesprach mit William E. Colby," *Der Spiegel* 4 (January 23, 1978), author's translation, pp. 69–115, quote at p. 75.
10   Quoted in *The Nation* (March 12, 1983), p. 301.
11   Frank Church, "Covert Action: Swampland of American Foreign Policy," *Bulletin of the Atomic Scientists* 32 (February 1976), pp. 7–11, quote at p. 8, reprinted in Loch K. Johnson and James J. Wirtz, eds., *Intelligence and National Security: The Secret World of Spies*, 3rd edn (New York: Oxford University Press, 2011), pp. 233–7.
12   See Jennifer Kibbe, "Covert Action and the Pentagon," in Loch K. Johnson, ed., *Strategic Intelligence, Vol. 3: Covert Action* (Westport, CT: Praeger, 2007), pp. 145–56; John Prados, "The Future of Covert Action," in Loch K. Johnson, ed., *Handbook of Intelligence Studies* (New York: Routledge, 2007), pp. 289–98; and Tim Shorrock, *Spies for Hire: The Secret World of Intelligence Outsourcing* (New York: Simon & Schuster, 2008).
13   Section 662(a) of the Foreign Assistance Act of 1974; Section 662 of the Foreign Assistance Act of 1961 (22 U.S.C. 2422).
14   Select Committee on Secret Military Assistance to Iran and the Nicaraguan Opposition, U.S. Senate, and House Select Committee to Investigate Covert Arms Transactions with Iran, U.S. House (the Inouye–Hamilton Committee), *Hearings and Final Report* (Washington, DC: Government Printing Office, 1987). The statutory responses came in the form chiefly of the 1991 Intelligence Authorization Act (see note 3). See also Malcolm Byrne, *Iran-Contra: Reagan's Scandal and the Unchecked Abuse of Presidential Power* (Lawrence: University Press of Kansas, 2014).
15   See Hugh Wilford, *The Mighty Wurlitzer: How the CIA Played America* (Cambridge, MA: Harvard University Press, 2008).
16   Testimony, "The CIA and the Media," Hearings, Subcommittee on Oversight, Permanent Select Committee on Intelligence, U.S. House

of Representatives (Washington, DC: Government Printing Office, 1979).

17 Author's interview with a CAS officer, Washington, DC (February 21, 1976).

18 Senior DDO officer, testimony, *Hearings*, Select Committee to Study Governmental Operations with Respect to Intelligence Activities (the Church Committee), *Final Report*, 94th Cong., 2nd Sess., Sen . Rept. No. 94–465 (Washington, DC: Government Printing Office, 1976), p. 31; see, also, Church Committee, *Alleged Assassination Plots Involving Foreign Leaders*, Interim Rept., S. Rept. No. 94–465 (Washington, DC: Government Printing Office, November 20, 1975), p. 181, note.

19 See Michael Grow, *U.S. Presidents and Latin American Interventions: Pressuring Regime Change in the Cold War* (Lawrence: University Press of Kansas, 2008).

20 David Wise and Thomas B. Ross, *The Invisible Government* (New York: Random House, 1964).

21 Tom Wicker et al., "CIA Operations: A Plot Scuttled," *New York Times* (April 28, 1966), p. A1.

22 Joint Chiefs of Staff, memo on SQUARE DANCE, dated October 30, 1964, and attached to a memo from R.C. Bowman to National Security Adviser McGeorge Bundy, 1964 National Security Files (November 12, 1964), Lyndon Baines Johnson Presidential Library, Austin, TX.

23 Stephen R. Weissman, "An Extraordinary Rendition," *Intelligence and National Security* 25 (April 2010), pp. 198–222.

24 Executive Order 12333, Sec. 2.11.

25 Former DCI Robert M. Gates, quoted by Walter Pincus, "Saddam Hussein's Death Is a Goal," *Washington Post* (February 15, 1998), p. A36.

26 Unsigned editorial, "Lethal Force under Law," *New York Times* (October 10, 2010), Wk. 7. See also Ken Dilanian and Courtney Kube, "U.S. Report Will Say Drones Have Killed Just 100 Civilians," *NBC News* (June 24, 2016). For the corrected figure in 2016, see the unsigned editorial, "The Secret Rules of the Drone War," *New York Times* (July 10, 2016), p. SR8. On the drone murder of Alaki, see Scott Shane, *Objective Troy: A Terrorist, a President, and the Rise of the Drone* (New York: Tim Duggan Books, 2015).

27 For accounts of U.S. drone attacks in the Middle East and Southwest Asia, see H. Gusterson, *Drone: Remote Control Warfare* (Boston: MIT Press, 2016); J. Kaag and Sarah S. Kreps, *Drone Warfare* (Cambridge, UK: Polity, 2014); Jane Mayer, "The Predator War," *The New Yorker* (October 26, 2009), pp. 36–45; Mark Mazzetti, *The Way of the Knife: The CIA, a Secret Army, and a War at the Ends of the Earth* (New York: Penguin, 2013); Shane, *Objective Troy*; and Chris Woods, *Sudden Justice: America's Secret Drone Wars* (New York: Oxford University Press, 2015). On the CIA rethinking the wisdom of its involvement in drone attacks, see Mark Mazzetti, "CIA to Focus More on Spying, a Difficult Shift," *New York Times* (May 24, 2013), p. A1.

28 "Lethal Force under Law" (see note 26 above).

29 Stansfield Turner, *Burn before Reading: Presidents, CIA Directors, and Secret Intelligence* (New York: Hyperion, 2005), p. 32.
30 John Ranelagh, *The Agency: The Rise and Decline of the CIA*, rev. edn (New York: Simon and Schuster, 1987), p. 220.
31 Church Commitee, *Final Report*, p. 31.
32 Daugherty, *Executive Secrets*, p. 140.
33 Author's interview with senior DO manager, Washington, DC (February 18, 1980).
34 Author's interview with a senior DO officer, Washington, DC (October 10, 1980).
35 George H. W. Bush, letter to the author (January 23, 1994); and author's interview with DCI R. James Woolsey, Langley, Virginia (September 29, 1993).
36 Author's interview, Washington, DC (March 21, 1995).
37 Deutch, DCI speech (see note 4).
38 Herman Kahn, *On Escalation: Metaphors and Scenarios* (New York: Praeger, 1965), p. 37.
39 A CIA intelligence officer, James A. Barry, suggested to the author (who agrees) that the demarcation of broad thresholds on the ladder is more useful than the exact steps within each threshold, since it is difficult to agree exactly about whether some specific rungs should be higher or lower than other rungs. The key point, he argues, is that "there are degrees of damage – physical, economic and psychological/moral – and that these must be clearly articulated in a discussion of proposed covert actions" (letter to the author, dated May 18, 1992).
40 See *Report of the Special Committee on Principles of International Law Concerning Friendly Relations and Co-operation among States*, UN Doc. A/6799 (1967), p. 161.
41 Lori Fisler Damrosch, "Politics across Borders: Nonintervention and Nonforcible Influence over Domestic Affairs," *American Journal of International Law* 83 (January 1989), pp. 6–13, quote at p. 11.
42 On this norm, see Damrosch, "Politics across Borders," pp. 6–13. The Murphy Commission was known more formally as the Commission on the Organization of the Government for the Conduct of Foreign Policy; see its *Report to the President* (Washington, DC: Government Printing Office, June 1975).
43 Damrosch, "Politics across Borders," p. 36.
44 George Ball, "Should the CIA Fight Secret Wars?" *Harper's* (September 1984), pp. 27–44, quote at p. 37.
45 A top-secret recommendation (since declassified) of the General Doolittle Committee, a part of the Hoover Commission in 1954, cited in Church Committee, *Final Report*, p. 9.
46 Ray Cline, former DDI at the CIA, quoted by Ball, "Should the CIA Fight Secret Wars?" pp. 39, 44.
47 Remarks, public lecture, University of Georgia, Athens, GA (May 4, 1986), author's notes.
48 On these ingredients for success, see Milt Bearden, "Lessons from Afghanistan," *New York Times* (March 2, 1998), p. A19.

49   Anthony Lewis, "Costs of the CIA," *New York Times* (April 25, 1997), p. A19.

50   Bearden, "Lessons from Afghanistan."

51   McGeorge Bundy, remark to the author, Athens, GA (October 6, 1987). In 2016, the media revealed that CIA weapons shipped to Jordan, a U.S. ally, for dispersal to rebels opposing the Syrian regime of President Bashar al-Assad, were stolen by members of the Jordanian intelligence service (the General Intelligence Directorate, or GID, also known as the Mukhabarat). The theft included thousands of Kalashnikov (AK-47) assault rifles with millions of rounds, mortars, rocket-propelled grenades, and antitank guided missiles. In 2013, President Obama had approved the program (codenamed TIMBER SYCAMORE), based on an apparently misplaced faith in the GID as a reliable intelligence liaison partner. In the past, though, Jordan had worked closely with the United States through a joint counterterrorism center in Jordan, as well as at a secret CIA prison outside of Amman where the Agency confined suspected terrorists. See Mark Mazzetti and Ali Younes, "Thefts Redirect Arms from C.I.A.," *New York Times* (June 27, 2016), p. A1. In 2009, a Jordanian physician serving as a CIA counterterrorism agent inside Al Qaeda also betrayed the United States by exploding a suicide vest he was wearing during a secret meeting with seven high-ranking CIA case officers (among them the Agency's COS stationed in Kabul), in a remote part of Afghanistan. All died in the attack (the most lethal against the Agency in twenty-five years), including a GID officer accompanying the double agent. On this tragic case of deception and murder, see Scott Shane and Eric Schmitt, "C.I.A. Deaths Prompt Surge in U.S. Drone Strikes," *New York Times* (January 23, 2010), p. A1.

52   W. Michael Reisman, remarks, "Covert Action," panel presentation, International Studies Association, annual meeting, Washington, DC (March 29, 1994).

53   Remarks, interview on "Larry King Live," CNN Television, Washington, DC (February 2, 1987).

54   Journalist Tom Friedman has observed that the United States treated the Arab world "as a collection of big, dumb gas stations, basically. We told them, 'Here's the deal. Keep your pumps open, your prices low, and be nice to the Jews. And you can do whatever you want out back' ....": Ian Parker, "The Bright Side," *The New Yorker* (November 10, 2008), pp. 52–65, quote at p. 61.

55   Daugherty, *Executive Secrets*, pp. 201, 211.

56   Stansfield Turner, author's interview, McLean, Virginia (May 1, 1991).

57   Remarks, Aspin–Brown Commission staff interview (1996). Similarly, former National Security Adviser Bundy has said that "if you can't defend a covert action if it goes public, you'd better not do it at all – because it will go public usually within a fairly short time span" [author's interview, Athens, GA (October 6, 1987)]. Stansfield Turner has also commented: "There is one overall test of the ethics of human intelligence activities. That is, whether those approving them feel

they could defend their decisions before the public if their actions became public" [*Secrecy and Democracy: The CIA in Transition* (Boston: Houghton Mifflin, 1985), p. 178].

58   Testimony, Hearings: Covert Action, the Church Committee, Vol. 7, pp. 50–5.

59   Roger Fisher, "The Fatal Flaw in Our Spy System," *Boston Globe* (February 1, 1976), p. A21.

Chapter 4   Counterintelligence: the hunt for moles

1   Theodore H. White, *Breach of Faith: The Fall of Richard Nixon* (New York: Atheneum, 1975), p. 133.

2   FBI counterintelligence officer, testimony, *Huston Plan Hearings*, Select Committee on Intelligence Activities (hereafter, Church Committee), U.S. Senate, 94th Cong., 1st Sess. (September 25, 1975), p. 137.

3   Author's interview with William C. Sullivan, Boston, MA (June 10, 1975); the quote is from C. D. Brennan of the FBI Counterintelligence Branch to William C. Sullivan, memorandum (June 20, 1969), cited in the *Huston Plan Hearings*, Church Committee, Exhibit 6, p. 23.

4   *Presidential Talking Paper*, prepared by Tom Charles Huston and used by President Richard Nixon, Oval Office (June 5, 1970), Church Committee files (February 2, 1975).

5   White, *Breach of Faith*, p. 133.

6   Tom Charles Huston, Memorandum to H. R. "Bob" Haldeman, the White House Chief of Staff (July 1970 – the precise day is unknown, but during the first two weeks of the month), *Huston Plan Hearings*, Church Committee, Exhibit 2, p. 2. Mail cover refers to an examination of the external contexts of a letter, such as the address and the date of postage – a first step before an intelligence agency decides to open a suspect's letter and read its contents.

7   Huston, Memorandum to H. R. "Bob" Haldeman, p. 3.

8   Richard M. Nixon, answer to Church Committee interrogatory No. 17 (March 3, 1976).

9   For a more detailed account, see Loch K. Johnson, *America's Secret Power: The CIA in a Democratic Society* (New York: Oxford University Press, 1989), pp. 133–56.

10   Testimony of Tom Charles Huston, *Huston Plan Hearings*, Church Committee, p. 45.

11   Executive Order 12333, Sec. 3.5, as amended on July 31, 2008.

12   Mary Anne Weaver, "The Stranger," *The New Yorker* (November 13, 1995), pp. 59–72.

13   See Beverly Gage, *The Day Wall Street Exploded: A Story of America in Its First Age of Terror* (New York: Oxford University Press, 2009). This crime was never solved.

14   Jo Thomas, "Letter by McVeigh Told of Mind-Set," *New York Times* (May 9, 1977), p. A1.

15 For an account, see Stuart A. Wright, *Patriots, Politics, and the Oklahoma City Bombing* (New York: Cambridge University Press, 2007).

16 In 2007, researcher Stuart A. Wright, drawing on a 2003 Associated Press investigation, charged that the federal Bureau of Alcohol, Tobacco and Firearms (ATF) had an informant inside the McVeigh camp who provided advanced warning about the Oklahoma City attack, but was ignored (*Patriots, Politics, and the Oklahoma City Bombing*, p. 183).

17 See *An Assessment of the Aldrich H. Ames Espionage Case and Its Implications for U.S. Intelligence*, Staff Report, Select Committee on Intelligence, U.S. Senate, S. Prt. 103–90, 103rd Cong., 2nd Sess. (Washington, DC: Government Printing Office, November 1, 1994); David Wise, *Nightmover: How Aldrich Ames Sold the CIA to the KGB for $4.6 Million* (New York: HarperCollins, 1993); and David Wise, *Spy: The Inside Story of How the FBI's Robert Hanssen Betrayed America* (New York: Random House, 2003).

18 Loch K. Johnson, *The Threat on the Horizon: An Inside Account of America's Search for Security after the Cold War* (New York: Oxford University Press, 2011).

19 See Paul J. Redmond, "The Challenges of Counterintelligence," in Loch K. Johnson, ed., *The Oxford Handbook of National Security Intelligence* (New York: Oxford University Press, 2010), pp. 537–54, quote at p. 541.

20 *Report on Terrorism in the United States*, Counterterrorism Center, Central Intelligence Agency, Langley, VA (July 1995), provided to the Aspin–Brown Commission in unclassified form (August 1995).

21 See Jane Mayer, *The Dark Side* (New York: Doubleday, 2008); and Amy B. Zegart, *Spying Blind: The CIA, the FBI, and the Origins of 9/11* (Princeton, NJ: Princeton University Press, 2007).

22 Richard A. Clarke, *Against All Enemies: Inside America's War on Terror* (New York: Free Press, 2004), p. 237.

23 John Earl Haynes, Harvey Klehr, and Alexander Vassiliev, with translations by Philip Redko and Steven Shabad, *Spies: The Rise and Fall of the KGB in America* (New Haven, CT: Yale University Press, 2009). See also Timothy Gibbs, "Catching an Atom Spy: MI5 and the Investigation of Klaus Fuchs," in Johnson, ed., *Oxford Handbook of National Security Intelligence*, pp. 555–68.

24 See, for example, Cleveland C. Cram, "Of Moles and Molehunters: A Review of Counterintelligence Literature, 1977–92," Center for the Study of Intelligence, CIA, *Report No. CSI 93–002* (October 1993).

25 See David C. Martin, *Wilderness of Mirrors* (New York: Harper & Row, 1980); and John Ranelagh, *The Agency: The Rise and Decline of the CIA*, rev. edn (New York: Simon & Schuster, 1987).

26 Redmond, "The Challenges of Counterintelligence."

27 For profiles of Kampiles and many of the other traitors mentioned here, see the useful compilation by Norman Polmar and Thomas B. Allen, eds., *The Encyclopedia of Espionage* (New York: Gramercy Books, 1997).

28   See David Wise, *The Spy Who Got Away: The Inside Story of Edward Lee Howard* (New York: Random House, 1988).
29   See Seymour M. Hersh, "The Traitor," *The New Yorker* (January 18, 1999), pp. 26–33.
30   See David Johnston and Tim Weiner, "On the Trail of a C.I.A. Official, From Asia Travel to Bank Files," *New York Times* (November 21, 1996), p. A1; and Walter Pincus and Roberto Suro, "Rooting Out the 'Sour Apples' Inside the CIA," *Washington Post*, National Weekly Edition (November 25–December 1, 1996), p. 30.
31   Tim Weiner, "Former South Korean Pleads Guilty in Spying Case," *New York Times* (May 8, 1997), p. A16.
32   Frederick L. Wettering, "Counterintelligence: The Broken Triad," *International Journal of Intelligence and Counterintelligence* 13 (Fall 2000), pp. 265–99, quote at p. 276.
33   For examples, see Percy Cradock, *Know Your Enemy* (London: John Murray, 2002); Michael S. Goodman, *Spying on the Nuclear Bear: Anglo-American Intelligence and the Soviet Bomb* (Stanford: Stanford University Press, 2007); Ranelagh, *The Agency*; and Athan Theoharis, *Chasing Spies* (Chicago: Ivan R. Dee, 2002).
34   Scott Shane, "A Spy's Motivation: For Love of Another Country," *New York Times* (April 20, 2008), p. WK 3.
35   Stan A. Taylor and Daniel Snow, "Cold War Spies: Why They Spied and How They Got Caught," *Intelligence and National Security* 12 (April 1997), pp. 101–25.
36   Reported by Shane, "A Spy's Motivation."
37   On Angleton, see Seymour M. Hersh, "The Angleton Story," *New York Times Magazine* (June 25, 1978), pp. 13ff.; William Hood, James Nolan, and Samuel Halpern, "Myths Surrounding James Angleton: Lessons for American Counterintelligence," *Working Group on Intelligence Reform, Consortium for the Study of Intelligence* (Washington, DC, 1994); Loch K. Johnson, "James Angleton and the Church Committee," *Journal of Cold War Studies* 15 (Fall 2013), pp. 128–47; Tom Mangold, *Cold Warrior: James Jesus Angleton, the CIA's Master Spy Hunter* (New York: Simon & Schuster, 1991); and Robin W. Winks, *Cloak & Gown: Scholars in the Secret War, 1939–1961* (New York: Morrow, 1987), pp. 322–438.
38   On Angleton's early suspicions about Philby, see Ranelagh, *The Agency*, p. 151.
39   See the argument in Redmond, "The Challenges of Counterintelligence," pp. 540, 547.
40   Hersh, "The Angleton Story."
41   Henry Brandon, "The Spy Who Came and Then Told," *Washington Post*, National Weekly Edition (August 24, 1987), p. 36.
42   Robert Jervis, "Intelligence, Counterintelligence, Perception, and Deception," in Jennifer E. Sims and Burton Gerber, eds., *Vaults, Mirrors, and Masks: Rediscovering U.S. Counterintelligence* (Washington, DC: Georgetown University Press, 2009), pp. 69–79, quote at p. 75.
43   The phrase comes from a line in T. S. Eliot's poem, "Gerontion" (1920).

44   Redmond, "The Challenges of Counterintelligence," p. 539.
45   Commission on the Intelligence Capabilities of the United States Regarding Weapons of Mass Destruction (the Silberman–Robb or WMD Commission), *Report to the President of the United States* (Washington, DC: Government Printing Office, 2005), p. 490.
46   Canadian intelligence scholar Wesley Warks notes in a similar vein: "Treason perpetually beckons and those with access to secrets will, on occasion, succumb to the temptations of leading a double life, and of the banalities of greed and folly": "For Love of Money," *Ottawa Citizen* (February 7, 2009), p. A16.
47   J. H. Plumb, *The Italian Renaissance* (Boston: Houghton Mifflin, 1961), pp. 102–3.
48   See Edward Jay Epstein, "The Spy War," *New York Times Sunday Magazine*, sec. 6 (September 28, 1980), p. 108.
49   Communication to the author (April 15, 2010).
50   See Mark Mazzetti, "Officer Failed to Warn CIA Before Attack," *New York Times* (October 20, 2010), p. A1.
51   Quoted by Ken Dilanian, "U.S. Counter-Terrorism Agents Still Hamstrung by Data-Sharing Failures," *Los Angeles Times* (October 5, 2010), p. A1.
52   Redmond, remarks to the Aspin–Brown Commission. Clapper offered similar observations several times in public statements, as he began to stress the cyber threat as early as 2013; see, for example, Mark Mazzetti and Scott Shane, "Spy Chief Calls Cyberattacks Top Threat to the U.S.," *New York Times* (March 13, 213), p. A1. One example of the cyber threat: Iran's Islamic Revolutionary Guards Corps has launched cyberattacks against dozens of U.S. banks and even attempted to take control of a small dam in a New York suburb: see David Sanger, "U.S. Indicts 7 Tied to Iranian Unit in Cyberattacks," *New York Times* (March 25, 2016), p. A3. An important ethical issue is how far the democracies should go in using highly aggressive cyberattacks against rivals. Reportedly, U.S. intelligence agencies, operating in a joint effort with Israeli intelligence, inserted a Stuxnet virus into key Iranian computers as a means for sabotaging Tehran's nuclear weapons program. The operation is said to have wiped out about 20 percent of that nation's nuclear centrifuges: see Isabel Kershner, "Meir Dagan, Israeli Who Disrupted Iranian Nuclear Program, Dies at 81," *New York Times* (March 18, 2016), p. B15; and David E. Sanger, *Confront and Conceal: Obama's Secret Wars and Surprising Use of American Power* (New York: Crown, 2012).
53   For the China quote (from James Lewis, a senior fellow at the Center for Strategic and International Studies in Washington), see Seymour M. Hersh, "The Online Threat," *The New Yorker* (November 1, 2010), pp. 44–55, quote at p. 49. The data on cyber-espionage come from Bill Gertz, "Chinese Espionage and Intelligence Activities At All Time High, Experts Say," *Asia Times*, Hong Kong (June 14, 2016); and Joseph Menn and Jim Finkle, "Chinese Economic Cyber-Espionage Plummets in U.S.," *Reuters* (June 20, 2016). On the Russian front,

a recent report based on osint imagery indicates that its Foreign Intelligence Service (SVR) has expanded dramatically in the past ten years, as displayed in a doubling of its floor space and a quadrupling of its parking capacity; based on data compiled by Allen Thomson and published in *Secrecy News* (July 13, 2016), p. 2. In 2016, U.S. counterintelligence accused Russian spies of hacking into the computers of the Democratic National Committee during the presidential election. Some knowledgeable observers believed that Russia's President, Vladimir V. Putin, had ordered the cyberattack as a means for finding information that would embarrass the Democratic Party and advance the fortunes of his preferred candidate, the GOP nominee Donald Trump. If true, the attack represented a serious and reckless attempt to manipulate an American presidential election; see David E. Sanger and Eric Schmitt, "Spy Agency Consensus Grows That Russians Hacked D.N.C.," *New York Times* (July 27, 2016), p. A1.

54 On the spy ring, see Clifford J. Levy, "Turncoat Aided in Thwarted Russian Spies, Article Says," *New York Times* (November 12, 2010), p. A6. On the relationship between cops and spies in the United States, see James E. Baker, *In the Common Defense: National Security Law for Perilous Times* (New York: Cambridge University Press, 2007).

55 Redmond, "The Challenges of Counterintelligence," p. 540.

56 See the essays on counterintelligence in the following "handbooks": Johnson, ed., *Oxford Handbook of National Security Intelligence.*; Loch K. Johnson, ed., *Strategic Intelligence, Vol. 4: Counterintelligence and Counterterrorism, Defending the National against Hostile Forces* (Westport, CT: Praeger, 2007); and Loch K. Johnson, ed., *Handbook of Intelligence Studies* (New York: Routledge, 2007). See also Raymond J. Batvinis, *The Origins of FBI Counterintelligence* (Lawrence: University Press of Kansas, 2007); and Theoharis, *Chasing Spies.*

57 Declassified CIA memorandum, Church Committee, p. 167.

58 Karen DeYoung and Walter Pincus, "Success Against al-Qaeda Cited," *Washington Post* (September 30, 2009), p. 1A.

59 George Tenet, public testimony, National Commission on Terrorist Attacks upon the United States (the 9/11 Commission), April 14, 2004, p. 5, cited by Zegart, *Spying Blind*, p. 113.

60 Jervis, "Intelligence, Counterintelligence, Perception, and Deception," p. 71.

61 Jervis, "Intelligence, Counterintelligence, Perception, and Deception," p. 77; see also Thaddeus Holt, *The Deceivers: Allied Military Deception in the Second World War* (New York: Scribner, 2004).

62 See Mayer, *The Dark Side.*

63 Duncan Campbell, "Afghan Prisoners Beaten to Death," *Guardian* (March 7, 2003), p. 1.

64 For arguments that harsh interrogation is inappropriate and yields poor results, see Loch K. Johnson, "Educing Information: Interrogation: Science and Art," *Studies in Intelligence* 51 (December 2007), pp. 43–6; William R. Johnson, "Tricks of the Trade: Counterintelligence Interrogation," *International Journal of Intelligence and*

Counterintelligence 1 (1986), pp. 103–33; Mayer, *The Dark Side*; and Ali H. Soufan (an FBI interrogator), "What Torture Never Told Us," *New York Times* (September 6, 2009), p. WK 9, who refers to this approach as "ineffective, unreliable, unnecessary and destructive."

65 Quoted by Toby Harden, "CIA 'Pressure' on Al Qaeda Chief," *Washington Post* (March 6, 2003), p. A1.

66 Letter written by George Washington in 1777, private collection, Walter Pforzheimer, Washington, DC, reprinted in the *Yale Alumni Magazine and Journal* (December 1983), p. 7.

67 Quoted in Paisley Dodds, "Chief of Britain's MI6 Takes Unusual Public Stand to Defend Spies' Work," *Washington Post* (October 29, 2010), p. A11.

68 Testimony, *Hearings*, Joint Committee to Investigate Covert Arms Transactions with Iran (the Inouye–Hamilton Committee), U.S. Congress (July 1987), p. 159.

69 Bill Moyers, "Moyers: The Secret Government, the Constitution in Crisis," *Public Affairs Television* (November 4, 1987).

70 Quoted in the *New York Times* (February 26, 1976), p. A1.

71 Raoul Berger, *Executive Privilege: A Constitutional Myth* (Cambridge, MA: Harvard University Press, 1974), p. 7.

72 See, for instance, the commentary by Senator (and former astronaut) John H. Glenn (D, Ohio), "The Mini-Hiroshima Near Cincinnati," *New York Times* (January 24, 1989), p. A27.

73 Berger, *Executive Privilege*, p. 14.

74 403 U.S. 713, 91 S.Ct. 2140, 29 L. Ed. 2nd 822 (1971); emphasis added.

75 See the series of *New York Times* articles published on October 24, 2010, especially pp. A1, A11.

76 For example, in a remark to the author, Athens, GA (July 4, 1983).

77 Author's interview with Senator Frank Church (D, Idaho), Washington, DC (October 16, 1976); see also his "Which Secrets Should Be Kept Secret?" *Washington Post* (March 14, 1977), p. A27. The Agee book, *Inside the Company: CIA Diary*, was published by Penguin (Harmondsworth, UK) in 1975 and made the author a pariah in the United States and many European democracies.

78 Quoted in Alistair Buchan, "Questions about Vietnam," in Richard Falk, ed., *The Vietnam War and International War*, Vol. 2 (Princeton, NJ: Princeton University Press, 1969), p. 345. With respect to not even the White House knowing about some intelligence activities, Clark Clifford (the author of the National Security Act of 1947 and an advisor to several presidents) has noted: "I believe on a number of occasions, a plan for covert action has been presented to the NSC and authority is requested for the CIA to proceed from point A to point B. The authority will be given and the action will be launched. When point B is reached, the persons in charge feel it is necessary to go to point C, and they assume that the original authorization gives them such a right. From point C, they go to D and possibly E, and even further"; testimony to the Church Committee, *Hearings on Covert Action*, U.S. Senate, Washington, DC (December 4, 1975), quoted in Loch K. Johnson, *A Season of Inquiry Revisited: The Church*

Committee Confronts America's Spy Agencies (Lawrence: University Press of Kansas, 2015), p. 148.

79 Daniel P. Moynihan, "System of Secrecy Has Served Liars Well," *Albany (NY) Times Union* (May 3, 1992), p. A17, reprinted in Center for National Security Studies, *First Principles* 17 (July 1992), pp. 11–12.

80 For his reflections on this experience, see Daniel P. Moynihan, *Secrecy* (New Haven, CT: Yale University Press, 1998). See also: Michael J. Glennon, *National Security and Double Government* (New York: Oxford University Press, 2015); and F.A.O. Schwarz, Jr., *Democracy in the Dark: The Seduction of Government Secrecy* (New York: Free Press, 2015).

81 Johnson, *A Season of Inquiry Revisited*.

82 NSA Deputy Director Benson Buffham, testimony, *Hearings: The National Security Agency and Fourth Amendment Rights*, Vol. 5, Church Committee, p. 45.

Chapter 5   Safeguards against the abuse of secret power

1 Author's interview with DCI James R. Schlesinger, Washington, DC (June 16, 1994).

2 *Myers v. United States*, 272 U.S. 52 293 (1926).

3 David M. Barrett, *The CIA and Congress: The Untold Story from Truman to Kennedy* (Lawrence: University Press of Kansas, 2005); for works that have found little meaningful accountability in these early days, see Harry Howe Ransom, *The Intelligence Establishment* (Cambridge, MA: Harvard University Press, 1970); and Jerrold L. Walden, "The CIA: A Study in the Arrogation of Administrative Power," *George Washington Law Review* 39 (January 1975), pp. 66–101. For more current accounts that continue to find Congress lacking in the department of intelligence oversight, see: Kathleen Clark, " 'A New Era of Openness?' Disclosing Intelligence to Congress under Obama," *Constitutional Commentary* 26 (2010), pp. 1–20; Jennifer Kibbe, "Congressional Oversight of Intelligence: Is the Solution Part of the Problem?" *Intelligence and National Security* 25 (February 2010), pp. 24–49; Anne Joseph O'Connell, "The Architecture of Smart Intelligence: Structuring and Overseeing Agencies in the Post–9/11 World," *California Law Review* 94 (December 2006), pp. 1655–1744; Amy B. Zegart, "The Domestic Politics of Irrational Intelligence Oversight," *Political Science Quarterly* 126 (Spring 2011), pp. 1–27; and Amy B. Zegart with Julie Quinn, "Congressional Intelligence Oversight: The Electoral Disconnection," *Intelligence and National Security* 25 (December 2010), pp. 744–66.

4 See the reporting of Seymour Hersh in the *Times* throughout the autumn and winter months of 1974, especially on December 22.

5 Church Committee, Select Committee on Intelligence Activities, U.S. Senate, 94th Cong., 1st Sess. (September 25, 1975), as well as two special reports: *Alleged Assassination Plots Involving Foreign Leaders*, Interim Rept., S. Rept. No. 94–465 (Washington, DC: Government

Printing Office, November 20, 1975); and *Covert Action in Chile, 1963–1973, Staff Report* (Washington, DC: Government Printing Office, December 18, 1975). The leading works about the Committee are Loch K. Johnson, *A Season of Inquiry* (Lexington: University Press of Kentucky, 1985), republished as *A Season of Inquiry Revisited: The Church Committee Confronts America's Spy Agencies* (Lawrence: University Press of Kansas, 2015); Frederick A. O. Schwarz, Jr. and Aziz Z. Huq, *Unchecked and Unbalanced: Presidential Power in a Time of Terror* (New York: New Press, 2007); and Frank J. Smist, Jr., *Congress Oversees the United States Intelligence Community, 1947–1989* (Knoxville, University of Tennessee Press, 1990).

6   Author's interview, Minneapolis, Minnesota (February 17, 2000). See, also, Walter F. Mondale, *The Good Fight: A Life in Liberal Politics* (New York: Simon & Schuster, 2010), Ch. 7.

7   Henry Steele Commager, "Intelligence: The Constitution Betrayed," *New York Review of Books* (September 30, 1976), p. 32.

8   On the seven Boland Amendments, each more restrictive, see "Boland Amendments: A Review," *Congressional Quarterly Weekly Online* (May 23, 1987), p. 1043; and Henry K. Kissinger, "A Matter of Balance," *Los Angeles Times* (July 26, 1987), p. V1.

9   See Barrett, *The CIA and Congress*, p. 459.

10   Joel D. Aberbach, "What's Happened to the Watchful Eye?" *Congress & the Presidency* 29 (2002), pp. 20–3, quote at p. 20.

11   Stephen F. Knott, "The Great Republican Transformation on Oversight," *International Journal of Intelligence and Counterintelligence* 13 (2002), pp. 49–63, quote at p. 57.

12   Marvin C. Ott, "Partisanship and the Decline of Intelligence Oversight," *International Journal of Intelligence and Counterintelligence* 16 (2003), pp. 69–94, quote at p. 87.

13   These quotes are from Charles Babington, "Senate Intelligence Panel Frayed by Partisan Infighting," *Washington Post* (March 12, 2006), p. A9.

14   L. Britt Snider, "Congressional Oversight of Intelligence after September 11," in Jennifer E. Sims and Burton Gerber, eds., *Transforming U.S. Intelligence* (Washington, DC: Georgetown University Press, 2005), p. 245. See, also, Snider's *The Agency and the Hill: CIA's Relationship with Congress, 1946–2004* (Washington, DC: Center for the Study of Intelligence, Central Intelligence Agency, 2008).

15   Bob Drogin, "Senator Says Spy Agencies are 'in Denial,' " *Los Angeles Times* (May 4, 2004), p. A1.

16   Kean Commission (led by former Governor Thomas H. Kean, R, New Jersey), *The 9/11 Commission: Final Report of the National Commission on Terrorist Attacks upon the United States* (New York: Norton, 2004).

17   See, respectively, Loch K. Johnson, *Secret Agencies: U.S. Intelligence in a Hostile World* (New Haven, CT: Yale University Press, 1996), p. 96; and Zegart, "The Domestic Politics of Irrational Intelligence Oversight."

18   Remarks, "Meet the Press," *NBC Television* (November 21, 2004).

19   Kean Commission, *The 9/11 Commission*, p. 420.

20   Gregory F. Treveton, *Intelligence in an Age of Terror* (New York: Cambridge University Press, 2009), p. 232.
21   Bill Gertz, *Breakdown* (Washington, DC: Regnery, 2002), p. 113.
22   On the Snowden affair, see Glenn Greenwald, *No Place to Hide: Edward Snowden, the NSA, and the U.S. Surveillance State* (New York: Metropolitan Books, 2014).
23   Quoted in Ken Dilanian, "NSA Weighed Ending Phone Program Before Leak," *Associated Press* (March 30, 2015).
24   Quoted in Darren Samuelsohn, "Hill Draws Criticism over NSA Oversight," *Politico* (March 2, 2014), p. 2.
25   Paul J. Quirk and William Bendix, "Secrecy and Negligence: How Congress Lost Control of Domestic Surveillance," *Issues in Governance Studies*, Brookings Institution, Washington, DC (March 2, 2015), pp. 9, 13.
26   The formal name of the panel is the President's Review Group on Intelligence and Communications Technologies, which urged that as a "central aspect of liberty" privacy must be protected; *Liberty and Security in a Changing World*, U.S. Government Printing Office, Washington, DC (December 12, 2013), p. 47.
27   Jack Goldsmith, "United States of Secrets (Part One): The Program," Transcript, *Nightline*, PBS Television (May 2015), p. 16.
28   See, respectively: Jennifer Steinhauer, "Senate Is Sharply Split Over Extension of NSA Phone Data Collection," *New York Times* (May 22, 2015), p. A15; and unsigned editorial, "Rand Paul's Timely Takedown on the Patriot Act," *New York Times* (May 22, 2015), p. A24.
29   Jonathan Weisman and Jennifer Steinhauer, "Patriot Act Faces Curbs Supported by Both Parties," *New York Times* (May 1, 2015), p. A1.
30   Jennifer Steinhauer, "Senate to Try Again Next Week after Bill on Phone Records Is Blocked," *New York Times* (May 24, 2015), p. A14.
31   Charlie Savage, "Surveillance Court Rules That NSA Can Resume Bulk Data Collection," *New York Times* (July 1, 2015), p. A14.
32   Lawrence Wright, "The Al Qaeda Switchboard," Comment, *The New Yorker* (January 13, 2014), p. 3.
33   For a chronology of the torture program, see Wilson Andrews and Alicia Parlapiano, "A History of the CIA's Secret Interrogation Program," *New York Times* (December 9, 2014).
34   Jane Mayer, "Torture and the Truth," *The New Yorker* (December 22, 2014).
35   Steven Aftergood, "CIA Torture Report: Oversight, but No Remedies Yet," *Secrecy News*, 2014/83 (December 10, 2014), p. 2.
36   A high-ranking HPSCI member remembers urging the CIA, in a letter to the Agency's General Counsel (Scott Muller) in 2003, not to destroy the interrogation videotapes [see Jane Harman (D, California), "America's Spy Agencies Need an Upgrade," *Foreign Affairs* (March/April 2015), p. 103].
37   Senator Dianne Feinstein, "Dianne Feinstein: The CIA 'Cannot Shove the Laws Aside,' " *Nightline*, p. 2.
38   Feinstein, "Dianne Feinstein," p. 1

39   Dianne Feinstein, remarks concerning the *Committee Study of the Central Intelligence Agency's Detention and Interrogation Program*, Senate Select Committee on Intelligence, U.S. Senate, 113th Cong., 2d Sess. (December 3, 2014; hereafter the *Senate Torture Report*), U,S. Senate floor (December 9, 2014).

40   Senator Chambliss retired from the Congress soon after the release of the torture report; he is now a member of the CIA's Advisory Board.

41   *Senate Torture Report*, Findings and Conclusions Section, p. 3. For a series of thoughtful essays on the Report, see Mark Phythian, editor, "An INS Special Forum: The US Senate Select Committee Report on the CIA's Detention and Interrogation Program," *Intelligence and National Security* 31/1 (January 2016), pp. 8–27.

42   See Adam Goldman, "Military Prosecutor: Senate Report on CIA Interrogation Program is Accurate," *Washington Post* (February 10, 2016), p. A1.

43   Remark to Eric Bradner, "John Brennan Defends CIA," *CNN Politics* (December 12, 2014).

44   President Barack Obama, Statement, White House (December 9, 2014).

45   Feinstein, "Dianne Feinstein," p. 4.

46   Quoted by Connie Bruck, "The Inside War," *The New Yorker* (June 22, 2015), p. 45.

47   Quoted anonymously by Jeremy Herb in *The Hill* (March 6, 2014), p. 11.

48   Bruck, "The Inside War," p. 46.

49   Bruck, "The Inside War," p. 48.

50   See Mark Mazzetti and Matt Apuzzo, "CIA Officers Are Cleared in Senate Computer Search," *New York Times* (January 15, 2015), p. A8.

51   Remarks to the Senate (December 9, 2014).

52   George J. Tenet, et al., "Ex-CIA Directors: Interrogations Saved Lives," *Wall Street Journal* (December 10, 2014).

53   David Ignatius, "The Torture Report's One Glaring Weakness," *Washington Post* (December 11, 2014). A senior CIA official has argued that when it came to keeping lawmakers informed about the interrogation program, their claim to have been misled is "farcical, not true....I can tell you, I had difficulty getting on the calendars of senators I wanted to brief. Their ardor for the truth is greater now than it was then, in some cases"; interview with Robert Grenier, former CIA/CTC Director, 2004-2006, *News Hour*, PBS Television (December 9, 2014)].

54   Michael Glennon, Fletcher School of Law and Diplomacy, remarks, Levin Center Conference on Intelligence Accountability, U.S. Senate (October 20, 2015).

55   See Amy Zegart, "INS Special Forum," p. 25. The denials of normative bias in the report were expressed during the Levin Center Conference by the leading Democratic staffer.

56   Dianne Feinstein, "NSA's Watchfulness Protects America," *Wall Street Journal* (October 13, 2013). In a Senate hearing, Feinstein spoke

in support of the NSA metadata collection, ruing "how little information" the United States had about Al Qaeda before the 9/11 attacks. "They will come after us," she said, "and I think we need to prevent an attack wherever we can"; Mattathias Schwartz, "Who Can Control NSA Surveillance?" *The New Yorker* (January 23, 2015)].

57 Feinstein, "Dianne Feinstein," p. 6.

58 Statement, U.S. Senate floor (December 9, 2014), cited by Professor Pfiffner in "INS Special Forum," p. 23. McCain, a former GOP presidential nominee, said elsewhere that he "totally agree[d] with the report…"; quoted by Matt Sledge and Michael McAuliff, "CIA Torture Report Approved by Senate Intelligence Committee," *Huffington Post* (October 13, 2012). Even D/CIA Brennan eventually ended up speaking out against the use of waterboarding in the future, declaring that "as long as I'm director of CIA, irrespective of what the president says, I'm not going to be the director of CIA that gives that order. They'll have to find another director"; John Brennan, public remarks, Brookings Institution, Washington, DC (July 13, 2016). Donald Trump, the 2016 Republican presidential nominee, said, though, that as the commander in chief he would use waterboarding against suspected terrorists and indeed "I'd bring back a hell of a lot worse than waterboarding"; quoted by Connie Bruck, "The Guantánamo Failure," *The New Yorker* (August 1, 2016), p. 34.

59 Harry H. Ransom, "Secret Intelligence Agencies and Congress," *Society* 123 (1975), pp. 33–6, quote at p. 38.

60 See, for example, Joel D. Aberbach, *Keeping a Watchful Eye: The Politics of Congressional Oversight* (Washington, DC: The Brookings Institution, 1990); Christopher J. Deering, "Alarms and Patrols: Legislative Oversight in Foreign and Defense Policy," in Colton C. Campbell, Nicol C. Rae, and John F. Stack, Jr., *Congress and the Politics of Foreign Policy* (Upper Saddle River, NJ: Prentice-Hall, 2003), pp. 112–38; and Loch K. Johnson, "Presidents, Lawmakers, and Spies: Intelligence Accountability in the United States," *Presidential Studies Quarterly* 34 (December 2004), pp. 828–37.

61 David Mayhew, *The Electoral Connection* (New Haven, CT: Yale University Press, 1974).

62 Matthew D. McCubbins and Thomas Schwartz, "Congressional Oversight Overlooked: Police Patrols and Fire Alarms," *American Journal of Political Science* 28 (1984), pp. 165–79.

63 Quoted by Philip Shenon, "As New 'Cop on the Beat,' Congressman Starts Patrol," *New York Times* (February 6, 2007), p. A18.

64 See Loch K. Johnson, John C. Kuzenski, and Erna Gellner, "The Study of Congressional Investigations: Research Strategies," *Congress & the Presidency* 19 (Autumn 1992), pp. 138–56. On the relationship between media reporting on scandals and intelligence failures, on the one hand, and a "shock" (fire-fighting) reaction on Capitol Hill, on the other hand, see Loch K. Johnson, "Intelligence Shocks, Media Coverage, and Congressional Accountability, 1947–2012," *Journal of Intelligence History* 13 (January 2014), pp. 1–21.

65   See Johnson, *A Season of Inquiry Revisited*; and Schwarz and Huq, *Unchecked and Unbalanced*.

66   U.S. Congress, *Report of the Congressional Committees Investigating the Iran–Contra Affair*, U.S. Senate Select Committee on Secret Military Assistance to Iran and the Nicaraguan Opposition and U.S. House of Representatives Select Committee to Investigate Covert Arms Transactions with Iran, S. Rept. 100–216 and House Rept. 100–433, 100th Cong., 1st Sess. (November 1987), chaired by Daniel K. Inouye (D, Hawaii) and Representative Lee H. Hamilton (D, Indiana).

67   *Preparing for the 21st Century: An Appraisal of U.S. Intelligence*, Report of the Commission on the Roles and Capabilities of the United States Intelligence Community (the Aspin–Brown Commission) (Washington, DC: Government Printing Office, March 1, 1996). For an account of the Commission's work, see Loch K. Johnson, *The Threat on the Horizon: An Inside Account of America's Search for Security after the Cold War* (New York: Oxford University Press, 2011).

68   Joint Inquiry into Intelligence Community Activities before and after the Terrorist Attacks of September 11, 2001, *Final Report*, U.S. Senate Select Committee on Intelligence and U.S. House Permanent Select Committee on Intelligence, led respectively by Senator Bob Graham (D, Florida) and Representative Porter J. Goss (R, Florida), Washington, DC: December 2002; and the Kean Commission, *The 9/11 Commission*.

69   *Intelligence Authorization Act for Fiscal Year 2005*, Report 108–558, Permanent Select Committee on Intelligence (the Goss Committee), U.S. House of Representatives, 108th Cong., 2nd Sess. (June 21, 2004), pp. 23–7.

70   *Report of the Commission on the Intelligence Capabilities of the United States Regarding Weapons of Mass Destruction*, led by Judge Laurence H. Silberman and former Senator Charles S. Robb (D, Virginia).

71   *Report on the U.S. Intelligence Community's Prewar Intelligence Assessments on Iraq* (the Roberts Report), Senate Select Committee on Intelligence (the Roberts Committee), U.S. Senate, 108th Cong., 2nd Sess. (July 7, 2003).

72   Title VI, Sec. 601, 50 U.S.C. 421; Public law 97–200.

73   Title VII, Intelligence Authorization Act for FY 1999; see Snider, *The Agency and the Hill*, pp. 71–2.

74   See Alfred Cumming, "Sensitive Covert Action Notifications: Oversight Options For Congress," *CRS Report for Congress*, Congressional Research Service (July 7, 2009), pp. 1–12.

75   Kathleen Clark, " 'A New Era of Openness?' Disclosing Intelligence to Congress under Obama," *Constitutional Commentary* 26 (2010), pp. 1–20, see p. 14.

76   Email communication to the author (May 28, 2010).

77   Clark, " 'A New Era,' " p. 13.

78   Cited by intelligence scholar Harry Howe Ransom, "Congress, Legitimacy and the Intelligence Community," paper, Western Political

Science Association, Annual Convention, San Francisco, California (April 20, 1976).

79 Quoted by Tom Braden, "What's Wrong with the CIA?" *Saturday Review* (April 5, 1975), p. 14.

80 While serving as D/CIA, Leon E. Panetta, said: "I do not want to just do a Gang of Four briefing – in other words, just inform the leaders of the party. My view is, and I said this at my confirmation hearings, I think it's very important to inform all the members of the Intelligence Committees about what's going on when we have to provide notification" [remarks during Q and A, Pacific Council on International Policy, California (May 18, 2009)].

81 Remark by constitutional scholar Raoul Berger, American Political Science Association, Annual Meeting, Chicago, Illinois (September 4, 1987; author's notes), in reference to the secret Nixon White House group known as "the plumbers" that attempted to stop leaks by using extralegal surveillance methods against political opponents – part of the Watergate conspiracy.

The single significant leak from the congressional Intelligence Committees came from HPSCI member Robert G. Torricelli (D, New Jersey) in 1995. He was upset to learn in a top-secret CIA briefing that the Agency had an asset in Guatemala who was a suspected murderer, including likely involvement in the death of the husband of an American citizen. Torricelli wrote a letter to President Bill Clinton in protest; but he later admitted to leaking this information to the media, as well, in hopes of putting pressure on the Agency to fire the asset (Colonel Julio Roberto Alpirez in the Guatemalan army) along with any other foreign agents with a record of gross human rights violations. However sound his reasoning about the abhorrent colonel, Torricelli had violated important intelligence nondisclosure rules. Further, his actions raised doubts in the minds of some about the reliability of Congress in handling classified information. The HPSCI leadership roundly chastised the Congressman, but no further action was taken. The next year, Torricelli ran for a U.S. Senate seat representing New Jersey and won. He withdrew from a re-election race in 2002, however, under a cloud of controversy over campaign funding irregularities that had hounded him since his initial election to the Senate in 1996.

82 Mike Soraghan, "Reyes Backs Pelosi on Intel Briefings," *The Hill* (May 1, 2009), p. 1.

83 See Addendum B, *Congressional Record*, vol. 126, part 20, 96th Cong., 2nd Sess. (September 17–24, 1980), esp. p. 17693.

84 *Congressional Quarterly Almanac*, vol. XLVII, 102nd Cong., 1st Sess. (1991), p. 482.

85 Douglas Jehl, "New Spy Plan Said to Involve Satellite Systems," *New York Times* (December 12, 2004), p. A1.

86 L. Britt Snider, former SSCI general counsel and CIA inspector general, as interviewed by Kibbe, "Congressional Oversight of Intelligence," p. 27.

87   Amy B. Zegart, testimony, "Congressional Oversight of Intelligence Activities," *Hearings*, Select Committee on Intelligence, U.S. Senate (November 2007), p. 47.

88   A member of the Senate Armed Services Committee, John McCain, is said to have told the 9/11 Commission that if his panel spent ten minutes considering the annual intelligence budget, it had been a good year; Jonathan Weisman, "Democrats Reject Key 9/11 Panel Suggestion," *Washington Post* (November 30, 2006), p. A17, cited in Kibbe, "Congressional Oversight of Intelligence," p. 30.

89   See David M. Barrett, "Congressional Oversight of the CIA in the Early Cold War, 1947–1963," in Loch K. Johnson, ed., *Strategic Intelligence, Vol. 5: Safeguards against the Abuse of Secret Power* (Westport, CT: Praeger, 2007), pp. 1–18; Loch K. Johnson, *America's Secret Power: The CIA in a Democratic Society* (New York: Oxford University Press, 1989); and Ransom, *The Intelligence Establishment*.

90   On the frequency and seriousness with which intelligence officers are questioned by lawmakers in public hearings, see Loch K. Johnson, "Playing Ball with the CIA: Congress Supervises Strategic Intelligence," in Paul E. Peterson, ed., *The President, the Congress, and the Making of American Foreign Policy* (Norman: University of Oklahoma Press, 1994), pp. 49–73.

91   For chronicles of these failures, see Tim Weiner, *Legacy of Ashes: The History of the CIA* (New York: Doubleday, 2007); and Amy Zegart, *Spying Blind: The CIA, the FBI, and the Origins of 9/11* (Princeton, NJ: Princeton University Press, 2007).

92   Daniel Patrick Moynihan, "Do We Still Need the CIA? The State Dept. Can Do the Job," *New York Times* (May 19, 1991), p. E17.

93   Quoted by Ann Davis, "GOP-Controlled Senate Expected to Give Less Scrutiny to War on Terror," *Miami Herald* (November 7, 2002), p. A1.

94   Interviewed by Cynthia Nolan, Washington, DC (October 15, 2003), "More Perfect Oversight: Intelligence Oversight and Reform," in Johnson, ed., *Strategic Intelligence, Vol. 5*, quote at pp. 126–7.

95   Remarks to the author by Representative Hamilton, University of Georgia, Athens, GA (April 9, 2008). See, also, *Report of the Congressional Committees Investigating the Iran–Contra Affair*.

96   Author's conversation with William J. Casey, Director's Dining Room, CIA Headquarters Building, Langley, VA (June 11, 1984).

97   The letter was dated April 9, 1984; Letters to the Editor, *Washington Post* (April 11, 1984), p. A17.

98   James Risen, *State of War: The Secret History of the CIA and the Bush Administration* (New York: Free Press, 2006), p. 9.

99   Richard C. Shelby, "September 11 and the Imperative of Reform in the U.S. Intelligence Community: Additional Views," Senator Richard C. Shelby, Vice Chairman, Senate Select Committee on Intelligence, *Joint Inquiry Report* (Washington, DC: U.S. Government Printing Office, December 10, 2002), p. 135.

100   For Graham's memoir, see Bob Graham with Jeff Nussbaum, *Intelligence Matters: The CIA, the FBI, Saudi Arabia, and the Failure of America's War on Terror* (New York: Random House, 2004).

101   K. Guggenheim, "Tenet Defends CIA's Pre-9/11 Efforts," *Washington Post* (October 17, 2002), p. A1.

102   Neil A. Lewis, "Senator Insists CIA Is Harboring Iraq Reports," *New York Times* (October 4, 2002), p. A12.

103   Graham, with Nussbaum, *Intelligence Matters*. The Director of the CIA, John O. Brennan, had this to say about these charges on "Meet the Press" (*NBC News*, May 1, 2016): "The 9/11 Commission took that joint inquiry [by the Graham-Goss Committee] and those 28 pages or so, and followed through on the investigation. And they came out with a very clear judgment that there was no evidence that indicated that the Saudi government as an institution, or Saudi officials individually, had provided financial support to Al Qaeda." Left unstated was the possibility that wealthy Saudis outside the government – with strong ties to the royal family – had provided financial support to the 9/11 terrorists.

   The twenty-eight pages were at last released on July 15, 2016, by HPSCI after being declassified by the Obama Administration with only a few redactions. The document revealed some contacts between the 9/11 hijackers and Saudi officials – "a catalog of meetings and suspicious coincidences," concluded a *New York Times* report on the release, including evidence of checks from Saudi royals to intermediaries in contact with the terrorists. In the words of the *Times* account, however, the evidence was "by no means a Rosetta Stone" that clearly implicated the Saudi government in the 9/11 attacks; Mark Mazzetti, "In 9/11 Document, View of Saudi Effort to Thwart U.S. Action on Al Qaeda," *New York Times* (July 16, 2016), p. A13. The twenty-eight pages could be read differently by different people, though, and Senator Graham remained a skeptic. "This [document] makes a very compelling case that the Saudis were the source of assistance to the 9/11 hijackers," he commented – *Bloomberg Business News* (July 15, 2016). An expert on the subject, Simon Henderson at the Washington Institute for Near East Policy, suggested that the evidence would not support the proposition that the royal family directly financed the 9/11 terrorists; however, "official Saudi money ended up in the pockets of the attackers, without a doubt"; see his "What We Know About Saudi Arabia's Role in 9/11," *Foreign Policy* (July 18, 2016).

104   Front-page stories on oversight in leading newspapers are rare; but, when they occur, they help boost the public's appreciation of this important government function; see, for example, Eric Schmitt and David Rohde, "2 Reports Assail State Dept. Role on Iraq Security: Oversight is Faulted," *New York Times* (October 23, 2007), p. A1.

105   Robert M. Gates, *From the Shadows* (New York: Simon & Schuster, 1996), p. 559.

106   Gary Hart, *The Good Fight: The Education of an American Reformer* (New York: Random House, 1993), p. 144.

Chapter 6   National security intelligence: shield and hidden sword of the democracies

1   This point is well made by David Kahn, "The Rise of Intelligence," *Foreign Affairs* 85 (September/October 2006), pp. 125–34; and John Keegan, *Intelligence in War: Knowledge of the Enemy from Napoleon to Al-Qaeda* (New York: Random House, 2003).

2   On the virtues of soft power, see Joseph S. Nye, Jr., *Soft Power: The Means to Success in World Politics* (New York: Public Affairs, 2004); and on public diplomacy, Kristin M. Lord, *Voices of America: U.S. Public Diplomacy for the 21st Century* (Washington, DC: Brookings Institution, November 2008). On the strengthening of American foreign policy across the board, see Loch K. Johnson, *American Foreign Policy and the Challenges of World Leadership: Power, Principle, and the Constitution* (New York: Oxford University Press, 2015).

3   See Business Executives for National Security (BENS), *Domestic Security: Confronting a Changing Threat to Ensure Public Safety and Civil Liberties* (Washington, DC, February 2015, and February 2016 update).

4   Barton Gellman, "U.S. Spied on Iraqi Military via U.N.," *Washington Post* (March 2, 1999), p. A1; Loch K. Johnson, *Bombs, Bugs, Drugs, and Thugs: Intelligence and America's Quest for Security* (New York: New York University Press, 2000), pp. 170–1.

5   Matthew Aid, expert on the NSA, comment, "Panel on Security Intelligence, and the Internet," CASIS (Canadian Association of Security and Intelligence Studies) International Conference, Ottawa, Canada (2009, author's notes).

6   Paul R. Pillar, a thoughtful former CIA National Intelligence Officer and Middle East expert, has also independently advanced the idea of an outside group of intelligence experts to assist SSCI and HPSCI with their oversight duties; see his *Intelligence and U.S. Foreign Policy: Iraq, 9/11, and Misguided Reform* (New York: Columbia University Press, 2011).

Suggested Readings

Absher, K.M., Desch, M.C., and Popadiuk, R. *Privileged and Confidential: The Secret History of the President's Intelligence Advisory Board*. Lexington: University Press of Kentucky, 2012.

Aid, M.A. *The Secret Sentry: The Untold History of the National Security Agency*. New York: Bloomsbury, 2009.

Aldrich, R.J. *The Hidden Hand: Britain, America and Cold War Secret Intelligence, 1945–1964*. London: John Murray, 2001.

Allen, M. *Blinking Red: Crisis and Compromise in American Intelligence After 9/11*. Washington, DC: Potomac Books, 2013.

Aspin–Brown Commission. *Preparing for the 21st Century: Appraisal of U.S. Intelligence, Report of the Commission on the Roles and Capabilities of the United States Intelligence Community*. Washington, DC: Government Printing Office, March 1, 1996.

Bamford, J. *The Puzzle Palace*. Boston, MA: Houghton Mifflin, 1984.

Bar-Joseph, U. "The Professional Ethics of Intelligence Analysis," *International Journal of Intelligence and Counterintelligence* 24 (Spring 2011), pp. 22–43.

Barrett, D.M. *The CIA and Congress: The Untold Story from Truman to Kennedy*. Lawrence: University Press of Kansas, 2005.

Barron, J. *Breaking the Ring*. Boston, MA: Houghton Mifflin, 1987.

Barry, J.A. "Covert Action Can Be Just," *Orbis* 37 (Summer 1993), pp. 375–90.

Betts, R.K. "Fixing Intelligence," *Foreign Affairs* 81 (January–February 2002), pp. 43–59.

Betts, R.K. *Enemies of Intelligence: Knowledge and Power in American National Security*. New York: Columbia University Press, 2007.

Born, H., Johnson, L.K., and Leigh, I., eds. *Who's Watching the Spies? Establishing Intelligence Service Accountability*. Washington, DC: Potomac Books, 2005.

Burrows, W.E. *Deep Black: Space Espionage and National Security*. New York: Random House, 1986.

Business Executives for National Security (BENS). *Domestic Security: Confronting a Changing Threat to Ensure Public Safety and Civil Liberties* (Washington, DC, February 2015, and February 2016 update).

Byrne, M. *Iran–Contra: Reagan's Scandal and the Unchecked Abuse of Presidential Power*. Lawrence: University Press of Kansas, 2014.

Central Intelligence Agency. *Factbook on Intelligence*. Washington, DC: Office of Public Affairs, 1991.

Chapman, P. *How the United Fruit Company Shaped the World*. Edinburgh: Canongate, 2008.

Church Committee. *Alleged Assassination Plots Involving Foreign Leaders: An Interim Report*. S. Rept. No. 94-465. Washington, DC: U.S. Government Printing Office, November 20, 1975.

Church Committee. *Final Report. Select Committee to Study Governmental Operations with Respect to Intelligence Activities*. U.S. Senate, 94th Cong., 2nd. Sess. (1976).

Church, F. "Covert Action: Swampland of American Foreign Policy," *Bulletin of the Atomic Scientists* 32 (February 1976), pp. 7–11.

Clapper, J.R., Jr. "Luncheon Remarks, Association of Former Intelligence Officers," *The Intelligence*, AFIO newsletter, McLean, Virginia (October 1995), p. 3.

Clapper, J.R., Jr. "The Role of Defense in Shaping U.S. Intelligence Reform," in L.K. Johnson, ed., *The Oxford Handbook of National Security Intelligence*. New York: Oxford University Press, 2010, pp. 629–39.

Clark, R.M. *The Technical Collection of Intelligence*. Washington, DC: CQ Press, 2011.

Clarke, R.A. *Against All Enemies: Inside America's War on Terror*. New York: Free Press, 2004.

Cohen, W.S., and Mitchell, G.J. *Men of Zeal*. New York: Penguin Press, 1988.

Colby, W.E., and Forbath, P. *Honorable Men: My Life in the CIA*. New York: Simon and Schuster, 1978.

Cole, D. and Dempsey, J.X. *Terrorism and the Constitution*. New York: The New Press, 2006.

Coll, S. *Ghost Wars*. New York: Penguin Press, 2004.

Commission on Government Secrecy. *Report*. Washington, DC: U.S. Government Printing Office, 1957.

Corson, W.R. *The Armies of Ignorance: The Rise of the American Intelligence Empire*. New York: Dial, 1977.

Cradock, P. *Know Your Enemy*. London: John Murray, 2002.

Crill, G. *Charlie Wilson's War*. New York: Grove Press, 2003.

Crumpton, H.A. *The Art of Intelligence: Lessons from a Life in the CIA's Clandestine Service* (New York: Penguin, 2012).

Daugherty, W.J. *Executive Secrets: Covert Action and the Presidency*. Lexington: University Press of Kentucky, 2004.

Farson, A.S., Stafford, D., and Wark, W., eds. *Security and Intelligence in a Changing World*. London: Frank Cass, 1991.

Fisher, L. *The Constitution and 9/11: Recurring Threats to America's Freedoms*. Lawrence: University Press of Kansas, 2008.

Fisher, L. *Defending Congress and the Constitution*. Lawrence: University Press of Kansas, 2011.

Ford, H.P. *Estimative Intelligence: The Purposes and Problems of National Intelligence Estimating*. Lanham, MD: University Press of America, 1993.

Freedman, L. "The CIA and the Soviet Threat: The Politicization of Estimates, 1966–1977," *Intelligence and National Security* 12 (January 1997), pp. 122–42.

Garthoff, D.F. *Directors of Central Intelligence as Leaders of the U.S. Intelligence Community, 1946–2005*. Washington, DC: Center for the Study of Intelligence, Central Intelligence Agency, 2005.

Garthoff, R.L. *Soviet Leaders and Intelligence: Assessing the American Adversary during the Cold War*. Washington, DC: Georgetown University Press, 2015.

Gates, R.M. "The CIA and American Foreign Policy," *Foreign Affairs* 66 (Winter 1987–88), pp. 215–30.

Gates, R.M. *From the Shadows*. New York: Simon and Schuster, 1996.

Gelb, L.H. "Should We Play Dirty Tricks in the World?" *New York Times Magazine* (December 21, 1975), pp. 10–20.

Gill, P. and Phythian, M. *Intelligence in an Insecure World*, 2d edn. Cambridge: Polity, 2012.

Gill, P., Marrin, S., and Phythian, M., eds. *Intelligence Theory*. London: Routledge, 2009.

Glennon, M.J. *National Security and Double Government*. New York: Oxford University Press, 2015.

Goldsmith, J. *The Terror Presidency*. New York: Norton, 2007.

Goodman, M.S. *Spying on the Nuclear Bear: Anglo-American Intelligence and the Soviet Bomb*. Stanford, CA: Stanford University Press, 2007.

Graham, B., with Nussbaum, J. *Intelligence Matters: The CIA, the FBI, Saudi Arabia, and the Failure of America's War on Terror*. Lawrence: University Press of Kansas, 2008.

Greenberg, K.J. *Rogue Justice: The Making of the Security State*. New York: Crown, 2016.

Greenwald, G. *No Place to Hide: Edward Snowden, the NSA, and the U.S. Surveillance State*. New York: Henry Holt, 2014.

Gusterson, H. *Drone: Remote Control Warfare*. Boston, MA: MIT Press, 2016.

Hamilton–Inouye Committee. *Report of the Congressional Committees Investigating the Iran–Contra Affair*. U.S. Senate Select Committee on Secret Military Assistance to Iran and the Nicaraguan Opposition and U.S. House of Representatives, Select Committee to Investigate Covert Arms Transactions with Iran, S. Rept. 100-216 and H. Rept. 100-433, 100th Cong., 1st Sess. (November 1987).

Hayden, M.V. *Playing to the Edge: American Intelligence in the Age of Terror*. New York: Random House, 2016.

Helms, R.M., with Hood, W. *A Look Over My Shoulder: A Life in the Central Intelligence Agency*. New York: Random House, 2003.

Herman, M. *Intelligence Power in Peace and War*. Cambridge, UK: Cambridge University Press, 1996.

Herman, M. "Ethics and Intelligence After September 2001," *Intelligence and National Security* 19 (Summer 2004), pp. 342–58.

Hitz, F. *The Great Game: The Myth and Reality of Espionage*. New York: Knopf, 2004.

Hughes, T.L. "The Power to Speak and the Power to Listen: Reflections in Bureaucratic Politics and a Recommendation on Information Flows," in T. Franck and W. Weisband, eds., *Secrecy and Foreign Policy*. New York: Oxford University Press, 1974, pp. 13–41.

Hughes, T.L. *The Fate of Facts in a World of Men: Foreign Policy and Intelligence-Making*, Headline Series, No. 233. Washington, DC: Foreign Policy Association, 1976.

Hulnick, A.S. "The Intelligence Producer–Policy Consumer Linkage: A Theoretical Approach," *Intelligence and National Security* 1 (May 1986), pp. 212–33.

Hulnick, A.S. *Fixing the Spy Machine: Preparing American Intelligence for the Twenty-First Century*. Westport, CT: Praeger, 1999.

Hulnick, A.S. "What's Wrong with the Intelligence Cycle?," in L.K. Johnson, ed., *Strategic Intelligence, Vol. 2: The Intelligence Cycle*. Westport, CT: Praeger, 2007, pp. 1–22.

Immerman, R.H. *The CIA in Guatemala: The Foreign Policy of Intervention*. Austin: University of Texas Press, 1982.

Inderfurth, K.F., and Johnson, L.K., eds. *Fateful Decisions: Inside the National Security Council*. New York: Oxford University Press, 2004.

Jeffreys-Jones, R. *The CIA and American Democracy*. New Haven, CT: Yale University Press, 1989.

Jeffreys-Jones, R. *In Spies We Trust: The Story of Western Intelligence*. New York: Oxford University Press, 2013.

Jervis, R. *Why Intelligence Fails: Lessons from the Iranian Revolution and the Iraq War*. Ithaca: Cornell University Press, 2010.

Johnson, L.K. *A Season of Inquiry: The Senate Intelligence Investigation*. Lexington: University Press of Kentucky, 1985.

Johnson, L.K. *America's Secret Power: The CIA in a Democratic Society*. New York: Oxford University Press, 1989.

Johnson, L.K. *Secret Agencies: U.S. Intelligence in a Hostile World*. New Haven, CT: Yale University Press, 1996.

Johnson, L.K. *Bombs, Bugs, Drugs, and Thugs: Intelligence and America's Quest for Security*. New York: New York University Press, 2000.

Johnson, L.K. "Bricks and Mortar for a Theory of Intelligence," *Comparative Strategy* 22 (Spring 2003), pp. 1–28.

Johnson, L.K. "Congressional Supervision of America's Intelligence Agencies: The Experience and Legacy of the Church Committee," *Public Administration Review* 64 (January/February 2004), pp. 3–14.

Johnson, L.K. "Educing Information: Interrogation, Science and Art," *Studies in Intelligence* 51 (December 2007), pp. 43–6.

Johnson, L.K. "A Framework for Strengthening U.S. Intelligence," *Yale Journal of International Affairs* 1 (Winter/Spring 2007), pp. 116–31.

Johnson, L.K., ed. *Handbook of Intelligence Studies*. New York: Routledge, 2007.

Johnson, L.K. *Seven Sins of American Foreign Policy*. New York: Longman, 2007.

Johnson, L.K., ed. *Strategic Intelligence*, 5 vols. Westport, CT: Praeger, 2007.

Johnson, L.K. "Glimpses into the Gems of American Intelligence: The *President's Daily Brief* and the National Intelligence Estimate," *Intelligence and National Security* 23 (June 2008), pp. 333–70.

Johnson, L.K., ed. *The Oxford Handbook of National Security Intelligence*. New York: Oxford University Press, 2010.

Johnson, L.K., ed. *Intelligence: Critical Concepts in Military, Strategic & Security Studies*, Vols. I–IV, New York: Routledge, 2011.

Johnson, L.K. *The Threat on the Horizon: An Inside Account of America's Search for Security after the Cold War*. New York: Oxford University Press, 2011.

Johnson, L.K. "James Angleton and the Church Committee," *Journal of Cold War Studies* 15 (Fall 2013), pp. 128–47.

Johnson, L.K., ed. "An *INS* Special Forum: Implications of the Snowden Leaks," *Intelligence and National Security* 29/6 (December 2014), pp. 793–810.

Johnson, L.K. "The Myths of Covert Action," *Virginia Policy Review* 7 (Winter 2014), pp. 5–64.

Johnson, L.K. *American Foreign Policy and the Challenges of World Leadership: Power, Principle, and the Constitution*. New York: Oxford University Press, 2015.

Johnson, L.K., ed. *Essentials of Strategic Intelligence*. Santa Barbara, CA: ABC-CLIO/Praeger, 2015.

Johnson, L.K. *A Season of Inquiry Revisited: The Church Committee Confronts America's Spy Agencies*. Lawrence: University Press of Kansas, 2015.

Johnson, L.K. "Congress and the American Experiment in Holding Intelligence Agencies Accountable," *Journal of Policy History* 28/8 (2016), pp. 494–514.

Johnson, L.K., and Wirtz, J.J., eds. *Intelligence and National Security: The Secret World of Spies*, 4th edn. New York: Oxford University Press, 2014.

Johnston, P. "No Cloak and Dagger Required: Intelligence Support to UN Peacekeeping," *Intelligence and National Security* 12 (October 1997), pp. 102–12.

Kaag, J. and Kreps, S. *Drone Warfare*. Cambridge, UK: Polity, 2014.

Keller, William W. *Democracy Betrayed: The Rise of the Surveillance Security State*. Berkeley, CA: Counterpoint, 2017.

Lowenthal, M.M. "The Policymaker–Intelligence Relationship," in L.K. Johnson, ed., *The Oxford Handbook of National Security Intelligence*. New York: Oxford University Press, 2010, pp. 437–51.

Lowenthal, M.M. *U.S. Intelligence: Evolution and Anatomy*, 2nd edn. Westport, CT: Praeger, 2015.

Lowenthal, M.M. *Intelligence: From Secrets to Policy*, 7th edn. Washington, DC: CQ Press, 2017.

Lowenthal, M.M., and Clark, R.M., eds. *The 5 Disciplines of Intelligence Collection*. Los Angeles: Sage/CQ, 2016.

MacEachin, D.J. *CIA Assessments of the Soviet Union: The Record vs. the Charges*. Langley, VA: Center for the Study of Intelligence: Central Intelligence Agency, 1996.

Macrakis, K. *Prisoners, Lovers, & Spies: The Story of Invisible Ink from Herodotus to al-Qaeda*. New Haven, CT: Yale University Press, 2014.

Mangold, T. *Cold Warrior: James Jesus Angleton, the CIA's Master Spy Hunter*. New York: Simon & Schuster, 1991.

Marrin, S. "Evaluating the Quality of Intelligence Analysis: By What (Mis)Measure," *Intelligence and National Security* 27 (December 2012), p. 896–912.

Martin, D. *Wilderness of Mirrors*. New York: Harper & Row, 1980.

Masterman, J.C. *The Double-Cross System in the War of 1939 to 1945*. New Haven, CT: Yale University Press, 1972.

Mayer, J. *The Dark Side: The Inside Story of How the War on Terror Turned into a War on American Ideals*. New York: Doubleday, 2008.

Mazzetti, M. *The Way of the Knife: The CIA, a Secret Army, and a War at the Ends of the Earth*. New York: Penguin, 2013.

Miller, R.A., ed. *US National Security, Intelligence and Democracy: From the Church Committee to the War on Terror*. New York: Routledge, 2008.

Millis, J.L. "Our Spying Success Is No Secret," Letter to the Editor, *New York Times* (October 12, 1994).

Mondale, W.F., Stein, R.A., and Fisher, C. "No Longer a Neutral Magistrate: The Foreign Intelligence Surveillance Court in the Wake of the War on Terror," *Minnesota Law Review* 100/6 (June 2016), pp. 2251–312.

Murray, W., and Gimsley, M. "Introduction: On Strategy," in W. Murray, A. Bernstein, and M. Knox, eds., *The Making of Strategy: Rulers, States and War*. New York: Cambridge University Press, 1994, pp. 1–23.

Nolte, W. "Keeping Pace With the Revolution in Military Affairs," *Studies in Intelligence* 48 (2004), pp. 1–10.

Nye, J.S., Jr. "Peering into the Future," *Foreign Affairs* 77 (July/August 1994), pp. 82–93.

Phythian, M., ed. "An *INS* Special Forum: The US Senate Select Committee Report on the CIA's Detention and Interrogation Program," *Intelligence and National Security* 31/1 (January 2016), pp. 8–27.

Phythian, M., and Gill, P. *Intelligence in an Insecure World*, 2nd edn. London: Routledge, 2012.

Pillar, P.R. *Terrorism and U.S. Foreign Policy*. Washington, DC: Brookings Institution, 2003.

Pillar, P.R. "The Perils of Politicization," in L.K. Johnson, ed., *The Oxford Handbook of National Security Intelligence*. New York: Oxford University Press, 2010, pp. 472–84.

Pillar, P.R. *Intelligence and U.S. Foreign Policy: Iraq, 9/11, and Misguided Reform* (New York: Columbia University Press, 2011).

Posner, R.A. *Not a Suicide Pact: The Constitution in a Time of National Emergency*. New York: Oxford University Press, 2009.

Powers, T. *The Man Who Kept the Secrets: Richard Helms and the CIA*. New York: Knopf, 1979.

Prados, J. *Safe for Democracy: The Secret Wars of the CIA*. Chicago: Ivan R. Dee, 2007.

Prados, J. *The Family Jewels: The CIA, Secrecy, and Presidential Power*. Austin: University of Texas Press, 2013.

Ranelagh, J. *The Agency: The Rise and Decline of the CIA*, rev. edn. New York: Simon & Schuster, 1987.

Ransom, H.H. *The Intelligence Establishment*. Cambridge, MA: Harvard University Press, 1970.

Reisman, W.M., and Baker, J.E. *Regulating Covert Action*. New Haven: CT: Yale University Press, 1992.

Richelson, J. *America's Eyes in Space: The U.S. Keyhole Spy Satellite Program*. New York: Harper and Row, 1990.

Richelson, J. *The Wizards of Langley: Inside the CIA's Directorate of Science and Technology*. Boulder, CO: Westview Press, 2001.

Richelson, J. *The U.S. Intelligence Community*, 5th edn. Boulder, CO: Westview Press, 2008.

Risen, J. *State of War: The Secret History of the CIA and the Bush Administration*. New York: Free Press, 2006.

Roosevelt, K. *Countercoup: The Struggle for the Control of Iran*. New York: McGraw-Hill, 1981.

Rusk, D. Testimony, Hearings, Government Operations Subcommittee on National Security Staff and Operations, U.S. Senate (December 11, 1963).

Rusk, D. *As I Saw It*, as told to R. Rusk and edited by D. Papps, New York: W.W. Norton, 1990.

Russell, R.L. *Sharpening Strategic Intelligence*. New York: Cambridge University Press, 2007.

Schwarz, F.A.O., Jr. "The Church Committee and a New Era of Intelligence Oversight," *Intelligence and National Security* 22 (April 2007), pp. 270–97.

Schwarz, F.A.O., Jr. "Intelligence Oversight: The Church Committee," in L.K. Johnson, ed., *Strategic Intelligence, Vol. 5: Intelligence and Accountability, Safeguards against the Abuse of Secret Power*. Westport, CT: Praeger, 2007, pp. 19–46.

Schwarz, F.A.O., Jr. *Democracy in the Dark: The Seduction of Government Secrecy*. New York: Free Press, 2015.

Schwarz, F.A.O., Jr., and Huq, A.Z. *Unchecked and Unbalanced: Presidential Power in a Time of Terror*. New York: The New Press, 2007.

Scott, L., and Jackson, P. "The Study of Intelligence in Theory and Practice," *Intelligence and National Security* 19 (Summer 2004), pp. 139–69.

Shane, S. *Objective Troy: A Terrorist, a President, and the Rise of the Drone*. New York: Duggan Books, 2015.

Sharp, D.H. *The CIA's Greatest Covert Operation: Inside the Daring Mission to Recover a Nuclear-Armed Soviet Sub* (Lawrence: University Press of Kansas, 2012).

Shorrock, T. *Spies for Hire: The Secret World of Intelligence Outsourcing*. New York: Simon & Schuster, 2008.

Sims, J.E. "Decision Advantage and the Nature of Intelligence Analysis," in L.K. Johnson, ed., *The Oxford Handbook of National Security Intelligence*. New York: Oxford University Press, 2010, pp. 389–403.

Snider, L.B. *The Agency and the Hill: CIA's Relationship with Congress, 1946–2004.* Washington, DC: Central Intelligence Agency, 2008.

Stuart, D.T. *Creating the National Security State: A History of the Law that Transformed America.* Princeton, NJ: Princeton University Press, 2008.

Tenet, G., with Harlow, B., Jr. *At the Center of the Storm: My Years at the CIA.* New York: HarperCollins, 2007.

Theoharis, A. *Chasing Spies.* Chicago: Ivan R. Dee, 2002.

Travers, R.E., "Waking Up on Another September 12th: Implications for Intelligence Reform," *Intelligence and National Security* 31/5 (August 2016), pp. 746–61.

Treverton, G.F. *Covert Action: The Limits of Intervention in the Postwar World.* New York: Basic Books, 1987.

Treverton, G.F. "Estimating beyond the Cold War," *Defense Intelligence Journal* 3 (Fall 1994), pp. 5–20.

Treverton, G.F. *Intelligence in an Age of Terror.* New York: Cambridge University Press, 2009.

Turner, M.A. *Why Secret Intelligence Fails.* Dulles, VA: Potomac Books, 2005.

Turner, S. *Secrecy and Democracy: The CIA in Transition.* Boston, MA: Houghton Mifflin, 1985.

Turner, S. *Burn before Reading: Presidents, CIA Directors, and Secret Intelligence.* New York: Hyperion, 2005.

U.S. Commission on the Roles and Responsibilities of the United States Intelligence Community (the Aspin–Brown Commission). *Preparing for the 21st Century: A Appraisal of U.S. Intelligence.* Washington, DC: U.S. Government Printing Office, 1996.

Wallace, R., and Smith, H.K., with Schlesinger, H.R. *Spycraft: The Secret History of the CIA's Spytechs from Communism to Al-Qaeda.* New York: Dutton, 2008.

Waller, D. *Disciples.* New York: Simon & Schuster, 2015.

Warner, M. *The Rise and Fall of Intelligence: An International Security History.* Washington, DC: Georgetown University Press, 2014.

Weiner, T. *Legacy of Ashes: The History of the CIA.* New York: Doubleday, 2007.

Weiner, T., Johnston, D., and Lewis, N.A. *Betrayal: The Story of Aldrich Ames, An American Spy.* New York: Random House, 1995.

Weissberg, J. *An Ordinary Spy.* New York: Bloomsbury, 2008.

Westerfield, H.B., ed. *Inside CIA's Private World: Declassified Articles from the Agency's Internal Journal, 1955–1992.* New Haven, CT: Yale University Press, 1995.

Wilford, H. *The Mighty Wurlitzer: How the CIA Played America.* Cambridge, MA: Harvard University Press, 2008.

Wirth, K.E. *The Coast Guard Intelligence Program Enters the Intelligence Community: A Case Study of Congressional Influence on Intelligence Community Evolution.* Washington, DC: National Defense Intelligence College, 2007.

Wirtz, J.J. *The Tet Offensive: Intelligence Failure in War.* Ithaca, NY: Cornell University Press, 1991.

Wise, D. *Nightmover.* New York: Random House, 1992.

Wise, D. *Spy: The Inside Story of How the FBI's Robert Hanssen Betrayed America*. New York: Random House, 2002.

Wise, D., and Ross, T. *The Invisible Government*. New York: Random House, 1964.

Woodward, B. *Plan of Attack*. New York: Simon & Schuster, 2004.

Wyden, P. *Bay of Pigs: The Untold Story*. New York: Simon & Schuster, 1979.

Zegart, A.B. "Cloaks, Daggers, and Ivory Towers: Why Academics Don't Study U.S. Intelligence," in L.K. Johnson, ed., *Strategic Intelligence, Vol. 1: Understanding the Hidden Side of Government*. Westport, CT: Praeger, 2007, pp. 21–34.

Zegart, A.B. *Spying Blind: The CIA, the FBI, and the Origins of 9/11*. Princeton, NJ: Princeton University Press, 2007.

Index

A-12 spy plane, 48
Aberbach, Joel D., 167
Abu Ghraib prison, 151
Abu Zubaydah *see* Zubaydah, Abu
accountability *see* intelligence
   oversight
active measures, 84
Acton, Lord, 7, 15, 216n
aerial terrorism, 4, 9, 67, 72, 126–7
Afghanistan
   and Al Qaeda, 3, 4–5, 48–9, 98, 99,
      100, 104, 112, 113, 114, 135, 143
   civilian casualties in, 99, 100, 149
   counterintelligence in, 48–9
   covert action in, 14, 84, 94–5, 98,
      99, 100, 102, 104, 105, 106, 112,
      113, 114
   mujahideen, 94, 112, 113
   Northern Alliance, 112, 114
   Soviet invasion of, 14, 67, 94, 104,
      105, 112, 113
   Taliban regime, 3, 4–5, 48–9, 81, 84,
      98, 99, 104, 112, 113, 114, 149,
      208
   use of torture in, 143
   war in, 25, 26, 42, 80, 95, 98, 104,
      114, 143, 149
Agee, Philip, 150
agents *see* assets
agents-in-place, 138–9, 140, 142
agents of influence, 91–2

agents provocateurs, 141
Aidid, Mohamed Ali Farrah, 102
Air Force intelligence unit, 18, 67
al-Awlaki, Anwar, 100, 102, 166
Alfred P. Murrah Federal Building
   (Oklahoma City), 123
Al Qaeda
   in Afghanistan, 3, 4–5, 48–9, 98, 99,
      100, 104, 112, 113, 114, 135, 143
   assassination plots against, 98, 99,
      100, 101, 102, 115
   collection of intelligence about, 4,
      48–9, 58, 80, 81
   covert action against, 95, 98, 99,
      100, 101, 102, 104, 114, 115, 208
   in Iraq 4, 115
   9/11 attacks, 1–4, 115, 126–7, 169
   in Pakistan, 4, 48–9, 80, 81, 99, 100,
      143
   in Somalia, 4, 80
   use of torture and renditions
      against, 142–3
   in Yemen, 4, 80, 101, 135
Allende, Salvador, 90, 93, 103, 163,
   188
Alwan, Rafid Ahmed ("Curve Ball"),
   50, 68, 78, 79
ambition instinct, 8–9
American Pilots Association, 126
Ames, Aldrich, 15, 123–5, 132, 134,
   138, 150, 184, 203, 209

Amiri, Shahram, 142
analysis *see* collection and analysis
Angleton, James, 131–3, 140
ante facto reporting, 188
anti-war movement, 116–21, 152–3, 163
Appropriations Committees, 26, 30, 155, 157, 186, 190, 191, 194, 209
Arab–Israeli War, 67, 73
Arbenz, Jacobo, 91, 94
Armed Services Committees, 26, 30, 186, 191, 192, 194, 209
Army intelligence unit, 18, 163
Aspin–Brown Commission, 37, 61, 76, 124–5, 133, 184, 192
Aspin, Les, 39, 79–80, 158–60, 184, 193, 212
assassination plots, 80, 95–103, 111, 113, 114, 166, 187
assets, 23, 45–6, 50–2, 57, 91–2, 107, 138–9, 149
Atta, Mohamed, 1

Backfire bomber, 40
al-Balawi, Humam Khali Abu-Mulal, 135
ballistic missiles, 53–4, 104, 128; *see also* weapons of mass destruction (WMD)
Barrett, David M., 162
Barrett, Richard, 49
Barry, James A., 231n
Bay of Pigs operation, 52, 75–6, 84, 94, 103, 114, 162
Bell, William, 129
Bennett, Donald, 118–20
Berger, Raoul, 147–8
Betts, Richard K., 68, 76
Biden, Joseph R., 34
Bin Laden, Osama, 4–5, 80, 100, 102
biological weapons, 47, 50, 111, 126; *see also* weapons of mass destruction (WMD)
Bissell, Richard, 75
Black, Cofer, 143
Black Panthers, 120
black propaganda, 88, 108
black sites (secret prisons), 142, 179

Blackwater, 25
Blair, Dennis C., 33–4, 138
blow back, 88, *89*, 108
Boland, Edward P., 87, 155–60, 186, 194, 196–7
Boland Amendments, 87, 105, 165, 166
bomber gap, 45
Branch Davidian sect, 123
Brandeis, Louis, 161–2
Brennan, John O., 76, 100, 175–8
British intelligence *see* MI6; United Kingdom (UK)
Brown, Harold, 184
Brzezinski, Zbigniew, 104
Buchanan, Pat, 117
Buckley, David, 178
Bunga (parasite), 92, 110
Bundy, McGeorge, 93, 113
Bureau of Intelligence and Research (INR), 19, 65
Burr, Richard, 102
Bush, George H. W., 74–5, 98, 105, 198
Bush, George W., 45, 51, 60, 69, 78, 99, 105, 153, 173, 189, 207
Bush Administration (1st), 98, 105, 170–1
Bush Administration (2nd), 19, 23, 59, 78, 101, 105–6, 127, 142–3, 153–4, 168, 170–2, 185, 186–7, 209
Butler Report (UK), xviii,

cable and telegram intercepts, 147, 153, 163
Cali drug cartel, 80
Cambodia, 104, 151
Cambridge Spy Ring, 132
Carlos the Jackal, 80
Carter, Jimmy, 104, 155, 156, 158
Carter Administration, 20, 46, 60, 62, 84, 104
case officers *see* operations officers
Casey, William J., 74, 77, 160, 196–8
Castro, Fidel, 52, 75–6, 90, 92–3, 96, 102, 113
Castro, Raoul, 113

Cavanagh, Thomas Patrick, 129
Center for Open-Source Intelligence, 24, 46
Central Intelligence Agency (CIA)
and appointment of chiefs of station, 33–4
assassination plots, 95–103, 111, 113, 114, 166, 187
attack on employees at Langley, 122
co-location of operations officers and analysts, 75–6, 207
counterintelligence, 118–21, 124–7, 131–3, 139–40, 141–3
Counterproliferation Center, 76
Counterterrorism Center, 126, 143
covert action, 14, 52, 83, 84–115, 163–6
Covert Action Staff, 85, 88, 96, 103
and the Cuban Missile Crisis, 52–5
definition of intelligence, 12–13
Directorate of Analysis, 23, 57, 75–6
Directorate of Operations, 20–3, 22, 57, 75–6, 85, 86, 96, 101, 104
Directorate of Science and Technology, 23, 68
Directorate of Support, 23
DNI not allowed office at, 31–2, 35, 75
domestic spying, 11, 23, 118–21, 152–3, 162–4, 182–4, 213–14
economic covert action, 92–3, 109, 110
establishment of, 26–30
and the Huston Plan, 118–21, 152
internal structure, 20–3, 21, 22
interrogation methods, 33, 101, 142–3, 151, 173–9, 209
and 9/11, 4, 79, 126–7, 140, 168, 184
numbers of operations officers, 49, 51
Office of Security, 140
Operation CHAOS, 23, 151, 152, 163, 182–4, 187
paramilitary activities, 52, 83, 93–103, 109, 110, 111

penetrated by Russian intelligence, 10, 15, 123–5
Phoenix Program, 98
political covert action, 91–2, 108–9
position in the Intelligence Community, 18, 19–23
Project Jennifer, 47–8
Project NIMBUS, 52
propaganda, 87–91, 94, 108, 114
relations with the FBI, 125, 127, 137–8, 139–40, 199
Reserve for Contingency Fund, 165
and the Senate Torture Report, 173–9
Special Activities Division, 85
Special Operations Group, 86, 96
treason within, 123–5, 129–30
use of torture, 33, 101, 110, 142–3, 145, 151, 152, 173–9, 185, 186, 209
Central Intelligence Group (CIG), 28, 30
Chambliss, Saxby, 174, 177
CHAOS Operation (CIA), 23, 151, 152, 163, 182–4, 187
"chatter," 74
"cheerleader" intelligence overseers, 192, 194, 196–7, 198, 210
cherry-picking, 73, 76
Chiefs of Station (COSs), 23, 33–4, 101
Chile, 85, 89–90, 91, 93, 97, 103, 163, 188
Chin, Larry Wu-tai, 130
China, 10, 61, 67, 71, 79, 88, 112, 130, 131, 136–7
Christian Democratic Party (Italy), 91
Chung, Dongfan, 130
Church, Frank, 68, 85, 163
Church Committee, 90, 96, 97, 103, 115, 121, 145, 153, 157, 163–4, 182–4, 193–4
Churchill, Winston, 72
Citizens Intelligence Advisory Board (CIAB), 210–13

civil liberties, 7–8, 11, 23, 120–1, 152–3, 170–3, 192; *see also* domestic spying
civil rights movement, 11, 152, 163, 164
civilian casualties, 99–100, 110, 111, 149
Clapper, James R., 24, 34, 35, 136
Clark, Kathleen, 187
Clarke, Richard A., 127
Clausewitz, Karl von, 6–7
"clientitis," 223n
Clifford, Clark, 28, 29, 84, 115
Cline, Ray, 88, 112
Clinton, Bill, 37, 45, 74, 77, 167, 192, 194
Clinton Administration, 20, 39, 59, 60, 63, 100, 105, 126–7, 185
Coast Guard Intelligence, 19
codebreaking, 18, 27, 57
Colby, William E., 42–3, 45, 47, 51, 56, 85, 98, 113, 133
Cold War, 10, 19–20, 23, 40, 44–5, 50, 51, 67, 85, 88–90, 91, 103, 112, 114, 123–4, 131, 145; *see also* communism; Russia/Soviet Union
collection and analysis
  analysis phase, 58–76, 207
  collection phase, 44–57, 206
  dissemination phase, 76–8, 207–8
  improvement of, 55–7, 78–81, 205–8
  intelligence cycle, 38–81, 205–8
  intelligence disciplines, 45–57
  intelligence reports, 59–75, 76–8
  as key intelligence mission, 9–10, 15, 205–8
  planning and direction phase, 39–43, 205–6
  processing phase, 57–8, 206
  weaknesses in, 27, 36–8, 59, 74, 78–9
co-location, 75–6, 207
combatant commanders (COCOMs), 41
Commager, Henry Steele, 164

communications intelligence (comint), 45
communism, 67, 85, 88, 90, 91, 94, 103, 104, 114, 118; *see also* Cold War
Congo, 96–7
Conrad, Clyde, 129
Constitution, 7–8, 11, 104–5, 143, 148, 152–3, 161–2, 164, 169
contras, Nicaraguan, 87, 196
Convention Against Torture, 173
Coons, Chris, 172
counterespionage (CE), 138–43
counterintelligence (CI)
  counterespionage activities, 138–43
  cybersecurity, 135–8
  definition, 121
  difficulty of catching spies, 131–3
  domestic use of, 118–21, 150–4, 162–4, 168, 170–3, 182–4, 185, 213–14
  failures in, 121–30, 168, 184–5, 198–9, 209
  as key intelligence mission, 10–11, 14–15, 208–9
  motivations for treason, 130–1
  oversight of, 152–4
  security activities, 134–8
  state secret protection, 144–52
  tradecraft, 133–43
counterproliferation, 76, 105
Counterproliferation Center, 76
counterterrorism, 10, 19, 44, 48–9, 58, 79, 80, 105, 133
Counterterrorism Center (CTC), 126, 143
covert action (CA)
  assassination plots, 95–103, 111, 113, 114, 166
  definition of, 84
  economic activities, 92–3, 109, 110
  environmental activities, 110, 115
  euphemisms for, 84
  evaluation of, 111–14
  funding for, 103, 104–5, 165
  guidelines for, 114–15, 208
  as key intelligence mission, 10, 14–15, 84–5, 208

covert action (CA) (*cont.*)
  HPSCI and SSCI briefings on,
    155–60, 164–6, 186–9
  implementation of, 86–7
  ladder of escalation, 106–11, *107*,
    208
  legal context, 84–5
  levels of use, 94–5, *95*, 103–6
  methods of, 87–103
  oversight of, 86–7, 155–60, 164–6,
    186–7
  paramilitary activities, 5, 10, 52,
    83, 93–103, 109, 110, 111
  political activities, 91–2, 106, 108–9
  and Presidential approval, 86–7,
    155–60, *159*, 164–6
  propaganda, 87–91, 94, 106, 108,
    114
  rationale, 85
Covert Action Staff (CAS), 85, 88, 90,
  96, 103
covert mail cover, 120, 163
Coyle, Philip E., 40
Cuba, *46*, 50–5, 64, 67, 75–6, 77, 84,
  90, 92–3, 94, 103, 96, 113, 162
Cuban Missile Crisis, 52–5
current intelligence, 60, 61, 70–1
Curve Ball *see* Alwan, Rafid Ahmed
  ("Curve Ball")
cyber-espionage, 136–7
cyber-hackers, 10, 42, 136–7
cyber-security, 135–8
cyber-warfare, 136
Cyprus, 67, 68
Czechoslovakia, 68

D-Day landings, 141, 203
Daesh see ISIS
Damrosch, Lori Fisler, 109
"dangles", 51, 141–2
data integration, 58, 135–6, 207
Daugherty, William J., 103, 114
deception operations, 140–1, 203
defectors, 139–40, 141–2
Defense Intelligence Agency (DIA),
  18, 31, 47, 118–20
democracy, and secrecy, 144, 148,
  149–52

Department of Defense (DoD),
  17–18, 28–9, 31–3, 36–8, 41, 54,
  65, 92–3, 99, 101, 148–9, 151
Department of Energy, 19, 47
Department of Homeland Security
  (DHS), 17, 19, 191
Department of Justice, 19, 101, 142,
  188
Department of State, 19, 53, 150
Department of Transportation,
  126
Department of Treasury, 19
Deputy Director for Operations
  (DDO), 20–2, 82–3, 174
Deputy Directors of National
  Intelligence (DDNIs), 20
Deutch, John, 24, 76, 105
Dicks, Norm, 195
Diem, Ngo Dinh, 97
diplomacy, 41, 80, 202, 203
Director of Central Intelligence
  (DCI), 16, 20, 24, 29–30, 77, 165,
  167–8, 184, 186–8, 189
Director of National Intelligence
  (DNI), 16–17, 20, 24, 30–5, 44, 64,
  75, 76, 99, 165, 203–4
Director of the CIA (D/CIA), 24,
  33–4, 99, 101, 165
Directorate of Administration (DA)
  see Directorate of Support (DS)
Directorate of Analysis (DA), 23, 57,
  75–6
Directorate of Intelligence (DI) *see*
  Directorate of Analysis (DA)
Directorate of Operations (DO), 20–3,
  22, 57, 75–6, 85, 86, 96, 101, 104;
  see also National Clandestine
  Service (NCS), 57
Directorate of Science and
  Technology (DS&T), 23, 68
Directorate of Support (DS), 23
disinformation, 10, 14, 88, 108, 132,
  140–1
dissemination *see* intelligence
  dissemination
domestic spying, 7–8, 11, 23, 118–21,
  150–4, 162–4, 168, 170–3, 182–5,
  213–14

dominant battlefield awareness
    (DBA), 41
Dominican Republic, 94, 97
double agents, 14, 50, 81, 139
drones *see* Unmanned Aerial Vehicles
    (UAVs)
Drug Enforcement Administration
    (DEA), 19
drugs-related operations, 19, 80, 99,
    105
Dulles, Allen, 26, 73, 91, 97, 187
Dulles, John Foster, 91
Dunlap, Jack E., 128
Durban, Richard, 69–70
Duvalier, François "Papa Doc", 97–8

economic covert action, 92–3, 109,
    110
economic espionage, 137
Egypt, 91, 112
Ehrlichman, John, 116–17
Eisenhower, Dwight D., 25–6, 86, 206
Eisenhower Administration, 24, 91,
    96–7, 103
El Salvador, 51, 104
electronic intelligence (elint), 45
"Elimination by Illumination"
    (proposed CIA operation), 90
Ellsberg, Daniel, 148–9
email intercepts, 18, 57; *see also*
    metadata collection program
embassies, 46, 50, 51, 56–7, 129, 135,
    140
"Enterprise, The", 87, 145, 166
environmental covert action, 110, 115
Environmental Intelligence Center,
    24
Ervin, Sam, 146
Ervin Committee, 146
executive privilege, 145–7, 179
Exon, James, 192–3
ex post facto reporting, 188
external consultants, 63–4
extraordinary renditions, 101, 110,
    142–3, 145, 152

false defector, 50, 139, 141
Federal Aviation Administration, 1

Federal Bureau of Investigation (FBI)
    counterintelligence, 118–20, 123–5,
        127, 129–30, 137–8, 139–40
    domestic spying, 151, 152–3, 163–4
    establishment of, 26
    and the Huston Plan, 118–20
    and 9/11, 4, 79, 127
    numbers of special agents, 49
    and the Oklahoma City bombing,
        123
    Operation COINTELPRO, 151,
        152–3, 163–4, 187
    penetrated by Russian intelligence,
        10, 123–5, 130
    position in the Intelligence
        Community, 19, 26
    relations with the CIA, 125, 127,
        137–8, 139–40, 199
    treason within, 123–5, 130
    and the Waco siege, 123
Federalist Papers, 7, 210
Federation of American Scientists
    Project on Government Secrecy,
    18
Feinstein, Dianne, 102, 174, 175, 177,
    178, 179
financial political incentives, 91,
    108–9
"finding," 156, 158–9, 164, 165–6, 167
"firefighting," 180–2, 185, 210
First Amendment (US Constitution),
    11, 120, 149, 150
Fisher, Roger, 115
Ford, Gerald R., 98, 147
Ford Administration, 146–7, 163
Foreign Affairs Committees, 191
foreign instrumentation signals
    intelligence (fisint), 45
foreign intelligence liaison, 80–1, 205
Foreign Intelligence Surveillance Act
    Court (FISA Court), 33, 101–2,
    153–4, 166, 168, 170, 172, 184,
    185
Foreign Intelligence Surveillance
    Court (FIS Court), 101–2, 153–4,
    172, 173
Foreign Relations Committees, 191,
    209

France, 5, 10, 130
Freedom of Information (FOIA)
    requests, 185
Fuchs, Klaus, 127, 131
funding see intelligence funding
fusion centers, intelligence, 58, 204

Gang of Eight, 186–7, 188, 189
Gang of Four, 186–7
"Gang of None," 187
Gates, Robert M., 33, 51, 167, 189,
    200
Gayler, Noel, 57, 118–20
Geneva Conventions, 173
geospatial intelligence (geoint), 18,
    36–7, 44–5, 46, 48–9, 52–4, 61,
    144
Germany, 6, 10, 50, 73, 91, 130, 141
Giancana, Sam, 96
Gill, Peter, 15–16
Gingrich, Newt, 167
Glennon, Michael, 179
Goldsmith, Jack, 171
Goldwater, Barry, 160, 193–4, 197–8
Gore, Al, 192
"gorillas in the stovepipes," 29
Goss, Porter, 198
Government Accountability Office
    (GAO), 191, 212
Graham, Bob, 69–70, 174, 198–9
Graham–Goss Committee, 184, 198–9
Grass, Günter, 85
Greece, 91, 94, 141
Greenglass, David, 127
GRU, 128
Guantánamo Bay, 175
"guardian" intelligence overseers,
    192, 193, 195–6, 197, 199–201,
    209–10
Guatemala, 85, 90–1, 94, 103, 111, 112
Gulf War, 24, 41, 98, 203

Hagel, Chuck, 70
Haiti, 94, 97–8, 105
Hall, James, 129
Hamilton, Lee H., 145, 195–6, 212
Hanssen, Robert, 123, 125, 138, 150,
    203

Hart, Gary, 201
Hayden, Michael V., 174, 176, 178,
    179
Haynes, John Earl, 127–8
Health Alteration Committee, 96
Hellfire missiles, 99, 101, 110
Helms, Richard, 73, 77, 93, 118–20,
    139, 188
Herbig, Katherine L., 131
Hiss, Alger, 128
Hitler, Adolf, 6, 73, 141
Hmung tribesmen, 94
Hoekstra, Peter, 189
Homeland Security, Department of
    see Department of Homeland
    Security (DHS)
Homeland Security Committee, 191
Hoover, J. Edgar, 26, 118–20, 139,
    152, 164, 214
Hoover Commission, 112
hostage-rescue operations, 109, 110
House Permanent Select Committee
    on Intelligence (HPSCI), 25, 56,
    102, 127, 150, 152, 154, 155–60,
    164–71, 173–4, 178–9, 184,
    186–99, 209–13
Houston, Lawrence R., 30
Howard, Edward Lee, 129, 150
Hughes, Howard, 47
Hughes–Ryan Act, 86, 87, 102, 105,
    156, 164–5, 185, 188, 189
Hulnick, Arthur S., 68
human intelligence (humint), 26, 33,
    37–8, 45–6, 48–57, 92, 144, 184,
    206
human nature, 7–9, 8
Hungary, 67, 94
Hurricane Katrina, 126–7
Hussein, Saddam, 36, 37, 41, 69, 70,
    78, 79, 98–9, 102
Huston, Tom Charles, 117–21, 214
Huston Plan, 117–21, 119
Hutton Report, xviii

Ignatius, David, 178–9
imagery intelligence (imint) see
    geospatial intelligence (geoint)
India, 198

India–Pakistan War, 67
indications and warnings (I & W), 12
Indonesia, 94, 97–8
information technology (IT), 206
Inouye, Daniel K., 155
Inouye–Hamilton Committee, 184
Inspector General Act (IG Act), 167,
    184
inspectors general (IGs), 15, 167, 178,
    184
intelligence agencies
  civilian, 19–23, 65
  cooperation with police, 137–8
  data integration, 58, 135–6, 207
  dissenting views among, 64–5
  domestic spying, 7–8, 11, 23,
      118–21, 150–4, 162–4, 168, 170–3,
      182–5, 213–14
  failures of, 4, 6–8, 27, 36–8, 59,
      67–8, 78–9, 121–30, 168, 182–5,
      198–9, 209
  funding of see intelligence funding
  generation of NIE proposals,
      61–2
  haphazard development of, 26–30
  horizontal and vertical integration,
      204
  key intelligence missions, 9–11, 13,
      205–9
  lack of coordination between,
      26–35, 133, 136, 204–5
  liaison with foreign intelligence
      services, 81, 205
  liaison with intelligence
      consumers, 65, 74, 77–8, 204,
      206, 207–8
  military, 17–19, 65
  organization of, 16–26, 17, 203–5
  oversight of see intelligence
      oversight
  reform of structure, 11, 30–5, 203–5
  reporting requirements for, 186–90
  see also individual agencies
intelligence analysis see collection
    and analysis
intelligence centers, 24
intelligence collection see collection
    and analysis

Intelligence Community
  civilian intelligence agencies,
      19–23
  intelligence centers and task
      forces, 24
  intelligence oversight boards, 24–5
  military intelligence agencies,
      17–19
  government organizations, 25–6
  overall structure, 16–26, 17
  private contractors, 25–6
  see also intelligence agencies
Intelligence Community
    Whistleblower Protection Act
    (1998), 152
intelligence cycle
  analysis phase, 58–76, 207
  collection phase, 44–57, 206
  dissemination phase, 76–8, 207–8
  planning and direction phase,
      39–43, 205–6
  processing phase, 57–8, 206
  summary diagram, 38
intelligence disciplines (ints), 45–57
intelligence dissemination, 76–8,
    207–8
intelligence funding, 9, 16, 18–19, 41,
    48, 55, 59, 103, 104–5, 165, 206
intelligence fusion centers, 58, 204
Intelligence Identities Act, 185
intelligence missions, 9–11, 13, 205–9
intelligence oversight
  agencies required to report,
      189–90
  and the Constitution, 7–8, 104–5,
      143, 161–2, 169
  and counterintelligence, 152–4
  and covert action, 86–7, 155–60,
      164–6, 186–7
  dynamic nature of, 196–9
  evolution of, 160–79
  failures of, 7, 166, 182–5, 209
  importance of, 7, 11, 209–10
  incentives for overseers, 199–201,
      209
  information to be reported, 189
  legislation enactment process,
      190–1

intelligence oversight (*cont.*)
  legislation on *see* Foreign
    Intelligence Surveillance Act;
    Hughes–Ryan Act; Inspector
    General Act; Intelligence
    Identities Act; Intelligence
    Oversight Acts
  lines of authority, 191–2, 209
  oversight boards, 15, 24–5, 152,
    212–13
  panels of inquiry, 163–4; *see also*
    individual panels
  persons to be kept informed,
    186–8
  proposed Citizens Intelligence
    Advisory Board, 210–13
  role of citizens, 213–14
  role of the HPSCI and SSCI, 25,
    155–60, 164–71, 173–9, 186–99,
    209–13
  role of the media, 162–4, 170, 174,
    177, 181–2, 200, 210
  roles played by overseers, 192–201,
    193, 196
  shock theory of accountability,
    180–5, *181*, 209
  term limits for HPSCI and SSCI
    members, 190
  timing of reports to Congress,
    188–9
Intelligence Oversight Acts, 87, 166,
  167, 184, 185, 187, 188–90
Intelligence Oversight Board (IOB),
  24, 25, 152, 212
intelligence planning and direction,
  39–43, 205–6
intelligence, politicization of, 73, 77,
  208
intelligence processing, 57–8, 206
Intelligence Reform and Terrorism
  Prevention Act (IRTPA), 30–2,
  34–5, 133
intelligence reports
  balance of current and research
    intelligence, 70–1
  critical review of, 63–4, 207
  dissemination of, 76–8, 207–8
  essential qualities of, 71–5

National Intelligence Estimates,
  61–70, 74–5
President's Daily Brief, 59–61
intelligence–risk relationship, 42–3,
  43
intelligence studies, xvi–ii, xviii
intelligence task forces, 24
intelligence to please, 77
intercepts *see* cable and telegram
    intercepts; covert mail cover;
    email intercepts; metadata
    collection program; telephone
    intercepts
International Telephone and
    Telegraph Corporation (ITT), 90,
    147
interrogation methods, 33, 101,
    142–3, 151, 173–9, 209; *see also*
    torture
Inter-Services Intelligence (ISI)
    (Pakistan), 81
Iran, 40, 46, 50, 68, 85, 87, 94, 103,
    111, 112–13, 139, 142, 144–6
Iran-*contra* affair, 85, 87, 94, 104–5,
    114, 144–5, 151, 160, 166, 182,
    184, 190, 196, 209
Iranian revolution, 40, 68, 113
Iraq
  absence of purported WMD, 6, 41,
    50, 59, 68, 69–70, 78, 79, 168,
    184–5
  and Al Qaeda, 4, 115
  assassination plots against
    Saddam Hussein, 98–9
  civilian casualties, 149
  covert action in, 94, 95, 98–9, 102,
    104, 115
  Gulf War, 24, 41, 98, 203
  intelligence collection in, 36–8, 41,
    48, 50, 68, 69–70, 78, 79
  Iraq war, 31, 41, 80, 95, 98–9, 104,
    105, 149, 151
  and ISIS, 5, 80, 102
  NIE controversy, 69–70, 78, 184–5
  outsourcing of security in, 25
  use of torture in, 151
  WikiLeaks release classified
    documents on, 149

Iraq war, 31, 41, 80, 95, 98–9, 104, 105, 149, 151
Iraqi Task Force, 24
iron pentagon, 25–6, 48, 206
iron triangle, 25–6
ISIS, 5, 42, 80, 95, 98, 99, 101, 102, 104, 106, 115, 133, 134, 136, 139, 208
Israel, 113, 129
Italy, 91, 134

Jervis, Robert, 133, 140
jihadist, xviii, 4, 136
Johnson, Lyndon B., 145
Johnson Administration, 89–90, 92, 96, 117
jointness, 73
Judiciary Committees, 191, 209

Kahn, Herman, 106
Kampiles, William, 129
Kansi, Mir Aimal, 122
Kant, Immanuel, 111
Kean, Thomas, 59
Kean Commission, 31, 51, 73, 169, 184, 191
Keating, Kenneth, 52
Kennan, George F., 72
Kennedy, John F., 53, 54, 75–6, 96, 140
Kennedy Administration, 52–3, 90, 92, 96, 103
Kent, Sherman, 66–7, 69, 77
Key Judgments (KJs), 64, 65, 70, 74
KGB, 85, 96, 118, 125, 128, 129, 132, 140
"King George's cavalry," 91
King, Martin Luther, 164
Klehr, Harvey, 127–8
Kleindienst, Richard, 146
Khrushchev, Nikita, 53, 132
Kim, Robert C., 130
Kissinger, Henry, 84, 93, 150, 192
Knott, Stephen F., 167
Korean War, 67, 94, 103, 104
Ku Klux Klan, 163
Kuwait, 36–7, 99

ladder of escalation, 106–111, *107*, 208
Lake, Anthony, 167–8
Land, Edward, 24
Langley, VA, 20, 31, 35, 62, 75–6, 99, 122, 189; *see also* Central Intelligence Agency (CIA)
Laos, 94, 111
Laurent, Sébastien, 11–12
leaks, 47, 87, 88, 144, 148–50, 153, 157, 170–1
"lemon-sucker" intelligence overseers, 192, 194–5, 197–9
Levi, Edward H., 147
Levin, Carl, 69–70
Lewis, Anthony, 112
Liberty Crossing, VA, 20, 31–3, 75
Libya, 5, 80, 98, 99, 101, 106, 130
Liddy, G. Gordon, 112
listening posts, 44, 48
"lone wolf" attacks, 5, 68
Lonetree, Clayton J., 129
Lowenthal, Mark M., 70–1
Lumumba, Patrice, 96–7

Madison, James, 7, 154, 169
Mafia, 96
MAGIC, 27
Mak, Chi, 130
Manhattan Project, 127
Marines intelligence unit, 18
Marshall, George Catlett, 72
Martins, Mark, 175
Matthews, Jennifer, 135
Mayer, Jane, 173
Mazzoli, Roman, 156, 157, 158–60, 193, 212
McCain, John, 169, 171, 179
McCone, John A., 53, 64, 77, 138
McConnell, Mike, 32–3, 57
McCubbins, Matthew D., 180
McFarlane, Robert C., 166, 178
McNamara, Robert S., 54–5
McNutt, Russell, 127
McVeigh, Timothy, 123
measurement and signatures intelligence (masint), 47

media, role in intelligence oversight, 162–4, 170, 174, 177, 181–2, 200, 210
media assets, 88, 108
metadata collection program, 25, 149, 150, 151, 170–3, 185, 186
MI6, 51, 78, 91, 132, 144
Military Intelligence Program (MIP), 18
Millis, John, 52
Mitchell, John, 93, 120
mock executions, 175
Mohammed, Khalid Sheikh, 143, 175
Mondale, Walter, 153, 163
Morgan Bank (Wall Street), 123
Mosman, Michael W., 173
Moss, John E., 147
Mossadeq, Mohammed, 94
Moussaoui, Zacarias, 127
Moyers, Bill, 145
Moynihan, Daniel Patrick, 79, 151, 195
mujahideen, 94, 112, 113
My Lai village massacre, 151
mysteries, 5–6, 39

National Clandestine Service (NCS), 23, 33; see also Directorate of Operations (DO)
National Command Authority (NCA), 16
National Counterproliferation Center, 76
National Counterterrorism Center (NCTC), 20, 44, 133
National Geospatial-Intelligence Agency (NGA), 18, 57
National Intelligence Board (NIB), 64
National Intelligence Council (NIC), 20, 34, 62–5
National Intelligence Estimates (NIEs)
    accuracy and inaccuracy of, 66–9
    improvements needed, 74–5
    incorporation of dissenting views, 64–5
    and internal liaison, 65

Iraq NIE controversy, 69–70, 78, 184–5
Key Judgments section, 64, 65, 70, 74
overview, 61
preparation process, 62–4
range of topics, 61–2
special NIEs, 66, 75–6
timing and frequency, 66, 66, 74–5
National Intelligence Managers (NIMs), 35, 63
National Intelligence Officers (NIOs), 62–5, 77
National Intelligence Priorities Framework (NIPF), 43
National Intelligence Program (NIP), 18
National Photographic Interpretation Center (NPIC), 37, 53
National Reconnaissance Office (NRO), 18, 130
National Security Act, 19, 29, 84–5, 115
National Security Agency (NSA)
    and appointment of chiefs of station, 34
    counterintelligence, 118–20, 128, 129, 134
    domestic spying, 25, 33, 147, 149, 150, 151, 152, 153–4, 163, 170–3, 185, 186
    funding, 16, 18, 48
    and the Huston Plan, 118–20
    intelligence processing, 57–8, 206
    metadata collection program, 25, 149, 150, 151, 170–3, 185, 186
    and 9/11, 4, 58
    Operation MINARET, 151, 153, 163, 187
    Operation PRISM, 170
    Operation SHAMROCK, 147, 151, 153, 163, 187
    position in the Intelligence Community, 18
    Snowden leak, 136, 145, 149, 150, 152, 170–1
    warrantless wiretaps, 33, 149, 151, 152, 153–4, 163, 185
    treason within, 128, 129, 134

National Security Council (NSC), 16, 60, 63, 85, 87, 99, 104, 146, 162, 166, 184, 189–90, 196
national security intelligence (NSI) and accountability, 11, 209–14
definitions of, 12–13, 16
holistic view of, 14–16
as organization, 13, 203–5
as process, 13
as secret information, 12–13
as set of missions, 9–11, 13, 205–9
national security letters (NSLs), 153
National Student Association, 162
Navy intelligence unit, 18
Negroponte, John D., 31–2
New York Times, 34, 142, 148–9, 153, 162–3, 164, 170, 172, 174, 181–2, 186
Ngo Dinh Diem, 97
Nicaragua, 14, 85, 87, 93, 94, 104–5, 144–5, 165, 166, 182, 196–7; *see also* Iran-*contra* affair
Nicolson, Harold J., 129–30
NIMBUS, Project, 52
9/11, 1–4, 6, 30–1, 58, 59, 67, 79, 100, 105–6, 115, 126–7, 140, 143, 168–9, 184, 198–9, 209
9/11 Commission *see* Kean Commission
Nixon, Richard, 90, 93, 116–20, 145, 146, 188
Nixon Administration, 73, 84, 90, 93, 103, 116–21, 148, 188
"nondiscernible microbioinoculator," 96
non-official cover officers (NOCs), 49–50, 56, 206
North Atlantic Treaty Organization (NATO), 5, 71, 85, 205
North Korea, 40, 50, 55, 79, 139, 152–3
Northern Alliance, 112, 114
Norway, 42
Nosenko, Yuri, 140
nuclear espionage, 127–8, 131
nuclear materials, 19, 47, 79, 147–8

nuclear weapons, 44, 53–4, 79, 104, 111, 198; *see also* weapons of mass destruction (WMD)
Nye, Joseph S., 44

Obama, Barack, 34, 106, 171–2, 175, 176
Obama Administration, 2–3, 59, 99–101, 104, 106, 149, 153, 171–2, 175, 187
Odom, William, 69
Office of Intelligence and Analysis, Department of Homeland Security, 19
Office of Intelligence and Analysis, Department of Treasury, 19
Office of Intelligence and Counterintelligence, 19
Office of National Security Intelligence, 19
Office of Security, 140
Office of the Director of National Intelligence (ODNI), 17, 30–5, 62, 75, 133, 189
official cover officers (OCs), 49–50
Ogonowski, Captain John, 1
Oklahoma City bombing, 123
O'Neill, Thomas "Tip", 155
open source intelligence (osint), 24, 46–7, 206
Operation CHAOS, 23, 151, 152, 163, 182–4, 187
Operation COINTELPRO, 151, 152, 163–4, 187
Operation MINARET, 151, 153, 163, 187
Operation PRISM, 170
Operation SHAMROCK, 147, 151, 153, 163, 187
Operation SQUARE DANCE (proposed), 92–3
operations officers, 23, 49–51, 55, 56–7, 75–6, 206
opportunity assessment, 41–2
oral briefings, 60
Organization of Petroleum Exporting Countries (OPEC), 67
Orlando shootings, 5, 68

Ortega, Daniel, 105, 196
"ostrich" intelligence overseers, 192,
    193–4, 197, 198, 210
Oswald, Lee Harvey, 140
outsourcing, 25–6
oversight, intelligence *see* intelligence
    oversight; Intelligence Oversight
    Acts; Intelligence Oversight
    Board

Pakistan, 4, 5, 48–9, 61, 80, 81, 98, 99,
    100, 106, 112, 122, 143
Panetta, Leon E., 33–4, 76, 176
Panetta Report, 176–7
paramilitary activities, 5, 10, 52, 83,
    93–103, 109, 110, 111
Pathet Lao, 94
Patriot Act, 100, 172
Paul, Rand, 172
Pearl Harbor, 6, 27
Pelton, Ron, 129
penetration, 10, 14, 130, 132, 138
Penkovsky, Oleg, 51, 53, 140
Pentagon *see* Department of Defense
    (DoD)
Pentagon Papers case, 148–9, 151
Perry, William J., 36–8
Persian Gulf Wars *see* Gulf War; Iraq
    War
personnel screening, 134
Peru, 80
Philby, Kim, 15, 132, 209
Philippines, 91
photographic interpretation, 37, 45,
    53, 57
Phoenix Program, 98
physical security, 135
Phythian, Mark, 15–16
Pike, Otis, 157, 163
Pike Committee, 145, 157, 163, 182–4,
    196
Pipes, Richard E., 63
Pitts, Earl, 130
plausible deniability doctrine, 86
Poindexter, John M., 144–5, 166
Poland, 94, 114
police, 137–8
"police patrolling," 180–2, 185

Policy Planning Staff (State
    Department), 72
political covert action, 91–2, 106,
    108–9
Pollard, Jonathan Jay, 129
polygraph tests, 23, 124, 130, 134
Portugal, 51
Predator drones, 48, 99, 101, 111
President, 16, 43, 59–61, 85, 86–7, 99,
    101, 145, 146, 151, 155–60, 164–6,
    187, 212
President's Daily Brief (PDB), 28,
    59–61, 72
President's Intelligence Advisory
    Board (PIAB), 24–5
President's Review Group, 171
prior restraint, 148–9
private contractors, 25–6, 87, 129, 130
processing of intelligence *see*
    intelligence cycle, processing
    phase
Project Jennifer, 47–8
Project NIMBUS, 52
propaganda, 87–91, 94, 106, 108, 114
provocation operations, 141–2

Qaddafi, Muammar, 98, 106

Radio Free Europe (RFE), 88–9
Radio Liberty (RL), 88–9
Ranelagh, John, 103
Ransom, Harry H., 180
Reagan, Ronald, 14, 74, 94, 98, 173
Reagan Administration, 14, 59, 67,
    87, 93–4, 103, 104–5, 145–6, 160,
    166, 189–90, 197
Reagan Doctrine, 14, 104
Reaper drones, 48, 99, 111
reconnaissance aircraft, 18, 44–5, 48,
    52–4, 86, 162
Redmond, Paul J., 124–5, 138
Reed, Harry, 177
Regan, Brian P., 130
renditions *see* extraordinary
    renditions
research intelligence, 61, 70–1
Reserve for Contingency Fund, 165
Ribbentrop, Joachim von, 73

Rice, Condoleezza, 69, 127
risk–intelligence relationship, 42–3,
    43
Roberts, Pat, 168–9, 170
Rockefeller, Jay, 178
Rockefeller, John D., 32, 168
Rockefeller, Nelson, 163
Rockefeller Commission, 96, 145,
    163, 164, 184
Rockwell, Norman, 164
Roosevelt, Franklin D., 6, 27
Rosenberg, Ethel, 127–8
Rosenberg, Julius, 128
Roselli, John, 96
Rumsfeld, Donald H., 33
Rusk, Dean, 39, 53, 55, 59, 150
Russia/Soviet Union
    Backfire bomber, 40
    collection of intelligence about,
        44–5, 47–8, 51, 52–5, 63–4, 67–8
    counterintelligence activities in
        Europe, 10, 15, 132
    counterintelligence activities in the
        US, 10, 15, 123–5, 127–30, 131–3,
        137–8, 141–2
    counterintelligence against, 125,
        138, 140
    covert action against, 85, 88–9, 92,
        94, 104, 105, 112, 113, 114
    and the Cuban Missile Crisis,
        52–5, 67
    fall of Soviet Union, 79
    intervention in Nicaragua, 14
    invasion of Afghanistan, 14, 67, 94,
        104, 105, 112, 113
    presence in Cuba, 52–5, 67
    propaganda aimed at, 88–9, 92,
        114
    shoots down US reconnaissance
        planes, 44, 86, 162
    suspected involvement in US
        anti-war movement, 117–21
    use of assassination, 95
    use of NOCs, 50
    see also Cold War
Russian/Soviet intelligence see GRU;
    KGB; Russia/Soviet Union; SVR
Rwanda, 39

San Bernardino shootings, 5, 68
Sandinistas, 87, 93, 104–5, 166, 196
satellite images, 18, 36–7, 44–5, 49
Saudi Arabia, 112, 199
Sawyers, John, 144
Schlesinger, Arthur M., 151
Schlesinger, James R., 161
Schneider, René, 97
Schwartz, Thomas, 180
Second Gulf War see Iraq War
Second World War, 6, 27–8, 73, 127,
    141, 203
Secretary of Defense (SecDef), 30, 31,
    33, 36–8, 99
secrets, 5–6, 139, 144–52
security activities, 134–8
security breaches see leaks
"self-licking ice cream cones," 65
Senate Select Committee on
    Intelligence (SSCI), 25, 69–70, 79,
    102, 127, 143, 150, 152, 154, 155,
    160, 164–71, 173–9, 184–99,
    209–13
Senate Torture Report, 173–9, 191,
    212
sensitive compartmented
    information facilities (SCIFs), 22
September 17th group, 141
Shaliskashvili, John, 36–7
SHAMROCK see Operation
    SHAMROCK
Shane, Scott, 130–1
Shelby, Richard C., 198
Shining Path, 80
Shultz, George P., 145
signals intelligence (sigint), 18, 34,
    45, 48–9, 55, 61, 118, 128, 129,
    144, 170, 185
Silberman–Robb Commission, 51,
    184
sleep deprivation, 143, 175
Snider, L. Britt, 168
Snow, Daniel, 131
Snowden, Edward J., 136, 145, 149,
    150, 152, 170–1
Snowe, Olympia, 179
Somalia, 4, 80, 102
South Korea, 130

Soviet Union *see* Russia/Soviet
    Union
Spann, Johnny Michael, 114
Special Activities Division (SA
    Division) *see* Covert Action Staff
    (CAS)
Special Forces, 87, 100, 114
Special National Intelligence
    Estimates (SNIEs), 66, 75–6
Special Operations Group (SOG), 86,
    96
Sputnik, 67
SQUARE DANCE *see* Operation
    SQUARE DANCE
SR-21 spy plane, 48
Stalin, Joseph, 6, 131, 132
state secret protection, 144–52
Stennis, John, 161, 186
Stewart, Justice Potter, 149
Stone, Geoffrey, 171
Stone, I. F., 128
"stonewalling," 147, 174, 199
student protests, 116–21
Suez crisis, 66
Sukarno, president of Indonesia,
    97–8
Sullivan, William C., 118–20
support to diplomatic operations
    (SDO), 41, 80
support to military operations
    (SMO), 41, 79, 104
Supreme Court, 146, 148–9, 212
surreptitious entry, 120
surreptitious surveillance, 141–2
surveillance satellites, 18, 24, 26,
    44–5, 48, 49, 129, 130
survival instinct, 8–9
SVR, 96, 125, 141
"swallows," 129
Syria, 80, 99, 101, 115, 134

tactical intelligence and related
    activities (TIARA), 18
Taliban, 3, 4–5, 48–9, 81, 84, 98, 99,
    104, 112, 113, 114, 149, 208
Taylor, Rufus, 30
Taylor, Stan, 131
Team A, Team B, 63, 207

technical intelligence (techint), 37,
    48–55, 144, 206
telemetry intelligence (telint), 45
telephone intercepts, 18, 33, 48–9,
    57–8, 61, 102, 145, 153–4, 163,
    168, 170, 185, 186, 209
Tenet, George J., 43, 45, 59, 60, 69–70,
    78, 140, 198–9, 207
Terms of Reference (TOR), 62
terrorist organizations, 19, 42, 44,
    48–9, 80, 95, 115, 136, 138, 141;
    see also Al Qaeda; ISIS
Thailand, 94
threat assessment, 40–3
torture, 33, 101, 110, 142–3, 145, 151,
    152, 173–9, 185, 186, 209
tradecraft, 45, 49, 50, 125, 177, 206
    counterintelligence tradecraft,
    133–43
"traffic analysis," 73–4
Trafficante, Santo, 96
translation, 57, 58, 74, 206
treason
    examples of, 127–30
    motivations for, 124, 125, 130–1
    within the CIA and FBI, 123–5,
    129–30
Treasury, Department of *see*
    Department of Treasury
Trotsky, Leon, 95
Trujillo, Rafael, 97
Truman, Harry S., 7–8, 27–30
Truman Administration, 28, 147
Turkey, 67, 68, 94
Turner, Stansfield, 20, 46, 114, 155–7,
    158–60, 186, 193

U-2 reconnaissance planes, 48, 52–4,
    86, 162
Udall, Mark, 171
United Arab Emirates (UAE), 100
United Fruit Company, 91, 112
United Kingdom (UK), 4, 10, 15, 42,
    51, 72, 78, 91, 112, 130, 132, 144,
    205
United Nations, 106, 205
United States Information Agency
    (USIA), 88

United States v. Nixon, 146
Unmanned Aerial Vehicles (UAVs), 18, 26, 48–9, 79, 99–100, 101, 102, 104, 110, 111, 166
USA Freedom Act, 153, 172, 185
USS *Cole*, 135
USS *George Washington*, 37
USS *Pueblo*, 150

Vance, Cyrus, 115
Vassiliev, Alexander, 127–8
Venezuela, 94
Venice Council of Ten, 134
Viet Cong, 94, 98
Vietnam War, 50, 67, 74, 94, 98, 103, 104, 148–9, 151, 163
Vietnam War protestors, 11, 23, 116–21, 152–3, 163
Village Voice, 157

Waco siege, 123
"walk-ins", 51, 140
Walker family, 128, 150
Warks, Wesley, 236n
Warner, Michael, 29–30
warrantless wiretaps, 33, 145, 149, 151, 153–4, 163, 166, 168, 170, 185, 186, 209
Warsaw Pact, 132
Washington, George, 144
Washington Post, 25, 58–9, 148–9, 174, 197
waterboarding, 143, 175
Watergate, 145, 146, 151, 188
"watch lists," 58
Waxman, Henry A., 180–1
weapons manufacturers, 25–6, 206
weapons of mass destruction (WMD), 6, 41, 42, 50, 52–4, 59, 68–70, 76, 78, 79, 111, 142, 168,

184–5; *see also* ballistic missiles; biological weapons; nuclear weapons
Weather, 120
Weber, Max, xvii
Webster, William H., 24, 114, 208
Weinberger, Casper, 145
Weisband, William, 128
"wet affairs," 95
whistle-blowers, 136, 149, 152, 170–1, 185
    see also Intelligence Community Whistleblower Protection Act (1998)
White, Theodore H., 116, 120
WikiLeaks, 149, 150, 151–2
wiretaps *see* cable and telegram intercepts; email intercepts; metadata collection program; telephone intercepts; warrantless wiretaps
"witting circle," 60, 186
Woolsey, R. James, 20, 39, 55, 74, 77
World Trade Center, 2
Wyden, Ron, 171

Xe Services, 25, 26

"Year of Intelligence" (1975), 162, 180, 195
"Year of the Spy" (1985), 130
Yemen, 4, 80, 100–1, 135, 166
Young Americans for Freedom (YAF), 117
Yugoslavia, 67, 108
Yurchenko, Vitaliy Sergeyevich, 141–2

Zegart, Amy B., 29, 169, 191
Zubaydah, Abu, 143, 175